CAUCASUS
ARMENIA
Caspian Sea
Aral Sea
R. Syr Darya
Turkestan
TRANSOXIANA
TURKESTAN
R. Oxus
Khiva
(Khwarazm)
Bukhara
Samarqand
Van
Tabriz
Ardabil
Mardin
Maraghah
Sultaniyyah
Mosul
Qazwin
Gunbad-i-Qabus
Nishapur
Tus
Mashhad
Merv
Balkh
Tehran
Rayy
Damghan
MESOPOTAMIA
Hatra
Samarra
Qum
Kashan
Ardistan
Na'in
Sultanabad
Baghdad
IRAQ
R. Tigris
Isfahan
Jundishapur
Ahwaz
Yazd
Najaf
Basra
Shiraz
Kerman
KHURASAN
Herat
Kabul
PERSIA
AFGHANISTAN
Persian Gulf
Multan
Lahore
PUNJAB
TIBET
NEPAL
R. Indus
SINDH
Karachi
Delhi
Tughlugabad
Agra
Jaipur
Fatehpur Sikri
R. Ganges
Lucknow
BENGAL
Ujjain
INDIA
ARABIA
Arabian Sea
Hyderabad
San'a
YEMEN
CEYLON
Turfan
Miran
CHINA

(Hueby-Ford)

£25

[illegible]

22/4

Islamic Science
An Illustrated Study

Islamic Science

An Illustrated Study

Seyyed Hossein Nasr

photographs by Roland Michaud

World of Islam Festival Publishing Company Ltd

First published 1976
ISBN 0 905035 02 X

Published and produced by the World of Islam Festival Publishing Company Ltd.

Designer: Colin Larkin
General Editors: Daphne Buckmaster and Halina Tunikowska
Indexers: Bronwen Gray and John Franklyn-Robbins
Line illustrations and diagrams: TAS David Hoxley Ltd
Set in 12/13pt. Monophoto Plantin 110

Colour origination: Westerham Press
Filmset by Westerham Press and printed in England by Westerham Press Ltd, Westerham, Kent

Other works by the author in European languages

An Introduction to Islamic Cosmological Doctrines, Cambridge (Mass.), Harvard University Press, 1964; new edition, London, Thames and Hudson, 1976.

Three Muslim Sages, Cambridge, Harvard University Press, 1964.

Iran (French and English editions), Paris, UNESCO, 1966; Tehran, 1971 and 1973.

Ideals and Realities of Islam, London, George Allen and Unwin, 1966; French translation as *Islam : Perspectives et réalités,* Paris, Buchet-Chastel, 1974; Italian translation as *Ideali e realità dell' Islam*, Milano, Rusconi editore, 1974.

Islamic Studies – Essays on Law and Society, the Sciences, and Philosophy and Sufism, Beirut, Librairie du Liban, 1967.

Science and Civilization in Islam, Cambridge, Harvard University Press, 1968; and New York, Mentor Books, 1970.

The Encounter of Man and Nature, The Spiritual Crisis of Modern Man, London, Allen and Unwin, 1968; paperback edition as *Man and Nature,* London, Allen and Unwin, 1976.

Sufi Essays, London, Allen and Unwin, 1972; Albany, State University of New York Press, 1973; Italian translation as *Il Sufismo*, Milano, Rusconi editore, 1974.

Jalal al-Din Rumi, Supreme Persian Poet and Sage, Tehran, High Council of Culture and Arts, 1974.

An Annotated Bibliography of Islamic Science, vol. I, Tehran, Imperial Iranian Academy of Philosophy, 1975.

With R. Beny, *Persia, Bridge of Turquoise,* Toronto, McClelland and Stewart, 1975.

Islam and the Plight of Modern Man, London, Longman, 1976.

Collaboration with Henry Corbin and O. Yahya in the *Histoire de la philosophie islamique,* Paris, Gallimard, 1964.

Contents

List of Illustrations

Transliteration

Arabic Letter	Transliteration
ء	'
ب	b
ت	t
ث	th
ج	j
ح	ḥ
خ	kh
د	d
ذ	dh
ر	r
ز	z
س	s
ش	sh
ص	ṣ
ض	ḍ
ط	ṭ
ظ	ẓ
ع	ʿ
غ	gh
ف	f
ق	q
ك	k
ل	l
م	m
ن	n
ه	h
و	w
ي	y
ة	t

Short Vowels	
ـَ	a
ـُ	u
ـِ	i

Long Vowels	
ـَا	ā
ـُو	ū
ـِي	ī

Diphthongs	
ـَوْ	aw
ـَيْ	ay
ـِيّ	iyy
ـُوّ	uww

Persian Letters	
پ	p
چ	ch
ژ	zh
گ	g

بســـم اللــــه الرحمــن الرحـــيم

In the Name of God Most Merciful and Compassionate

Preface

Islamic science, which is taken in this work to include disciplines concerned with the study of the cosmos, embraces a wide spectrum of intellectual activity, from the study of plants to algebra, carried out over more than a millennium by many races and peoples spread over the middle belt of the earth from Spain and Morocco to eastern Asia. Because of its traditional character, this science is not limited in scope or meaning as is the modern discipline with the same name. The Islamic sciences, even in the more limited sense considered here, which excludes the religious and many branches of the philosophical sciences, are concerned at once with the world of nature, of the psyche and of mathematics. Because of their symbolic quality, they are also intimately related to metaphysics, gnosis and art, and because of their practical import they touch upon the social and economic life of the community and the Divine Law which governs Islamic society. Considering these factors, it becomes evident with what a vast subject the student of Islamic science is faced and why as yet no complete study of the subject has been carried out.

Its extensive influence upon the Latin and Renaissance West has, since the eighteenth century, caused numerous studies in European languages to be devoted to the various facets of Islamic science, studies of which a complete bibliography has been made for the first time only recently (S. H. Nasr with the collaboration of W. Chittick, *An Annotated Bibliography of Islamic Science*). To this must be added the not inconsiderable amount of writings in the Islamic languages themselves. Nevertheless, a great deal of the subject remains unknown, and throughout the libraries of the world there are numerous treatises on the Islamic sciences which have never received any attention.

Basing themselves on the available results of research carried out so far, several scholars have attempted to write histories of Islamic science, including the classical reference work of G. Sarton, *An Introduction to the History of Science*, A. Miéli, *La science arabe et son rôle dans l'évolution scientifique mondiale*, and more recently the works of F. Sezgin and M. Ullmann. There is also the work of S. H. Nasr, *Science and Civilization in Islam* which combines a historical and morphological study of Islamic science with selections of actual Islamic scientific texts rendered into English.

The present work is, however, the first ever written on Islamic science in which the study and analysis of the texts is combined with illustrations from sources throughout the Islamic world. It is written on the occasion of the major Festival of the World of Islam in London, one of whose main features is the first exhibition ever organized of

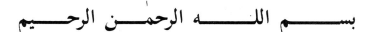

Islamic science anywhere and being held at the Science Museum of that city. It is written with the hope not only of providing a complete picture, to the extent possible, of Islamic science with appropriate illustrations, but also of complementing the exhibition with whose organization we have also been closely associated.

The perspective of this work, as of our other writings, is that of the Islamic tradition. We have sought to present the Islamic sciences as they have been viewed and still continue to be viewed to a large extent by those who have lived, breathed and died, and continue to do so, within the Islamic Universe and who have belonged, and still belong, to this Universe through both their hearts and their minds. The work is thus in many ways a complement to *Science and Civilization in Islam*, which is also written in the same perspective but with literary rather than visual illustrations.

We wish to thank M. Roland Michaud, the perspicacious and gifted French photographer, who is responsible for most of the photographs, and also Mr Robert Harding, the well-known and experienced British photographer, for their assistance to us in preparing most of the illustrated material for the book. We also wish to thank Mr Haddad-Adel who helped us with locating many manuscripts, Dr William Chittick and Mr Peter Wilson who read over the text and made helpful suggestions, Mr Colin Larkin whose talents are responsible for the artistic lay-out of the book, Mr John Knight-Smith who helped in many stages of the work, Mrs Daphne Buckmaster who edited the work and Mrs I. Hakemi who prepared the typescript for publication. Finally, it is necessary to mention that the whole plan for this and other books which complement it in the World of Islam Festival Series was originally conceived by the Director of the Festival, Mr Paul Keeler. Without his aid the work for this volume could not have been achieved.

Seyyed Hossein Nasr
Tehran
Shawwāl, 1395
October, 1975

Part One
The General Background

Chapter I
Islam and the Rise of the Islamic Sciences

No understanding of the Islamic sciences is possible without a comprehension of Islam itself, the life-giving force of a vast civilization one of whose fruits is the sciences. These sciences did not come into being accidentally among peoples who happened to be Muslim but were produced in the form that they *were* produced because those who brought them into being were Muslims and breathed within an Islamic universe.

The Islamic revelation, like all major manifestations of the Divine Logos, not only produced a religion in the sense of an ethical and social code but also transformed a segment of the cosmos and the minds of those who have lived within that cosmic sector. The phenomena which formed the subject matter of the Islamic sciences as well as the minds of the men who studied these phenomena have always been determined by a particular spiritual 'style' and transformed by a special type of grace (*barakah*) issuing directly from the Quranic revelation.[1] No serious study of the Islamic sciences can thus be carried out without some reference, no matter how brief, to the principles of Islam and the conditions created in time and space by Islam for the cultivation of the sciences.[2]

Islam, this last revelation of the Eternal and Unique Truth in the present cycle of human history, brought a message which encompasses all of human life, both what man does and what he makes. But before being concerned with doing and making, Islam is most of all concerned with what man is, or rather with how man can become what he really is in his profoundest and primordial nature (*fiṭrah*), namely, a theomorphic being created to reflect the Divine in all Its Majesty and Beauty. To achieve this end, Islam brought a metaphysical doctrine of the highest order and numerous sciences related inextricably to that supreme *scientia sacra* contained in the

1. We have provided ample arguments for the organic relation between Islam and the Islamic sciences, particularly those of nature, in many of our writings, arguments which cannot be repeated in an illustrated study such as the present one. See especially our *An Introduction to Islamic Cosmological Doctrines*, Cambridge (U.S.A.), 1964 (new edition, London, in press); and *Science and Civilization in Islam*, Cambridge (U.S.A.), 1968 and New York, 1970.

2. For a more extensive treatment of the basic elements of Islam, especially as they pertain to the sciences, see F. Schuon, *Understanding Islam*, trans. by D. M. Matheson, London, 1961 and Baltimore, 1972; F. Schuon, *Dimensions of Islam*, trans. by P. Townsend, London, 1970; T. Burckhardt, *An Introduction to Sufi Doctrine*, trans. by D. M. Matheson, Lahore, 1959; S. H. Nasr, *Ideals and Realities of Islam*, London, 1967.

inner dimensions of the Quran, and made accessible through various rites and forms which are also of a sacred nature and derive directly from the revelation. The doctrine is based on the Unity of the Principle (*al-tawḥīd*) and the interrelatedness of all that has been brought into being by the creative act (the *kun* of the Quran).[3] Its human complement is the doctrine of the Universal Man (*al-insān al-kāmil*) in whom the fullness of the human state is realized and through whom multiplicity returns to Unity.[4]

Upon the basis of the nature of ultimate reality as reflected in pure doctrine Islam has promulgated laws, called the *Sharī'ah*, governing human life whose aim is to enable man to live in conformity with this Reality. It has also brought into being a sacred art whose goal is to reflect that Reality in the world surrounding man during his terrestrial journey. Like all integral traditions, Islam is thus a total way of life, aimed at remoulding man's nature to enable him to become what he *is* eternally in the Divine Presence, and transforming the manner of man's doing and making to bring them into conformity with his role as God's vice-gerent in this world and with his ultimate destiny as a being made for immortality.

The unifying perspective of Islam has never allowed various forms of knowledge to be cultivated independently of each other. There has, on the contrary, always been a hierarchy of knowledge in which every form of knowledge from that of material substances to the highest metaphysics is organically interrelated, reflecting the structure of Reality itself. Moreover, Islamic spirituality has always been sapiential and gnostic in nature,[5] so that the quest for knowledge has possessed a particular religious aura even among common people in a way that is rarely found to this extent in other traditions. The rise of the Islamic sciences and their later development is inconceivable without the ever present spirit of the Islamic revelation, and the manner this revelation has moulded the minds, actions and surroundings of the men and civilizations responsible for the creation and cultivation of the sciences.

On a more outward plane the particular manner in which Islam spread and the whole unfolding of its history are also of course of paramount importance for an understanding of the rise and later growth of the Islamic sciences. The Prophet Muḥammad – upon whom be peace – unified Arabia in his twenty-three years of prophethood. The four caliphs who followed – Abū Bakr, 'Umar, 'Uthmān and 'Alī – called 'the rightly guided' (*khulafā' rāshidūn*) – consolidated the newly founded 'world of Islam' (*dār al-islām*) and spread its boundaries to Central Asia on the one hand and North Africa on the other. But the perfect norm of social and political life established by the Prophet was put under great tension and stress by centrifugal forces latent within Arab society and by the passions and short-comings of men, which had been checked momentarily by that blinding Divine intervention in human history which is Islam.

A fall from this early period of intense religious fervour in which sanctity and political authority were combined began with the death of 'Alī. Henceforth the caliphate became less 'apostolic' and more 'political' in character although still of a completely religious nature, there being no secularism in Islam. The Umayyad caliphate following upon the wake of the assassination of 'Alī by a member of the *Khawārij*[6] ruled for nearly a century, to be followed by the Abbasids, the Umayyads of Andalusia, the Fāṭimids, and numerous sultanates and princely states ranging from the powerful Seljuks who ruled over nearly all of Western Asia to hardly noticed local dynasties. Gradually Persia and North Africa became politically independent in fact if not in theory until with the Mongol invasion even the theoretical political unity symbolized by the Abbasid caliphate came to an end and the Islamic world became polarized into the three vast empires of the

3. 'But His command, when He intendeth a thing, is only that He saith unto it: Be! (*kun*) and it is' (Quran, XXXVI, 82; Pickthall translation).

4. On these two pillars of all Islamic doctrine, see Nasr, *Science and Civilization in Islam*, chap. 13; also al-Jīlī, *De l'homme universel*, trans. by T. Burckhardt, Lyon, 1953.

5. This does not mean that Islamic spirituality has excluded the element of love. It is only a question of accent, for no complete spiritual path can exclude the three basic elements of fear, love and knowledge.

6. The *Khawārij* opposed both 'Alī and Mu'āwiyah at the battle of Siffin and remained for centuries a revolutionary force which fought against both the Sunnis and the Shī'ites. See E. Adib Salem, *Political Theory and Institutions of the Khawārij*, 1957; and H. Laoust, *Les schismes dans l'Islam*, Paris, 1965.

Ottomans, Safavids and Moguls. But this pattern of apparent political turmoil and upheaval did not destroy the unity and stability of Islamic society protected by both the *Sharī'ah* and a sacred art, each of which in its own way enabled the Muslims to breathe in an Islamic universe whose horizons guarded a continuity that is hardly imaginable in an anti-traditional world.

Meanwhile during these periods Islam grew geographically in a continuous manner and spread in three basic phases to its present boundaries. In the first phase up to the early Abbasid period the heartland of the Islamic world from Spain to Central Asia was conquered and consolidated. During the second period from around the 7th/13th to the 10th/16th centuries[7] Islam spread, this time completely peacefully and mostly by means of Sufism, to the Indian sub-continent and the Indonesian archipelago. And since the last century Islam has been spreading steadily in Africa. In fact throughout its history, and despite various political ups and downs, Islam has grown steadily geographically, never receding in any territory with the exception of the Iberian peninsula, which after eight centuries of rule the Muslims lost to the Christians. But the main arena in which the Islamic sciences were cultivated and developed was for the most part that earliest part of *dār al-islām* spreading from Central Asia and Persia to Spain, the land which has always remained, especially in its central regions, the intellectual and geographical heartland of the Islamic world, the land in which before everywhere else the message of the Islamic revelation was consolidated into forms and institutions governing human society.

* * *

The central theophany of the Islamic revelation from which have been drawn the principles of both knowledge and action is the Holy Quran, to which must be added the prophetic *Ḥadīth*,[8] that is, the Prophet's commentary and extension of the teachings of the Book of God.[9] The Quran and *Ḥadīth* together are the fountainhead of all that is Islamic in whatever domain it might be. More specifically, these sources have played a double role in the creation and cultivation of the sciences. First of all the principle, not of course the details, of all science is considered by Muslims to be contained in the Quran, and there is an esoteric interpretation of the Holy Book which makes possible the unveiling of its mysteries and penetration into its inner meaning wherein reside the principles of all the sciences.[10] Secondly, the Quran and the *Ḥadīth* have created an atmosphere for the cultivation of the sciences by emphasizing the virtue of pursuing all knowledge that is in one way or another a confirmation of Divine Unity. Therefore, a whole metaphysics and cosmology have issued from the bosom of the Quran and the *Ḥadīth* and have acted as the basis upon which all the Islamic sciences have been constructed.[11] They have also created a particular atmosphere which has fostered and encouraged all intellectual activity that is in conformity with the spirit of Islam as reflected in the Quran and the *Ḥadīth*. The importance of the *dicta* contained in these

7. Throughout this work the dates on the left refer to the Islamic lunar calendar and those on the right to the Christian calendar.

8. *Ḥadīth* in Arabic literally means 'saying', but when used generally in a religious context it refers to the sayings of the Holy Prophet in Sunnism and of the Holy Prophet and the Imāms in Shī'ism. See Nasr, *Ideals and Realities of Islam*, chap. 3.

9. When the Holy Prophet was asked how he should be remembered after his death, he answered, 'Read the Holy Quran'. The text of the Quran, which is the word of God and divinely inspired in both form and meaning, contains something of the trace of the soul of the Holy Prophet. The *Ḥadīth* is, therefore, bound in a most intimate manner with the Quran. In fact without it much of the Quran would be incomprehensible.

10. It needs to be emphasized that this has nothing to do with trying to harmonize the Book of God with 'modern science' by trying to show how one verse explains the nature of the atom and the other microbes. This sterile type of activity, which was common among Christians with regard to the Bible in 19th century England and America and which has had some adherents among Muslims during this century in their study of the Quran, stems only from an enfeebled intellectual position and its shallowness is displayed by the speed with which it falls out of vogue. See S. H. Nasr, *Islam and the Plight of Modern Man*, London, 1976, chap. 11.

11. This is true not only of the 'transmitted sciences' (*al-'ulūm al-naqliyyah*), with which we are not so much concerned in this book, but also of the 'intellectual sciences' (*al-'ulūm al-'aqliyyah*), which form the main subject matter of our present study. On the division of the Islamic sciences into these categories see Nasr, *Science and Civilization in Islam*, pp. 59ff. We shall also deal briefly with this subject in the next chapter of the present work.

Figure 1. Verses from the Holy Quran concerning knowledge.

آية الكرسى «سورهٔ بقره «٢» آيهٔ ٢٥٧»

اَللهُ لَا اِلٰهَ اِلَّا هُوَ الْحَىُّ الْقَيُّومُ لَا تَأْخُذُهُ سِنَةٌ وَلَا نَوْمٌ لَهُ مَا فِى السَّمٰوَاتِ وَمَا

فِى الْاَرْضِ مَنْ ذَا الَّذِى يَشْفَعُ عِنْدَهُ اِلَّا بِاِذْنِهِ يَعْلَمُ مَا بَيْنَ اَيْدِيهِمْ وَمَا

خَلْفَهُمْ وَلَا يُحِيطُونَ بِشَيْءٍ مِنْ عِلْمِهِ اِلَّا بِمَا شَاءَ وَسِعَ كُرْسِيُّهُ السَّمٰوَاتِ

وَالْاَرْضَ وَلَا يَؤُدُهُ حِفْظُهُمَا وَهُوَ الْعَلِىُّ الْعَظِيمُ ٭

Figure 1a. Allah! There is no God save Him, the Alive, the Eternal. Neither slumber nor sleep overtaketh Him. To Him belongeth whatsoever is in the heavens and whatsoever is in the earth. Who is he that intercedeth with Him save by His leave? He knoweth that which is in front of them and that which is behind them, while they encompass nothing of His knowledge save what He will. His throne includeth the heavens and the earth, and He is never weary of preserving them. He is the Sublime, the Tremendous.

٭ اَللهُ نُورُ السَّمٰوَاتِ وَالْاَرْضِ مَثَلُ نُورِهِ كَمِشْكٰوةٍ

فِيهَا مِصْبَاحٌ اَلْمِصْبَاحُ فِى زُجَاجَةٍ اَلزُّجَاجَةُ كَاَنَّهَا

كَوْكَبٌ دُرِّىٌّ يُوقَدُ مِنْ شَجَرَةٍ مُبَارَكَةٍ زَيْتُونَةٍ لَا شَرْقِيَّةٍ

وَلَا غَرْبِيَّةٍ يَكَادُ زَيْتُهَا يُضِىءُ وَلَوْ لَمْ تَمْسَسْهُ نَارٌ

نُورٌ عَلٰى نُورٍ يَهْدِى اللهُ لِنُورِهِ مَنْ يَشَاءُ وَيَضْرِبُ اللهُ

الْاَمْثَالَ لِلنَّاسِ وَاللهُ بِكُلِّ شَيْءٍ عَلِيمٌ

Figure 1b. Allah is the Light of the heavens and the earth. The similitude of his light is as a niche wherein is a lamp. The lamp is in a glass. The glass is as it were a shining star. (This lamp) is kindled from a blessed tree, an olive neither of the East nor of the West, whose oil would almost glow forth (of itself) though no fire touched it. Light upon light. Allah guideth unto His light whom He will. And Allah speaketh to mankind in allegories for Allah is Knower of all things.

هَلْ يَسْتَوِى الَّذِينَ يَعْلَمُونَ وَالَّذِينَ لَا يَعْلَمُونَ

اِنَّمَا يَتَذَكَّرُ اُولُوا الْبَابِ

سُورَةُ زُمَّر آيَة ٩

Figure 1c. Are those who know equal with those who know not? But only men of understanding will pay heed.

سَنُرِيهِمْ آيَاتِنَا فِى الْآفَاقَ وَفِى اَنْفُسِهِمْ حَتَّى يَتَبَيَّنَ لَهُمْ اِنَّهُ الْحَقَ

سُورَةُ فُصِّلَتْ آيَة ٥٣

Figure 1d. We shall show them our portents on the horizons and within themselves until it will be manifest unto them that it is the Truth.

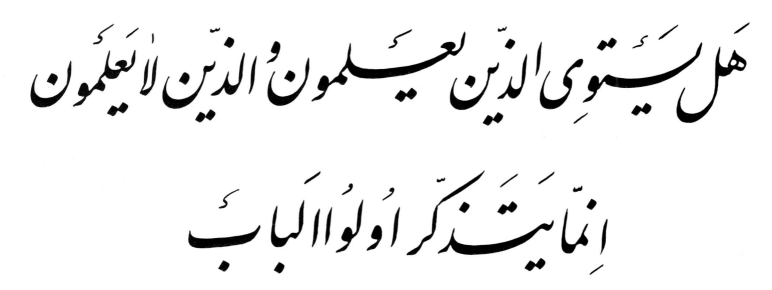

Figure 2. Sayings of the Holy Prophet pertaining to knowledge.

قَالَ رَسُولُ ٱللَّهِ : طَلَبُ ٱلْعِلْمِ فَرِيضَةٌ عَلَى كُلِّ مُسْلِمٍ .

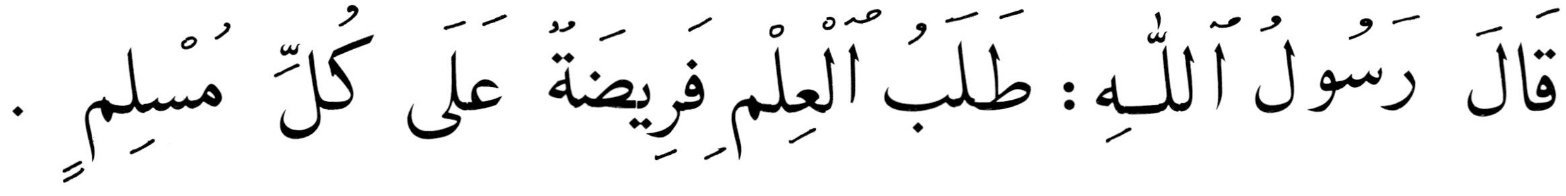

Figure 2a. The Holy Prophet has said: 'The quest of knowledge is obligatory for every Muslim'.

قَالَ رَسُولُ ٱللَّهِ : إِنَّ ٱلْعُلَمَاءَ وَرَثَةُ ٱلْأَنْبِيَاء

Figure 2b. The Holy Prophet has said: 'Verily the men of knowledge are the inheritors of the prophets'.

قَالَ رَسُولُ اللّٰهِ : اُطْلُبُوا ٱلْعِلْمَ مِنَ ٱلْمَهْدِ اِلَى ٱللَّحْدِ

Figure 2c. The Holy Prophet has said: 'Seek knowledge from the cradle to the grave'.

two basic sources of Islam for an understanding of the Islamic sciences in their organic link with the Islamic religion and the civilization created by Islam can hardly be overemphasized, for these sayings have moulded the minds of Muslim men of learning over the ages and have provided for them a source of both knowledge and inspiration.

* * *

Islamic science came into being from a wedding between the spirit that issued from the Quranic revelation and the existing sciences of various civilizations which Islam inherited and which it transmuted through its spiritual power into a new substance, at once different from and continuous with what had existed before it. The international and cosmopolitan nature of Islamic civilization, derived from the universal character of the Islamic revelation and reflected in the geographical spread of the Islamic world (*dār al-islām*), enabled it to create the first science of a truly international nature in human history.

Islam became heir to the intellectual heritage of all the major civilizations before it save that of the Far East, and it became a haven within which various intellectual traditions found a new lease upon life, albeit transformed within a new spiritual universe. This point must be repeated, particularly since so many people in the West wrongly believe that Islam acted simply as a bridge over which ideas of Antiquity passed to mediaeval Europe. As a matter of fact nothing could be further from the truth, for no idea, theory or doctrine entered the citadel of Islamic thought unless it became first Muslimized and integrated into the total world view of Islam. Whatever could not make its peace (*salām*) with Islam was sooner or later dispelled from the arena of Islamic intellectual life or relegated completely to the margin of the tapestry of the Islamic sciences.[12]

Before the rise of the Islamic sciences many civilizations had come and gone and produced sciences of various domains of reality and with different orders of perfection. The vast proto-history of science which leads to the deepest recesses of human history and which reveals with each new discovery astounding achievements need not concern us here.[13] It is to the immediate predecessors of Islamic science that we must turn. The two outstanding river civilizations of Egypt and Mesopotamia had already produced medicine and mathematics of extraordinary quality before the Greek philosophers and scientists came upon the stage to theorize about them and to develop them further. Basing themselves upon this long tradition of the study of the heavens as well as the world of nature, the Greeks in turn produced Thales, Pythagoras, Plato and Aristotle within a relatively short period of less than three centuries before the centre of their scientific activity shifted to Alexandria. There in the soil of Egypt, at the moment of the twilight of Greek power and the dying gasps of ancient Egyptian civilization, a new synthesis of Greek, Egyptian and Oriental learning was achieved leading to one of the most prolific periods of the history of science, which produced such men as Euclid, Ptolemy and indirectly Galen, figures who entered Islamic civilization almost as if they had been Muslim teachers and masters.[14] It is important for an understanding of Islamic science to realize that the Graeco-Hellenistic heritage reached Islam not directly from Athens but through Alexandria, that Plato was seen mostly through the ideas of the Neoplatonists and Aristotle through Alexander Aphrodisias and Themistius. Alexandrian science, in its combining of mystical elements with rigorous logic, in synthesizing various scientific traditions, in basing all the sciences upon a hierarchy related to the 'mode of knowledge' and in many other ways, is a historical anticipation of Islamic science and in fact became transformed into Islamic science in the same manner that the Alexandria of Ptolemy and Origen became transformed into the jewel of Islamic Egypt, the

12. See Nasr, *op. cit.*, pp. 21ff.

13. Recent studies have unveiled amazing intellectual and more specifically scientific achievements going back to the Palaeolithic period. See J. Servier, *L'homme et l'invisible*, Paris, 1964; and G. Di Santillana and E. von Dechend, *Hamlet's Mill*, New York, 1967.

14. Those Hellenic and Hellenistic masters who were in conformity with the Islamic perspective and who were integrated into the Islamic intellectual universe were so thoroughly Muslimized that to this day their names are given to numerous children all over the Islamic world. In any Muslim city such as for example Tehran there are certainly more Aristotles, Euclids and Galens than in an Anglo-Saxon city (the modern Greeks themselves are of course an exception in their usage of these ancient names).

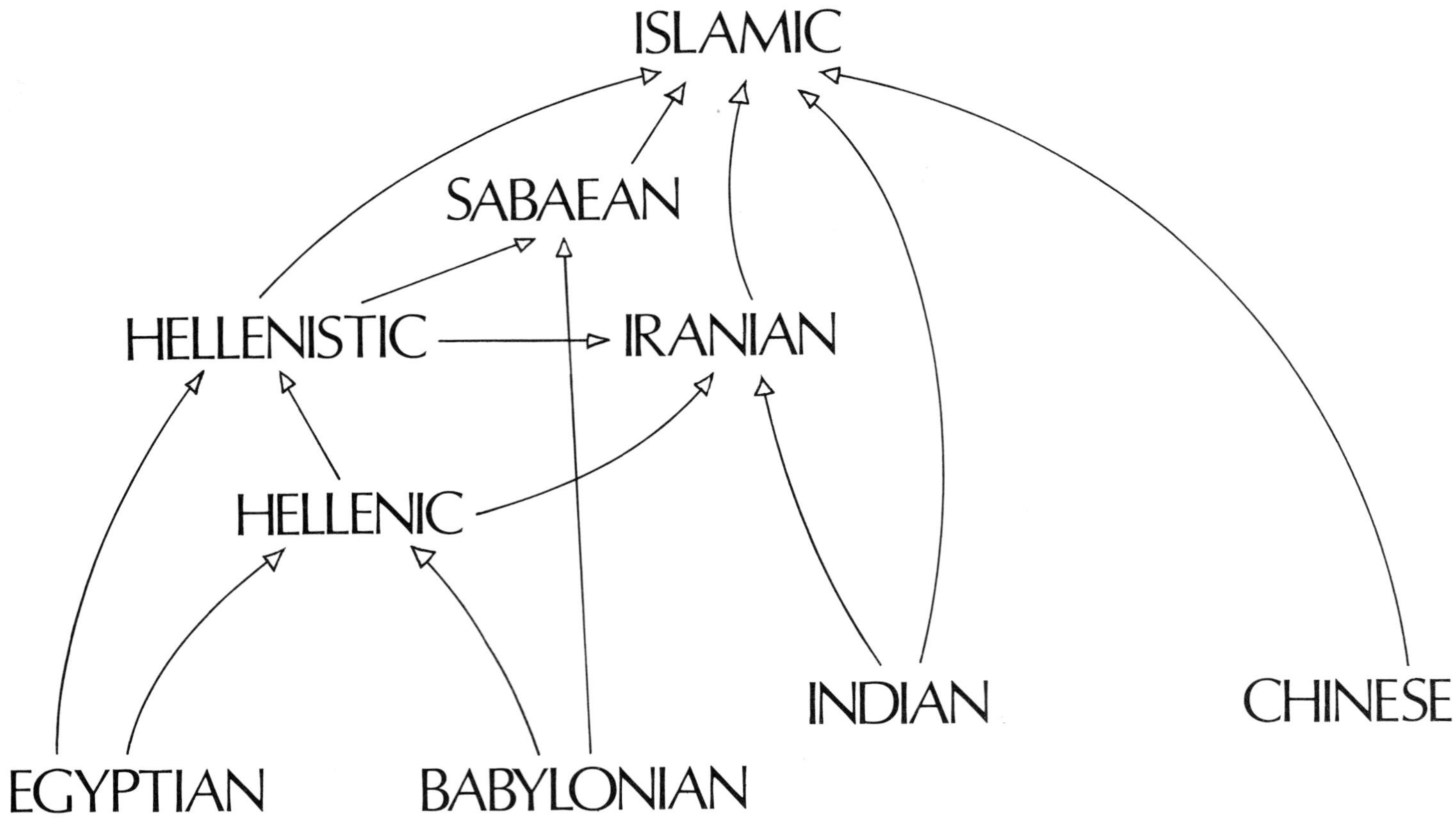

Figure 3. Scheme depicting the transmission of science and learning from the civilizations of Antiquity to the Islamic world.

home of such masters as Ibn 'Aṭā'allāh al-Iskandarī.

But the transmission of the Graeco-Hellenistic tradition to Islam was not a direct one. Several centuries of Christian history lie between the golden age of Alexandria and the rise of Islam. Alexandria was to become transformed into a major intellectual centre of early Christianity, then to undergo severe rivalries with other centres of Christian power, especially Constantinople and Antioch, and finally to bear witness to the death of its scientific activity under the pressure of Byzantine emperors, a death which is symbolized forcefully by the hanging of Hypatia, the daughter of Heron, in one of the squares of the city and the burning of its fabulous libraries.[15] But before this tragic end the main intellectual activity of Alexandria had been transmitted to Antioch thanks to the fierce rivalry that had come into being between the Monophysite and Nestorian Churches of the East on the one hand and the Byzantine Church on the other.[16] Furthermore rivalries between the Byzantines and the Sassanids, who naturally supported any schismatic movement against the Byzantines, pushed the centres of learning of the eastern churches ever more eastward to Edessa, Nisibis and finally to within the boundaries of the Persian Empire itself.

But the Christian centres of the Near East where Greek was taught and Syriac used as the language of science and learning were not the only channels which linked the intellectual life of Antiquity to that of Islam. There developed among the people of Harran a religious cult later

15. Research during the past few decades has shown clearly that the libraries of Alexandria had been destroyed for the most part long before the Islamic conquest of Egypt and that by the 1st/7th century there was little left for the Muslims to either burn or preserve.

16. It is remarkable how internal theological dispute between various Christian churches helped to transmit the scientific heritage of the ancient world to Islam. See L. DeLacy O'Leary, *How Greek Science Passed to the Arabs*, London, 1964; and M. Meyerhof, 'Von Alexandrien nach Baghdad', *Sitzungsberichte der Preussischen Akademie der Wissenschaften, Phil. Hist. Klasse*, 1930 (23): 389–429. See also R. Walzer, *Greek into Arabic*, Oxford, 1962, where the actual process of translation and transmission is discussed in several essays.

known to Muslims as Sabaeanism[17] that combined elements drawn from Babylonian religion with the more esoteric aspects of the Greek tradition. The Ḥarrānians were heirs, therefore, to the astronomical and astrological teachings of the Babylonians as well as to Neopythagoreanism and Hermeticism. Independent of Christian centres of learning they transmitted to the Muslims many aspects of the Graeco-Hellenistic heritage, and independent of the Greek world certain aspects of Babylonian mathematics and astronomy which are reflected in Muslim sources but have not been found in Greek ones.

As far as the Persian world is concerned, it too transmitted to Islamic civilization many sciences, some of its own and some ultimately of Greek and Indian origin. During the Sassanid period the Persians developed Jundishapur, near the present day Persian city of Ahvaz, as a university centre which in fact grew steadily until it became heir to both Antioch and Edessa, a haven for men of learning everywhere, and by the time of the fall of the Sassanids without doubt the most important centre of learning in Western Asia, particularly in the field of medicine. Jundishapur was a cosmopolitan gathering place where Persian, Greek and Indian men of learning met and worked together. In many fields, especially in medicine, this school more than any other was the living link between Islamic science and the ancient world. Meanwhile the Persians themselves showed special interest and made important discoveries in astronomy on the one hand and pharmacology on the other at the same time that they cultivated avidly both the Indian and the Greek sciences. Persia made major contributions to nearly every facet of Islamic civilization, became one of its major centres and played a central role in its creation. But in the field of science Persia played a triple role as far as transmission was concerned: it transmitted its own scientific tradition to Islam, as seen in such works as the *Royal Astronomical Tables* (*Zīj-i shahriyā*r); it made available certain aspects of Greek learning to Muslims which had been translated into Pahlavi or even Syriac but taught in centres of learning within Persia such as Jundishapur; and finally it passed on to Islam many of the Indian sciences, especially medicine, astronomy and natural history, which had been cultivated by the Sassanids. A particularly outstanding example of this latter role is the *Kalīlah wa Dimnah*, which was first translated from Sanskrit into Pahlavi and then by Ibn Muqaffaʿ into Arabic, becoming rapidly one of the masterpieces of Arabic literature and at the same time a source for Muslim natural history.[18]

As for India itself, its scientific tradition, especially in mathematics (including astronomy) and medicine reached Islam not only through Sassanid Persia but also thanks to a number of Indian men of learning who were invited to Baghdad and other Islamic intellectual centres. Of course the Indian sciences entered into the Islamic world again through the writings of al-Bīrūnī in the 5th/11th century and soon after through the numerous works of Amīr Khusraw. But as far as the genesis of Islamic science is concerned it was mostly as a result of the translation of certain basic texts of mathematics and astronomy such as the *Brāhmasphuṭasiddhānta* of Brahmagupta and a few medical works, particularly concerning drugs and poisons, that Indian science made a visible effect upon Islamic science and became one of the notable elements that contributed to its birth.

Finally, a word must be said of the Far East. It is true that no traces of the Chinese scientific tradition are visible within *dār al-islām* at the moment of the founding of the Islamic sciences and that we must wait until after the Mongol invasion for the official transmission of Chinese scientific works through their translation into Persian and Arabic. But there is no doubt that there was some kind of earlier contact even with China. The transmission to the Muslims of such important Chinese technological inventions as the making of paper and the appearance of certain definitely Chinese elements such as the *Ming-Tang* in early Islamic alchemy are witness

17. This should not be confused with the Sabaean or Mandaean cults of Iraq and Southern Persia which continue to this day. On the Sabaeans of Harran the classical work of D. Chwolson, *Die Ssabier und der Ssabismus*, 2 vols., St. Petersburg, 1856, is still valuable. See also E. Drower, *The Mandaeans of Iraq and Iran*, Oxford, 1937.

18. See S. H. Nasr, 'Natural History' in M. M. Sharif (ed.), *A History of Muslim Philosophy*, vol. II, Wiesbaden, 1966, pp. 1316–1332.

to contacts which were not merely bound to business transactions through land or sea but which possessed an intellectual and scientific aspect. There is no doubt, however, that the Far Eastern element in the foundation of the Islamic sciences does not compare in any way with the Greek, Indian or Persian, which formed for the most part the *materia prima* upon which Islam imposed a new intellectual and spiritual form, creating through this wedding the Islamic sciences.

* * *

The actual process of transmission of the sciences of ancient civilizations from such languages as Greek, Syriac, Sanskrit and Pahlavi into Arabic is one of the most remarkable instances of cultural transmission in human history, to be compared only with such other major processes of translation and transmission as the rendering of the Buddhist sutras into Chinese, and Arabic works into Latin. But in both quantity and quality the translation of works into Arabic surpasses perhaps all other episodes of a similar nature. Without outward compulsion but driven most of all by an inner need to *know*, in conformity with the 'gnostic' nature of Islamic spirituality,[19] the young and extremely virile Islamic civilization channelled its energies into the vast enterprise of translation, establishing such well known academies as the *Bayt al-ḥikmah* of al-Ma'mūn for this purpose. The existence of religious minorities within *dār al-islām*, minorities whose scholars were eminently suited for the task of translation, facilitated the process as did the fact that many scientific works had already been rendered into Syriac, a Semitic language which was the sister of Arabic.

Nevertheless the translation of the majority of the important scientific works of Antiquity into Arabic within a period of about 150 years stretching from the 2nd/8th to the 4th/10th centuries was no mean task. Thanks to such masters of translation as Ḥunayn ibn Isḥāq[20] and to the concerted effort of caliphs, princes and viziers, the main scientific works of such men as Hippocrates, Aristotle, Theophrastus, Euclid, Ptolemy, Dioscorides, Galen and many others were rendered into a precise Arabic. Moreover this was done with the help of an oral tradition which has made of these translations something that is often more true to the original Greek, Syriac or whatever other language was involved than most modern translations. Thanks to this movement Arabic became the most important scientific language of the world for many centuries[21] and the ground was prepared for the rapid growth of the Islamic sciences properly speaking. The translations provided the *materia prima* upon which the Muslim mind pondered and which it moulded into the substructure for the Islamic sciences that soon came into being as a body of knowledge at once distinct and related to the age-old intellectual traditions which it had inherited and adopted as its own thanks to the synthesizing and integrating power of the Islamic revelation. Henceforth this science, while revealing the traits of its historical origins, has been more than anything else the crystallization of the study of the cosmos and its parts from the perspective of Islam as reflected in the most principial manner in the Quran and the prophetic traditions.

19. On the summary of various reasons offered by historians and scholars for the translation of works into Arabic see S. H. Nasr, *Ma'ārif-i islāmī dar jahān-i mu'āṣir*, Tehran, 1353 (A. H. solar), introduction.

20. See O. Bergstrasser, *Ḥunain ibn Isḥak und seine Schule*, Leiden, 1913.

21. One should not, however, forget the great importance of Persian especially for the later period of Islamic history.

Chapter II
The Islamic Educational System

The cultivation of the Islamic sciences depended upon a vast educational system which embraced both formal and informal education and which made possible the encouragement and transmission of knowledge in all its forms. The educational system was of course based on the traditional Islamic concept of knowledge and learning. It emphasized most of all the religious sciences but included nearly all other forms of knowledge from theodicy to pharmacology. Islam considers knowledge (*'ilm*) as something sacred because ultimately all knowledge concerns some aspect of God's theophanies. It is this sacred view of knowledge that has imbued the whole Islamic educational system to this day making it even institutionally inseparable from specific religious organizations and institutions such as the mosque, the Sufi centre and places run by means of endowments (*awqāf*).[1] This view has made the relation between the teacher and the student of traditional schools a most intimate and spiritual one, and teachers have enjoyed a reverence hardly imaginable in modern societies. There is in fact a well-known saying attributed to 'Alī ibn Abī Ṭālib – upon whom be peace – which states, 'I have become the slave of him who has taught me a single word.'[2] The whole affair of education has always been at the heart of Islamic civilization as one of its basic pillars because it has been inseparable from the tradition itself which forms the marrow and the backbone of the whole of Islamic civilization.

Because of this inseparable link the Islamic concept of knowledge is based upon the two fundamental axes of unity and hierarchy. Like existence itself, with which knowledge is ultimately identical,[3] the sciences or forms of knowledge are ultimately one, and at the same time belong to a hierarchic order. Knowledge is not random as it appears in the profusion of profane knowledge today when there is no longer an organic link between man's various modes and

1. The institution of *awqāf* is vast and embraces nearly every facet of traditional Islamic society, but its relation to schools, libraries and other specifically educational institutions is particularly strong. On the institution of *awqāf* see M. Gaudefroy-Demombynes, *Les Institutions musulmanes*, Paris, 1950.

2. *'Man 'allamanī ḥarfan fa qad ṣayyaranī 'abdan'.* Obviously this 'word' is very far removed from the vast stream of information, most of it useless, that bombards people today in an atmosphere in which knowledge has become completely de-sacralized.

3. This basic doctrine was made fully explicit in later centuries from two different perspectives in the majestic doctrines of Ibn 'Arabī and Mullā Ṣadrā.

ways of knowing. The Islamic sciences and the intellectual perspectives cultivated in Islam have always been seen in a hierarchy[4] which leads ultimately to the knowledge of the One, of the supreme 'Substance', this being itself from another point of view the Substance of all knowledge.[5] That is why whenever confronted with sciences originally cultivated by other civilizations Muslim intellectual authorities sought to integrate them into the Islamic scheme of the hierarchy of knowledge. And that also is why the greatest Muslim gnostics, philosophers and scientists from al-Kindī, al-Fārābī and Ibn Sīnā to al-Ghazzālī, Naṣīr al-Dīn al-Ṭūsī and Mullā Ṣadrā were concerned with the question of the classification of the sciences.

The Muslims saw two main channels open before man for the acquiring of formal knowledge: the path of revealed truth, which after its revelation is transmitted from one generation to the next in a form which the Muslims called 'the transmitted sciences' (*al-ʿulūm al-naqliyyah*), and knowledge acquired through the God-given intelligence of man on both the level of the intellect and reason[6] and which the Muslims came to call the 'intellectual sciences' (*al-ʿulūm al-ʿaqlīyyah*). To these two classes of formal knowledge, together usually referred to as 'acquired knowledge' (*al-ʿilm al-ḥuṣūlī*), must be added the sapiential wisdom, the gnosis which results from vision (*kashf*) and the actual 'tasting' of the truth (*dhawq*, in Latin *sapere*, to taste, which is the root of *sapientia*) and which the Muslims have usually called 'presential knowledge' (*al-ʿilm al-ḥuḍūrī*).

Faced with the great array of various pre-Islamic sciences made available through translation along with the vast river of both exoteric and esoteric sciences that had flowed from the inexhaustible ocean of the Quranic revelation, Muslim intellectual authorities set out to classify the sciences, hoping in this way to elucidate their hierarchy and contribute to the solution of the problem of the harmony between reason and revelation, or religion and science. Al-Kindī was perhaps the first to turn to this problem in his *Fī aqsām al-ʿulūm* (*On the Types of the Sciences*). But it was the work of his successor in the Peripatetic school, Abū Naṣr al-Fārābī, the 'Second Teacher', which wielded a much wider influence over the curricula of Muslim universities and even those of the West. The *Kitāb iḥṣāʾ al-ʿulūm* (*The Enumeration of the Sciences*) of al-Fārābī reflects at once the Aristotelian classification of the sciences as transmitted to Muslims through the commentary of John Philoponos upon the *Isagoge* of Porphyry and the desire to harmonize this concept with that derived from the Quran and especially the *Sharīʿah*. This work not only influenced later Muslim authors but became also widely known in the West thanks to the translation of Dominicus Gundisalvi, and is cited by many Latin authors such as Peter of Abano.[7]

With the continuous development of the Islamic sciences new branches and forms of science came into being and at the same time the sciences which were taken over from the pre-Islamic civilizations were ever more Muslimized and fitted into the Islamic hierarchy of knowledge. Both these tendencies are reflected in the later schemes of classification to which dozens of separate treatises or chapters have been devoted by such masters as Ibn Sīnā, the Ikhwān al-Ṣafāʾ, al-Ghazzālī and Ibn Rushd and even by the remarkable historian of the 8th/14th century Ibn Khaldūn who in his *Muqaddimah* (*Prolegomena*) to the general study of history gives an elaborate account of the classification of the Islamic sciences after their period of maturity.[8]

From the time of Ibn Khaldūn onward several philosophical and scientific encyclopaedias appeared in both Arabic and Persian, and later also in Turkish, in which the classification of the sciences are discussed. Some of these works like the *Durrat al-tāj* of Quṭb al-Dīn al-Shīrāzī are more concerned with philosophy and others like the *Tadhkirah* of Dāʾūd al-Anṭākī more with the

4. On the hierarchy of various intellectual perspectives in Islam see S. H. Nasr, *Three Muslim Sages*, Cambridge (U.S.A.), 1964, introduction.

5. As stated so forcefully by F. Schuon, 'The substance of knowledge is Knowledge of the Substance . . .', 'Atmā-Māyā', in *Studies in Comparative Religion*, Summer, 1973, p. 130.

6. The distinction between these two instruments of knowledge is as fundamental to Islamic thought as is the distinction between *intellectus* and *ratio* in the traditional schools of ancient and mediaeval philosophy.

7. See D. M. Dunlop, *Arabic Science in the West*, Karachi, 1958, pp. 88–89.

8. See Ibn Khaldūn, *The Muqaddimah: An Introduction to History*, trans. by F. Rosenthal, 3 vols., New York, 1958, vol. 2, pp. 436ff. A summary of his classification is given by Nasr, *Science and Civilization in Islam*, pp. 62ff.

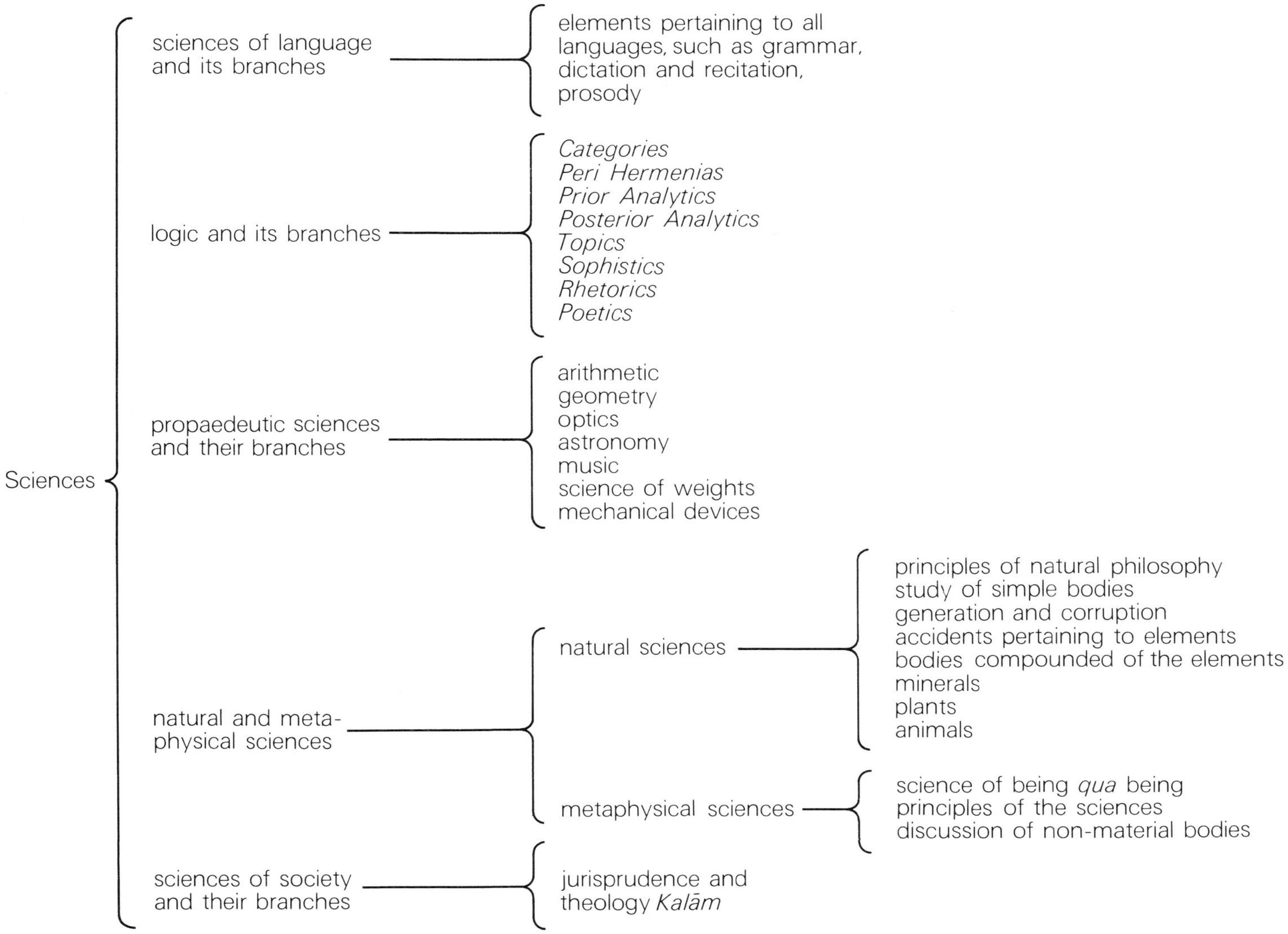

Figure 4a. The classification of the sciences according to the *Iḥṣā' al-'ulūm* of al-Fārābī.

sciences. One of the most complete and widespread of these encyclopaedias which mentions nearly all the sciences cultivated in Islamic civilization is the *Nafā'is al-funūn* (*Precious Elements of the Sciences*) of Shams al-Dīn al-Āmulī written during the 9th/15th century. The numerous sciences outlined by Āmulī and the classification upon which the work is based reflect the spectrum and the hierarchy of the Islamic sciences after their full flowering and centuries of development.

The Muslims became faced once again in the 13th/19th century with the onslaught of Western science, which has since threatened both the Islamic hierarchy of knowledge and the harmony of its educational system, wreaking havoc with them to an extent that is unprecedented in Islamic history. Al-Fārābī became known as the 'Second Teacher' (*al-mu'allim al-thānī*) because he gave order to the sciences and classified them. To a lesser extent Mīr Dāmād performed the same function in Safavid Persia and gained the title of the 'Third Teacher'. Today Islam is truly in need of a 'Fourth Teacher'[9] to re-establish the hierarchy of knowledge so essential to the Islamic perspective and to classify the sciences once again in such a way as to prevent the sacred from being inundated by the profane and the ultimate goal of all knowledge from being forgotten amidst the glitter of quickly changing forms of science which

9. See S. H. Nasr, 'Chirā Fārābī-rā mu'allim-i thānī khwāndahand', *Fārābī Commemoration Volume*, Tehran, Tehran University (in press).

The Classification of the Sciences according to the *Nafā'is al-funūn fī ᶜarā'is al-ᶜuyūn* by Shams al-Dīn Muḥammad al-Āmuli

First classification

- Sciences
  - philosophical sciences (which are the same at all periods)
    - theoretical
      - metaphysics (supreme science)
      - mathematics (intermediate science)
      - natural philosophy (lower science)
    - practical
      - pertaining to the individual — ethics
      - pertaining to the collectivity
        - economics
        - politics
  - non-philosophical sciences (which are not the same at all periods)
    - religious
      - intellectual
      - transmitted
    - non-religious

Figure 4b

Second classification

- Sciences
  - early *(awā'il)*
    - practical philosophy (including ethics, politics and economics)
    - theoretical philosophy (including logic, prime philosophy, metaphysics, science of natural bodies and all branches of natural philosophy)
    - principles of mathematics (including arithmetic, geometry, astronomy and music)
    - branches of natural philosophy (including medicine, alchemy, natural magic, etc.)
    - branches of mathematics (including all branches of astronomy such as the science of *anwā'*, mathematical geography, mechanical devices, chess and backgammon)
  - late *(awākhir)*
    - literature
    - sciences of law *(sharᶜiyyāt)*
    - Sufism
    - sciences of 'daily discourse' *(muḥāwarī)* such as history, biography, genealogy, etc.

Figure 4c

Figures 4b and 4c. Two different classifications of the sciences according to the *Nafā'is al-funūn fī 'arā'is al-'uyūn* by Shams al-Dīn Muḥammad al-Āmulī.

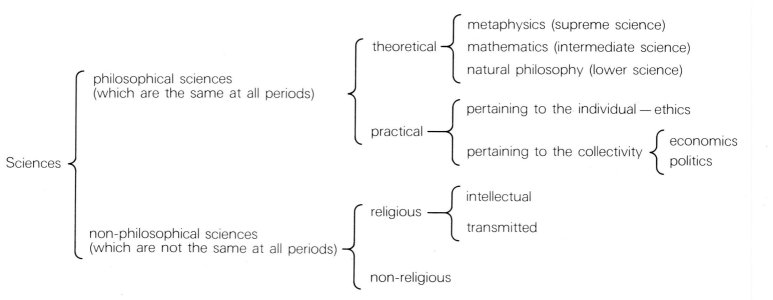

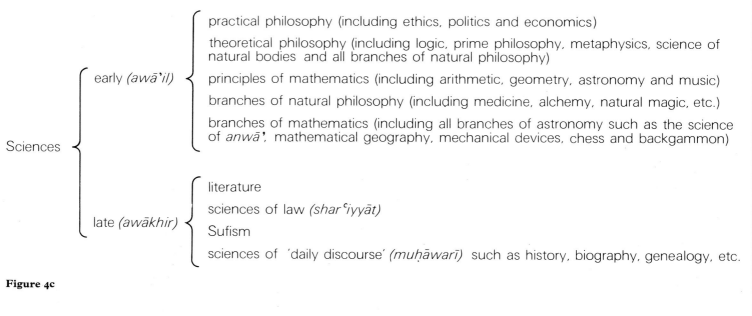

move ever more rapidly without approaching any closer to the centre of the circle of universal existence.[10]

* * *

The centres in which the Islamic sciences have been taught over the ages have been an integral aspect of Islamic civilization, participating in its formal unity in the same way that the content of the sciences became integrated into the all embracing intellectual unity of Islam. From the beginning the mosque was at once the religious and social centre of the Islamic community as well as the centre for learning. To this day Quranic schools (where the fountainhead of all the Islamic sciences, namely the Quran, is taught to the young) are connected with the local mosques in various quarters of Muslim cities.

But historically there gradually developed a distinct institution called *madrasah* (literally 'the place for lessons') which grew alongside the mosque and is still closely associated with it. At the beginning certain parts of mosques were used for lessons in religious sciences, each master occupying a corner or pillar of his own which in fact often became associated with his name. Then as teaching became formalized and extended, buildings were often erected specifically for teaching purposes, with mosques attached to them. In either case, however, both architecturally and intellectually the mosque and the *madrasah* have never been dissociated from each other and some of the greatest Muslim centres of learning such as al-Azhar are even now both mosques and schools, reflecting the profoundly religious character of learning in Islam.

The *madrasah* developed into a full-fledged university around eleven hundred years ago, a university in which a variety of subjects from religious law to astronomy were taught regularly. Some of the earliest Islamic educational institutions dating from this period of genesis in fact still survive, the best examples being perhaps the Qarawiyyīn in Fez, the Zaytuniyyah in Tunis and al-Azhar in Cairo.[11] Other outstanding *madrasahs*, such as those of Qum, Mashhad, Samarqand, Isfahan, Najaf, San'a', Lucknow and the like belong to later periods of Islamic history, but are profoundly connected to the earlier *madrasahs*. Likewise the mediaeval European universities and their *curricula* reflect their close relation with the Muslim universities, which they emulated consciously.

As far as the intellectual sciences are concerned, they have not always been taught in all the

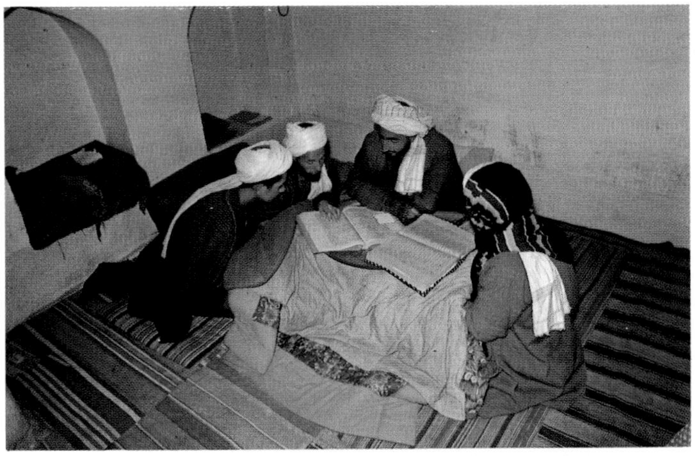

Plate 1. Students studying the Quran with a master in Afghanistan.

Plate 2. The Qarawiyyīn Mosque and School, Fez, Morocco.

10. See S. H. Nasr, *Islam and the Plight of Modern Man*, chap. 1.

11. On al-Azhar, which is the most thoroughly studied of Muslim universities, see B. Dodge, *Muslim Education in Medieval Times*, Washington, 1962.

Plate 3. Interior of the Gawharshād Mosque and School in Mashhad, Iran.

Plate 4. A general view of Shīr-dar *madrasah* on Registan Square in Samarqand.

Figure 5. A general view of the inner courtyard of al-Azhar University, Cairo.

Plate 5. Miniature depicting a traditional scene of instruction.

madrasahs, especially during the past few centuries. The mainstay of the curriculum of the *madrasahs* has always been the religious sciences. Nevertheless, many of the intellectual sciences such as philosophy, logic and mathematics *have* been taught in various *madrasahs* over the ages and are still taught today. This is especially true of the Persian *madrasahs*, where traditional philosophy is taught even now and where through the Safavid period mathematics was also taught on a serious level.[12]

But the *madrasah* was far from being the only centre for the study and the transmission of the sciences. The hospitals, for example, played an important educational role and many of the leading hospitals such as those of Rayy and Baghdad in the 4th/10th century had medical schools attached to them with regular programmes for students; medical dissertations had to be written by those who wanted to receive their medical certificate.[13] The traditional hospitals, some of the best examples of which survive

12. The whole philosophy of education involved in the traditional *madrasah* is of the utmost significance even today but cannot be dealt with in a book such as this. See A. L. Tibawi, *Islamic Education: its Traditions and Modernization into the Arab National Systems*, London, 1972. As for the 'decay' of many of the sciences in the Islamic world from the 11th/17th and 12th/18th centuries onward (and not the 7th/13th century as most Western historians of science imagine) it is without doubt directly related to a gradual loss of interest in such subjects as mathematics in the *madrasahs* and the deleting of more advanced courses on these subjects from the curriculum of the *madrasahs*.

13. On the educational aspect of Muslim hospitals see C. Elgood, *A Medical History of Persia*, Cambridge, 1951; and M. Z. Siddiqi, *Studies in Arabic and Persian Medical Literature*, Calcutta, 1959, pp. xxiiiff. Also M. Najmābādī, *Tārīkh-i ṭibb dar Īrān-i pas az Islām*, Tehran, 1353 (A. H. solar), part eight; and Ahmed Isa Bey, *Histoire des bimaristans (hôpitaux) à l'époque islamique*, Cairo, 1928.

today strangely enough in the Indo-Pakistani sub-continent, like that of Hyderabad, Deccan, have been throughout Islamic history a major scientific institution, combining the curing of patients with extensive teaching of medicine, pharmacology and allied subjects.[14]

Another important scientific institution which complemented the hospital and in which both research and teaching took place was the observatory. In fact it can be said without exaggeration that the observatory as a scientific institution owes its birth to Islamic civilization.[15] While in the early Islamic period the observatory was of a small size and usually associated with a single astronomer, from the 7th/13th century and the building of the Maraghah observatory by Naṣīr al-Dīn al-Ṭūsī, it became a major scientific institution in which numerous scientists gathered

Figures 6 and 7. Master physician (possibly Ibn Sīnā) teaching medicine.

Figure 8. A figure purported to be Ibn Sīnā (Avicenna) teaching a group of students.

14. A living example of this in contemporary form can be seen in the Hamdard institutes of Delhi and Karachi established by two of the leading traditional physicians (*ḥakīms*) of the Islamic world, the brothers Ḥakīm ʿAbd al-Ḥamīd and Ḥakīm Muḥammad Saʿīd.

15. See A. Sayīlī, *The Observatory in Islam*, Ankara, 1964.

Plate 6. General view of Bayazid II *Külliye* – a university complex consisting of mosque, *madrasah* and hospital – in Edirne, Turkey.

Plate 7. Osmania Hospital, Hyderabad, Deccan, India.

Plate 8. Miniature showing students studying astronomy with their teacher.

to work and teach together. The Maraghah observatory served as the source of inspiration and model for the Ulugh-Beg observatory in Samarqand and the Istanbul observatory of the Ottoman period where Taqī al-Dīn worked. These observatories in turn served as models for the several observatories constructed by Jai Singh in the 12th/18th century in India in such cities as Delhi and Jaipur and also were the model for the early European observatories such as those used by Tycho Brahe and Kepler. An analysis of the astronomical instruments in these 10th/16th and 11th/17th century European observatories and their comparison with earlier Muslim instruments reveals the close nexus between the Muslim and later European observatories.

The formal and public institutions of learning so far mentioned are not, however the only ones to consider when discussing the important centres for the teaching and the transmission of the sciences in Islam. Much of the transmission of learning, especially of more esoteric knowledge, has taken place and continues to take place in private circles not accessible to the public at large. These circles include first of all the Sufi centres (*khānaqāh* in Persian and *zāwiyah* in Arabic), where not only initiatic and spiritual practices take place but also many of the esoteric and sometimes even exoteric sciences are taught. The Sufi centres became especially important as centres of formal learning after the Mongol invasion, when they were forced to fulfil the role of the *madrasahs* destroyed by the Mongol onslaught as well as their own proper function of training the adepts spiritually.

There are also private circles connected with a particular teacher, meeting either at his house or the house of one of his disciples. Much of traditional learning is carried out today in the Islamic world in such private circles whose great propaedeutic importance can hardly be overestimated. Moreover, the occult sciences such as alchemy or geomancy have always been taught in such completely private circumstances. The *atelier* of an alchemist is almost always his home or the house of an adept, and it is here that those considered by the alchemist as capable of mastering the royal art have been and are to this day trained. The same could be said of the other esoteric and occult sciences, the former being also taught in Sufi centres but the latter almost exclusively in completely private places and gatherings. The channels of learning are like

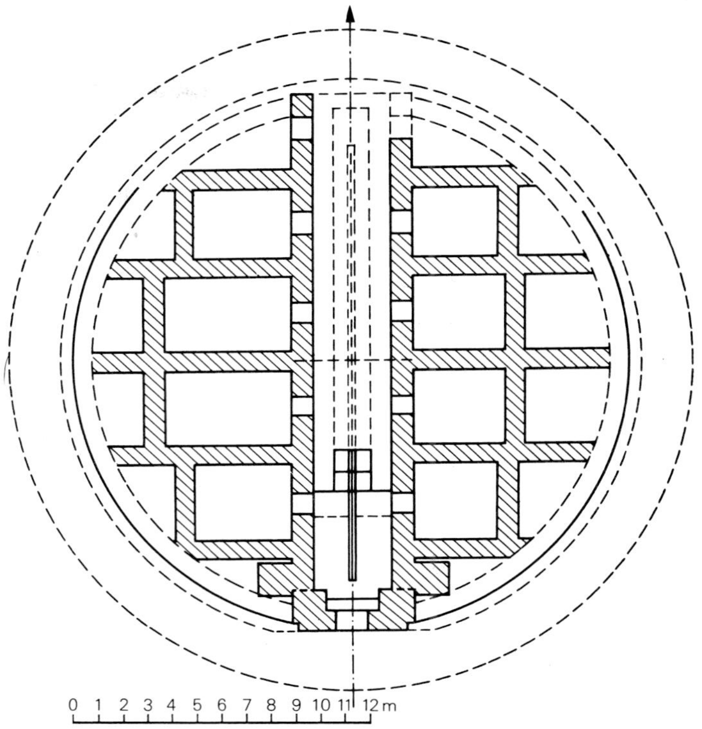

Figure 9a

Figure 9. (a) The horizontal and (b) the vertical cross-section of the Maraghah Observatory based on recent excavations by Azarabadegan University, Tabriz, Persia.

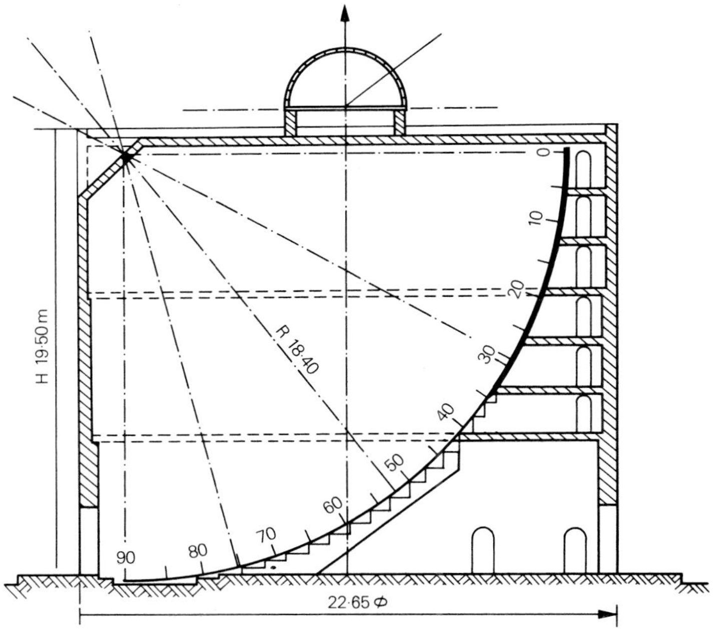

Figure 9b

arteries and veins in the body of Islamic society, some externally visible and others hidden. But together they have always played the vital role of enabling the life-giving blood of knowledge to flow through the body of the community, to rejuvenate it constantly and to preserve its vitality, enabling it to fulfil the function for which it has been destined by its very acceptance of the celestial norm of the Islamic revelation.

Plate 9. Inside a Sufi *khānaqāh*.

Part Two

The Islamic Sciences The Qualitative Study of the Universe

Chapter III
Cosmology, Cosmography and Geography

No understanding of the Islamic sciences or for that matter the sciences of any other tradition is possible without a consideration of the cosmology to which the branches of the traditional sciences are related like so many limbs belonging to a living organism. Even modern science, whether realized fully by its cultivators or not, functions within a world view created by 17th century rationalism and has been inseparable from this philosophical background since the scientific revolution.[1] So much more is the reliance upon a 'theoretical' background true of the Islamic sciences which are but applications and aspects of traditional Islamic cosmology and therefore of the metaphysical principles of the tradition of which the cosmological sciences themselves are expressions and reflections upon the cosmic plane.[2]

The cosmos is at once continuous and discontinuous with respect to its Origin, the Origin which is Pure Being and ultimately the Absolute and Infinite Reality which stands beyond even Being. As Being, the Origin is like the Sun of which all existents in the cosmos are rays. But the Origin is also Substance with respect to which the whole of the Universe is but a series of accidents, and

1. Modern science is related to the rationalistic universe emanating from the philosophical world view of the 17th century through its reliance upon human reason as the ultimate criterion of truth, its limiting of reality to the physical domain and its restricting of the relation between man and nature to the level of the senses and of reason analyzing the results of sense perception. Traditional sciences are related to metaphysical and cosmological principles in relying upon the language of symbolism, in basing themselves upon the hierarchic nature of the cosmos, in considering the analogies which exist between the macrocosm and the microcosm and in relying upon the Intellect, which pierces through phenomena to their noumenal essences, in addition to reason and the senses. See H. Butterfield, *The Origins of Modern Science*, New York, 1951; E. A. Burtt, *The Metaphysical Foundations of Modern Science*, New York, 1954; and F. Brunner, *Science et réalité*, Paris, 1954.

2. On the meaning of the cosmological perspective see T. Burckhardt, 'Nature de la perspective cosmologique', *Etudes Traditionnelles*, vol. 49, 1948, pp. 216–219.

Essence of which all cosmic forms are but reflections and theophanies.[3] The various cosmological schemes developed within Islam and the cosmos sanctified by the Islamic revelation are so many ways of depicting the relationship between the Origin and the Universe in its multiple levels of existence extending from the spiritual through the animic to the material (the *rūḥ*, *nafs* and *jism* of Islamic cosmologists and philosophers, corresponding to the *spiritus*, *anima* and *corpus* of the cosmologists of Antiquity). They are means of depicting this relationship in a 'space' which transcends purely physical space and also a 'time' which is beyond profane time, that is, within the matrix of the universal hierarchy which stands 'above' the terrestrial plane here and now and with respect to the 'rhythms' associated with the Substance or the phases of the 'Breath of the Compassionate'[4] which determines from on high the cycles (*adwār*) of universal existence and cosmic events associated with cosmic history and also with eschatology.[5]

Islamic cosmology is directly related to the principles of the Islamic revelation and to the metaphysics which issues forth from the esoteric message of the Quran and the inner teachings of the Prophet which are its complement.[6] It is not a generalization of the physical sciences or the extension of a terrestrial physics to the confines of the visible Universe. It has in fact nothing to do with what passes for cosmology today. Islamic cosmology aims at providing a vision of the cosmos which enables man to pierce through the visible world to the higher states of existence and creating a science of the cosmic domain which acts as a ladder to allow man to mount to the 'roof of the cosmos', to use the well-known phrase associated with the works of Rūmī,[7] and even beyond it to behold Metacosmic Reality which transcends all the planes of cosmic manifestation. The Origin or Principle of the Universe is at once Being, consciousness and bliss (*wujūd*, *wujdān* and *wajd* in Arabic)[8] and these qualities flow in the arteries of the cosmos precisely because the cosmos is a manifestation of the Principle. Traditional cosmologies are means of gaining knowledge of this positive aspect of the cosmos; in the bosom of metaphysical doctrines and with the aid of appropriate methods of realization they enable men to gain access to that consciousness and experience, that bliss which is already a foretaste of paradise.

To fulfil the role assigned to it within Islamic civilization, Islamic cosmology naturally

3. See F. Schuon, *Logic and Transcendence*, trans. by P. Townsend, New York, 1975, chap. 5. 'Substance may be compared to the centre of a spiral, and Essence to the centre of a system of concentric circles; one may also say that the notion of Substance is nearer to that of the Infinite and the notion of Essence nearer to that of the Absolute; again, there is in Substance an aspect of feminity and in Essence an aspect of masculinity.' *ibid.*, p. 76.

4. Sufis speak of the very 'stuff' or substance of the Universe as the 'Breath of the Compassionate' (*nafas al-raḥmān*) which passing through the 'essences' (*al-a'yān al-thābitah*) produces created beings like human breath which produces words and sounds by passing through the vocal cords. Man imitates on the human plane the act of creation through his speech and for that reason the word in the form of invocation (*dhikr*) plays such a central role in the 'reversal' of the cosmogonic act and the return of man to his Origin. On the *dhikr* see F. Schuon, *The Transcendent Unity of Religions*, trans. P. Townsend, New York, 1975, pp. 137 and 145–46.

5. In exoteric discussions of eschatology in Islam, rhythms of the manifestations of the Substance, or what would correspond to the days in the life of Brahma in Hinduism, are usually passed over in silence, but they are discussed in esoteric schools, in both Sufism and various forms of Shī'ism.

6. The cosmology based upon traditional Islamic sources is concerned with all the states of being below the Divine Names and Qualities, beginning with the Spirit (*al-Rūḥ*), which is the 'Divine Centre' of the cosmos, extending to the four archangels, the eight angels connected with the Divine Throne, and then the various angelic hierarchies and ending with the psychic and finally physical worlds. These 'worlds' have been depicted in various fashions, perhaps the most central being the 'Five Divine Presences' (*al-ḥaḍarāt al-ilāhiyyat al-khams*) of Ibn 'Arabī. See F. Schuon, *Logic and Transcendence*. pp. 97–100; and Schuon, *Dimensions of Islam*, chap. 11.

7. Concerning the *Mathnawī* of Rūmī it has been said,

> These words are the ladder to the firmament.
> Whoever ascends it reaches the roof –
> Not the roof of the sphere that is blue,
> But the roof which transcends all the visible heavens.

See S. H. Nasr, 'Rumi and the Sufi Tradition', *Studies in Comparative Religion*, Spring, 1974, p. 89.

8. It is not accidental that these terms possess the same root in Arabic.

وهذِهِ صُورَةُ فَرَسِ حيزُومْ فَرَسِ السَّيِّدِ مِنْهُ
جِبْرِيلْ عَلَيْهِ الصَّلَاةُ وَالسَّلَامُ

Plate 10. A miniature image of the horse of the Archangel Gabriel.

Plate 11. The nocturnal ascent (*al-mi'rāj*) of the Holy Prophet.

has made use of numerous forms of symbolism and has had recourse to many different means through which the end in view could be achieved. In fact it could not be otherwise seeing that Islam had to create a world-wide civilization and integrate within its fold people of different psychological and mental constitutions. In all forms of cosmology, however, the aim has remained the same, namely to transform the cosmos and its parts into an 'icon' which can be contemplated and a mirror in which the One can be revealed within the matrix of multiplicity itself. Beginning with the Universe which has become transformed by the Quranic revelation, the Universe in which the Archangel Gabriel descended and the Prophet made his nocturnal ascent (*al-miʿrāj*) to the Divine Proximity, Islamic cosmology has made use of such diverse elements as Quranic symbolism, concepts and symbols drawn from the doctrinal formulations of Sufism (itself developed to a large extent from the Quran and *Ḥadīth*), theosophical and philosophical descriptions of the cosmos, numerical symbolism and traditional astronomy. Islamic cosmology, therefore, displays many facets and forms but all leading to a single inner content. The meaning of all the cosmological schemes in Islam has remained the same, namely the relating of multiplicity to Unity, of existence to Being, of each creature on a particular level of existence to the higher levels and finally to the Divine Names and Qualities in which are to be found the principle and the 'end' of all cosmic manifestation.

No single 'event' is more central to the understanding of Islamic cosmology than the nocturnal ascent or *al-miʿrāj* of the Blessed Prophet from Mecca to Jerusalem and then vertically through all the states of being to the Divine Throne (*al-ʿarsh*) itself, an 'event' which is described in the Holy Quran and depicted by numerous miniaturists as well as described by countless writers and poets.[9] The Prophet Muḥammad – upon whom be peace – is himself the symbol of all that is positive in the cosmos, and the second *Shahādah* of Islam, *Muḥammadun rasūl Allāh* (Muḥammad is the Messenger of God) means esoterically among other things that the whole cosmos, in its positive aspect as symbol and not in its privative aspect as veil, comes from God. The nocturnal ascent of the Universal Man is therefore at once a return of the cosmos to its Source, the model for the spiritual life, and a delineation of the cosmos and hence the principal model for all Islamic cosmology. All the versions of the description of the cosmos to be found in various forms of Islamic cosmology are of the cosmos which was 'experienced' by the Prophet in his nocturnal journey and in fact Islamicized through this very journey as well as by the descent of the Holy Quran.[10]

The Muslim sages have elaborated Islamic cosmology in numerous treatises, sometimes making use of Quranic angelology alone and at other times incorporating into their works cosmological sciences drawn from other traditions but in conformity with the Islamic perspective. This is to be seen especially in the writings of Ibn ʿArabī, who was like a sea into which the rivers of Pythagoreanism, Platonism and Hermeticism flowed and in which they became completely intermingled with purely Islamic esotericism. The symbolism of the Arabic alphabet, the astrological signs, numerical symbolism and the science of the Divine Names became synthesized in his writings into a pattern of unity that is characteristic of the synthesizing genius of this great master of Islamic gnosis.

Similar to the cosmology described by Ibn ʿArabī but enclosed within the more particular world of Shīʿism are the schemes found in the writings of Sayyid Ḥaydar al-Āmulī, who was a disciple of Ibn ʿArabī as well as an outstanding Shīʿite theosopher and theologian. He also had a particular love for geometric patterns and made use of them as symbols of his cosmological doctrines. He designed *mandalas* to be contemplated by the adept, complicated patterns in which the twelve Imāms of Shīʿism enter into the cosmic scheme to play a major role as so many epiphanies of the Logos and reflections of the

9. Among them may be mentioned the Persian Sufi poet Sanāʾī whose *Miʿrāj-nāmah* along with several other Muslim sources most likely served as a source of inspiration for the *Divine Comedy* of Dante. See the well-known works of M. Asín Palacios, *La escatologia musulmana en la Divina Comedia*, Madrid, 1919; and E. Cerulli, *Il 'Libro della scala' e la questione delle fonti arabospagnole della Divina Comedia*, Vatican, 1949.

10. The 'night of power' (*laylat al-qadr*), during which the Quran was revealed, and the 'night of ascent' (*laylat al-miʿrāj*) complement each other and signify from the cosmological point of view the Islamicization of the cosmos in the descending and ascending orders, or from the cosmogonic and initiatic points of view.

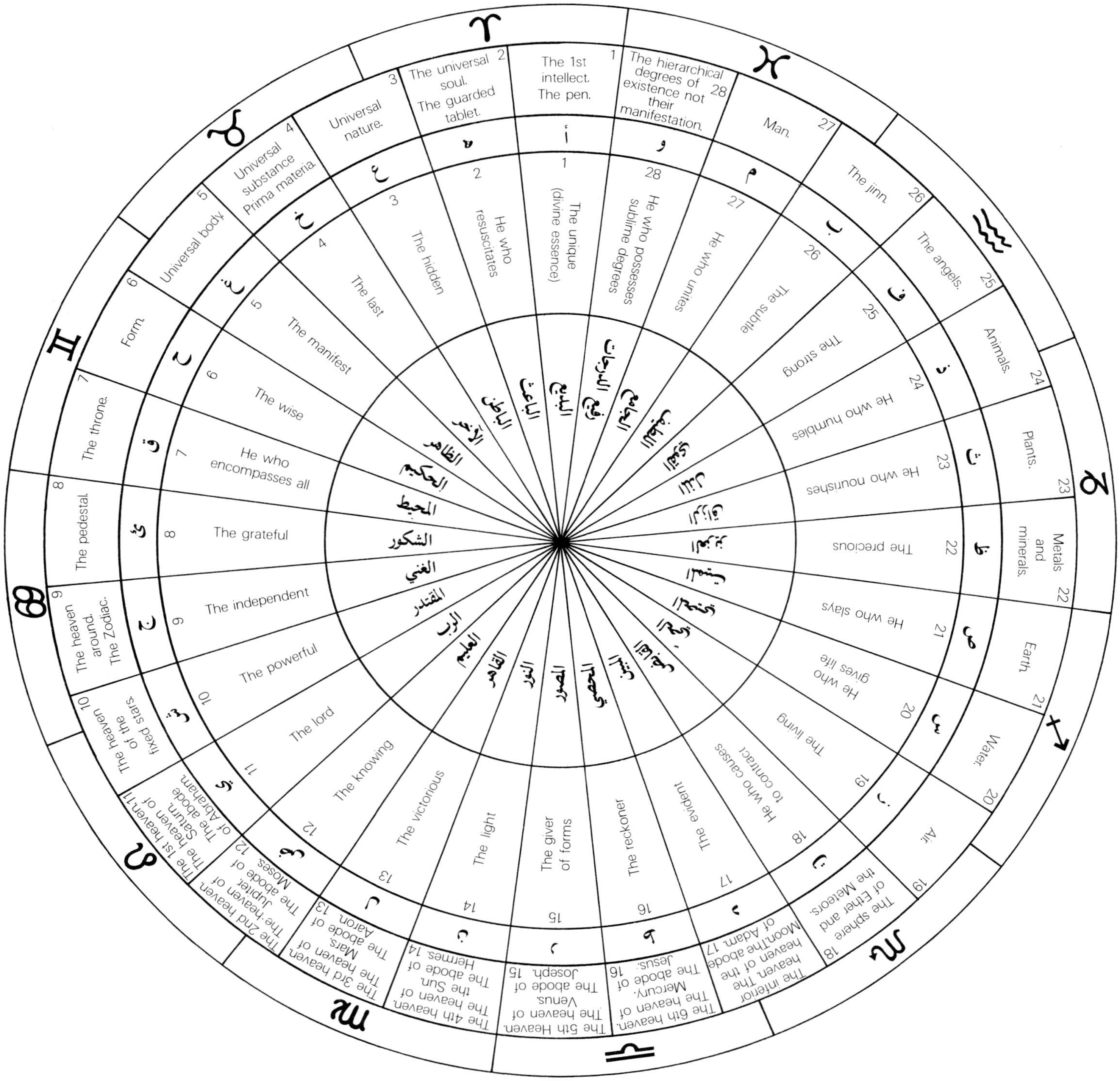

Figure 10. The macrocosmic deployment of the Divine Names in their correspondence with cosmological and astrological states and signs, according to Ibn ʻArabī.

Figure 11. The correspondence between the Prophets, the Imāms and the cosmic hierarchy according to Sayyid Ḥaydar al-Āmulī.

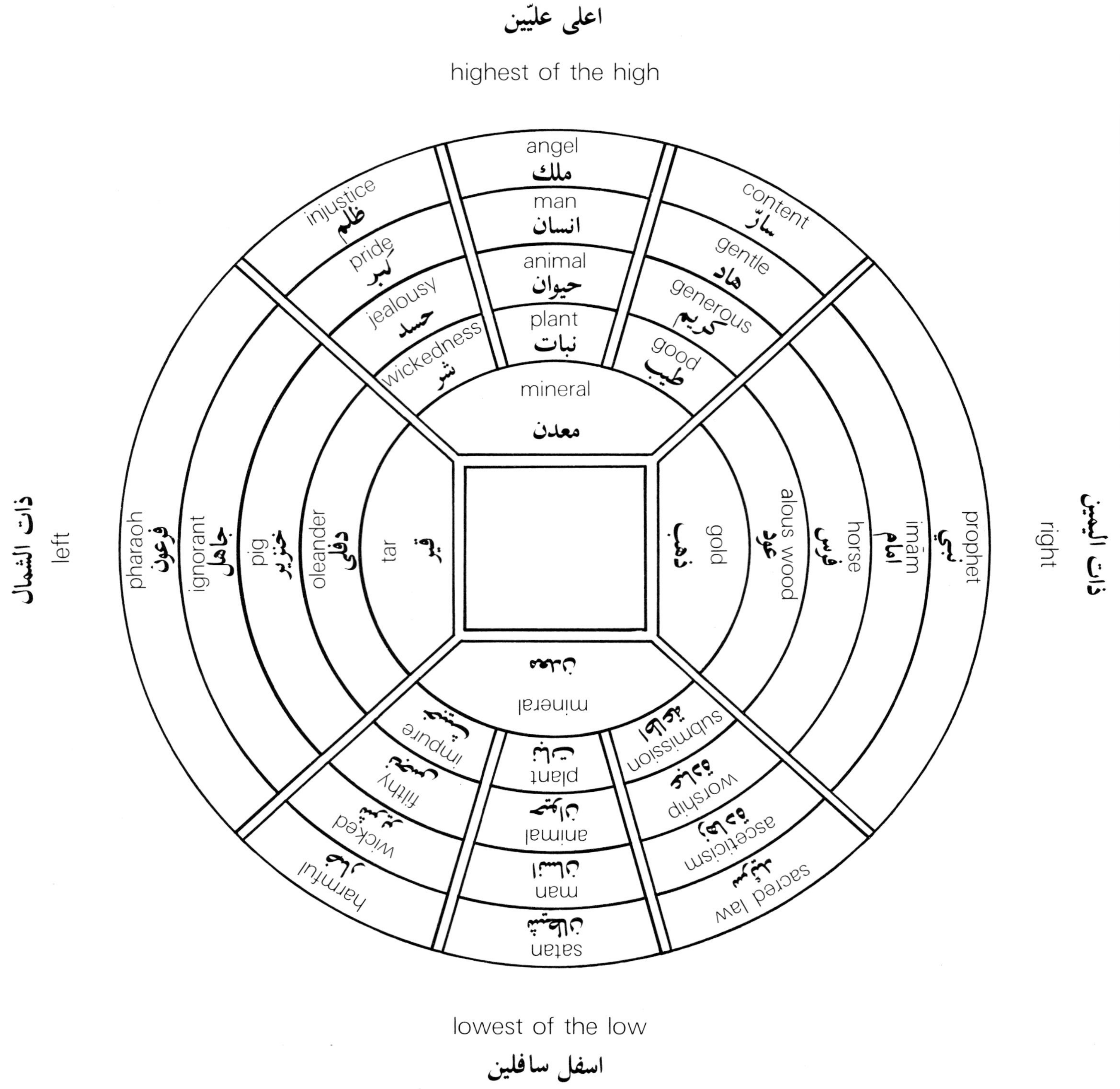

Figure 12. The cosmic hierarchy according to the *Epistles* of the Ikhwān al-Ṣafā'.

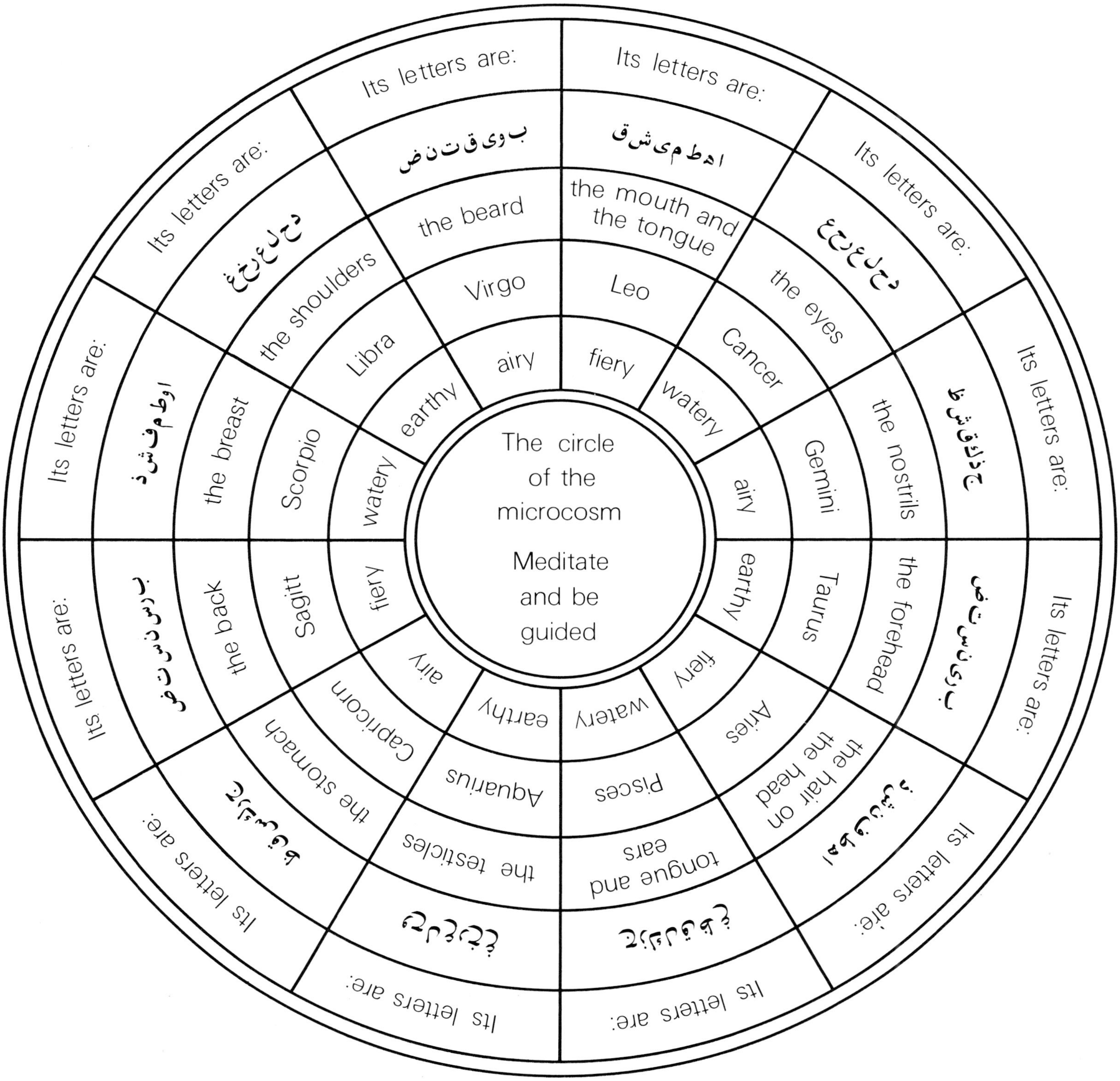

Figure 13. The correspondence between the elements, the astrological signs, the parts of the human body and the letters of the Arabic alphabet according to Shams al-Dīn al-Būnī.

Divine Light. The number twelve naturally plays a central role in these patterns, which unify angelology, imamology and astronomy in grand schemes unveiling the contours of the Islamic cosmos with its particular Shīʿite colour.

Another form of Islamic cosmology is to be found in the writing of those schools which were devoted to the science of the symbolism of numbers and letters and which often combined the Aristotelian doctrine of the three kingdoms and the Pythagorean philosophy of numbers with Islamic metaphysics while making use of the sciences concerned with the symbolism of the Arabic alphabet as well as the symbolism of certain words and phrases. In the case of the Ikhwān al-Ṣafā', whose *Epistles* reflect closely the thought of certain circles within Shīʿism, especially Ismāʿīlism, and which are related in many ways to the Jābirean corpus, there is to be found more than anything else a Pythagoreanism combined with Aristotelian natural philosophy and integrated into the matrix of Islamic esotericism, while in the works of such men as Shams al-Dīn al-Būnī certain Hermetic and also magical ideas enter into the picture.

Cosmology deals with the content and cosmography with the external form and description of the cosmos. In the Islamic world there developed numerous cosmographies based upon the traditional cosmologies. One type of cosmography is to be found in the class of writings known as the *Wonders of Creation* (*ʿAjā'ib al-makhlūqāt*) by such men as Abū Yaḥyā Zakariyyā' al-Qazwīnī. These books begin with the angelic world and end with plants and minerals. Moreover, they combine mythology with scientific description within the hierarchic Universe described in the cosmological works. These works, which are usually of a popular nature, have served as background for both popular literature and numerous miniature paintings. Other cosmographies such as those contained in the works of astronomers and mathematicians like al-Bīrūnī and Quṭb al-Dīn al-Shīrāzī are of a much more scientific nature being closely allied to the astronomy and physics developed by Muslim scientists but also staying within the bounds of the traditional Universe of Islamic cosmology.

In all of their diverse forms Islamic cosmology and cosmography have served as background, matrix and principle for the various Islamic sciences from geography to alchemy. They have made possible the linking of the particular sciences to the principles of the Islamic revelation and the creation of an integral civilization by Islam in which the various sciences have been cultivated without disrupting its unity, a civilization in which nature has been studied without destroying the harmony between man and his natural and cosmic environment.

Plate 12. The Angel of Death, Izrā'īl.

Geography and Geodesy

Muslim studies in geography extend from a symbolic and sacred geography which views the earth as an image of the spiritual world to the most exact mathematical measurements of geographic coordinates and quantitative geomorphic studies. Cast within the world view of Islam and centred most of all upon the vast confines of *dār al-islām*, the science of geography drew from many

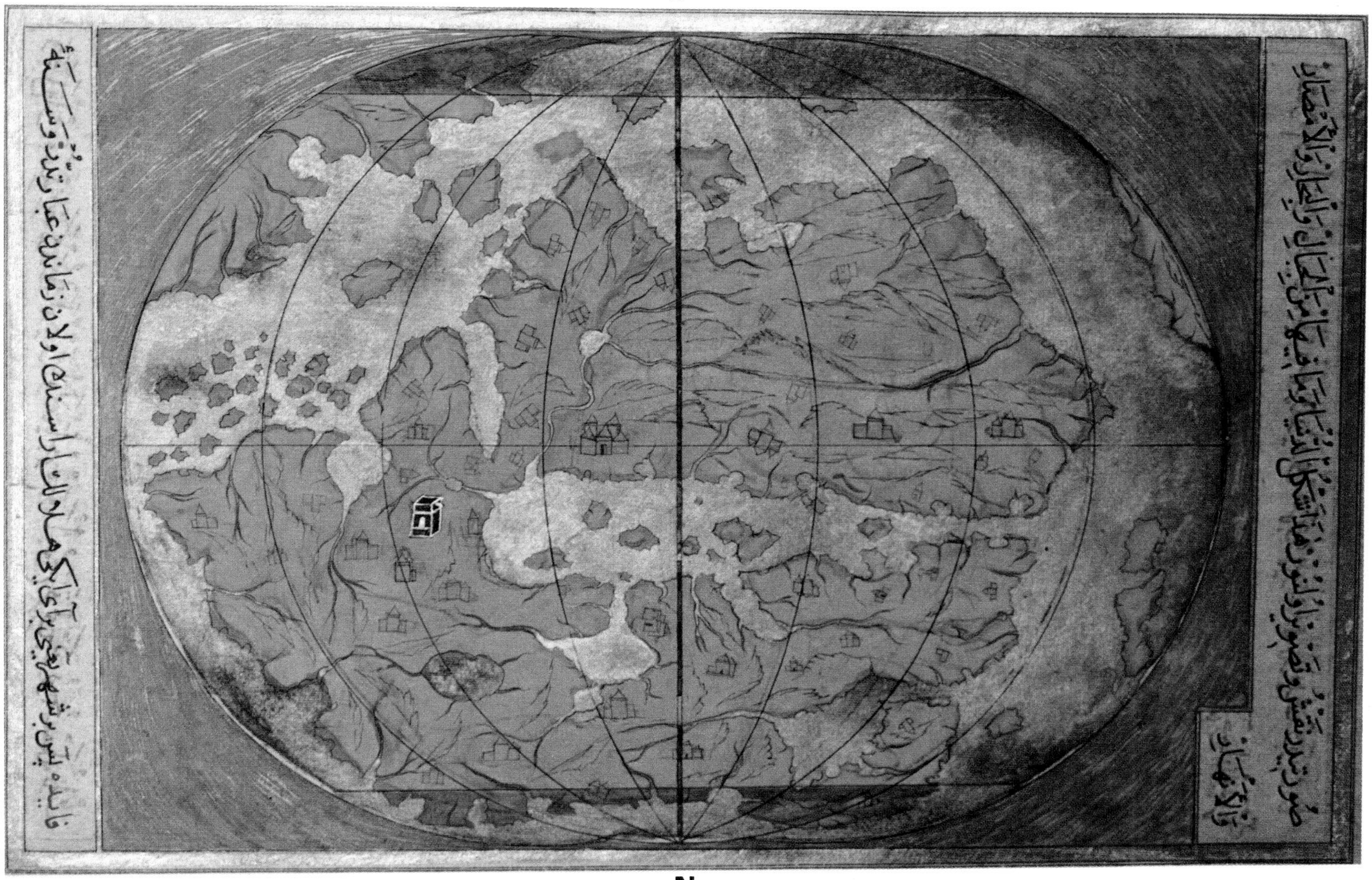

Plate 13. The Ka'bah at the centre of the inhabitable world.

sources, such as Babylonia, Greece, India and especially Persia. Pre-Islamic Persian geography had already influenced pre-Islamic Arabic geographical ideas, as the Arabic word *barzakh*, which comes from Pahlavi *farsang*, reveals, and it played a central role in early Islamic geography as well. The ancient Persians saw the earth as an angel and possessed a highly developed 'visionary geography'.[11] Their division of the world into seven circular 'regions' (*kishwars*) was a terrestrial reflection of the sevenfold spiritual hierarchy and left its deep effect upon geographers of the Islamic period,[12] who were fully aware of the symbolic significance of seven in both the Greek scheme of the climates and the Persian scheme of the *kishwars*. Likewise, the central cosmic mountain of the ancient Persians became transformed into the Mount Qāf mentioned in the Quran, and at least among a great number of Islamic geographers the central region of the world was conceived in a new fashion so as to encompass Mecca, the centre of the Islamic world and the point where for Muslims the heavenly axis touches the terrestrial plane. In 'Islamicizing' the natural world about it Islam in fact incorporated much of the symbolic and sacred geography of the traditions before it, sanctifying them anew through the power of the new revelation. How many mountains, lakes and other distinct *loci* can be found today in the Islamic world which are of particular religious significance now and were also of special religious significance in the traditions which preceded Islam!

While sacred geography goes back mostly to the origins of the Islamic revelation and its early expansion within the land destined to become the

11. See H. Corbin, *Terre céleste et corps de résurrection*, Paris, 1961, pp. 41ff.

12. See S. H. Nasr, 'La cosmographie en Iran préislamique et islamique, le problème de la continuité dans la civilisation iranienne', in *Arabic and Islamic Studies in Honor of Hamilton A. R. Gibb*, Leiden, 1965, pp. 521ff. Some of the ideas contained in old Persian world maps have even entered into apocryphal *Ḥadīth* literature.

Figure 14.

Figure 15.

Figures 14 and 15. Map of the world and the seven climes according to al-Bīrūnī.

home of classical Islam, descriptive and quantitative geography, which is considered as 'scientific' geography today, begins essentially in the Abbasid period with the translation of Indian, Persian and Greek geographical texts. The rendering into Arabic of the *Sūryasiddhānta* as well as other Indian astronomical texts acquainted Muslims with Indian geography, from which they learned most of all the calculation of longitudes from Ujjain. As for Persian sources, although no names of specific geographical works have survived, the knowledge of Sassanid geography among Muslims was widely extended, as can be seen in the names of many areas such as the Indian Ocean, which they called *baḥr al-fārs*, the 'Persian Sea', following Sassanid examples. The Iranian influence was particularly strong in maritime literature, as can be seen in the survival of numerous Persian words such as *bandar* (port) and *nākhudā* (captain of a ship) in Arabic geographical works.

As far as Greek sources are concerned, the Muslims had an intimate acquaintance with the *Geography* of Ptolemy, which was translated several times into Arabic, as well as the geography of Marinos of Tyre. Moreover, they were familiar with such works as the *Timaeus* of Plato and the *De Caelo* and *Meteorology* of Aristotle with all the geographical knowledge these texts contained. The descriptive geography of such men as Strabo, however, was never translated into Arabic. Islamic works drew from Greek sources mostly for mathematical geography and from Persian sources for descriptive geography. Thanks to the ease of travelling over the vast areas covered by *dār al-islām*, Islam produced its own Strabo's and gained a great deal more knowledge of geography than was ever accessible to the civilizations preceding it, a knowledge which it then fitted into the theoretical patterns inherited from both the Greeks and the Persians.

The earliest Islamic geographical works properly speaking belong to the early 3rd/9th century, especially to the reign of al-Ma'mūn.

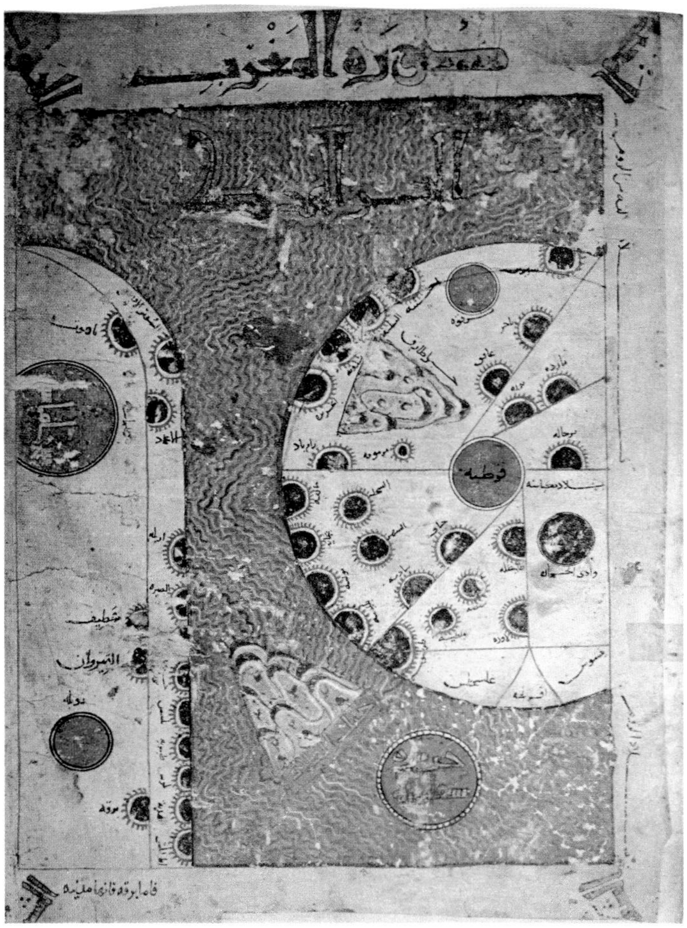

Plate 14

Plate 14. Spain and North Africa according to the map of al-Istakhrī.

Plates 15a and 15b. The Persian Gulf according to the map of al-Istakhrī.

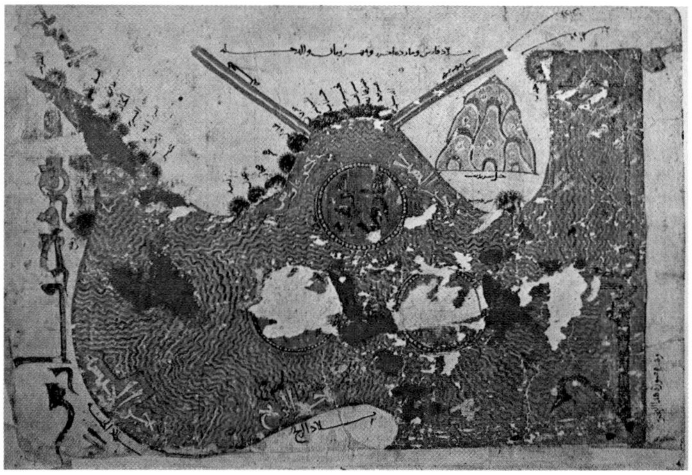

Plate 15a

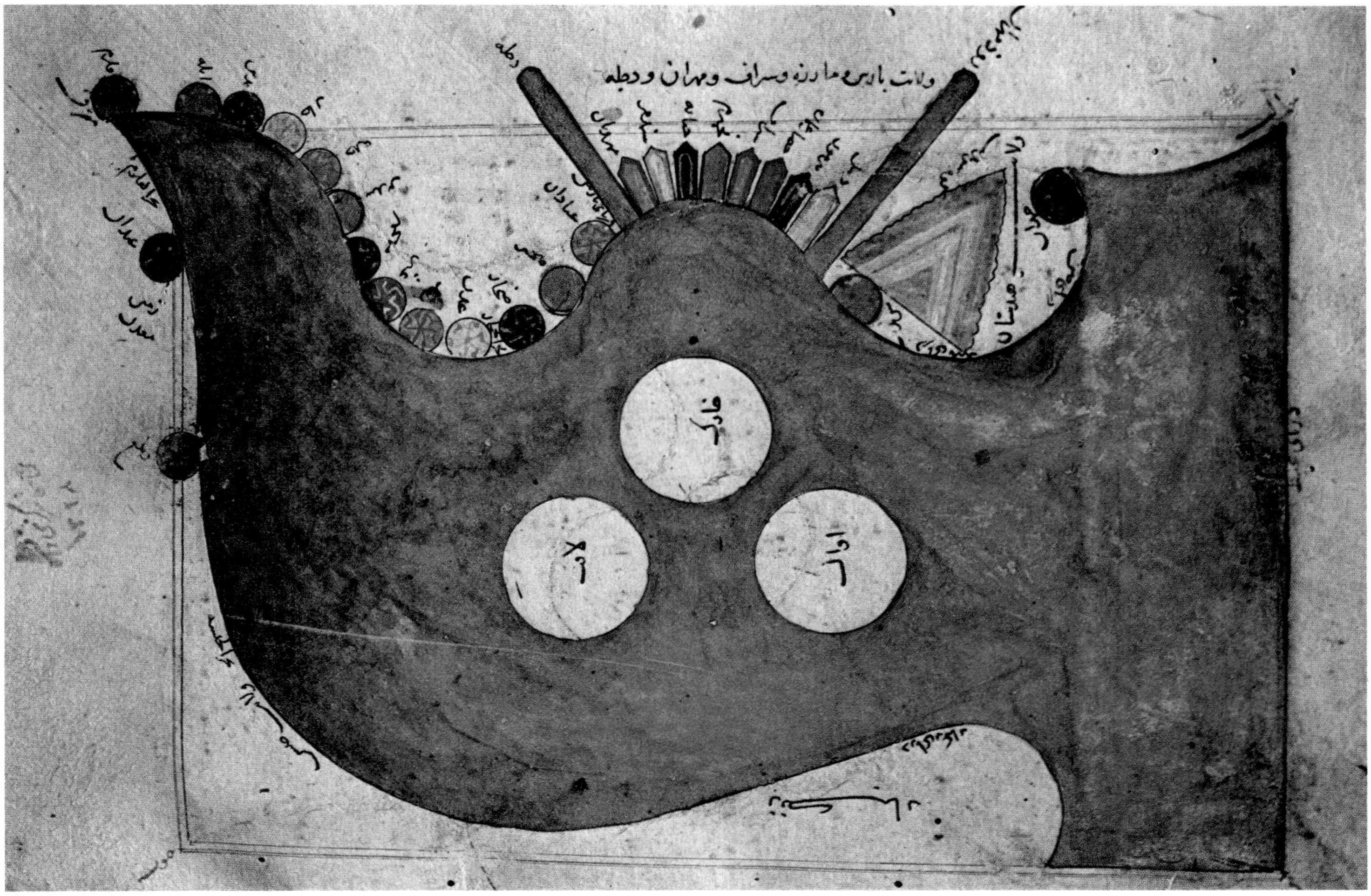

Plate 15b

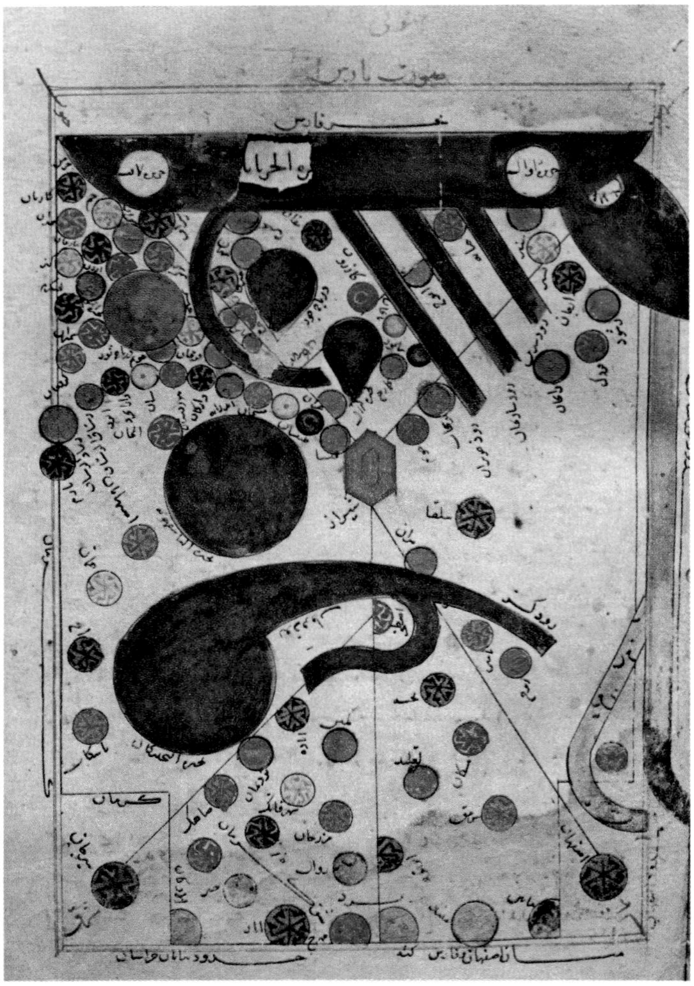

Plate 16. The province of Fars according to the map of al-Istakhrī.

During his caliphate the map of the world was drawn, entitled 'the Ma'mūnic map' (*al-ṣūrat al-ma'mūniyyah*), which is now lost but which was seen by Abu'l-Ḥasan al-Mas'ūdī who considered it more accurate than that of Ptolemy. During this time also several other major works on geography appeared on the scene, some written by philosophers such as al-Kindī and Aḥmad al-Sarakhsī and others contained in the astronomical works of such men as Abū 'Abdallāh al-Battānī, Abu'l-'Abbās al-Farghānī and Ibn Yūnus. These works were both descriptive and mathematical, the descriptive works being often in the form of itineraries such as the *al-Masālik wa'l-mamālik* of Ibn Khurdādhbih,[13] and the mathematical works following mostly upon the model of Ptolemy. Of the latter group the most important in this early period is without doubt the *Ṣūrat al-arḍ* (*The Figures of the Earth*) of Muḥammad ibn Mūsā al-Khwārazmī. Also among works of this period dealing extensively with mathematical geography may be mentioned *al-A'lāq al-nafīsah* (*The Book of Precious Things*) of Ibn Rustah.

During the 4th/10th and 5th/11th centuries geography developed extensively as actual observations of various parts of the world, accumulation of earlier studies and continuous research by Muslim scientists themselves made possible a notable expansion of the horizons of geography. Great historians such as Aḥmad al-Ya'qūbī also wrote on geography as an adjunct to history. Natural historians like Abu'l-Ḥasan al-Mas'ūdī, who has been called the Muslim Pliny, combined cosmology, history and geography in a single encyclopaedia entitled *Murūj al-dhahab* (*Prairies of Gold*) which set an example for centuries to follow.

This was also the period during which the first Persian work on geography, called *Ḥudūd al-'ālam* (*Limits of the World*), was written by an anonymous author based on the earlier work of Abū Isḥāq al-Istakhrī who belonged to a class of geographers like Abū Zayd al-Balkhī and Ibn Ḥawqal. These latter figures tried to give a more distinct Islamic colour to geography and usually limited themselves to Islamic lands.

A new chapter was also opened in the field of the geography of the seas during this formative period as Arab and Persian sailors made extensive journeys to such far away lands as Java, Sumatra and China, not to speak of India. From this seafaring there issued both popular tales and scientific descriptions contained in such works as the *Akhbār al-Ṣīn* (*Reports on China*) and *Akhbār al-Hind* (*Reports on India*) of Sulaymān the Merchant and the famous *'Ajā'ib al-hind* (*Wonders of India*)[14] of Buzurg ibn Shahriyār

Plate 17. Western Asia and the Eastern Mediterranean according to the map of Ibn Ḥawqal.

Plate 18. Central Asia and Transoxiana according to the map of Ibn Ḥawqal.

13. See F. E. Peters, *Allah's Commonwealth*, New York, 1973, pp. 344ff. For Islamic geography in general see Nafis Ahmad, *Muslim Contributions to Geography*, Lahore, 1947; also S. Maqboul Ahmad and Fr. Taeschner, *'Djughrāfiyā'*, in *Encyclopaedia of Islam* (new edition). See furthermore, the important study of A. Miquel, *La géographie humaine du monde musulman jusqu'au milieu du 11ᵉ siècle,* Paris, 1967, in which (pp. 4–33) special attention is paid to the diverse sources for the study of geography among Muslims.

14. For this *genre* of writing in English translation see J. O'Kane, *The Ship of Sulaiman*, London, 1972.

Plate 17

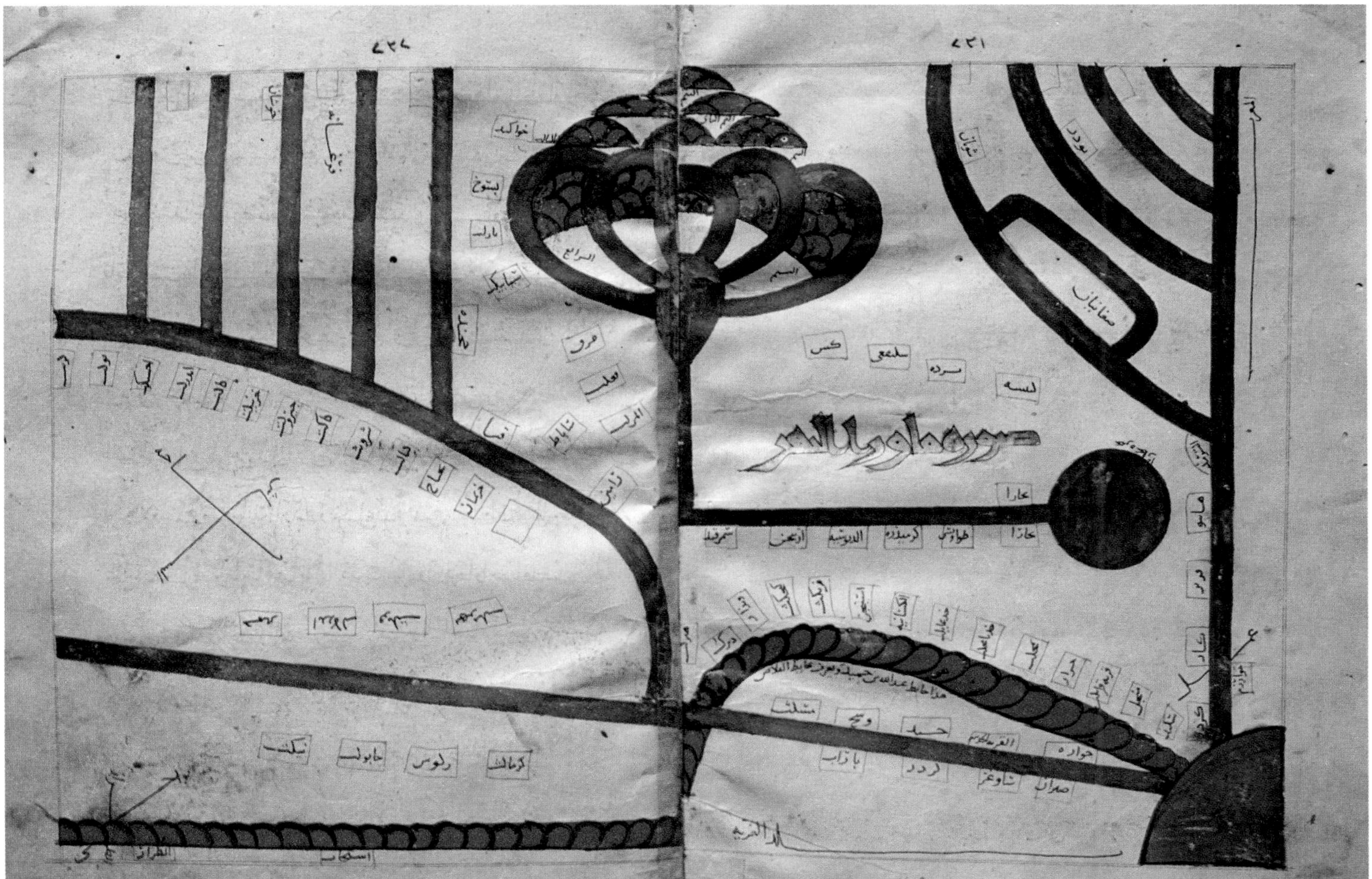

Plate 18

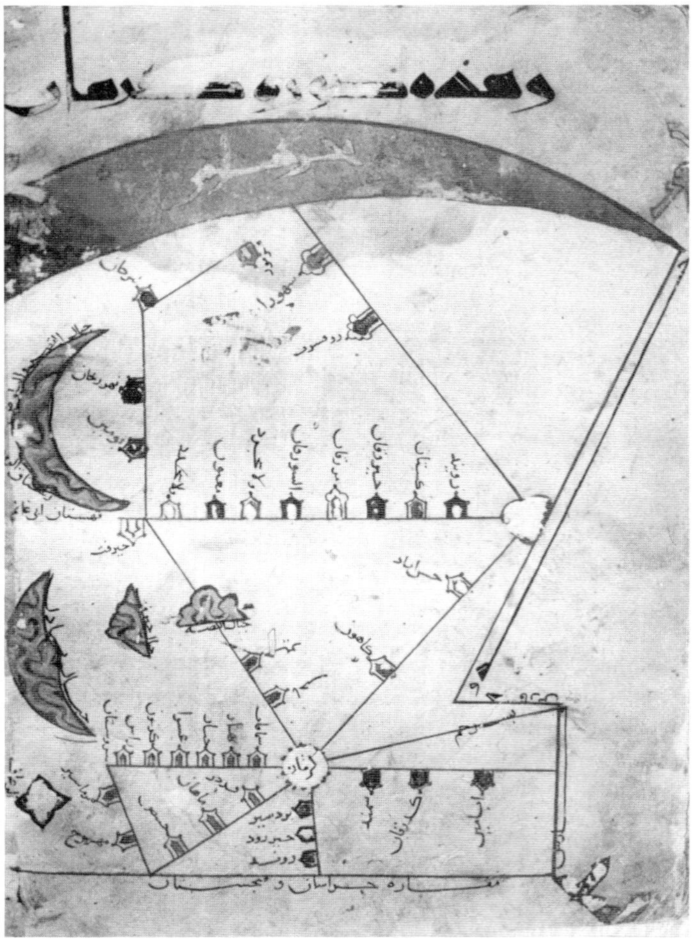

Figure 16. A map of Kerman and its vicinity.

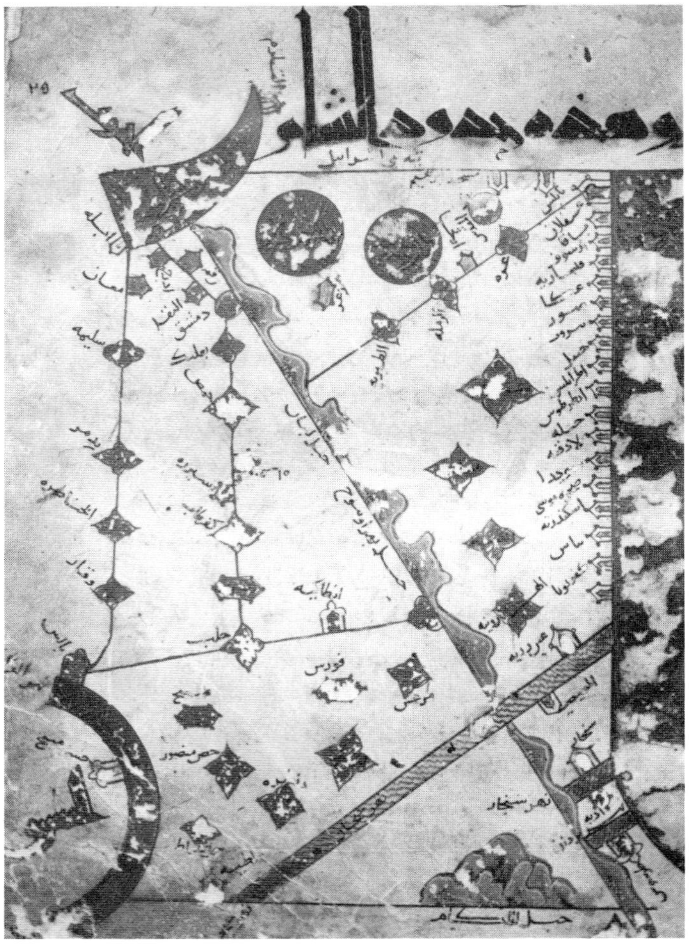

Figure 17. A map of Palestine, Syria and the Lebanon.

Rāmhurmuzī. The knowledge gained by these means brought Muslims face to face with the deficiencies which existed in the Greek material they had inherited and had a role to play in the new synthesis the Muslims were able to make from Greek, Persian and Indian geography and their own observations and studies.

The height of Islamic geographical studies of this early period is to be found in the writings of the peerless Abū Rayḥān al-Bīrūnī, at once master of mathematical, descriptive and cultural geography. Not only is al-Bīrūnī's *Taḥdīd nihāyāt al-amākin* (*The Determination of the Coordinates of Cities*)[15] the foremost Islamic work on mathematical geography, but throughout the incomparable *India*, the *Chronology of Ancient Nations* and the *Mas'ūdic Canon* numerous pages are devoted to geography discussed with the precision and care that characterize all of the works of this master scientist and scholar.

From the 6th/12th century until the beginning of the European expansion during the Renaissance marks the period of elaboration and systematization in geography among Muslims during which such cosmographical encyclopaedias as the *Nukhbat al-dahr* (*The Selection of the Age*) of Shams al-Dīn al-Dimashqī and *'Ajā'ib al-buldān* (*The Wonders of the Lands*) of Zakariyyā' al-Qazwīnī saw the light of day. But it was also the age which saw original geographers such as Abu'l-Fidā' and especially Abū 'Abdallāh al-Idrīsī, the Moroccan geographer who served at the court of Roger II in Sicily, for whom he wrote his *Kitāb al-rujārī* (*The Book of Roger*). The world map prepared by al-Idrīsī, based upon both Hellenistic and earlier Islamic sources, marks the

15. See al-Bīrūnī, *The Determination of the Coordinates of Cities*, trans. by Jamil Ali, Beirut, 1967. See also the extensive and valuable commentary of E. S. Kennedy to this work, *A Commentary upon Biruni's Kitab Tahdid Nikayat al-Amakin*, Beirut, 1973.

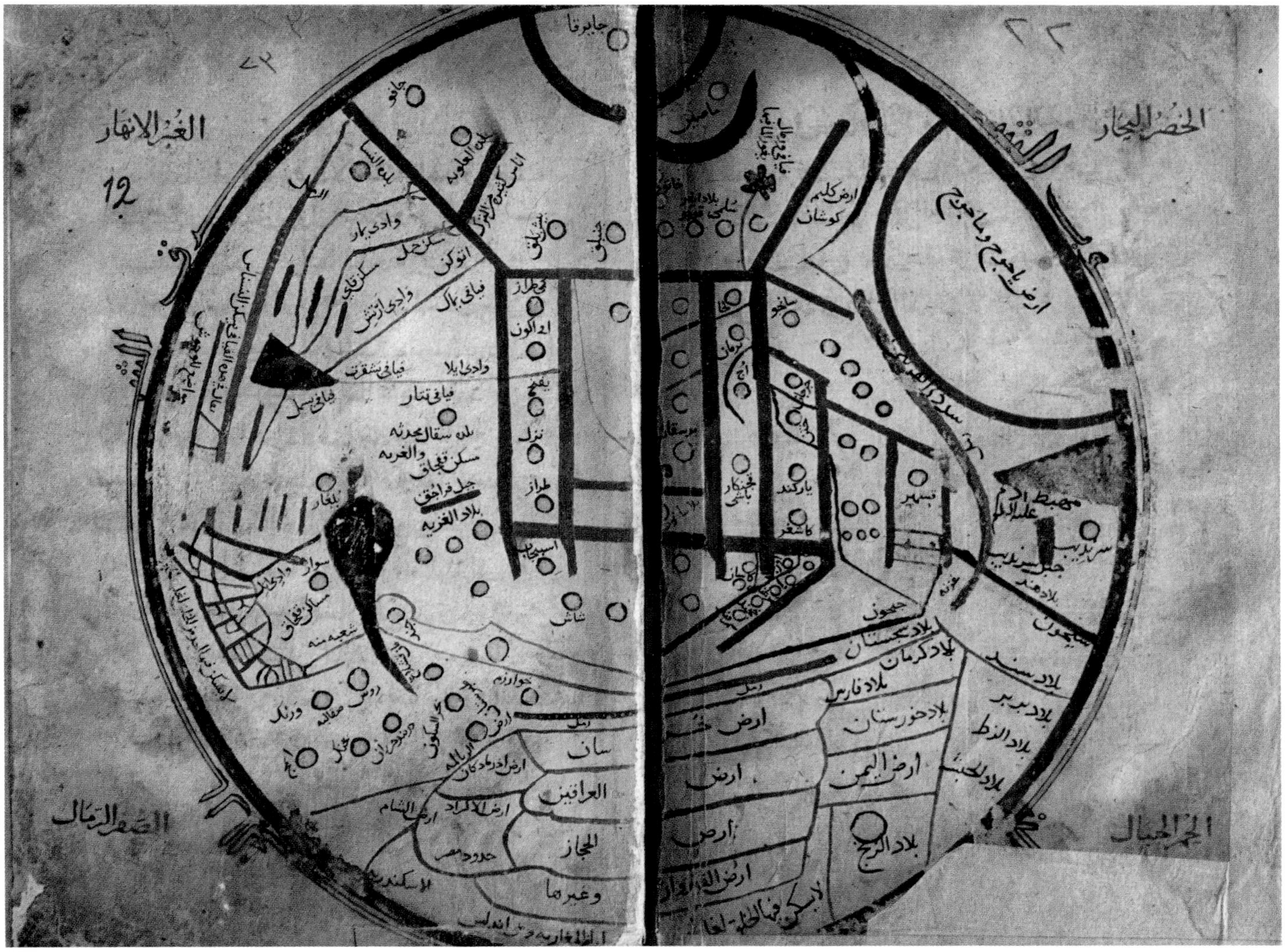

Plate 19. The Muslim lands of Western Asia according to the map of Kāshgarlī Maḥmūd.

height of cartography in Islam and the apogee of Islamic geography in this domain.

Also to this period belongs the incomparable geographical dictionary of Yāqūt entitled *Mu'jam al-buldān* (*Dictionary of the Lands*), which is still an indispensable tool of research for modern scholars. This work incorporated a great deal of local information which had been collected within the works on local history and geography so typical of this age. Of course not all the descriptions of this period were local, for this was also the age of great travellers, foremost among them Ibn Baṭṭūṭah, who set out from Tangiers and reached as far east as India and possibly China. In his remarkable *Tuḥfat al-nuẓẓār* (*The Gift of Observers*, usually known as *Travels*)[16] he provides extensive geographical and topographical information, not to speak of material on history, religion, ethnography and the like, which make of this work one of the most outstanding in the mediaeval period.

Just before the advent of the European Renaissance Muslims made notable advances in nautical geography as seen in the well-known *al-'Umdat al-mahriyyah* (*The Pillars of al-Mahrī*) of Sulaymān al-Mahrī and especially *Kitāb al-fawā'id fī uṣūl 'ilm al-baḥr wa'l-qawā'id* (*The Book of Benefits Concerning the Principles and Foundations of the Science of the Sea*) of Ibn Mājid.[17] The influence of works of this period in

16. See H. A. R. Gibb (trans.), *The Travels of Ibn Baṭṭūṭah*, 2 vols., Cambridge, 1958–62.

17. See G. R. Tibbetts, *Arab navigation in the Indian Ocean before the coming of the Portuguese, being a translation of Kitāb al-fawā'id fī uṣūl al-baḥr wa'l-qawā'id, together with an introduction on the history of Arab navigation, . . . and a glossary of navigational terms*, London, 1971.

the West is reflected in such meteorological terms as typhoon (from the Arabic *ṭūfān*) and monsoon (from *mawsim*). Ibn Mājid also guided the boat of Vasco de Gama from Malindi in East Africa to Calicut in India. But the very entrance of the Portuguese upon the scene signalled the decline of Muslim sea power and also nautical geography at least until the Ottoman period.

From the 9th/15th century onward geographical works continued to be written mostly in Persian by the Persians and Indians and also in Persian, Turkish and occasionally Arabic by the Ottomans. The most original geographical work of the period belongs to the Ottoman writers. Some like Ibn al-ʿĀshiq, the author of *Manāẓir al-ʿālam* (*Views of the World*) followed the models of earlier works like the *ʿAjāʾib al-makhlūqāt* (*The Wonders of Creation*) of al-Qazwīnī but added new material on Anatolia and the Balkans not found in earlier Muslim sources. Others like the *Khiṭāy-nāmah* (*Treatise on China*) of Sayyid ʿAlī Akbar Khiṭāʾī gave a fresh geographical description of the journey to China.

But the most amazing geographical contribution of this period is perhaps the cartographical works of Pīr Muḥyī al-Dīn Raʾīs, produced in the early 10th/16th century, containing maps of Africa and America, which

Plate 20a

continue to astonish modern scholars. The second Ra'īs, Sayyid 'Alī, entitled Kātib-i Rūm, also made worthy contributions to marine geography in his *al-Muḥīṭ* (*The Circumference*). This late Ottoman tradition of geography reached its height with the *Jihān-nümā* of the 11th/17th century author Ḥājjī Khalīfah, which clearly reflects the transition from mediaeval to modern geography and which was completed and printed in the 12th/18th century with the help of European sources. This work was contemporary with the monumental *Seyāḥat-nāmah* (*Travel Accounts*) of Ewliyā Čelebi in which a synthesis is made of the geography of the day. In geography as in few other fields Islamic science not only developed and transmitted some of the fruit of its endeavours to the West, but also drew from Renaissance and even later Western sources before the onslaught of the West upon the Islamic world. It also made this transition in a manner that was not totally disruptive as was the case in so many other of the sciences.

Plate 20a. An Ottoman compass.

Plate 20b. A Syrian compass.

Plate 20c. A late Persian compass.

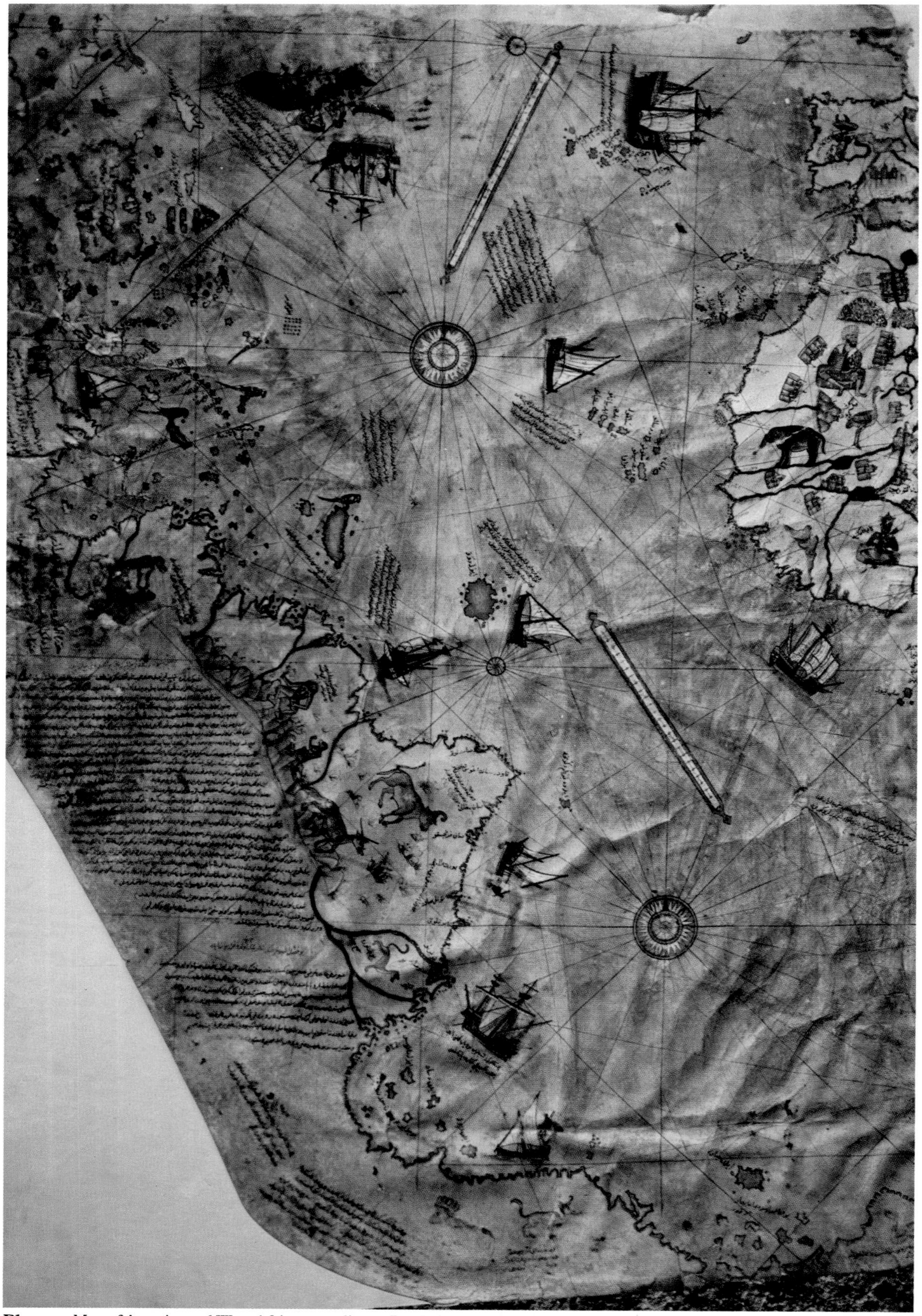

Plate 21. Map of America and West Africa according to Pīri Ra'īs.

Figure 18. Europe and North Africa according to Pīri Ra'īs.

Figure 18

As far as geodesy is concerned the Islamic geographers made major contributions to it as well, and in fact al-Bīrūnī may be considered as the founder of the science of geodesy.[18] Muslims were interested in mathematical studies of the features of the surface of the earth as well as in determining the latitude and longitude of cities, the height of mountains, the diameter of the earth, etc., from the moment they inherited the Greek, Indian and Persian works on the subject. But they were also interested in some of these problems for the practical purpose of orientating themselves in the direction of Mecca and finding the various times of day in order to perform the prescribed prayers and to fast properly. Treatises on how to determine the length of day abound in Islamic languages, as do works on ways of determining the direction of Mecca from various latitudes and longitudes.

But Muslims did not remain content with only these problems, despite their central importance. They spent much effort in refining means of measuring latitudes and longitudes of cities and other geographical features. Already during the 3rd/9th century they had measured a degree of latitude at about 36°N to be 2877 feet basing themselves on simultaneous observations at Palmyra and Raqqa. Al-Bīrūnī, who devoted about fifteen books to geodesy and mathematical geography, improved on these measurements, while Ibn Yūnus, almost his contemporary, devoted careful studies to the measurement of longitudes. By the 7th/13th century Abu'l-'Alī al-Marrākushī had composed his *Jāmi' al-mabādī wa'l-ghāyāt* (*Sum of the Beginnings and the Ends*) as well as his treatise on astronomical instruments which caused Sarton to describe his works as 'the most important contribution to mathematical geography – not only in Islam but anywhere.'[19]

As far as the measurement of the diameter of the earth is concerned the Muslims knew earlier Greek and Indian methods. But a new effort at measurement was made in the Sinjar plain of Syria in the 3rd/9th century by a team under the direction of the sons of Mūsā ibn Shākir which improved upon the earlier measurements. Likewise, the astronomers al-Battānī and al-Farghānī measured the diameter of the earth. But again it was al-Bīrūnī who in several of his works described means of measuring the diameter of the earth and finally carried out the method himself while in India, coming up with the answer of about 25,000 miles, which would have been very accurate if the earth were not a geoid.[20] Al-Bīrūnī also devised ingenious methods of measuring mountains and other elevations so that he truly deserves to be named the founder of geodesy, a science which numerous Islamic geographers and astronomers pursued in the centuries which followed him.

18. See S. H. Barani, 'Muslim researches in geodesy', *Islamic Culture*, vol. 6, 1932, pp. 363–369.

19. G. Sarton, *An Introduction to the History of Science*, vol. II, Baltimore, 1931, pp. 41–42.

20. See S. H. Nasr, *An Introduction to Islamic Cosmological Doctrines*, pp. 128–130. Also S. H. Barani, *ibid.*

Chapter IV
Natural History

Geology – Mineralogy – Botany – Zoology

The analytical approach of modern science during the past few centuries and especially since the nineteenth century has eclipsed almost completely the knowledge of the unity and interrelatedness of the natural order, a unity to which in fact science has turned its back in quest of ever more refined quantitative knowledge. As a result, natural history, which embraces the various 'kingdoms' of nature in a global view based upon their undeniable organic unity, has been nearly forgotten despite the long tradition of natural history in the West. Only the catastrophic ecological crisis which has come to the surface during the past decade has caused a belated interest, within certain circles, in natural history as the repository of a *wisdom* concerning nature, a wisdom of which the modern world is in profound need if it is to regain the vision of nature as a totality and an organic whole.

In Islamic civilization, natural history has always played a central role as the integrating and all-embracing matrix within which particular descriptive sciences of nature have been cultivated, from mineralogy to zoology. It has sought to integrate particular forms of knowledge of the natural order into universal principles of a metaphysical and cosmological nature. And it has sought to study nature not only with respect to other physical and biological forms and *vis-à-vis* man's relation to these forms but most of all as the 'signs' or 'portents' (*āyāt*) of God to be contemplated rather than simply analyzed.[1] It has nurtured a perspective which is close to that of such Western scientists as Jean Bodel and John Ray, who studied nature as the *vestigia Dei* and wrote on natural history for the 'glory of God'.

Muslim writings on natural history range from encyclopaedias such as the *'Uyūn al-akhbār* (*The Most Essential Information*) of Ibn Qutaybah[2] to the cosmographical *compendia* of such men as al-Qazwīnī and al-Dimashqī, to historico-cosmographical works such as those of al-

1. On Islamic natural history see S. H. Nasr, 'Natural History', in M. M. Sharif (ed.), *A History of Muslim Philosophy*; also E. Wiedemann, *Aufsätze zur Arabischen Wissenschaftsgeschichte*, 2 vols., Hildesheim, 1970, in which numerous articles are devoted to various aspects of natural history.

2. The zoological section of this important early encyclopaedia of natural history has been rendered into English. See F. S. Bodenheimer and L. Kopf, *The Natural History Section from a Ninth Century 'Book of Useful Knowledge', The 'Uyun al-Akhbar of Ibn Qutayba*, Paris, 1949.

Plate 22. Aristotle teaching.

Mas'ūdī, to literary works such as those of al-Jāḥiẓ, to philosophical treatises such as the *Shifā'* (*The Book of Healing*) of Ibn Sīnā, in which major sections are devoted to the subject. The treatises on natural history also vary as to content, some emphasizing descriptions of nature, others symbolic and mythological narratives, and yet others the cosmological and philosophical aspects of the study of nature. But they are all united in their interest in the interrelation between natural forms, the inner forces (*nafs* or 'soul') which governs each kingdom and the significance of natural forms as guideposts to a knowledge beyond the world of nature, this being both metaphysical and moral. Muslim natural historians were thus concerned, beyond their descriptive studies of animals, plants, rocks and mountains, with both the symbolic significance of the natural world and the lessons man can learn morally and spiritually from the study of natural forms.[3]

The underlying theme of the works on natural history, which recurs over and over again, is the 'three kingdoms' (*mawālīd*) and the various 'souls' which dominate, move and determine the life patterns of each kingdom. The Muslims adopted elements from Aristotle and other Greek sources and integrated them into a total science of the Universe which embraced the whole 'chain of being', beginning with the angels and ending with the saint in whom creation returns to its source.[4] It was in fact Ibn Sīnā who in his *Shifā'* treated all the three kingdoms systematically for the first time in a single work, adding to the zoological studies of Aristotle and the botany of Theophrastus his own study of the mineral kingdom which in its Latin version as *De Mineralibus* was considered for many centuries in the West to be a work of Aristotle.[5]

As for the various souls and their faculties, this doctrine was also adopted from the works of the Alexandrian commentators upon the *De Anima* of Aristotle but was elaborated and

3. The Muslims inherited the traditions of natural history of both the Greeks, principally Aristotle and Pliny, and the Indians and Persians. The latter school emphasized likewise the moral and spiritual lessons to be learned from nature. This type of natural history was transmitted to Islam most of all through the *Kalīlah wa Dimnah (The Tales of Bidpai)* which was translated from Sanskrit into Pahlavi, from Pahlavi into Arabic and from Arabic into Persian and many other languages both Islamic and Western.

4. See S. H. Nasr, *An Introduction to Islamic Cosmological Doctrines*, pp. 4ff.; also Nasr, *Science and Civilization in Islam,* chap. 13.

5. See E. J. Holmyard and D. C. Mandeville, *Avicennae. De congelatione et conglutinatione lapidum, being sections of the Kitāb al-Shifā'*, Paris, 1927. Muslims strangely enough did not have a thorough knowledge of the *Botany* of Theophrastus, in contrast to the zoological works of Aristotle, which they knew well. But that did not prevent them from integrating the science of the world of plants and animals as envisaged separately by the earlier Greek scientists into a whole embracing all the three kingdoms.

systematized by Muslim philosophers, especially al-Fārābī and Ibn Sīnā. The 'faculty psychology' of Muslim philosophers and natural historians meant that the life-giving force found within nature came from a reality beyond the material world itself. In fact the various 'souls' are so many aspects and powers of the one World Soul which is responsible for the qualitative differentiation between forms and their life patterns. Otherwise the material aspect of natural forms is no more than so many combinations of the four elements, fire, air, water and earth. It is the wedding of a particular soul to each combination of the elements that constitutes its particular character and gives each being its distinct features, just as from another point of view the totality of each natural form is a reflection of an archetype belonging to the spiritual empyrean.

The various faculties of the souls which dominate the three kingdoms can be summarized as follows:[6]

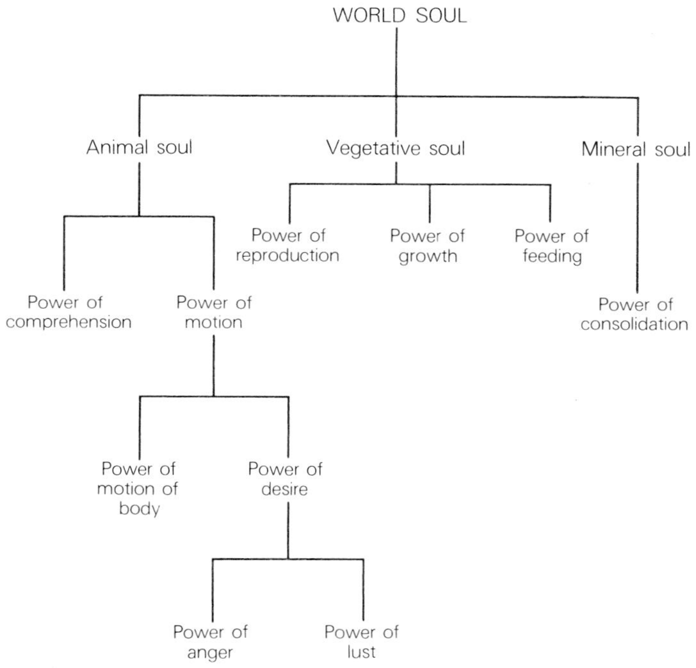

Each mineral, plant and animal possesses some of these faculties and grows in perfection to the degree that these faculties become more fully manifest in it. Only in man are all these faculties present in their fullness in addition to the 'rational faculty' (*al-nafs al-nāṭiqah*) which distinguishes man from the animals in a fundamental and not just an accidental manner.

Geology

The home of the above-mentioned kingdoms is the earth, so Muslim natural historians usually turned to a study of geology before discussing any of the three kingdoms. It is surprising to realize how many geological observations and ideas which came to be substantiated during later centuries were already known to Muslims. Of course the Muslim scientists never operated within a deistic world in which the hands of God were, so to speak, cut off from His creation. They therefore did not need to have recourse to such hypotheses as uniformitarianism and 'horizontal' biological evolution, which parade as scientific 'facts' today but which are in reality a means by which secularized man fills the gap created by his banning of the Divine Cause from the natural order.

Muslim writings on geology, which are usually found in the same sources as those of natural history and of course also in works on mineralogy, show a clear understanding of the gradual character of geological change, of the major transformations which have taken place on the surface of the earth, including the changing of lands into sea and of sea into land, of the importance at the same time of many cataclysms such as violent earthquakes, which have transformed the sculpture of the surface of the earth, and of the importance of rocks as a record of the earth's geological history.[7] Concerning the importance of records contained in rocks, al-Bīrūnī, one of the foremost of Muslim geologists, writes, 'We have

6. The most extensive treatment of the various faculties in Islamic sources is to be found in the *Ṭabī'iyyāt* of the *Shifā'* of Ibn Sīnā. See J. Bakoš, *La psychologie d'Avicenne*, Prague, 1956. Also E. Gilson, 'Les sources gréco-arabes de l'augustinisme avicennant', in *Archives d'Histoire Doctrinale et Littéraire du Moyen Age*, vol. IV, 1929, pp. 5–149. See also Nasr, 'Natural History', p. 1326.

7. On the main geological ideas of the Ikhwān al-Ṣafā', al-Bīrūnī and Ibn Sīnā see Nasr, *An Introduction to Islamic Cosmological Doctrines*, pp. 87–88; 141–144; 244–246.

As far as earthquakes are concerned many special works have been devoted to them. See for example Jalāl al-Dīn al-Suyūṭī, *Kashf al-ṣalṣalah 'an waṣf al-zalzalah*, ed. by 'Abd al-Laṭīf al-Sa'dānī, Fez, 1971. Translated with annotations by S. Najjar as 'Kashf aç-çalçala 'an waçf az-zalzala (Traité du tremblement de terre)', *Cahiers du Centre Universitaire de la Recherche Scientifique* (Rabat), no. 3, 1973–74.

to rely upon the records of rocks and vestiges of the past to infer that all these changes should have taken place in very very long times and under unknown conditions of cold and heat.'[8]

Muslim students of geology were also fully aware of the origin of fossils. Usually in Western histories of geology and palaeontology it is mentioned that after millennia of confusion concerning the origin of fossils, suddenly in the 12th/18th century a clear scientific explanation was provided. Actually nothing could be further from the truth if Islamic sources are taken into account. The *Epistles* of the Brethren of Purity written in the 4th/10th century had already described fossils as remains of sea animals which had become petrified in a place which is now land but which had been a sea in bygone ages.

Similarly, Muslim scientists were fully aware of many major geological phenomena such as weathering, the difference in the degree of resistance of various mountain formations to the weathering process, the accumulation of sand created by wind and water in their endless action upon rocks, and finally the coming into being of sedimentary rocks through this process. Ibn Sīnā described carefully his own observations along the banks of the River Oxus concerning the gradual petrification and solidification of clay, and explained the formation of sedimentary rocks correctly.[9]

Perhaps the most remarkable geological observation ever made by a Muslim scientist, however, is al-Bīrūnī's identification of the Ganges Plain in India as a sedimentary deposit. After studying extensively all aspects of India including its natural forms al-Bīrūnī wrote in his unique work *Taḥqīq mā li'l-hind* (*India*): 'One of these plains is India, limited in the south by the above-mentioned Indian Ocean, and on three sides by lofty mountains, the waters of which flow down to it. But if you see the soil of India with your own eyes and meditate on its nature, if you consider the rounded stones found in the earth however deeply you dig, stones that are huge near the mountains and where the rivers have violent current, stones that are of smaller size at a greater distance from the mountains and where the streams flow more slowly, stones that appear pulverized in the shape of sand where the streams begin to stagnate near their mouths and near the sea – if you consider all this, you can scarcely help thinking that India was once a sea, which by degrees had been filled up by the alluvium of the streams.'[10]

One cannot discuss geology among Muslims without mentioning their special interest in underground waters and water systems. This is particularly true of Persia where Islam inherited the vast underground water system (*qanāts*) from the Sassanids. But Muslim scientists did not remain content simply with the practical applications of this system to agriculture. They also made scientific studies which are related to both hydrology and geology, one of the most remarkable being that of al-Karajī (usually known as al-Karkhī).[11] In the work of al-Karajī, as in similar treatises, one observes that wedding between theoretical and practical knowledge and also between various disciplines ranging from mathematics to geology which characterizes Islamic science in all its major facets.

Mineralogy

The study of the three kingdoms usually begins with mineralogy, which in Islam is closely interrelated with alchemy, chemistry and metallurgy on the one hand and medicine on the other. Works concerned with mineralogy in various Islamic languages are usually lapidaries with numerous references not only to mineralogy but also to petrography and metallurgy. Moreover, works on alchemy are also concerned with mineralogy, and often it is not easy to draw a clear distinction between them. Even the term *ḥajar* (stone) which is used in the title of many lapidaries also refers to the Philosophers' Stone and is as much of a petrographical term as an alchemical one.

The Muslims inherited a vast literature on mineralogy and related fields from the Greeks, Persians and Indians, works or fragments associ-

8. Z. Validi Togan, *Biruni's Picture of the World, Memoirs of the Archaeological Survey of India*, vol. 53, Calcutta, 1937–1938, pp. 57–58.

9. See N. Sāte' al-Hosrī, 'Les Idées d'Avicenne sur la géologie', *Millénaire d'Avicenne, Congrès de Baghdad*, 1952, pp. 454–463.

10. *Alberuni's India*, trans. by E. C. Sachau, London, 1910, vol. I, p. 198.

11. See al-Karagi (Mohammad), *La civilisation des eaux cachées*, traduit par A. Mazahéri, Nice, 1973.

ated with such names as Sokatos, Xeuskrates, Bolos Demokritos and Alexander of Tralles, as well as Zoroaster, Jāmāsp and Manūchihr. Moreover, such important medical and pharmacological sources as Dioscorides and Galen, and religious works such as the Pahlavi *Dātəstān-i̤ dēnīk*, served also as sources of knowledge of mineralogy among Muslims. But the two most important and influential works which determined much of the colour of lapidaries written by Muslims are the *Lapidary of Aristotle*, which exists in many recensions,[12] and the pseudo-Aristotelian *Kitāb sirr al-asrār*, whose Latin translation by Roger Bacon under the title of *Secretum Secretorum* was well known in the West. Both works are compilations from Persian, Syriac and Greek sources of late Antiquity having little to do with the mineralogy of the immediate school of Aristotle. Both deal primarily with the occult properties of substances, especially minerals.[13]

Works written by Islamic scientists and scholars on mineralogy and related fields begin in the 3rd/9th century with two treatises by the philosopher-scientist al-Kindī, *Risālah fī anwāʿ al-jawāhir al-thamīnah wa ghayrihā* (*Treatise on Various Types of Precious Stones and Other Kinds of Stones*) and *Risālah fī anwāʿ al-ḥijārah wa'l-jawāhir* (*Treatise on Various Types of Stones and Jewels*). Al-Kindī also wrote an important treatise on metallurgy and the art of making swords, this being the first book of its kind in Arabic.[14] These works were followed by treatises on the subject of minerals and stones by al-Jāḥiẓ, Naṣr ibn Yaʿqūb al-Dīnawarī, the philosopher and physician Muḥammad ibn Zakariyyā' al-Rāzī, the Ikhwān al-Ṣafā', who devoted one of their *Epistles* to it, and Muḥammad ibn Aḥmad al-Tamīmī whose *Kitāb al-murshid* (*The Guide-Book*) is a major work on minerals, stones and metals and is quoted by numerous later authors.[15]

But the most outstanding works in this field belong to Ibn Sīnā and al-Bīrūnī. The first dealt extensively with the process of generation and the description of metals and minerals and their classification in his *Shifā'* (*The Book of Healing*)[16] and also in the second book of the *Qānūn* (*Canon*); the second wrote the *Kitāb al-jamāhir fī maʿrifat al-jawāhir* (*The Book of the Multitude of Knowledge of Precious Stones*), which is considered by many as the most notable Muslim work on the subject.[17] In this unique work, al-Bīrūnī combines the philological, mineralogical, physical, medical, and even philosophical approaches, and he studies minerals from all these points of view. He even makes careful measurements of the specific weights of minerals, something which belongs more to the realm of physics than mineralogy and which we shall therefore treat later, in our chapter on physics.

Contemporary with al-Bīrūnī in the late 4th/10th and the 5th/11th century studies on mineralogy began to appear in the Maghrib, where Maslamah ibn Waddāḥ al-Qurṭubī al-Majrīṭī devoted a major section to minerals in his *Rawḍat al-ḥadā'iq wa riyāḍ al-ḥaqā'iq* (*The Garden of Gardens and Meadow of Truths*). Even the great Andalusian Sufi Ibn ʿArabī devoted a chapter to the esoteric qualities of stones in his *Tadbīrāt al-ilāhiyyah fī iṣlāḥ mamlakat al-insāniyyah* (*Divine Measures for the Restoration of the Human Kingdom*).

12. See J. Ruska, *Das Steinbuch des Aristoteles*, Heidelberg, 1912.

13. On the sources for Muslim mineralogical works see M. Ullmann, *Die Natur- und Geheimwissenschaften im Islam*, Leiden, 1972, pp. 95ff.

14. The treatise is called *Risālah fī anwāʿ al-suyūf al-ḥadīd* (*Treatise on Various Kinds of Steel Swords*). See *A Treatise on Swords and Their Essential Attributes, a Rare and Original Work of al-Kindī, the Great Arab Philosopher*, ed. by R. M. N. Ehsan Elahie, Lahore, 1962.

15. For a scholarly and thoroughly documented history of mineralogy among Muslims see Ullmann, *op. cit.*, pp. 114ff.

16. See Holmyard and Mandeville, *De congelatione et conglutinatione lapidum*. Ibn Sīnā divided minerals into four classes (*aqsām*): stones (*aḥjār*), sulphurs (*kabārīt*), salts (*amlāḥ*) and solubles (*dhā'ibāt*).

17. For this reason numerous studies have been devoted to various aspects of this work. See for example, F. Krenkow, 'The Chapter on Pearls in the Book of Precious Stones by al-Biruni', *Islamic Culture*, vol. 15, 1941, pp. 399–421; and vol. 16, 1942, pp. 11–36; and Taḳī al-Dīn al-Hilālī, 'Die Einleitung zu al-Bīrūnīs Steinbuch', in *Sammlungen orientalistischer Arbeiten*, Heft 7, Leipzig, 1941. For other studies on this work see Ullman, *op. cit.*, p. 121, ft. nt. 1; and S. H. Nasr, *al-Biruni: An Annotated Bibliography*, Tehran, 1974, pp. 87–94.

Work on mineralogy continued in the 6th/12th and 7th/13th centuries with treatises by such men as Abu'l-'Abbās al-Tīfāshī, Naṣīr al-Dīn al-Ṭūsī and Abu'l-Qāsim al-Qāsānī (Kāshānī).[18] Likewise, the compilers and cosmographers who followed, such men as al-Qazwīnī, Ḥamdallāh Mustawfī, Shams al-Dīn al-Akfānī, Ibn al-Athīr, Ibn al-Jawzī and Dā'ūd al-Anṭākī all devoted sections of their writings to mineralogy, drawing mostly from the earlier sources of the 4th/10th and 5th/11th centuries.

Even after the Muslim world became divided into several empires, works in this field continued, often of a more local character, but nevertheless based on the earlier sources, which were widely known throughout the Islamic world. In the 9th/15th century the Persian scientist Muḥammad ibn Manṣūr Shīrāzī, who lived in India, wrote a treatise in Persian on precious stones, and in the 12th/18th century the Persian Sufi and scholar Shaykh 'Alī Ḥazīn, who had also migrated to India, continued this tradition with another Persian work, this time on pearls. In the Ottoman world also works of this kind were written, such as the treatise of Yaḥyā ibn Muḥammad al-Ghaffārī, in Turkish but based on the text of Ṭūsī, and that of Muḥammad ibn al-Mubārak al-Qazwīnī, written in Persian for Sultan Selim I. In Persia itself most of the interest in mineralogy in this later period was in the direction of either medicine or alchemy. As for the Maghrib a major work on the subject appeared in the 11th/17th century by Imām Aḥmad al-Maghribī, who drew heavily upon al-Anṭākī. This tradition has survived to this day in the Islamic world in 'folk' medicine, in the use of jewels and in many other aspects of daily living, while the theoretical foundations of this ancient science of minerals became gradually replaced by modern theories in the 13th/19th century.

The Muslim lapidaries are based on a view of the Universe very different from that of modern science and cannot be understood if seen only from the perspective of a purely quantitative science. In these works the qualitative aspect of stones is as real as their quantitative aspect. The colour, brilliance, texture and form of a stone belong as much to its ontological reality as do its weight or size. Moreover, there is a *sympatheia* between various orders of being which cannot be reduced to external, measurable relations and which determines the role of certain stones in calming the soul or causing joy or evoking other psychological states. If these treatises wander from 'scientific' descriptions of a particular stone to occult properties which appear as fantasy from the point of view of modern science, it is precisely because modern man has lost sight of that *sympatheia* between various objects and levels of cosmic existence which causes interactions and effects to take place, effects which cannot be determined by quantitative means alone. The 'science of the properties of things' was never limited in the Muslim mind to what was measurable, although it naturally included this aspect of things. Rather, the 'science of the properties of things' (*'ilm khawāṣṣ al-ashyā'*), which is so closely interwoven with mineralogy, is based on a vast vision of reality according to which the outward and the inward, the manifest and the occult aspects and properties of things, are all real and react with each other and with man in a Universe through whose arteries the Spirit never ceases to flow.

Botany

As in mineralogy so in botany the Muslims inherited a vast body of knowledge from Greek, Roman, Babylonian, Persian and Indian sources which they synthesized and made the basis for their own studies of the plant world. Muslim interest in plants was extensive for both agricultural and medical reasons. In fact in the earliest Muslim works on the sciences such as the *Kitāb al-ḥudūd* (*The Book of Limits*) of Jābir ibn Ḥayyān, botany (*'ilm al-nabāt*) and agriculture (*'ilm al-filāḥah*) are classified together and only later appear as separate sciences. Likewise, the earliest pharmacological studies are inseparable from the study of botany.[19] Moreover, Muslim studies on botany range from the most 'scientific' descriptions to the study of the occult properties

18. Both Ṭūsī and Kāshānī wrote in Persian, the first the *Tanksūkhnāma-yi Īlkhānī* (*The Īl-khānid Treatise on Mineralogy*) and the second *'Arā'is al-jawāhir wa nafā'is al-aṭāyib* (*Brides of Jewels and Gems of Delicacies*) which also contains an important section on the technology of tiles. But it seems that both works are based on an earlier 5th/11th century model.

19. On the history of Islamic botany see H. F. Meyer, *Geschichte der Botanik*, vol. III, Konigsberg, 1856; F. Sezgin, *Geschichte der Arabischen Schrifttums*, vol. IV, Leiden, 1971, pp. 303ff.; M. Ullmann, *Die Natur- und Geheimwissenschaften in Islam*, pp. 62ff.

بیاشامند خفاق را عظیم موافق بود و اکر با شراب بیاشامند قوانج را بکشد میذرنبد نوعی از زبرد
است و طبیعت ان سرد است در دوم و خشک است در اول باصره را قوت دهد و دیکر منافع در صفت
زمرد کفته یشود و زبر العقار بر مصحفونیا است و کفته یشود در حمول کثوث است و کفته یشود رجاج
بیار سی که بیینه کوید
در اول و خشک است
چون با روغن زنبق طلا
و لطافی بود و سفیدی چشم
بیفزاید و چون بسوزانند
سوخته نبود و سحق کرده
چون با شراب بیاشامند
بید که بغایت سحق کنند و صفت سوختن وی در کوره آهنکران نهند و بدهند تا نزدیک که اختن
پس بمیان در آب قلی انذازند و بعد از ان سحق کنند و مستعمل کنند و کوبینه سوختن وی چنان
است که سحق کنند و بر روی صحیفه از آهن کنند سران کشوده بود و آتش فخم در شیب ول
کنند مقدار سه ساعت و دایم تحریک ان کنند بعد از ان سحق کنند نمک و مستعمل کنند

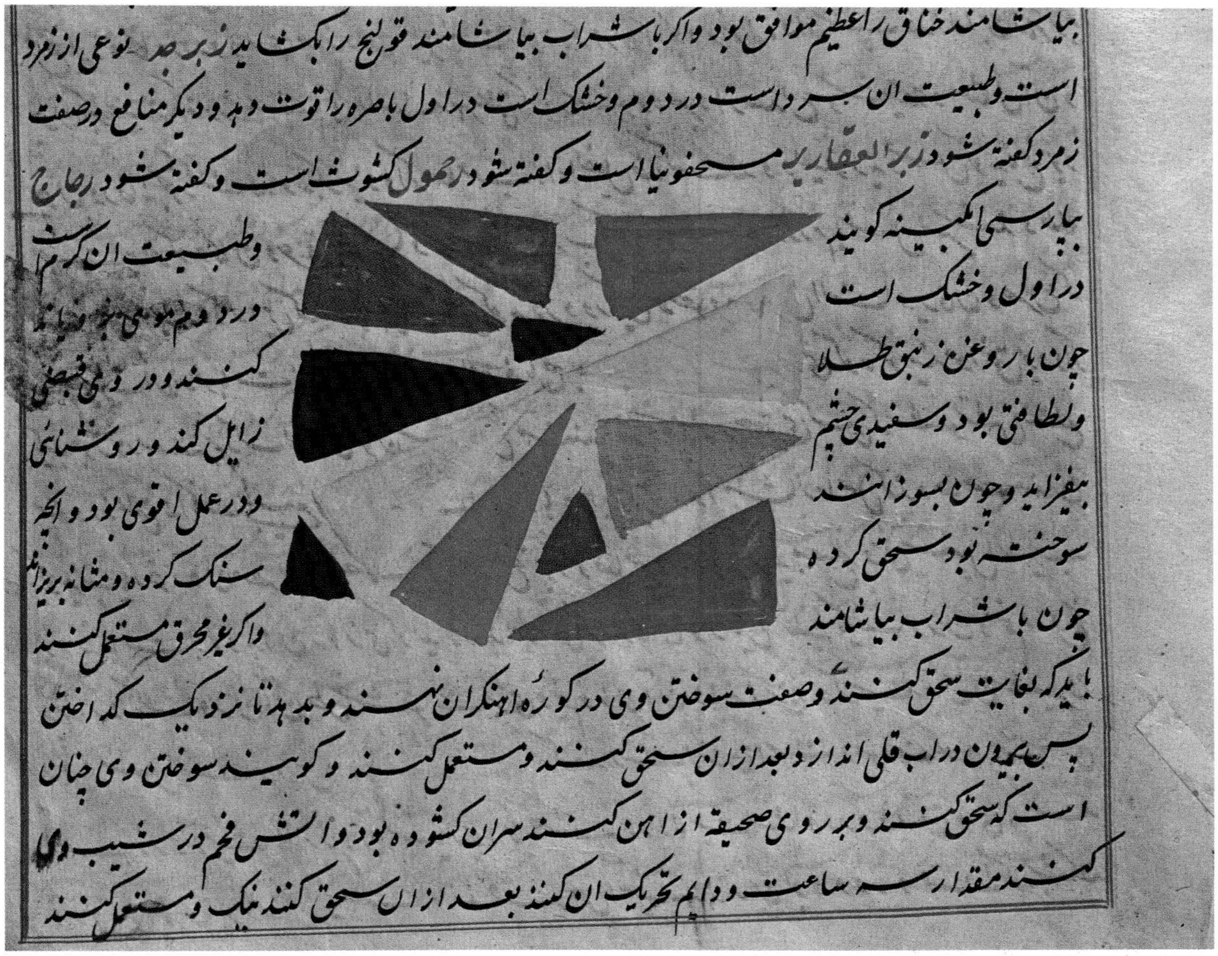

Plates 23 and 24. Illustrated pages of the mineralogical section of a treatise on the *Ikhtiyārāt-i badī'i* of 'Alī ibn al-Ḥusayn, Zayn al-'Aṭṭār.

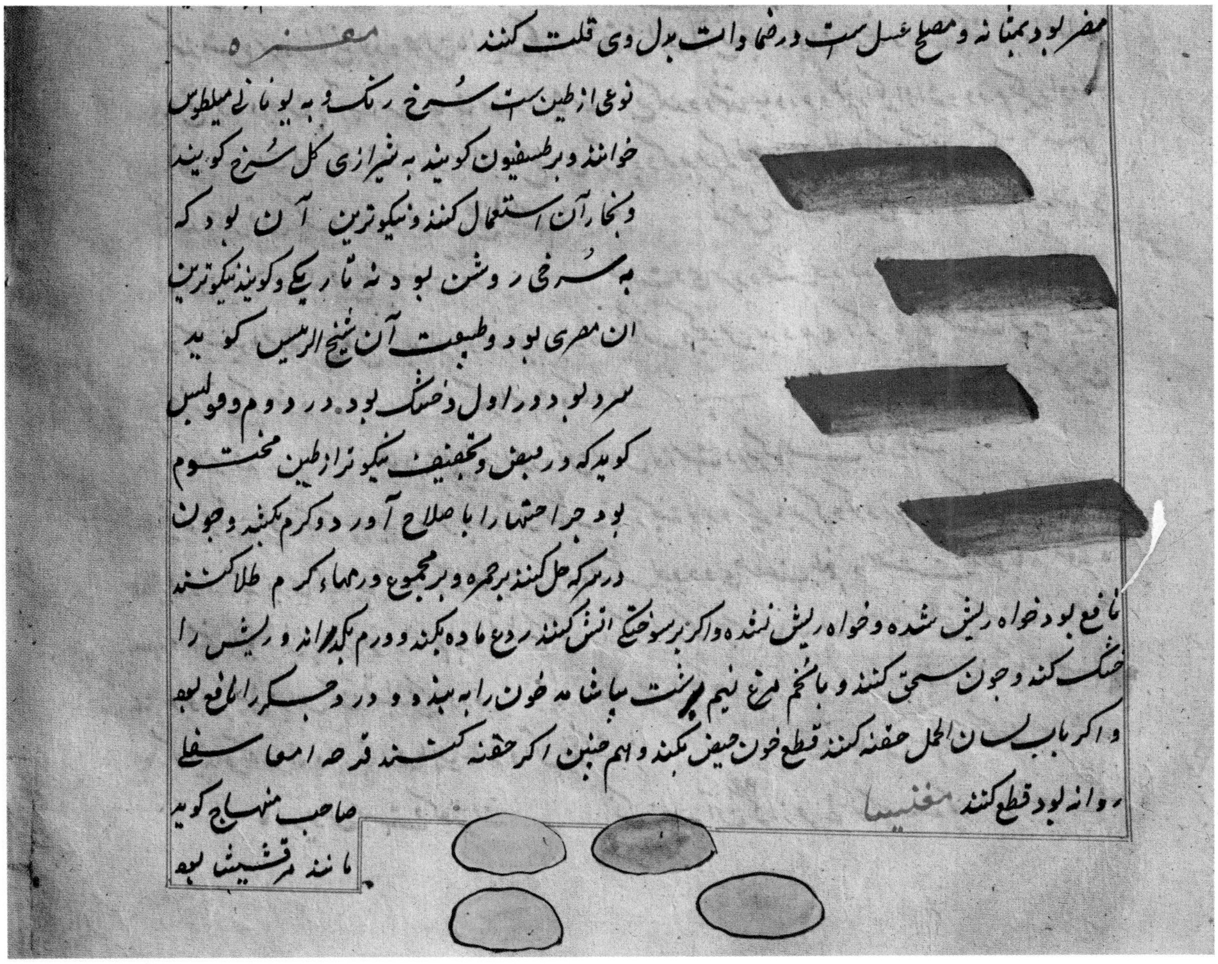

of plants, as well as their symbolic and spiritual significance in the cosmos.

The most important pre-Islamic sources from which Muslim botanists drew information include the *Book of Agriculture* of Pseudo-Apollonios, an agricultural treatise attributed to Demokritos, the works of Aristotle and Theophrastus, the famous and influential *De Plantis* also attributed to Aristotle, the pharmacological works of Dioscorides and Galen, as well as the writings of Apollonios of Tyana. Of special significance for the rise of both botany and agriculture is the *Nabataean Agriculture* of Ibn Waḥshiyyah, concerned with ancient agricultural practices of the Near East combined with considerations belonging to the occult sciences, a work which exercised an immense influence upon later Muslim authors.[20] Mention must also be made of Persian botanical knowledge, which reached the Muslims through both oral transmission and the pharmacopoeia.

Islamic works on botany begin in the 2nd/8th century with the treatises of Jābir ibn Ḥayyān on botany and agriculture. Also the philologists and grammarians of this period such as Abū Naḍr ibn Shumayl and Abū Zayd al-Anṣārī from Basra and Ibn al-Sikkīt from Kufa were interested in plants and assembled information about their morphology and properties as well as names. Of a similar nature is the *Kitāb al-nabāt wa'l-shajar* (*The Book of Plants and Trees*) of Abū Sa'īd al-Aṣma'ī.

From the 3rd/9th century onward medical works in Arabic also begin to appear with important sections devoted to plants and their medical benefits. The *Firdaws al-ḥikmah* (*Paradise of Wisdom*) of 'Alī ibn Rabban al-Ṭabarī is noteworthy from this point of view as are several treatises of Ḥunayn ibn Isḥāq and during the following century of Rāzī, Ibn Juljul and 'Alī ibn 'Abbās al-Majūsī.

But the most important botanical treatise of the 3rd/9th century is probably the *Kitāb al-nabāt* (*The Book of Plants*) of Abū Ḥanīfah al-Dīnawarī. This work, which combines a philological, historical and botanical approach in its study of plants, is marked by its thoroughness and the care taken in the description of each specimen. It was read widely by later authors and has been quoted numerous times over the centuries.

In the 4th/10th century several philosophical studies of plants appeared. The Ikhwān al-Ṣafā' devoted one of their *Epistles* to the morphology, genesis and manner of growth of plants as well as the numerical symbolism of their various parts and their place in the total cosmic order. Likewise, Ibn Sīnā in the seventh chapter (*fann*) of the *Tabī'iyyāt* (*Natural Philosophy*) of his *Shifā'* (*Book of Healing*) dealt extensively with plants from both a philosophical and scientific point of view.[21] In Spain also the philosophers were interested in botany. Ibn Bājjah was an authority in this field and wrote two works on the subject, the *Kitāb al-tajribatayn* (*The Book of the Two Experiences*) dealing with the medical properties of herbs and the *Kitāb fi'l-nabāt* (*The Book on Plants*) with their physiology. Even Ibn Rushd had a special interest in botany and wrote a commentary on the *De Plantis*.

Andalusia and the Maghrib in general were also witness at this time to a series of major works related to plants, but from either the agricultural point of view, as with Ibn al-'Awwām, or the pharmacological perspective, as with al-Ghāfiqī and Ibn al-Bayṭār. But these works are so important for botany itself that they must be mentioned here, although they are concerned, properly speaking, with other disciplines. These works systematized Muslim botanical knowledge up to the 6th/12th and 7th/13th centuries and are especially strong in their descriptions of the flora of Andalusia. Similarly in works that appeared at the same time in the eastern lands of Islam emphasis is naturally placed upon the flora of those regions. For example, the *Kitāb al-i'tibār* (*The Eastern Key*) of 'Abd al-Laṭīf al-Baghdādī[22] is particularly rich in its description of the plants of Egypt.

Plate 25. The opening page of the treatise on simples (drugs) by Ibn al-Bayṭār.

Plate 27. An illustration of an anthropomorphous flower from a Persian botanical treatise.

Plate 28. Vine from a Persian botanical treatise.

20. There is a strange combination of astrology, magic and botany in this work which has attracted many Western as well as Muslim scholars to its study. For a summary of present-day knowledge of Ibn Waḥshiyyah see Sezgin, *op. cit.*, pp. 318–329. See also J. Hammer-Purgstall, *Ancient Alphabets and Hieroglyphic Characters Explained, with an Account of the Egyptian Priests, their Classes, Initiation and Sacrifices*, London, 1806.

21. Ibn Sīnā of course also dealt with plants in his pharmacological studies as did al-Bīrūnī in his *al-Ṣaydalah*. But these works will be treated later in the chapter on medicine.

22. See *The Eastern Key – Kitāb al-ifādah wa'l-i'tibār of 'Abd al-Laṭīf al-Baghdādī*, trans. by Kamal Hafuth Zand and John A. and Ivy E. Videau, London, 1965.

Plate 25

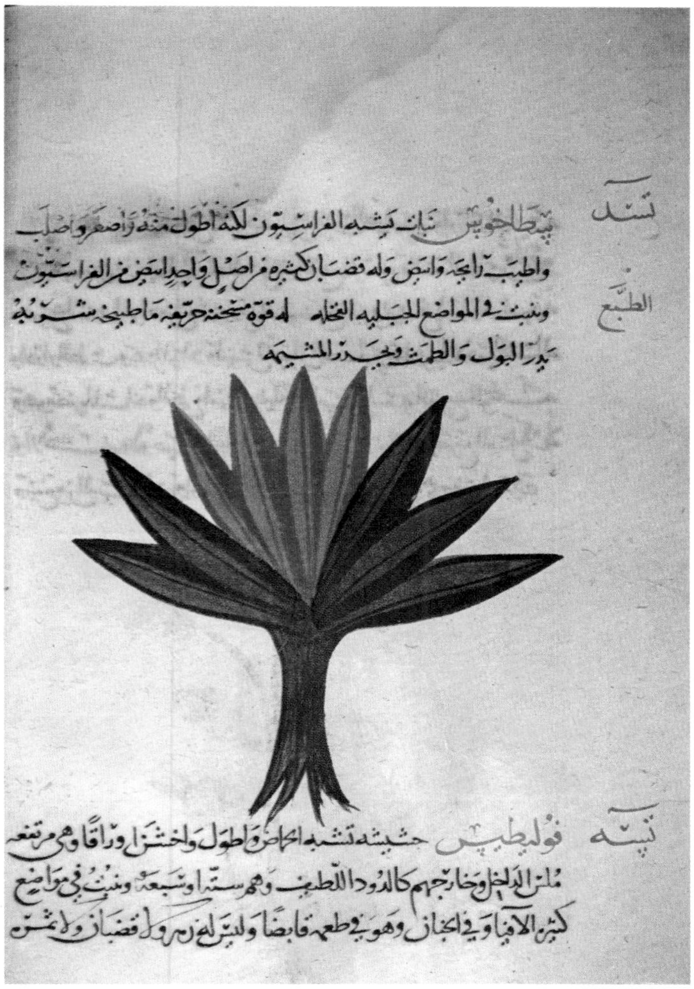

Plate 26. An illustration of a variety of sorrel.

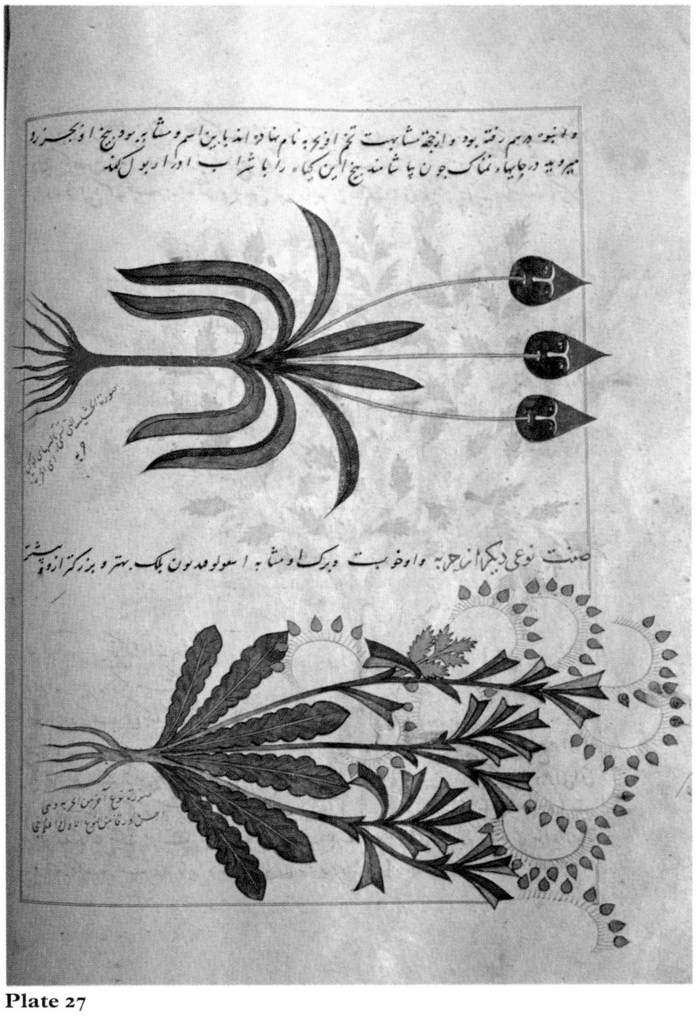

Plate 27

Plate 28

Plate 29. An illustration of the iris and white lily.

From the 8th/14th century onward compilations of earlier studies and encyclopaedic works began in botany as in so many other fields of the Islamic sciences. The encyclopaedias of al-Qazwīnī, Shams al-Dīn al-Nuwayrī, Ḥamdallāh Mustawfī, the *Tuḥfat al-ʿajā'ib* (*The Gift of Wonders*) attributed to Ibn al-Athīr, al-Juzūlī, ʿUmar ibn al-Wardī and many others devote special chapters to the study of plants, basing themselves mostly on the earlier studies mentioned above.

During the later Islamic centuries, the most important works of botany appeared mainly in Persian but also in Arabic and occasionally Urdu in the Indian sub-continent, where the profusion of vegetation offered a new opportunity for Muslim botanists to add a fresh chapter to the history of Islamic botany. Most of these later works have been neglected until now by the outside world, and even by scholars of other Muslim countries. But they display by their number as well as quality the richness of this later phase of botany which, while basing itself on the ideas of earlier Islamic botany, found itself in a new environment with a richness of flora and fauna not encountered by the earlier masters of this science who were accustomed to the drier climates and less varied plant life of Persia and the Arab lands.

Muslim studies on botany deal mostly with such questions as the classification of plants, their physiology, genesis and modes of growth, the description of their parts, their relation to geographical and climatic conditions and their medical as well as 'occult' properties. Also Muslim authors insisted upon studying the plant world with the aim of drawing spiritual and moral lessons from it as well as of contemplating its forms as parts of the *vestigia Dei*. It is noteworthy to remember the importance of plants in the Islamic paradise, the participation of plants in the resurrection discussed so extensively by Mullā Ṣadrā and others and the role of stylized plants in the sacred art of Islam. The spiritual significance of trees and flowers in Persian and Spanish gar-

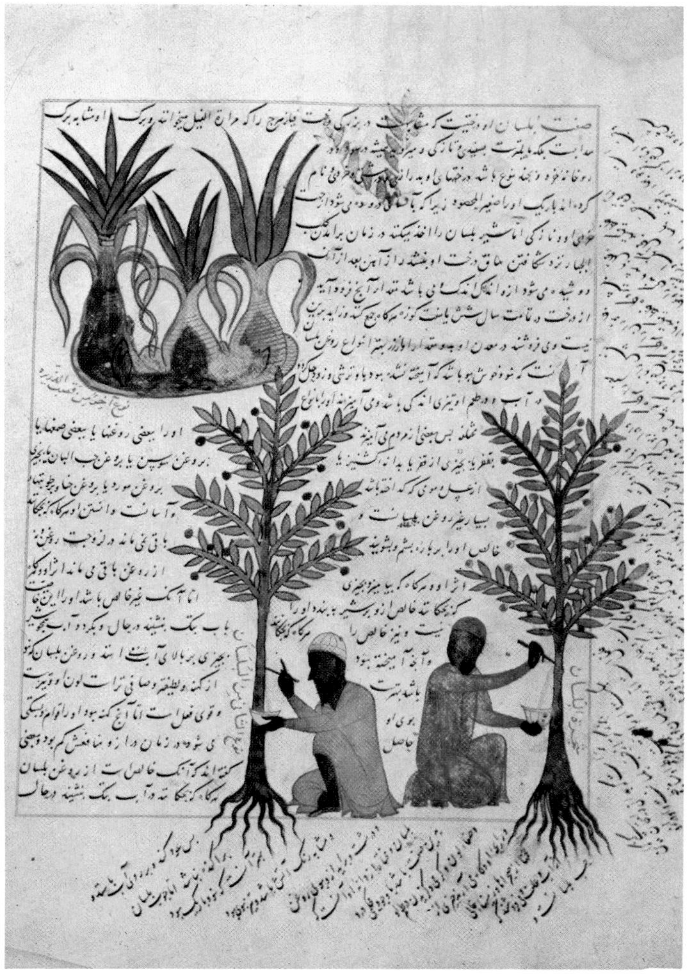

Plate 30. The tapping of a balsam tree.

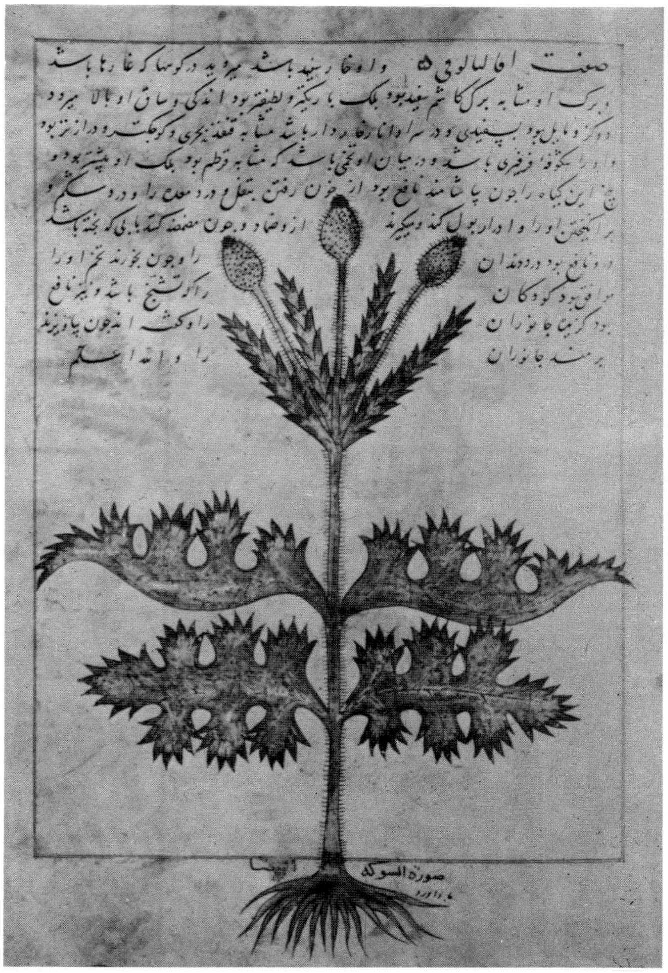

Figure 19. An illustration of the thistle.

dens, or in Arabic and Persian poetry, as well as in other aspects of Islamic art and in fact in the general life of Muslims, is inseparable from those aspects of botany which deal with the physical and medical properties of herbs. It is in fact all of these aspects together, from the most outward physical descriptions to the esoteric significance of the tree of Paradise, which together constitute the science of plants (*'ilm al-nabāt*) as it came into being and developed in the Muslim world over the centuries.

Zoology

The study of zoology in its broadest sense among Muslims involves nearly every facet of Islamic civilization, from jurisprudence to literature and from art to medicine. Not only did the Muslims have an intimate acquaintance with the life and habits of domesticated animals, which in fact provide to this day the basis for the life of nomads – whether they be in Morocco, Arabia, or Persia – but they also lived with the animal kingdom in an intimacy which permitted its world to enter the inmost chamber of Islamic spirituality as expressed in art and literature and as depicted religiously in the role played by animals in both the *Sharī'ah* and in eschatology. The very act of sacrifice, through which alone a Muslim can feed upon the animal kingdom, has sanctified animal life for Muslims, and the injunctions of the *Sharī'ah* have placed many duties and responsibilities upon the shoulders of man in his treatment of animals. And even beyond everyday life and their utility to man animals play an important role in the Islamic paradise and also in this world as symbols of various spiritual realities and as theophanies. Many Western scholars have assumed that since Muslims did not produce systematic works on zoology, they lacked substantial knowledge of the animal kingdom. Such a superficial judgment limits the study of animals solely to the model developed later in the West. It is as if one were to say that the American Indians knew nothing about eagles because they did not write treatises on their anatomy, whereas in reality their knowledge of what an eagle really is transcends infinitely all the zoological treatises written on this solar bird. The same is true *mutatis mutandis* of Islam, although Muslims in addition to their symbolic study of animals also did write 'scientific' treatises about them.

The pre-Islamic Arabs already had much knowledge of certain animals such as the camel and the horse, as did the Persians, who were also to make major contributions to zoological studies during the Islamic period. The Muslims in general inherited three different traditions connected with the animal kingdom: the pre-Islamic Arabic, the Graeco-Alexandrian and the Indo-Persian. The early Arabic tradition combined interest in animals with questions of philology and genealogy. The Graeco-Alexandrian sources included a treatise on zoology attributed to Hippocrates, the *Historia animalium* of Aristotle translated into Arabic by Yaḥyā ibn al-Biṭrīq, the treatise on animals of Theomnestos of Magnesia, the *Sirr al-khalīqah* (*The Book of the Secret of Creatures*) attributed to Apollonios of Tyana and certain Byzantine works.

The Indo-Persian tradition differed profoundly from the Greek, especially from the detailed descriptive and analytical works of Aristotle. The Oriental sources on animals were more concerned with the spiritual and moral

Plate 31. The lion and the jackal from the *Kalīlah wa Dimnah*.

Plate 32. Elephants from the *Kalīlah wa Dimnah*.

Plate 33. Owls from the *Kalīlah wa Dimnah*.

significance of animal life than the anatomy and classification of animals. The main work belonging to this tradition, namely the *Kalīlah wa Dimnah* (*Tales of Bidpai*), which became a major literary masterpiece of both Arabic and Persian, reveals clearly the concern to learn not only *about* but also *from* animals and to study animals as creatures who share in man's ultimate destiny and who have much to teach man concerning the wisdom of God and man's duties on earth.

The Islamic tradition of zoology came into being by unifying the traditions Islam inherited from the Greeks, the pre-Islamic Arabs and the Indo-Persian world.[23] The earliest works dating from the 2nd/8th century were mostly lexicographical in nature and were concerned especially with camels and horses. During the 2nd/8th and 3rd/9th centuries, philologists from both Basra and Kufa, men like Abū Naḍr ibn Shumayl, al-Aṣma'ī, Ibn al-A'rābī, Abū 'Ubayd ibn Sallām and Abū Ḥātim al-Sijistānī, all wrote on zoology.[24] Likewise, many of the Mu'tazilite theologians of this period, such as the well-known figures Bishr ibn al-Mu'tamir and Abū Isḥāq al-Naẓẓām, showed special interest in zoology.

But of course the foremost Mu'tazilite author who wrote on zoology was the celebrated literary figure al-Jāḥiẓ, whose *Kitāb al-ḥayawān* (*The Book of Animals*) is the most famous of its kind in Islam. Al-Jāḥiẓ assembled all the knowledge that existed before him from Arabic and Persian as well as Greek sources. He knew the studies of Aristotle and in fact referred to him and even criticized him. For al-Jāḥiẓ the goal of the study of zoology could not but be the demonstration of the existence of God and the wisdom inherent in His creation. Al-Jāḥiẓ made of zoology a branch of religious studies without, however, remaining oblivious to natural and scientific observations of the animal kingdom. He studied about 350 animals, which he described and classified into four categories according to the way they move. He was also, like Aristotle, much interested in animal psychology. In fact had his treatment of animals been more orderly he would have been worthy – to quote Pellat, the well-known modern Western authority on him – to stand as one of the foremost contributors to the science of zoology along with Aristotle and Buffon.[25]

The philosopher al-Kindī was also interested in zoology and wrote several treatises on animals, as was his successor al-Fārābī, who in his classification of the sciences considered zoology as an independent discipline. But in the 3rd/9th and early 4th/10th century the most important contributions to zoology still came from compilers and natural historians rather than philosophers. This was the period when Ibn Qutaybah wrote his *'Uyūn al-akhbār* (*The Most Essential Information*) with an important section devoted to zoology[26] and when the *'Ajā'ib al-hind* of Buzurg ibn Shahriyār Rāmhurmuzī described for the first time in the Islamic world many exotic animals belonging both to the Indian world and to the mythology connected with that world. This is also the period when the influential *Kitāb nu'ūt al-ḥayawān* (*The Book of the Qualities of Animals*) attributed to Aristotle was assembled.

From the middle of the 4th/10th century onward, however, philosophical works became the main repository for zoological studies. One of the longest epistles of the Ikhwān al-Ṣafā' is devoted to animals. In this important treatise the Ikhwān make a profound study of animals in the total chain of being and also classify them according to several criteria, including the number of senses each animal has developed, the way each species is generated and the habitat of each species. They also analyze in detail the organs of many animals according to a perspective which is thoroughly teleological and which combines the approach of Aristotle with that of the Indo-Persian sources.[27] Moreover, they devote a long section, exceptional in length alone within all the epistles, to 'the dispute between man and the animals'. This beautifully written story, which is

23. On the sources and history of zoology among Muslims see '*ḥayawān*' by Ch. Pellat *et al.* in the new edition of the *Encyclopaedia of Islam*; F. Sezgin, *Geschichte des Arabischen Schrifttums*, vol. III, pp. 343ff.; and M. Ullmann, *Die Natur- und Geheimwissenschaften im Islam*, pp. 5–60.

24. During the same period Jābir ibn Ḥayyān also wrote a treatise on animals which is, however, lost and known only through citations from it in later works.

25. See Pellat, *op. cit.*, p. 312.

26. See F. S. Bodenheimer and L. Kopf, *The Natural History Section from a 9th Century 'Book of Useful Knowledge'*.

27. See Nasr, *An Introduction to Islamic Cosmological Doctrines*, pp. 93–95.

extremely timely today in the light of the ecological crisis, discusses the reasons given by man for his right to dominate and destroy the animal kingdom, and the response of the animals, which nullifies all the arguments of man based upon his purely human advantages such as the power of ratiocination or invention. Only when animals see that among men there are saints, who in returning to God also fulfil the deepest purpose of the creation of the animal kingdom, do they agree to obey man and to serve him.[28] The moral of the story is that man has the right to dominate animals only on condition that he remain conscious of his vice-gerency (*khilāfah*), of his being God's representative on earth and from another point of view the representative of all earthly creatures before God. Otherwise, he has no cogent reason whatsoever to rule and dominate other creatures and in fact will pay dearly for usurping a function to which he is not entitled save as the child of that Adam who, as the Holy Quran asserts,[29] was taught the 'names' of all things.

The philosopher Ibn Sīnā also devoted a major section of his *Shifā'* (*The Book of Healing*), namely the eighth chapter of the 'Natural Philosophy' (*Ṭabī'iyyāt*), to animals, and dealt especially with animal psychology and their physiology.[30] Also in Spain both Ibn Bājjah and Ibn Rushd were interested in zoology, the first having written a separate treatise on zoology and the second commentaries upon the *De Partibus animalium* and *De generatione animalium* of Aristotle.

As in botany so in zoology, from the late 7th/13th and early 8th/14th centuries there began to appear a series of encyclopaedic works with major sections devoted to animals. In fact this was the beginning of a very active period in the composition of notable works devoted to zoology.[31] Al-Qazwīnī, in his cosmography, devoted a special section to animals, in which he divided the animal kingdom according to each animal's means of defence. Likewise al-Dimashqī, al-Nuwayrī, al-Jīldakī in his *Durrat al-ghawwāṣ* (*The Pearl of the Pearl-Diver*), Ḥamdallāh Mustawfī, Aḥmad ibn Yaḥyā al-'Umarī in his *Masālik al-abṣār* (*Voyages of the Eyes*), the anonymous *Tuḥfat al-'ajā'ib wa ṭurfat al-gharā'ib* (*Gift of Wonders and Present of Marvels*), 'Alā' al-Dīn al-Juzūlī in his *Maṭāli' al-budūr* (*Ascensions of the Full Moon*) and al-Qalqashandī in his *Subḥ al-a'shā'* (*Dawn for the Weak-Sighted*), all devoted notable sections to the study of animals.

Plate 34. Birds of India from the *Bābur-nāmah*.

28. See Ikhwān al-Ṣafā', *Dispute between Man and the Animals*, trans. J. Platts, London, 1869.

29. 'And He taught Adam all the names.' Quran, II, 31.

30. This section became famous in the West as an independent work under the title *Abbreviatio Avicennae de animalibus*, translated by Michael Scot.

31. We do not mean to imply that after Ibn Rushd no specific treatises on animals appeared, as the well-known *Ṭabāyi' al-ḥayawān* (*On the Nature of Animals*) of Sharaf al-Zamān al-Marwazī and *Manāfi' al-ḥayawān* (*The Uses of Animals*) of Ibn al-Durayhim show. The encyclopaedic and cosmographic type of work became, however, the main vehicle for natural history from the 8th/14th century onward.

Plate 35. A buzzard by Manṣūr.

Plate 36. A partridge by Muḥammad ʿĀlim.

Plate 36

The foremost Muslim work of the later period, however, is the *Ḥayāt al-ḥayawān al-kubrā* (*The Great Book on the Life of Animals*) of Kamāl al-Dīn al-Damīrī written in the late 8th/14th century.[32] This work, which systematized all the studies which had preceded it, soon became, after the work of al-Jāḥiẓ, the most popular Muslim treatise on animals and was translated into Persian and Turkish. Al-Damīrī did not attempt a new classification of the animal kingdom, but in an orderly fashion made a study of the philological aspects of the names of animals, their religious and juridical status according to the *Sharīʿah*, traditions relating to them, their medical benefits and even magical use and significance in the interpretation of dreams. Because of its thoroughness and the combining of the religious, literary and scientific perspectives in studying animals, the *Ḥayāt al-ḥayawān* soon found a special place among Muslims. It was read by young and old alike, in order to learn of the wisdom of God and to gain better acquaintance with the animal world. It was consulted even for juridical purposes for the specific religious reason of knowing more about animals mentioned in the Holy Quran.[33] It was a source of folklore and finally an inspiration for numerous artists who illustrated its text. Altogether al-Damīrī's work is the most complete and systematic extant work on zoology in the Islamic world.

During the last four or five centuries some treatises on zoology have appeared in Persian and Turkish as well as Arabic[34] all written in the classical heartland of the Islamic world, but in this as in other domains of natural history the most interesting new works of this period belong to India. The Mogul Emperor Jahāngīr himself devoted sections of his *Tūzuk-i Jahāngīrī* or *Jahāngīr-nāmah* (*The Book of Jahāngīr*) to natural history. Of these the most noteworthy concerns animals, which he described carefully.[35] His studies were made more valuable by the fact that miniaturists who were at the Mogul court, especially Manṣūr, drew miniatures of these same animals, producing works of great beauty which, without being naturalistic,[36] captured the inner qualities and the very genius of the species in question. The illustrations to the descriptions in works such as those of Jahāngīr (although of an earlier period) are the first forms of Persian, Arabic and Turkish as well as Mogul miniatures and are like an extension of the art of calligraphy. They have never occupied the place which painting holds in Western art. But in the field of natural history and especially zoology they have played an important role of both an artistic and scientific nature and are a vivid reminder that not only is Islamic art a 'science'[37] but that Islamic science is in the most profound sense an art, a sacred art which enables man to contemplate the visible cosmos as an icon revealing the spiritual world beyond it.

Plate 37. A hunting hawk.

32. Numerous studies have been devoted to this work by J. de Somogy. See for example, 'Ad-Damīrī's Ḥayāt al-ḥayawān. An Arabic Zoological Lexicon', *Osiris*, vol. 9, 1950, pp. 33–43.

33. The Egyptian scholar Jalāl al-Dīn al-Suyūṭī made a poetic summary of this work which was translated into Latin and incorporated into the *Hierozoicon* composed in 1663. This latter work tried to study the animals which are mentioned in the Bible in the same way that al-Damīrī had done for those mentioned in the Quran and Islamic traditions.

34. Notable among Arabic works of the later period is the *Kitāb al-mustaṭraf* (*The Book of Novelties*) of Muḥammad ibn Aḥmad al-Ibshīhī with a long section devoted to animals.

35. See M. A. Alvi and A. Rahman, *Jahangir – the Naturalist*, New Delhi, 1968. The study of animals by Muslims continued in India even after Jahāngīr, and in the 12th/18th century the great Persian Sufi saint and poet 'Alī Ḥazīn wrote his work *Khawāṣṣ al-ḥayawān* in Persian while he was in India. There are numerous manuscripts in Indian libraries on this subject, mostly in Persian, which attest to activity in this field. Unfortunately most of them have not as yet been studied.

36. Islamic art is opposed to all forms of naturalism and in fact the external emulation of natural forms. Based on Unity, this art seeks to reflect Unity upon the plane of multiplicity rather than to paint an image, be it even a sacred one. See T. Burckhardt, *Sacred Art, East and West*, trans. by Lord Northbourne, London, 1967, chap. 4, where the principles of Islamic art are fully explained with unparalleled clarity.

37. Echoing the well-known dictum of St Thomas that *ars sine scientia nihil.*

Plate 37

Muslim interest in the animal kingdom is seen not only in art but also in literature. This is reflected most clearly in Persian literature, which in fact influenced Arabic and Turkish profoundly in this domain. Animals as symbols of cosmic qualities and of spiritual attitudes and as moral teachers to men are to be found already in Pahlavi works. But it is Persian which is particularly rich in this respect. In epics such as the *Shāh-nāmah* (*Epic of Kings*) of Firdawsī, in tales such as the *Jawāmiʿ al-ḥikāyāt* (*Collected Stories*) of al-Awfī, and in folk literature such as the *Sindbād-nāmah* (*The Story of Sinbad*), animals play a major role. Moreover, in Sufi literature, animals occupy a special position as man's companions during his earthly journey. The *Ḥadīqat al-ḥaqīqah* (*The Garden of Truth*) of Sanā'ī, the numerous works of 'Aṭṭār, especially the *Manṭiq al-ṭayr* (*The Conference of the Birds*), in which the flight of thirty birds to their original abode symbolizes the journey of the soul towards God, the *Mathnawī* of Rūmī and the *Bahāristān* (*The Garden of Spring*) of Jāmī all attest to the role of animals on the highest level as elements necessary to the cosmic equilibrium and as theophanies of God's Names and Qualities which the traveller upon the spiritual path 'encounters' and integrates into his being on his journey beyond the cosmic crypt.

At the other extreme one finds the study of animals for practical matters, ranging from hunting to medicine.[38] Muslims developed especially the

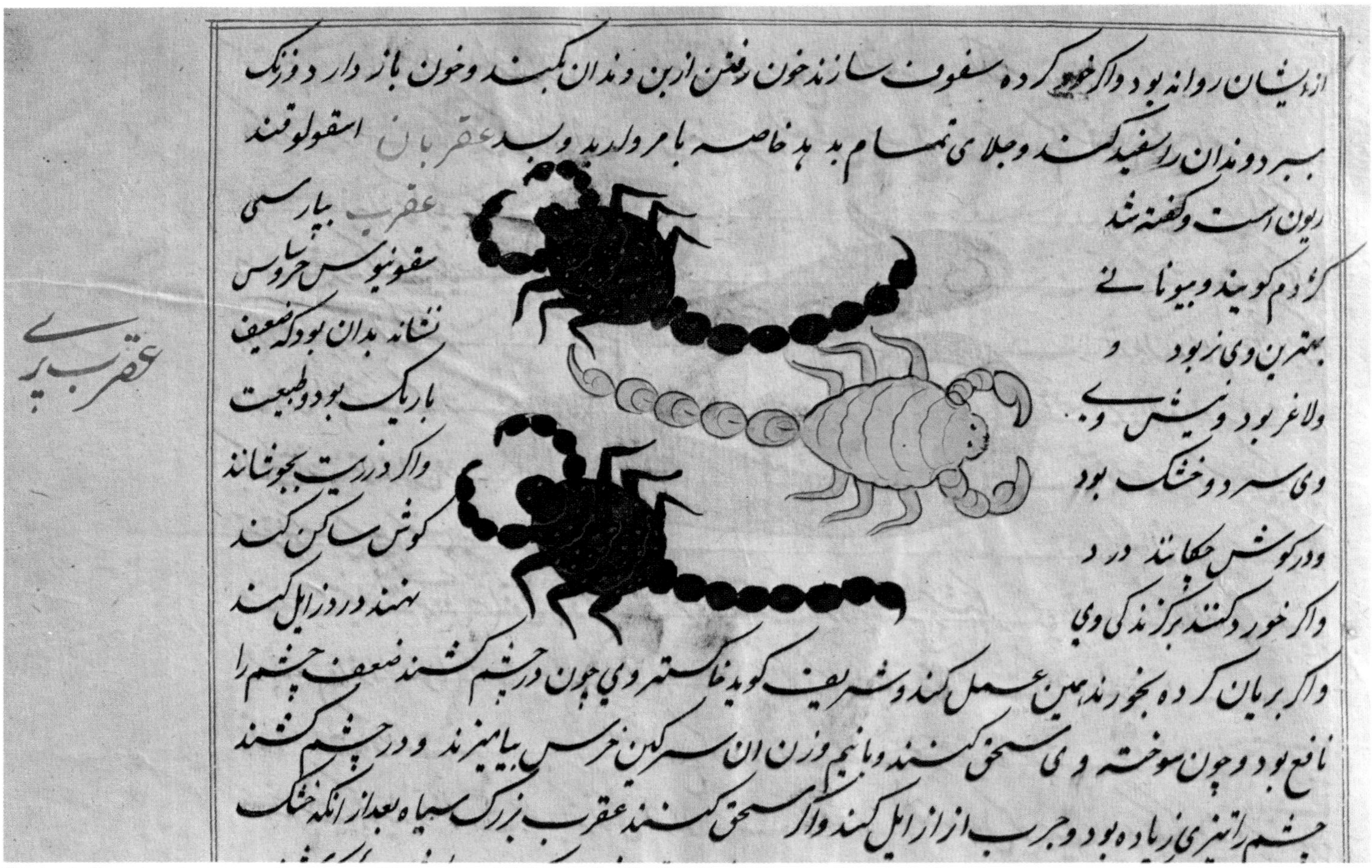

Plate 38. Scorpions from a treatise on natural history, the *Ikhtiyārāt-i badīʿī* of 'Alī ibn al-Ḥusayn, Zayn al-'Aṭṭār.

38. It is in the nature of Islamic civilization to integrate the sacred and the temporal, the sublime and the practical. There is no art for art's sake nor science for science's sake in Islam. Everything is for an end, which includes what is most 'useful' to man as an earthly creature and as a being destined for immortality. That is why there is so much zoology in Islamic sources, not only in the manner expected by Western students of Aristotle or Buffon and Cuvier but also in a manner that stretches from the way a Rūmī conceives of a lion or an Ibn 'Arabī of a griffin to the way in which Ibn Sīnā discusses the medical use of various animal products.

field of hippology, in which they wrote numerous treatises, such as those of al-Aṣma'ī, 'Abd al-Mu'min al-Dimyāṭī, al-Jawālīqī and Ibn al-Mundhir.[39] It is interesting to add in this case the special love of the nomadic Turks for horses, upon whom they even 'bestowed' sanctity. The horse of Sultan 'Uthmān II, which was buried at Usküdar, was known as the 'saint of horses' (*At-Ewliyāsī*) and sick horses were brought there for cure. Muslims also excelled in ornithology, especially in the study of hawks. Numerous treatises were composed on this subject, mostly in Persian, some of which are still read in the West in courses on ornithology.[40]

Practical concerns also led the Muslim physicians and pharmacologists to study animals. From 'Alī ibn Rabban al-Ṭabarī, to Rāzī, Ibn Sīnā, 'Īsā ibn 'Alī, Ibn Bukhṭīshū', Ibn al-Bayṭār, Dā'ūd al-Anṭākī and the later Ottoman, Safavid and Mogul medical authorities, the Muslims devoted considerable attention to both veterinary medicine and the use of animals in the treatment of man. A major source for the study of zoology among Muslims must be sought in Muslim medical works.

Altogether it can be said that despite the accusation of some scholars that Muslims did not cultivate zoology extensively, the study of animals occupies a very important chapter in the whole of Islamic civilization. It is related to the arts, from carpet weaving to poetry, to medicine and allied subjects, to general studies of natural history, and even to the esoteric and spiritual meditations on the cosmos and the Reality beyond. The Muslims have always had a profound awareness that animals along with plants and minerals are an

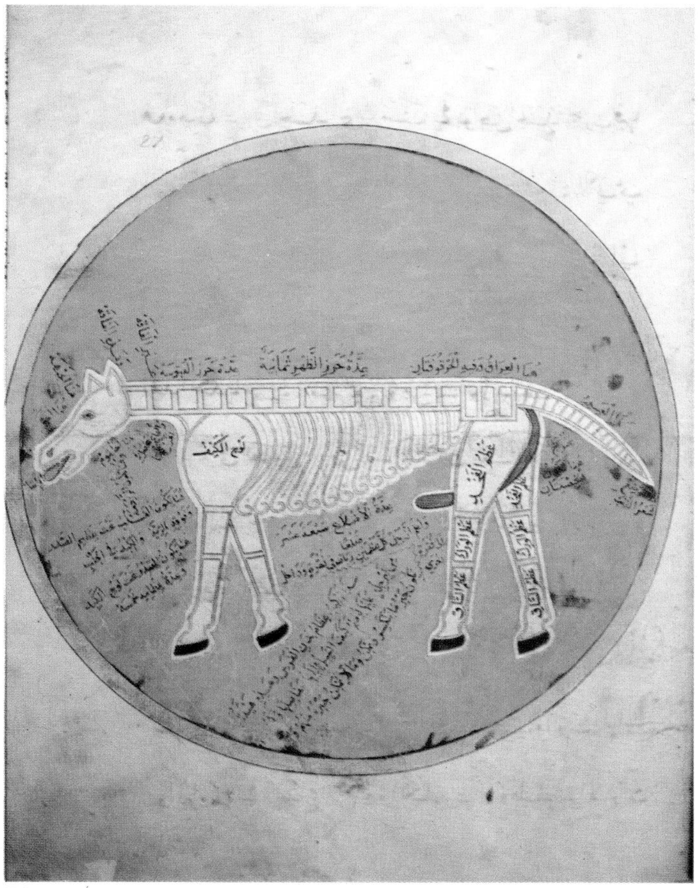

Plates 39 and 40. An anatomical study of the horse.

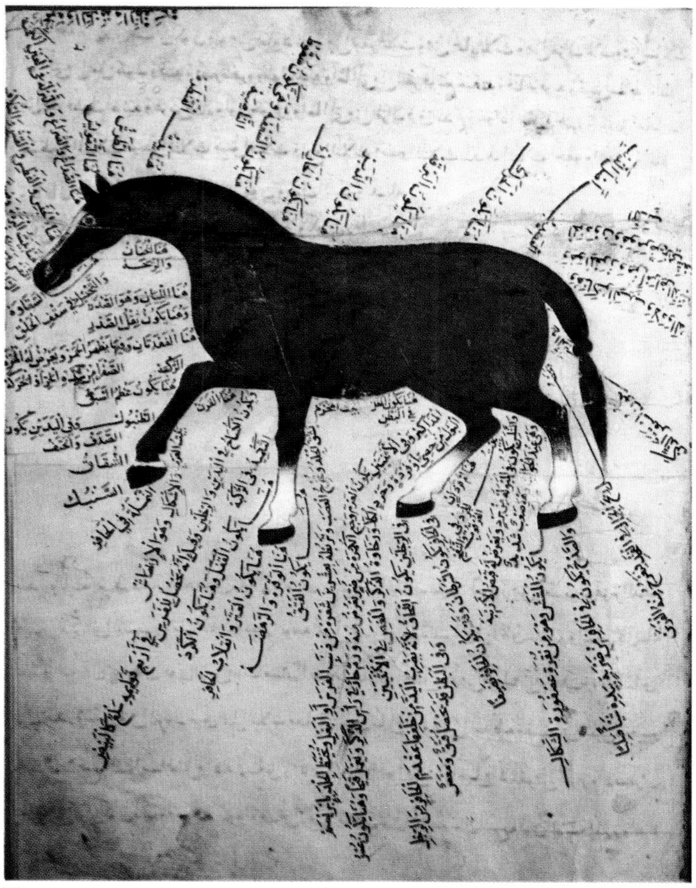

Plate 40

39. See the article '*faras*' by F. Viré in the *Encyclopaedia of Islam* (new edition).

40. See the article '*bayzara*' by F. Viré in the *Encyclopaedia of Islam* (new edition).

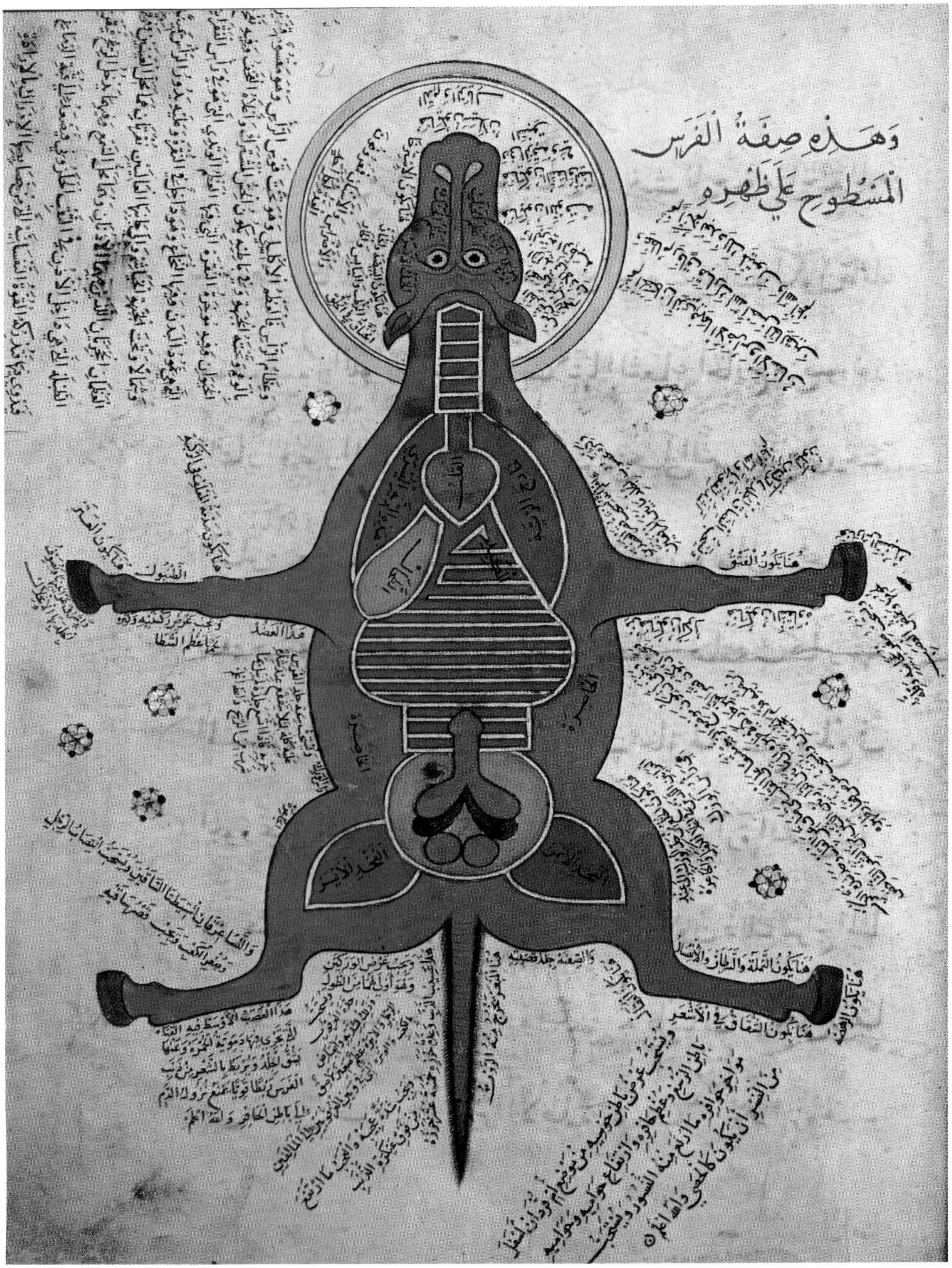

Plate 41. An anatomical study of the horse.

essential component of that equilibrium which virgin nature manifests so openly and which Islamic art recaptures in its sacred structures. They have known that animals must be studied not only to be utilized but also to be better understood for their own sake, so that through them man may gain greater knowledge of the Divine Wisdom and also come to know better his own inner nature, which is a total reflection of the Divine Names and Qualities as the animals are partial but often more direct reflections. Through the study of the animal kingdom man is therefore more fully able to realize his vice-regal role and become aware of the great responsibility he must exercise as the central being in the terrestrial environment *vis-à-vis* the animal and plant kingdoms.

Natural History and the Gradation of Being

One of the recurrent themes in Muslim studies on natural history is the gradation of beings within the three kingdoms, which in fact re-echoes a universal traditional doctrine,[41] and along with the correspondence between the microcosm and the macrocosm forms the basic doctrinal background for the study of the various forms manifested within nature. Such authors as the Ikhwān al-Ṣafā' and Ibn Sīnā go to great pains to divide and sub-divide each kingdom according to a scale which reveals an ever greater degree of perfection. The mineral world ranges from the most opaque substances to those which resemble plant life, and plant life likewise stretches from moss and algae, which resemble mineral growth, to palm trees, in which there is a differentiation of the sexes. The same holds true for the animal kingdom, at whose apex are creatures which resemble man in certain aspects of their intelligence. Muslim authors studied this gradation from the point of view of the reflection of cosmic qualities rather than just anatomical resemblances. That is why the Ikhwān al-Ṣafā' considered the elephant and not the monkey as the creature which stands just below man in the scale of being.[42]

Furthermore, Muslim authors were also aware that in the 'great chain of being' certain life forms preceded others in *time* on the surface of the earth. But they never believed in the theory of evolution in the modern sense according to which through some mysterious fashion the greater 'evolves' from the lesser.[43] Evolutionary theory as usually understood is a means to fill the void created by modern man's cutting off the hands of God from His creation. For the Muslims, however, any form of deism is absurd and God never ceases to act within the world He has brought into being. The scale of creatures and the gradation of being has been, therefore, from the beginning considered by Muslim authorities as a vertical hierarchy 'always' present in a Now which is above temporality while also becoming manifested in time at different moments of cosmic history through what might be called the successive dreams of the World Soul. The 'great chain of being' was formulated not to explain away the Divine Cause but to enable man to ascend towards the Source while being fully aware of the total cosmic equilibrium of which natural forms provide such striking evidence.

41. See A. K. Coomaraswamy, 'Gradation, Evolution and Reincarnation', chapter 6 of his *Am I my Brother's Keeper?* (*The Bugbear of Literacy*, London, 1949), New York, 1947.

42. See Nasr, *An Introduction to Islamic Cosmological Doctrines*, p. 70.

43. Some Western scholars have, however, tried to read 19th century evolutionary ideas into Islamic texts. See for example, Fr. Dieterici, *Der Darwinismus im X. und XI. Jahrhundert*, Leipzig, 1878; see also J. Z. Wilczynski, 'On the presumed Darwinism of Alberuni eight hundred years before Darwin,' *Isis*, vol. 50, part 4, Dec., 1959, pp. 459–466.

Part Three
The Cosmos and Its Mathematical Study

Chapter V
Mathematics

Mathematics and the Islamic Perspective

Any first-hand knowledge of Islamic civilization and particularly the Islamic sciences reveals the 'privileged position' of mathematics in the Islamic tradition. There are crystalline and geometric aspects to Islamic art and architecture, a love of arithmetic and numerical symbolism in both the plastic and auditory arts – especially poetry and music – an 'algebra' of language and of thought so clearly reflected in Arabic and also in many other Islamic languages, and numerous other tangible manifestations which make plain the central role of traditional mathematics in Islamic art and civilization and on the highest level in the spiritual 'style' of Islam so directly reflected in its sacred art.

This love for mathematics, especially geometry and number, is directly connected to the essence of the Islamic message, which is the doctrine of Unity (*al-tawḥīd*). God is One; hence the number one in the series of numbers is the most direct and most intelligible symbol of the Source. And the series of numbers themselves is a ladder by which man ascends from the world of multiplicity to the One. As a treatise summarizing the views of the Ikhwān al-Ṣafā' says, 'Verily the form of numbers in the souls of men corresponds to the forms of existents in the *hylé*. It is a sample from the upper world. Through its knowledge the ascetic reaches gradually the other mathematical and natural sciences and metaphysics. The science of numbers is the root of the sciences, the element of wisdom, the origin of the divine sciences, the pillar of meaning, the first elixir and the great alchemy.'[1]

There is indeed a profound affinity between the Pythagorean concept of numbers and of geometric figures and certain intellectual perspectives within Islam. Pythagoras was Islamicized rapidly, for there existed already in the Islamic universe a dimension which could be described as 'Abrahamic Pythagoreanism', one in which the symbolic role of numbers and figures appeared in dazzling clarity, illuminated by Islamic gnosis which is precisely a blinding message of the One. Here we are not concerned so much with a question of historical borrowing as with spiritual and morphological affinity. The numerical symbolism of the letters of the Arabic alphabet connected with the sacred and esoteric science of *al-jafr* is said to

1. *Risālat al-jāmi'ah,* ed. Dj. Saliba, Damascus, 1949, vol. I, p. 9. For the philosophy of mathematics among Muslims see also Mīr Dāmād, *Jadhawāt*, Tehran, 1302 (A. H. lunar), pp. 81ff.

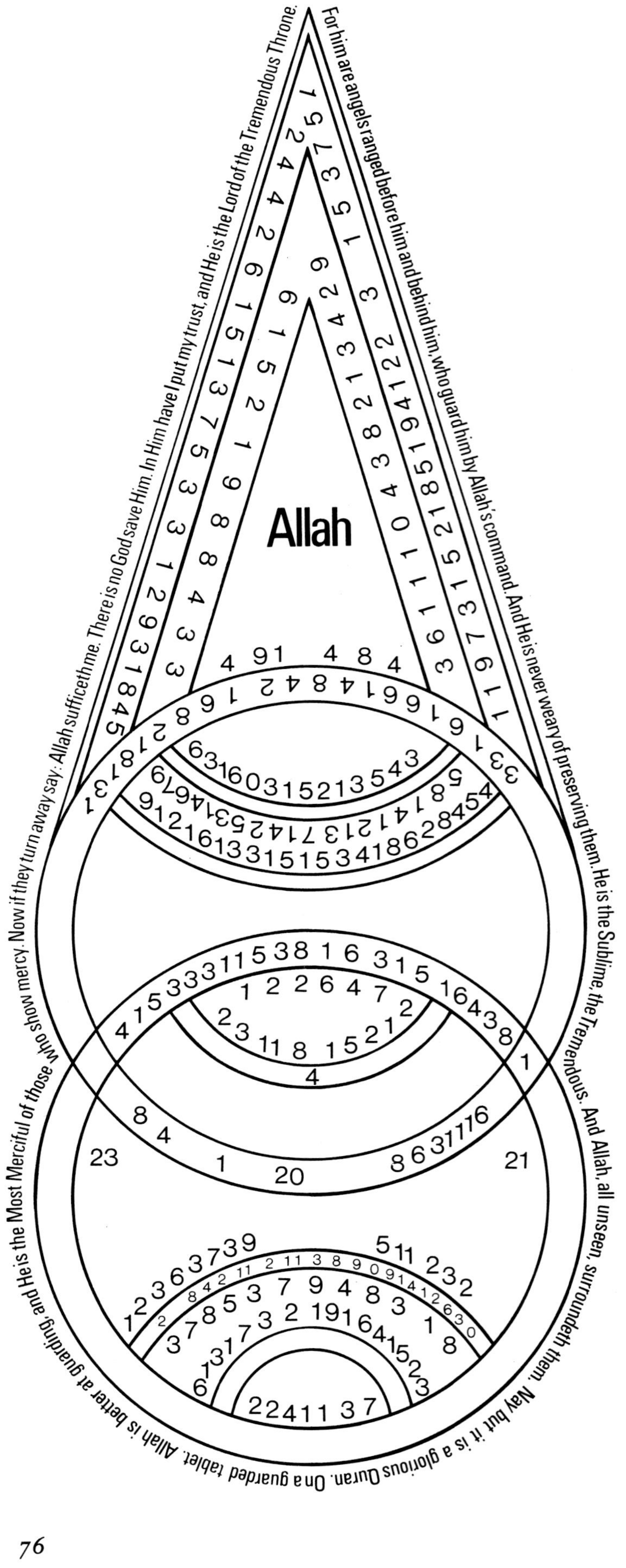

Figure 20. Cosmological and magical schemes relating Quranic verses to the symbolism of numbers according to Shams al-Dīn al-Būnī.

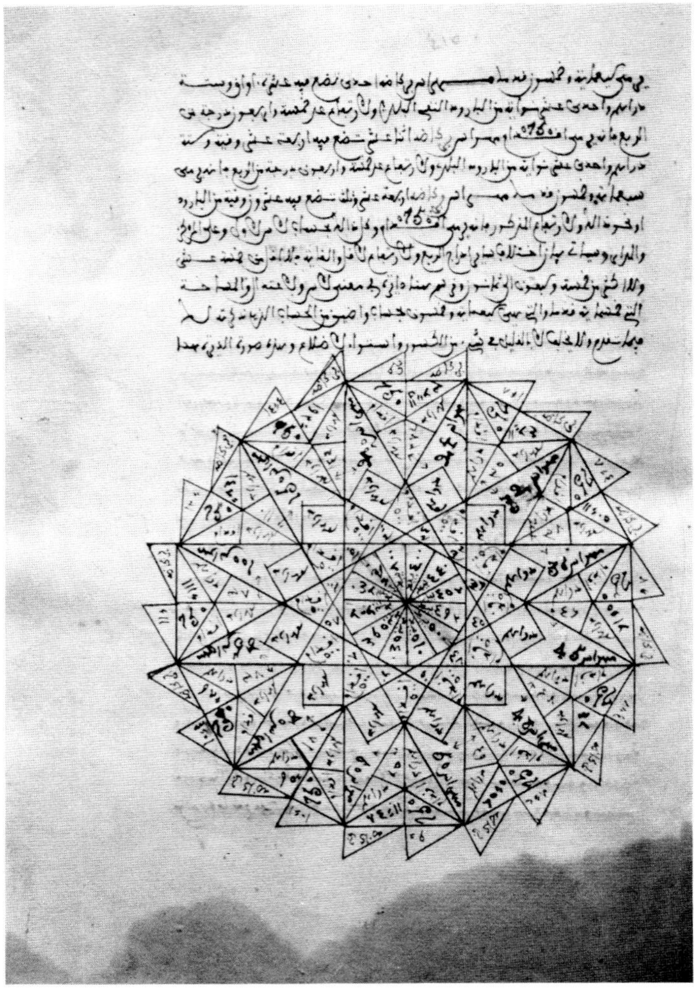

Figure 21. Geometric and numerical patterns used as the basis for the construction of various devices and instruments.

have been codified by 'Alī ibn Abī Ṭālib and is inseparable from the form and inner meaning of certain passages of the Holy Quran. The traditional mathematics of the Pythagoreans only provided a powerful aid for the expression of a message which comes from the source of the Islamic revelation itself and a spiritual and dialectic style which is also inseparable from its sacred form.

That is why, from sublime treatises on metaphysics to pottery used in homes, one is faced everywhere in the Islamic world with an order and a harmony directly related to the world of mathematics understood in its traditional sense.[2] Likewise, it is because of this element within the total spectrum of Islamic spirituality that Muslims became attracted to the various branches of mathematics early in their history and made so many contributions to the mathematical sciences for nearly a millennium.

The major sources for Islamic mathematics were Greek, as well as Persian and Indian. These sources, especially the Greek, included moreover the rich Babylonian tradition of mathematics, which bestowed upon the world the sexagesimal system. The Persian sources reflected mostly the Indian ones and were embedded in astronomical treatises. Likewise the knowledge which Muslims received from India in the domain of mathematics was contained for the most part within the astronomical compendia known as the *siddhāntas* and referred to in Muslim sources as *sindhinds*. Of these, perhaps the most important for both Islamic mathematics and astronomy are the *Brāhmasphuṭasiddhānta* of Brahmagupta and the *Āryabhaṭīya* of Āryabhaṭa which systematizes the earlier *siddhāntas*.

As for the Greek sources, they include most of the major works of Greek mathematics such as the *Elements* and *Data* of Euclid; the *Conics, The Section of the Ratio,* and the *Determinate Section* of Apollonios Pergaeus; the *Spherics* of Theodosius of Tripoli; the all-important *Introduction to Arithmetic* of Nichomachus of Gerasa[3] and the *Spherics* of Menelaus, along with the works of Heron, Theon and other important Alexandrian mathematicians and commentators. Also of special significance for Islamic mathematics is Archimedes, almost all of whose writings, such as *The Sphere and the Cylinder*, *The Measurement of the Circle, The Equilibrium of Planes* and *Floating Bodies,* were translated into Arabic. In fact there are many works in Arabic either by Archimedes or attributed to him for which there is no original Greek.[4] Altogether, it may be said with safety that the Muslims inherited nearly all the important mathematical ideas developed in ancient Mesopotamia, Egypt, Greece and the Hellenistic world as well as in Persia and India and made of this vast heritage the basis for the development of Islamic mathematics.

Numerals

Whenever Westerners think of Islamic civilization, one of the first elements which comes to mind is the Arabic numerals, which reached the West in the 4th/10th century from the Islamic world and brought about such a profound transformation in the West that some historians have compared their far-reaching significance to that of the new methods of harnessing the power and speed of the horse and the settling of the northern regions of Europe. It is, therefore, essential to

2. There is of course a principial difference between traditional mathematics, which is concerned with the symbolic and qualitative aspects of numbers and figures as well as their quantitative aspect, and modern mathematics, which is limited to the latter aspect. On traditional mathematics see S. H. Nasr, *An Introduction to Islamic Cosmological Doctrines*, pp. 45ff.; Fabre d'Olivet, *The Golden Verses of Pythagoras*, New York, 1917; and the numerous works of H. Kayser, such as *Bevor die Engel sangen,* Basel, 1953; *Der hörende Mensch,* Berlin, 1932; and *Akroasis, die Lehre von der Harmonik der Welt,* Stuttgart, 1947, which applies Pythagorean mathematics and music to various sciences of nature. For a summary of the views of H. Kayser see S. Levarie and E. Levy, 'The Pythagorean Table', *Main Currents in Modern Thought*, March–April, 1974, pp. 117–129.

3. This work, translated by Thābit ibn Qurrah into Arabic, had a particularly deep influence on the formulation of the philosophy of mathematics among Muslims, especially upon the first epistle of the Brethren of Purity. See R. Goldstein's translation of this epistle in 'A Treatise on Number Theory from a Tenth Century Arabic Source', *Centaurus*, vol. 10, 1964, pp. 129–134.

4. On the sources for Islamic mathematics see J. Vernet, 'Mathematics, Astronomy, Optics', in J. Schacht and C. E. Bosworth (eds.), *The Legacy of Islam,* Oxford, 1974, pp. 461ff.; also F. Sezgin, *Geschichte der Arabischen Schrifttums,* vol. V, Leiden, 1975, pp. 1ff.

unravel the complicated history of these numerals before delving into various branches of mathematics.

Anyone who travels through the Islamic world today realizes that in the eastern lands of Islam extending as far West as Egypt, the numerals used are, with slight variations, as follows[5]:

٠ ١ ٢ ٣ ٤ ٥ ٦ ٧ ٨ ٩

In North Africa, however, the numerals are the same as those which Westerners call Arabic numerals, whose forms reveal their historical relation with the numerals now in use in the eastern Islamic countries.

The Muslims originally used finger computation (*ḥisāb al-yad*)[6] before learning of the Indian numerals and the 'dust-board' system (*ḥisāb al-ghubārī*) early in the 2nd/8th century from Indian and Persian sources.[7] But even after learning of these new methods of reckoning the method of finger computation continued. Moreover, the Muslims inherited the sexigesimal system from ancient Babylonia, which continued to be used, especially by astronomers, even after the decimal system had been adopted. The *ḥisāb al-jummal*, using letters to symbolize numbers and based on the sexigesimal system, spread widely throughout the Islamic world over the centuries. The sexigesimal system in fact came to be known as the 'arithmetic of astronomers' (*ḥisāb al-munajjimīn*), and as late as the 9th/15th century Sibṭ al-Māridīnī wrote an entire work in this system entitled *Raqā'iq al-ḥaqā'iq fī ma'rifat al-daraj wa'l-daqā'iq* (*Delicacies of Truth Concerning Knowledge of Degrees and Minutes*). As far as the decimal system is concerned, the Muslims in fact fused various methods of reckoning into a system which was based on the Indian numerals and the place-system.

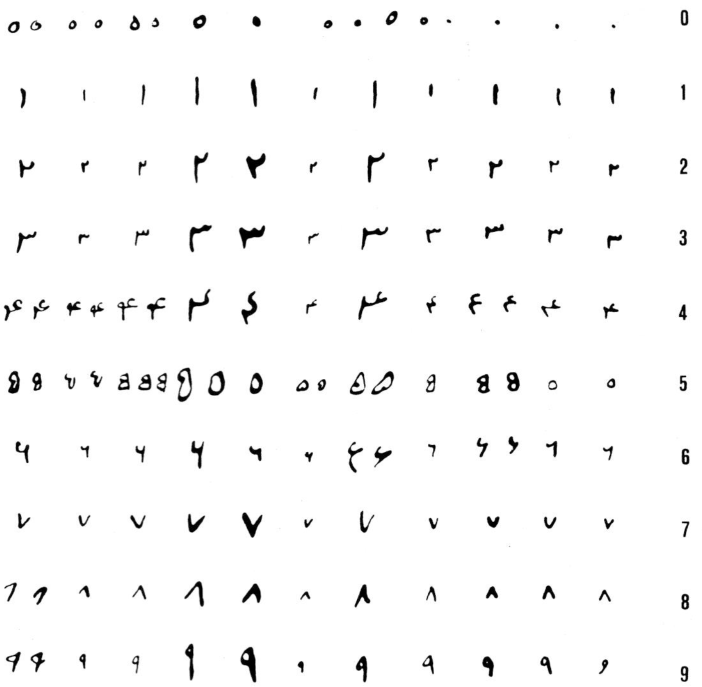

Figure 22. The development of the Arabic numeral.

The means whereby the Indian numerals became transformed into the Arabic numerals, which themselves are based on the *ghubārī* system, is not known in detail. But it is known that the Muslims gradually developed the 'Arabic numerals' from the Indian numerals they had learned from Sanskrit sources early in the Islamic period in Persia and other eastern lands of Islam and then, having developed this system, went back for the most part to the Indian system, while the newly developed system spread to the Maghrib and from there to the West.[8]

The work in which Indian numerals were used and transmitted to the West for the first time is *al-Jam' wa'l-tafrīq bi ḥisāb al-hind* (*Addition and Subtraction in Indian Arithmetic*) of Muḥammad ibn Mūsā al-Khwārazmī, the original of which is

5. These numbers are of Indian origin and therefore called Indian numbers (*al-arqām al-hindiyyah*) in Arabic. See the classical study of D. E. Smith and L. C. Karpinski, *The Hindu-Arabic Numerals*, Boston, 1911.

6. See A. Sa'dān, Abu'l-Wafā' al-Buzjānī, '*Ilm al-ḥisāb al-'arabī (Ḥisāb al-yad)*, Amman, 1971.

7. On the dust-board system, which is thus called because it made use of a board on which dust was spread so that numbers could be traced upon it, see M. Souissi, '*ḥisāb al-ghubār*' in the *Encyclopaedia of Islam* (new edition).

Naṣīr al-Dīn al-Ṭūsī in fact wrote a treatise entitled *Jawāmi' al-ḥisāb bi'l-takht wa'l-turāb* (*Summaries of Arithmetic through Board and Dust*). The dust-board method still survives as a 'folk' practice in certain regions along with other popular methods of calculation such as the *siyāq* system which is still fairly prevalent in the bazaars of Persia.

8. See R. Irani, 'Arabic Numeral Forms', *Centaurus*, vol. 4, no. 1, 1955, pp. 1–12.

lost but which survives in translation. The Toledan translation of this work known as *Algorismi de numero indorum* had a profound effect upon the West and bestowed upon Western languages such terms as algorithm in English (from the name of al-Khwārazmī himself) and *guarismo* in Spanish, as well as the word cipher (from the Arabic *ṣifr* or zero).

In the 4th/10th century Abu'l-Ḥasan al-Uqlīdusī wrote his *Kitāb al-fuṣūl fi'l-ḥisāb al-hindī* (*The Book of Chapters Concerning Indian Arithmetic*),[9] in which he applied Indian schemes of calculation to methods of finger reckoning and tried to change dust-board methods so as to make them applicable to ink and paper. Contemporary with him Abu'l-Wafā' freed the Indian numerals from the dust-board techniques, while in the following century Abu'l-Ḥasan al-Nasawī wrote another important treatise on Indian numerals entitled *Kitāb al-muqni' fi'l-ḥisāb al-hindī* (*The Satisfying Book on Indian Arithmetic*) first in Persian and later in Arabic.[10] By the 5th/11th century, therefore, the decimal system and the two methods of reckoning connected with it had become fully established among Muslims and through them had reached the West, bringing about a transformation which influenced nearly all aspects of life and thought from pure mathematics to commerce and trade.[11]

Number Theory and Computation

Interest in the science of numbers and reckoning among Muslims goes back to the earliest Islamic centuries. At the beginning the Muslims distinguished between *'ilm al-'adad* (science of numbers) and *'ilm al-ḥisāb* (science of reckoning), following the Greeks, but the latter often included for Muslims the science of algebra, which they themselves developed.[12] During the later centuries the two names were used almost interchangeably while the name *arithmāṭiqī* derived from the Greek was also employed by certain authors. In any case most Muslim mathematicians wrote of the science of numbers, but relatively few treatises were devoted solely to this science.

The concern with the science of numbers among Muslims was closely connected with the study of magic squares and amicable numbers,[13] which were also applied to various occult sciences from alchemy to magic. As far as magic squares are concerned, they entered into alchemical speculation in the writings of Jābir ibn Ḥayyān and were studied mathematically by the Ikhwān al-Ṣafā', who knew squares up to 36 components. The celebrated authority on the occult sciences, Shams al-Dīn al-Būnī, carried out further studies on them and found the general formula for larger squares. As for amicable numbers, their general rule was discovered by Thābit ibn Qurrah.

From such preoccupations came the study of numerical series, with which so many mathematicians were concerned. For example, in the 4th/10th century al-Karajī in his *Kitāb al-fakhrī* (*The Book Dedicated to Fakhr al-Dīn*) devoted a notable section to numerical series, while his near contemporary al-Bīrūnī wrote numerous studies on them. The best known study of al-Bīrūnī on the subject is the famous chess-board problem which is as follows: the man who invented the game of chess was commanded by the ruler to whom he presented it to demand a favour. The man asked to be given the amount of grain which would correspond to the number of grains on a chess-board arranged in such a way that there would be one grain in the first square, two in the second, four in the third, and so on up to the 64 squares. The ruler first accepted, but soon realized that there was not that much grain in his whole kingdom. This problem, whose form is

9. On this important and recently discovered author see A. Sa'dān (ed.), Abu'l-Ḥasan al-Uqlīdusī, *al-Fuṣūl fi'l-ḥisāb al-hindī*, Amman, 1973; also *idem*, 'The Earliest Extant Arabic Arithmetic', *Isis*, vol. 57, 4, 1966, pp. 475–490.

10. Nasawī is also well-known for his treatise on falconry in Persian entitled *Bāz-nāmah*. See Abu'l-Qāsim Qorbānī, *Nasawī-nāmah*, Tehran, 1351 (A.H. solar).

11. On the development of numbers and the history of mathematics among Muslims see A. P. Yuschkewitsch, *Geschichte der Mathematik im Mittelalter*, Leipzig, 1964 (original Russian version, 1961).

12. See A. I. Sabra, "*ilm al-ḥisāb*', in the *Encyclopaedia of Islam* (new edition).

13. Two numbers are called amicable if one of them is equal to the sum of the divisors of the other, such as the numbers 220 and 284, which were known to the Ikhwān al-Ṣafā'.

Plate 42. The Ikhwān al-Ṣafā' (Brethren of Purity).

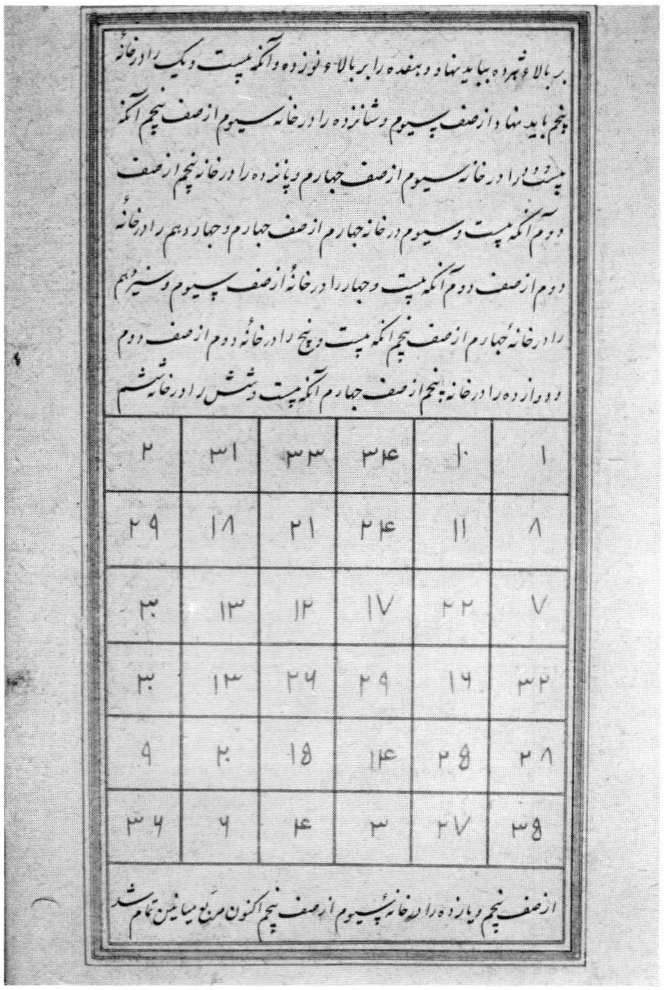

Figure 23. Magic square of 36 squares.

typical of mathematical problems found in Muslim texts, was solved by al-Bīrūnī. In modern connotation it would be $\sum^{64} 2^i - 1 = 2^{64} - 1$. Al-Bīrūnī found the answer to be 18, 446, 744, 073, 709, 551, 615.[14]

The study of numbers and numerical series as well as computation reached its peak with Ghiyāth al-Dīn Jamshīd al-Kāshānī, the outstanding Persian mathematician, whose amazing contributions to the science of numbers are only now becoming known after centuries of neglect. Kāshānī not only invented the decimal fraction,[15] the approximate method for calculating problems which have no exact solution, and the iterative algorism, and made a remarkably accurate calculation of π; but he must also be considered the first person to have invented a calculating machine.[16] He was also the first to have solved the binomial known by the name of Newton. The solution of the binomial

$$(a+b)^n = a^n + cn^1 a^{n-1} b + cn^2 a^{n-2} b^2 \ldots + cn^n b^n$$

is found in his *Miftāḥ al-ḥisāb* (*Key to Arithmetic*), which is perhaps the most important

14. This problem is cited as an example by al-Bīrūnī in his *Chronology of Ancient Nations*. See E. Sachau, 'Algebraisches über das Schach bei Biruni', *Zeitschrift der deutschen morgenlandischen Gesellschaft*, vol. 29, 1876, p. 148; see also A. Qorbānī, *Bīrūnī-nāmah*, Tehran, 1353 (A.H.solar), pp. 234ff.

15. Al-Uqlīdusī seems to have invented them, but they were forgotten for centuries until re-discovered and introduced into the mainstream of mathematics by Kāshānī.

16. See E. S. Kennedy, 'A fifteenth-century planetary computer: al-Kashī's *Ṭabaq al-manāṭeq*', *Isis*, vol. 41, 1950, pp. 180–183; vol. 43, 1952, pp. 42–50. A word must also be said concerning the abacus. This instrument, which is in wide use in the Islamic world and which differs from the one used in the Far East and elsewhere, is probably also a Persian or Arabic invention, whose origin in time, however, is not known. It may be very ancient; in fact some have suggested that the Babylonians may have had some form of abacus.

Muslim work on the science of numbers.[17] Kāshānī is also the author of *al-Risālat al-muḥīṭiyyah* (*The All-Embracing Treatise on the Circumference*) which is a masterpiece in arithmetic based on the sexagesimal system.[18]

Interest in the science of numbers was not limited to Persia, although most of the activity there was concentrated into the Safavid period, with the appearance of the works of such figures as Shaykh Bahā' al-Dīn 'Āmilī and Mullā Muḥammad Bāqir Yazdī. 'Āmilī was particularly influential because he was a truly universal genius, at once mathematician, architect, theologian, poet, Sufi and alchemist, and his works were widely read. It is not accidental that Suter concluded his now classical work on Islamic mathematicians with him and noted the importance of his *Khulāṣat al-ḥisāb* (*The Summary of Arithmetic*) for number theory.[19]

Elsewhere in the Islamic world a series of important figures appeared almost contemporary with Ṭūsī and Kāshānī. Foremost among them was Abu'l-'Abbās ibn Bannā' al-Marrākushī who lived in the 7th/13th century and produced some seventy books on all branches of mathematics, foremost among them the *Talkhīṣ a'māl al-ḥisāb* (*Summary of Arithmetic Operations*), which is among the best Muslim works on the subject.[20] Also from the Maghrib one may mention Ibn Ḥamzah al-Maghribī, who lived in the 10th/16th century and wrote the *Tuḥfat al- i'timād* (*Gift of Confidence*) in Turkish on number theory. He laid the foundation for the invention of the logarithm through the study of numerical series, as had Mullā Bāqir Yazdī, his contemporary in Persia.

As for the middle part of the Islamic world, there, too, several notable figures devoted studies to the science of numbers. Abu'l-'Abbās ibn al-Hā'im al-Miṣrī, who lived in the 8th/14th century, wrote on both arithmetic and algebra. A century later Badr al-Dīn al-Māridīnī composed his *Tuḥfat al-bāb fī 'ilm al-ḥisāb* (*Gift of the Gate concerning the Science of Arithmetic*), which contains a discussion of number theory and fractions.

When we glance over Muslim works in number theory and computation we observe several important achievements. One is the development of the philosophy of numbers and of mathematics in general, which unveils a concept of mathematics very different from that prevalent today. Secondly there is the new definition given by Muslims to number itself, expanding the definition provided by Eudoxos through recourse to continuous fractions by means of which a ratio is expressed. For example,

$$\sqrt{2}:1 = 1 + \cfrac{1}{2 + \cfrac{1}{2 + 1 \ldots}}$$

In such a procedure, if the fraction is terminated, the ratio is rational, and if not, it is irrational. Khayyām, who discussed this matter, almost made of the irrational itself a number, saying that the irrational can be 'interpreted' as a number. Also Ṭūsī asserted that every ratio can be regarded as a number.[21]

Finally the Muslims developed techniques of computation far beyond what had existed before. This is to be seen especially in the circle of Naṣīr al-Dīn al-Ṭūsī at Maraghah, where a precision of one in ten million was attained for the table of tangents. To have a large number of mathematicians work on problems together, to coordinate their computation and finally to develop a means of checking error as one progresses is no easy task. But this is precisely what was achieved in Persia in the 7th/13th century, although the means whereby it was done are not as yet fully known. Be it as it may, it represents a major achievement of Islamic mathematics.

17. For an analysis of this important work see P. Luckey, 'Die Rechenkunst bei Gamšīd b. Mas'ūd al-Kāšī, mit Rückblicken auf die altere Geschichte des Rechnens', *Abhandlungen für die Kunde des Morgenlandes*, XXXI, I, 1951; the extensive commentary on this work along with its translation into Russian by Rosenfeld, Segal and Yuschkewitsch, Moscow, 1956; and A. Qorbānī, *Kāshānī-nāmah*, Tehran, 1350 (A.H. solar), part three.

18. This work was translated and commented upon extensively by P. Luckey in his 'Der Lehrbrief über den Kreisumfang', *Abhandlungen der deutschen Akademie der Wissenschaften zu Berlin*, no. 6, 1953.

19. See H. Suter, *Die Mathematiker und Astronomen der Araber und ihre Werke*, Leipzig (*Abhandlungen zur Geschichte der mathematische Wissenschaften*, vol. 10), 1900; 'Nachtrage und Berichtigunger', vol. 14, 1902, pp. 155–185; reprinted Ann Arbor, 1963.

20. See Qadrī Ḥāfiẓ Ṭuqān, *Turāth al-'arab al-'ilmī fī'l-riyāḍiyyāt wa'l-falak*, Cairo, 1963, pp. 429–432.

21. See E. S. Kennedy, 'The Exact Sciences in Iran under the Seljuqs and Mongols', in *Cambridge History of Iran*, vol. V, ed. by J. A. Boyle, Cambridge, 1968, p. 663.

Geometry

The study of geometry among Muslims begins with the classical Greek sources, especially Euclid and Apollonios, with which Muslim mathematicians became acquainted early in the Abbasid period. Interest in geometry in Baghdad was incited most of all, however, through the works of the sons of Mūsā, or Banū Mūsā, especially their *Kitāb ma'rifah misāḥat al-ashkāl* (*The Book of Knowledge of the Area of Figures*), upon which Naṣīr al-Dīn al-Ṭūsī was later to write a commentary. This work was also translated into Latin and influenced Fibonacci and Thomas Bradwardine. The Banū Mūsā also wrote an important recension of the *Conics* of Apollonios. Also in the 3rd/9th century Thābit ibn Qurrah wrote on cubatures and quadratures and used the method of exhaustions in a manner which anticipates the development of integral calculus. Thābit also advanced the study of parabolas and in his *Quadrature of the Parabola* used integral sums to find the area of a segment of a parabola.

During the 4th/10th century Abu'l-'Abbās al-Nayrīzī, the Latin Anaritius, followed the work of Thābit and also that of Abū 'Abdallāh al-Māhānī, writing an important commentary upon Euclid, which made use of the works of Heron, Simplicius and other Alexandrian mathematicians. Another important work on geometry of this period is the *Fī mā yaḥtāj ilayhī al-ṣāni' min a'māl al-hindisah* (*What the Artisan Needs of Geometric Operations*) of Abu'l-Wafā' al-Buzjānī in which the various applications of geometry are thoroughly discussed. Also of importance during this period are the works of Abū Sahl al-Kūhī, who sought to solve those problems posed by Archimedes and Apollonios which lead to equations higher than the second degree, and Ibn al-Haytham, the great physicist, who worked on isoperimetry.

In the 5th/11th century the great impetus given to geometry during the previous century continued. Abu'l-Jūd, who corresponded with al-Bīrūnī on mathematical questions, devised a geometric method to divide the circle into nine equal parts. His contemporary Abū Sa'īd al-Sijzī

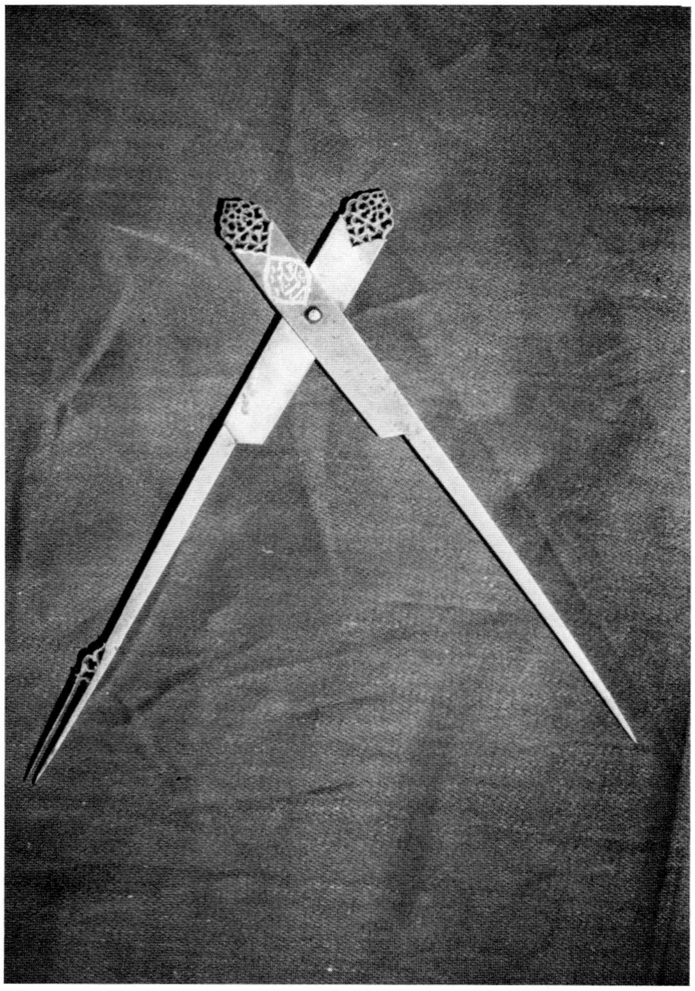

Figure 24. Steel compass made for the Persian king Shāh 'Abbās.

studied conic sections and trisected an angle by means of the intersection of a circle and a hyperbola.

A new chapter was opened in the study of geometry when Khayyām, and following him Ṭūsī, re-examined the fifth postulate of Euclid concerning the parallel line theorem, which concerns the very foundation of Euclidean geometry. Khayyām in his treatise *Fī sharḥ mā ashkala min muṣādarāt kitāb Uqlīdus* (*Concerning the Difficulties of Euclid's Elements*)[22] considers the quadrilateral ABCD with sides AB and DC equal to each other and both perpendicular to BC, which is the birectangular quadrilateral associated in the history of Western mathematics with Saccheri. In this quadrilateral, angles A and D are equal and

22. See E. S. Kennedy, *op. cit.*; also B. A. Rosenfeld and A. P. Yuschkewitsch, *Omar Xaiiām, Traktāti*, Moscow, 1961, where the text of the treatise appears with translation and commentary in Russian. See also the extensive analysis of this problem in J. Homā'ī. *Khayyāmi-nāmah*, vol. I, Tehran, 1346 (A.H.solar). Ṭūsī preceded Western mathematicians in the discussion of yet another problem. His *Jawāmi' al-ḥisāb* contains the earliest reference to what has come to be known as Pascall's triangle.

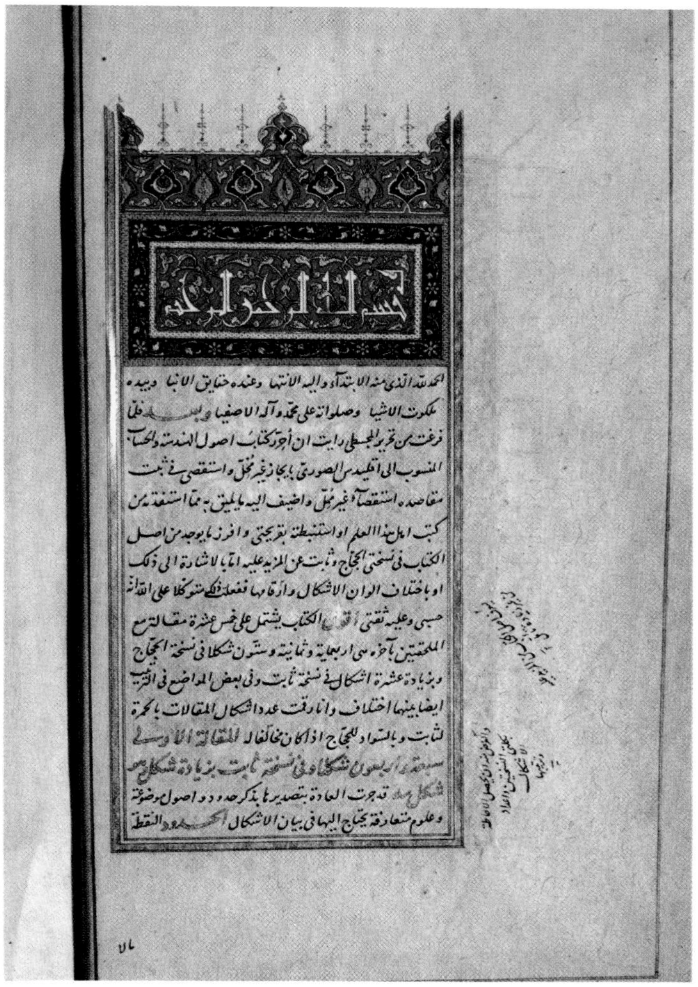

Plate 43. The opening page to the commentary on the *Elements* of Euclid by Naṣīr al-Dīn al-Ṭūsī.

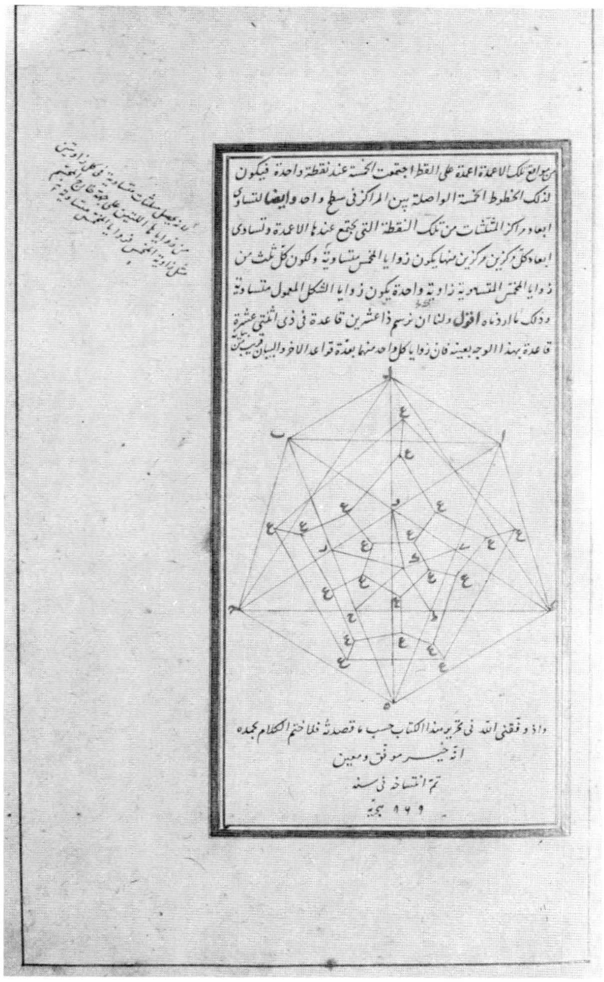

Figure 26. Final page of al-Ṭūsī's commentary on the *Elements* of Euclid.

Figure 25. Rectangle related to the fifth postulate of Euclid.

must be acute, obtuse or right angles. Khayyām proves that only the third can be true, thus asserting the fifth postulate of Euclid. Both Khayyām and Ṭūsī realized that if the first possibility were to be true, the sum of the angles of a triangle would be less than 180°. Neither Khayyām nor Ṭūsī followed their research in this domain to its end, and non-Euclidean geometry, including that of Lobachevskii, was left for Western geometers to deal with. But Khayyām realized the special character of the fifth postulate and pointed to the principle which defines this geometry as a coherent and distinct system, corresponding because of its symbolic nature to the profoundest aspects of physical reality.

Altogether, in the domain of geometry, both plane and solid, Muslims followed the path laid out by the Greek mathematicians, solving many of the problems which had been posed but remained unsolved by their predecessors. They also related geometry to algebra and sought geometric solutions for algebraic problems. Finally, they devoted special attention to the symbolic aspects of geometry and its role in art and architecture, keeping always in view the qualitative geometry which reflects the wisdom of the 'Grand Architect of the Universe'.

Plane and Spherical Trigonometry

Although Greek mathematicians, especially Hipparchus, had calculated a table of chords, trigonometry – both plane and solid and based on the relation of the sides and angles of a right triangle – was invented by Muslims. It was Muslim mathematicians who for the first time formulated the trigonometric functions explicitly. In fact the word 'sine' is the direct translation of the Arabic word *jayb*.[23]

Already in the 3rd/9th century trigonometry was used by al-Battānī in his astronomical works. He also helped advance spherical trigonometry. Ḥabash al-Ḥāsib, another astronomer of the period, was the first to use tangents (*ẓill*) and also had knowledge of the sine, cosine and cotangent functions. The most notable advance in trigonometry during the early period was made, however, by Abu'l-Wafā' al-Buzjānī whose *Almagest*, not to be confused with that of Ptolemy, was concerned mostly with trigonometry. Abu'l-Wafā' was the first person to give a demonstration of the sine theorem for a general spherical triangle. He knew the equations:

$$\sin(a \pm b) = \sin a \cos b - \cos a \sin b$$

$$2\sin^2\frac{a}{2} = 1 - \cos a$$

$$\sin a = 2\sin\frac{a}{2} \times \cos a$$

It was also he who first invented the secant (*quṭr al-ẓill*) and not Copernicus as is usually believed. Al-Buzjānī was also the first to discover the relation

$$\frac{\sin a}{\sin A} = \frac{\sin b}{\sin B} \quad \frac{\sin c}{\sin C}$$

in a non-perpendicular spherical triangle.

Intense interest in trigonometry existed also among other mathematicians of this period such as Abū Naṣr al-'Irāq, Abū Maḥmūd al-Khujandī and Ibn Yūnus, each of whom made new contributions to the field, the last having discovered that

$$\cos a \cos b = \tfrac{1}{2}[\cos(a+b) + \cos(a-b)].$$

But it was again al-Bīrūnī who wrote the most masterly work on the subject. Despite its title, his *Maqālīd 'ilm al-hay'ah* (*Keys to the Science of Astronomy*), as recently discovered, is the first independent work on spherical trigonometry.[24] Al-Bīrūnī also calculated the approximate value of a diagonal of one degree and in his *Mas'ūdic Canon* was the first to give a demonstration that for a plane triangle

$$\frac{a}{\sin A} = \frac{b}{\sin B} = \frac{c}{\sin C}.$$

Trigonometry, like most other branches of mathematics, underwent an eclipse in the 5th/11th and 6th/12th centuries and was fully revived by Naṣīr al-Dīn al-Ṭūsī, whose *Kitāb shikl al-qiṭā'* (*Book of the Figure of the Sector*) is of fundamental importance to the history of trigonometry. Ṭūsī synthesized the works of the earlier masters such as Abu'l-Wafā' and al-Bīrūnī and gave all the six trigonometric functions based on a triangle and independent of the Menelaus Theorem. He also presented those functions independent of astronomy. In fact until the recent discoveries by Qorbānī concerning al-Bīrūnī's *Maqālīd* . . . the work of Ṭūsī was considered the first independent treatise on trigonometry.

In any case whether it be the works of Ṭūsī or Bīrūnī, there is no doubt that trigonometry as studied even now was developed completely and established as an independent science by Muslim mathematicians. It is, therefore, strange indeed that in many Muslim countries today even the names of the trigonometric functions, which were originally Arabic, are changed into their French or English equivalents, and this science is presented in the schools of the Islamic world as if it were imported along with gun powder and modern physics from the Occident.

Algebra

As in trigonometry so in algebra Muslims must be considered as the founders of this science whose very name (from the Arabic *al-jabr*) reflects its origin.[25] Muslims made use of Greek (mostly Diaphontos) and Indian sources as well as Babylonian ones, which had reached them through Hebrew works, especially the *Mishnat ha-Middot*, but it was the early Muslim mathematicians of the 3rd/9th century leading to Muḥammad ibn Mūsā al-Khwārazmī who firmly established this branch of mathematics, which is closely related to certain metaphysical principles so central to Islamic doctrines. The first Muslim

23. See Sabra, *op. cit.*

24. Qorbānī, *Bīrūnī-nāmah*, pp. 402ff.

25. Likewise the unknown in an algebraic equation, which to this day is called x, is derived by means of Spanish from the Arabic word *shay'*, which is used for the unknown in Arabic treatises on algebra.

work on algebra, the *Kitāb al-mukhtaṣar fī ḥisāb al-jabr wa'l-muqābalah* (*The Book of Summary Concerning the Process of Calculating Compulsion and Equation*) of al-Khwārazmī in fact has given this science its name, the word *jabr* in the title meaning restoration and amplification of something incomplete and *muqābalah* the balancing of two sides of an equation.[26] This work was translated into Latin by Robert of Chester and was responsible for the introduction of algebra into the West.[27]

In the 4th/10th century the brilliant start made by al-Khwārazmī was pursued by a number of outstanding mathematicians. Abū Kāmil al-Shujā' resolved equations with up to five unknowns. Abū 'Abdallāh al-Māhānī studied a problem posed by Archimedes in his *The Sphere and the Cylinder*: 'To cut a sphere by a plane in such a way that the two parts are in a given proportion to each other'.[28] He tried to solve the equation $x^3+a=cx^2$ resulting from this problem, an equation which has become synonymous with his name. Abū Ja'far al-Khāzin solved this equation after al-Māhānī by means of the intersection of conics.

Another important algebraist of the 4th/10th century, al-Khujandī, wrote a treatise showing that it is impossible to solve the equation $x^3+y^3=z^3$ where x, y, and z are whole numbers. This is a special case of Fermat's proposition. Abu'l-Jūd followed this work and was the first to solve third degree equations through geometric solutions. Al-Karajī, who lived a few years earlier, had in the meantime written one of the foremost Muslim works on algebra, the already mentioned *Kitāb al-fakhrī* (*The Book Dedicated to Fakhr al-Dīn*).[29] Woepcke, who first introduced this book to the West, showed that most of Fibonacci's works were influenced by al-Karajī. In al-Karajī one finds a discussion of indeterminate algebra as well as indeterminate analysis. As an example one can cite the following problem with four unknowns discussed by al-Karajī (using modern notations):

$$x+1=2(y-1)$$
$$y+2=3(z-1)$$
$$z+3=4(v-3)$$
$$v+4=5(x-4)$$

Several centuries of the development of algebra culminated in the well-known *Algebra* of 'Umar Khayyām, the most famous Oriental poet in the West thanks to the imaginative translation of his quatrains by Fitzgerald, but rarely seen by the public at large as one of the outstanding mathematicians of history. Khayyām classified algebraic equations up to the third degree in a rigorous and systematic manner and solved them through geometric means.[30] In its thoroughness, clarity and manner of exposition as well as its mathematical content the *Algebra* of Khayyām must be counted as one of the masterpieces of Islamic mathematics and is still of value as a model for the way that algebra should be taught to young students.

After Khayyām the study of algebra gradually declined among Muslims and although works continued to be written on the subject they never reached the level of al-Karajī and Khayyām.

26. See G. Anawati, 'Science', in P. M. Holt, A. K. S. Lambton and B. Lewis, (eds.), *The Cambridge History of Islam*, vol. II, Cambridge, 1970, pp. 750ff. See also the already cited histories of mathematics of Yuschkewitsch, and Rosenfeld as well as Ṭuqān.

27. See L. C. Karpinski, *Robert of Chester's Latin Translation of the Algebra of al-Khwarizmi*, New York, 1915. See also F. Rosen, *The Algebra of Muhammad ben Musa*, London, 1831. There were other early Muslim works on algebra such as that of Ibn Turk but none had the influence of al-Khwārazmī's famous treatise.

28. See J. Vernet, *op. cit.*, p. 468.

29. Selections of this book were translated and thoroughly analyzed by F. Woepcke in his *Extrait du Fakhri*, Paris, 1853. Al-Karajī's other major mathematical work, the *Kāfī fi'l-ḥisāb* (*The Sufficient Book in Arithmetic*) also includes sections devoted to algebra. See A. Hochheim, *Kāfī fi'l-Ḥisāb* (*Genügendes über Arithmetik*), Halle, 1878–1880.

For a summary history of algebra, including Muslim contributions and those of al-Karajī, see D. E. Smith, *History of Mathematics*, vol. I, New York, 1951, pp. 283ff.

30. This work has been translated into European languages and analyzed several times. See F. Woepcke, *L'algèbre d'Omar Alkhayyāmī*, Paris, 1851; W. E. Story, *Omar as a Mathematician*, Boston, 1918; D. S. Kasir, *The Algebra of Omar Khayyam*, New York, 1931; and H. J. J. Winter and W. 'Arafat, 'The Algebra of 'Umar Khayyām', *Journal of the Royal Asiatic Society of Bengal*, vol. XVI, 1950, no. 1, pp. 27–78. See also Nasr, *Science and Civilization in Islam*, pp. 160ff. A thorough study of the mathematics of Khayyām has been made in Persian by Gh. Muṣāḥab in his *Ḥakīm 'Umar Khayyām bi 'unwān-i 'ālim-i jabr*, Tehran, 1339 (A.H. solar).

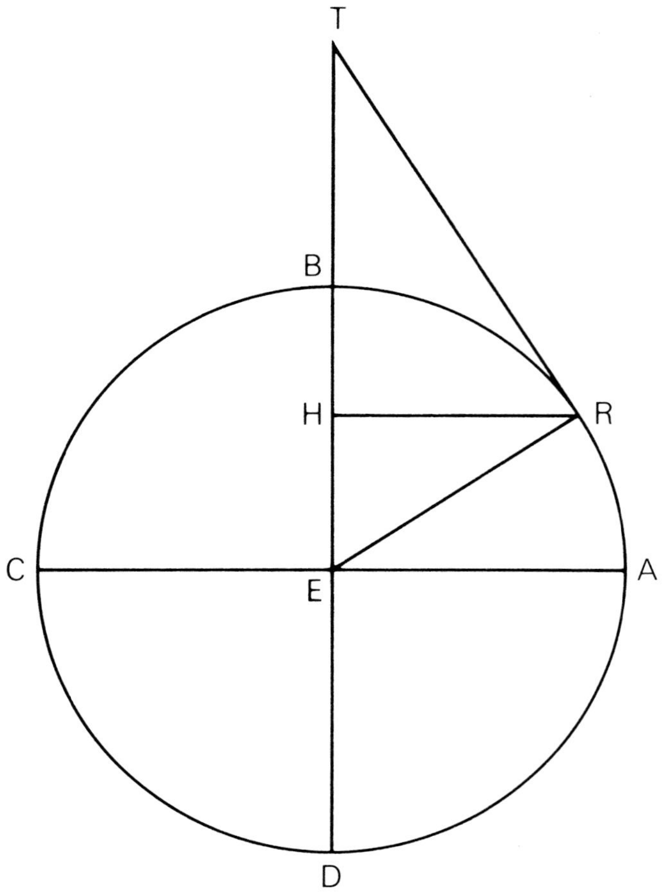

Figure 27. The solution of an algebraic problem by Khayyām. 'The problem is to find the point R on the quadrant AB in such a way that

$$AE : RH = EH : HB$$

Assume that in the triangle ERT, ET = ER + RH. Then the triangle ERT is a right triangle whose hypotenuse is equal to the sum of one of its sides and the perpendicular to the hypotenuse. Khayyām assumes that if the height of this triangle = x, and the hypotenuse is taken to be 10, then

$$x^3 + 200x = 20x^2 + 2000$$

which is solved through conic intersections.'

As a noteworthy work of the later period one might mention the *Kashf al-asrār 'an 'ilm al-ghubār* (*The Unveiling of Mysteries Concerning the Science of the 'Dust-Board'*) of Abu'l-Ḥasan al-Bastī known as al-Qalṣādī, a 9th/15th century author from Andalusia. This work is the first which revealed to Europeans the fact that Muslims used algebraic signs such as ج for root (*jadhr*), ش for unknown (*shay'*), م for square (*māl*) etc. In the eastern lands of Islam also a few treatises on algebra of some interest were written, but most of the new developments in the late centuries were in the domain of number theory rather than algebra. In fact with Khayyām algebra reached a perfection beyond which a step could not be taken until the invention of descriptive geometry and the opening of a new chapter in the science of algebra in the 17th century, a chapter which, however, was based on the forgetting of the very metaphysical principles which have always dominated the horizon of all Islamic mathematics.

Mathematics and Islamic Art and Architecture

Anyone who has gained some familiarity with Islamic art and architecture realizes that mathematics plays a special role in these art forms, a role which is more central and extensive than what is found in other living traditions. Not only do the music and poetry of the Islamic peoples follow strict mathematical principles[31] similar to other traditional forms of these arts, but also the plastic arts – from patterns on carpets to the ornaments of mosques – have a relation to the world of geometry and numbers which is more direct than that found in the sacred art of other traditions. In fact some have denied that Islam has developed an art of any importance because it has produced neither painting nor sculpture to compare with what is found in mediaeval Christendom or India. And to most modern Westerners geometric patterns and mathematical rhythms hardly appear as having any relation with sacred art.

Figure 28. A flute player. From an Arabic treatise on music.

Figures 29, 30 and 31. Pages from the section on music of the Persian encyclopaedia *Durrat al-tāj* of Quṭb al-Dīn al-Shīrāzī.

31. Numerous treatises in Arabic and Persian deal with the mathematical aspect of poetry and music. Music in particular, in its theoretical aspect, was always considered as a branch of mathematics, much as in the *Quadrivium* of the mediaeval West. Many leading Muslim philosophers and scientists, such as Ibn Sīnā, Khayyām and Quṭb al-Dīn al-Shīrāzī, devoted treatises to music, and some like al-Fārābī were leading theoreticians of music. Unfortunately limitations of space do not allow us to devote a separate chapter to this subject.

Concerning music among Islamic peoples see R. D'Erlanger, *La musique arabe*, 5 vols., Paris, 1930–1939 (which deals, however, mostly with Persian rather than Arabic music); the numerous works of H. G. Farmer such as *The Sources of Arabian Music*, Glasgow, 1940; N. Caron and D. Safvat, *Iran* (collection *Les traditions musicales*, vol. 2), Paris, 1966; A. Shiloah (ed. and trans.), Ibn 'Alī al-Kātib, *La perfection des connaissances musicales*, Paris, 1972; and the translation of the important treatise of the Ikhwān al-Ṣafā' on music including its effect on the body and the soul by A. Shiloah, 'L'épître sur la musique des Ikhwān al-Ṣafā'', *Revue des Etudes Islamiques*, 1965, pp. 125–162; 1967, pp. 159–193.

Figure 28

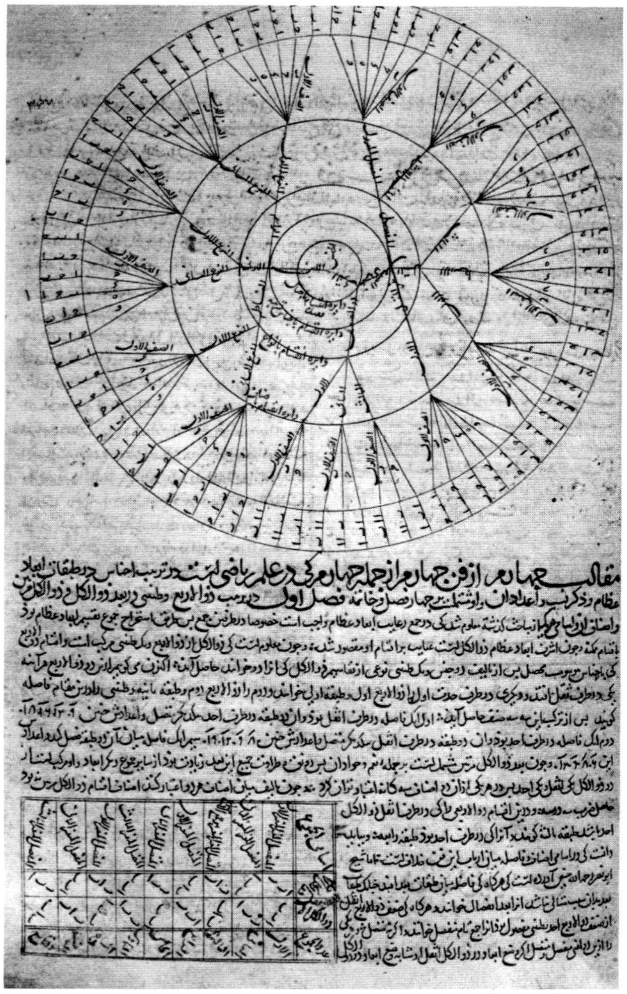

Figure 30

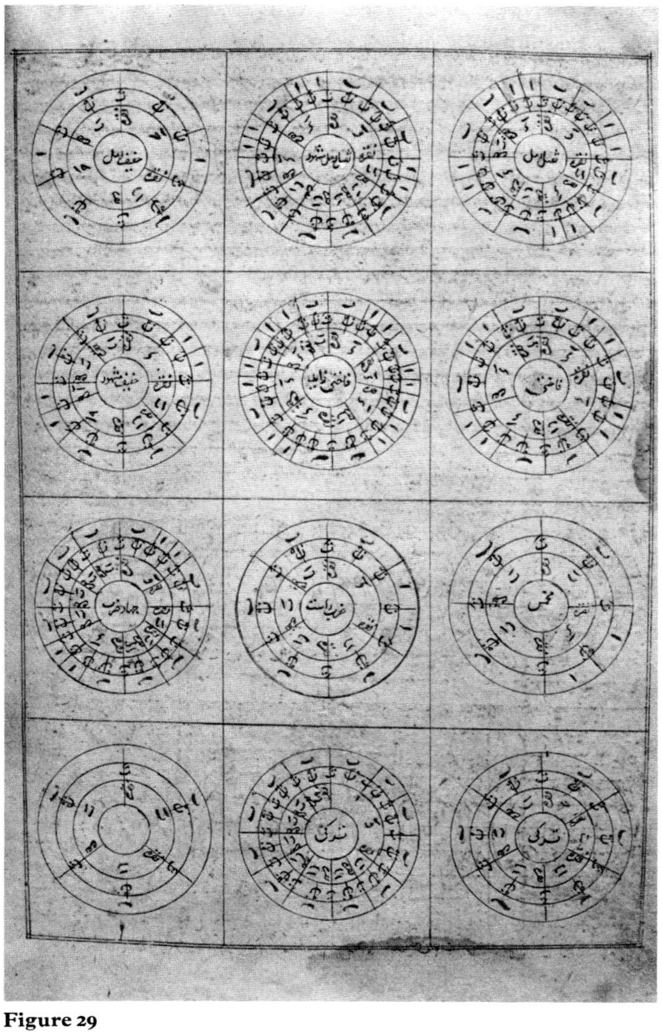

Figure 29

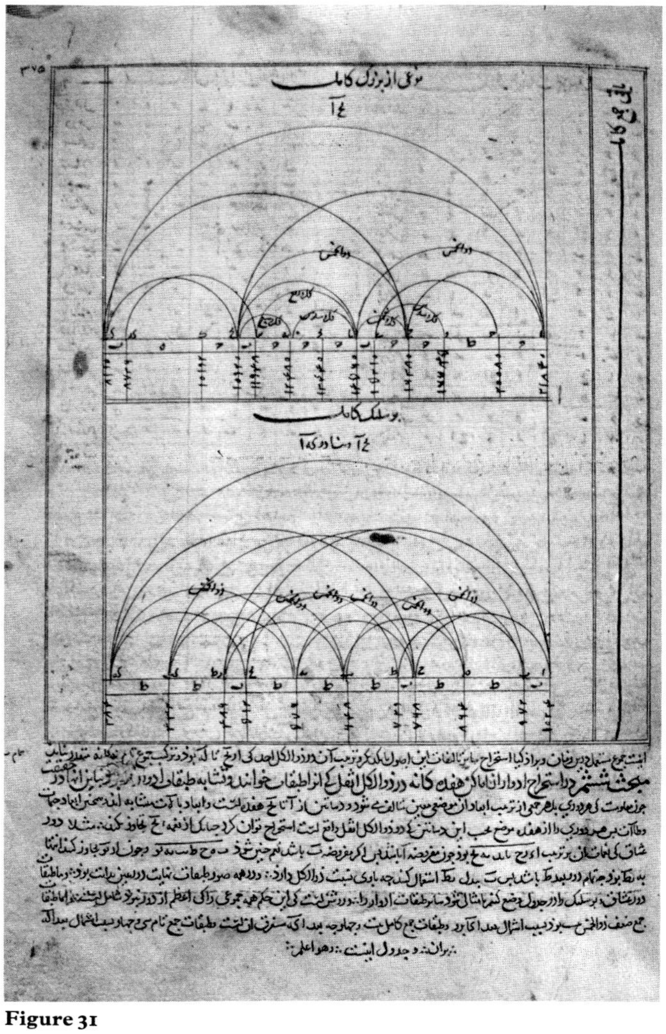

Figure 31

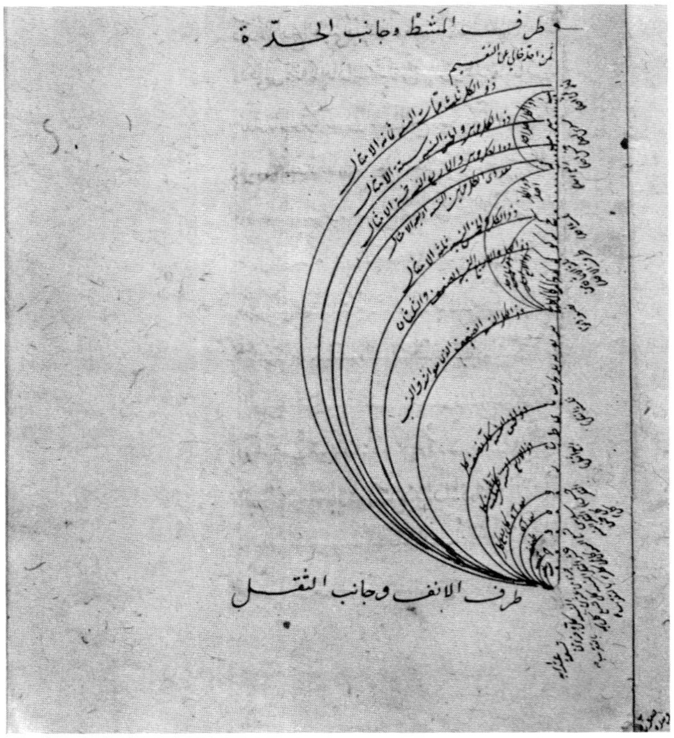

Figure 32. The division of the chord from a treatise on music.

Actually this judgement is due to a complete forgetting of the Pythagorean doctrine of mathematics as summarized especially by Nichomachus and reflected even in the writings of certain early Christian theologians such as Clement of Alexandria.[32] If one studies these traditional sources, which express the same truths concerning the world of mathematics as those that determined the Islamic vision of things, it becomes evident that number and figure exist on three levels of reality: in the Divine Intellect as archetypes in the principial domain; in the intermediate world of the mind, which Nichomachus refers to as 'scientific'; and in the external world, corresponding to 'concrete', quantitative numbers and figures. The modern world knows only the second and third levels, whereas Islam has remained always aware of all three. The use of mathematics in Islamic art and architecture is not only the result of an 'aniconic' tendency away from the 'concrete' toward the 'abstract'. Rather, it is also a means whereby the archetypes are reflected upon the material plane, making the material transparent and capable of acting as a ladder toward the spiritual realities, which are the most concrete realities of all, realities compared to which physical realities are no more than abstractions. The use of mathematics in Islamic art is a way whereby the material is sacralized by virtue of reflecting the archetypal world. It is also the means whereby man becomes aware of the origin as well as the fundamental structure of the physical world that surrounds him and is able to penetrate into the very mystery of God's creation.[33]

Mathematics in Islam has not been bound to the world of 'matter' as is modern mathematics. It has in fact been related more to the world of life forms and beyond that to the archetypal world. As a result it has been able to reveal the principle of the physical world rather than the structure of its constitutive parts as in modern physics. Moreover, it has been able to aid in the realization of a harmony, balance and awareness of the effusion of multiplicity from Unity and the return of all multiplicity to Unity which characterize Islamic spirituality and are manifested in the most direct manner in Islamic art and architecture. Nowhere is the sacred character of mathematics in the Islamic world view more evident than in art, where with the help of geometry and arithmetic matter is ennobled and a sacred ambience created wherein is directly reflected the ubiquitous Presence of the One in the many.

32. The three kinds of Pythagorean number are treated fully in the existing works of Nichomachus, which include his *Manual of Harmony*, *Introduction to Arithmetic* and parts of the *Theologumena Arithmetica* which have survived in the compilation of Iamblichus of Rome.

The three meanings of numbers have also been dealt with in several contemporary works. In addition to the writings of H. Keyser mentioned above see R. Allendy, *Le symbolisme des nombres*, Paris, 1948; M. Ghyka, *Le nombre d'or*, Paris, 1931; and L. Bosman, *The Meaning and Philosophy of Numbers*, London, 1932.

33. As one of the foremost Western students of Islamic architecture in its relation to mathematics, Keith Critchlow, has shown, certain complicated patterns of Islamic art are identical with the internal structure of various natural substances discovered by modern science. Critchlow has said that it seems that Muslims discovered the inner structure of matter without splitting molecules and atoms. This can in fact be easily explained if one understands the traditional role of number and figure, the hierarchy of universal existence and the principle that the 'heart' of physical objects can only be understood in an ultimate sense through a knowledge of their archetypes, rather than by means of indefinite analysis and division, although every analytical study of a legitimate nature reflects again the archetype of the object in question on its own level of reality.

Plate 44. Colour, form and geometry in Islamic art.

Plate 45. The use of geometry to depict the spatial and temporal aspects of cosmic reality.

BERYL

$Be_3\,Al_2\,Si_6\,O_{18}$

Figure 33. *Ars sine scientia nihil.*

Chapter VI
Astronomy and Astrology

'And He it is Who hath set for you the stars (*al-nujūm*) that ye may guide your course by them amid the darkness of the land and the sea' (V; 98, Pickthall translation).

'It is not for the sun to overtake the moon, nor doth the night outstrip the day. They float each in an orbit (*falak*)' (XXXVI; 39).

'Lo! in the creation of the heavens (*samāwāt*) and the earth, and the difference of night and day . . . are signs (of Allah's sovereignty) for people who have sense' (II; 164).

'He it is Who created for you all that is in the earth. Then turned He to the heavens and fashioned it as seven heavens (*samāwāt*) (II; 29).

'And We have made the sky (*al-samā'*) a roof withheld (from them). Yet they turn away from its portents' (XXI; 32).

'And when the sun is overthrown,
And when the stars (*al-nujūm*) fall,
And when the hills are moved' (LXXXI; 1–3).

These verses from the Holy Quran are only a few among numerous references made in the Holy Book of Islam to the heavens and celestial phenomena in general. As the last religion in the present cycle of humanity, Islam is also in a fundamental sense a return to the primordial tradition (*al-dīn al-ḥanīf*). This basic truth is naturally reflected in the Holy Quran, many of whose verses point to a return to the primordial revelation which is none other than the 'book of creation' or virgin nature itself. The 'signs' (*āyāt*) of this 'Book' become transparent once again in the pages of the Holy Quran. Hence, there is continuous reference to the world of creation to complement the verses, which specifically concern man on the one hand and the purely principial domain on the other. And Muslims speak of the created world as the 'Quran of creation' (*al-Qur'ān al-takwīnī*) and of the written Quran as the 'recorded Quran' (*al-Qur'ān al-tadwīnī*).[1] None of the sacred texts of the various traditions speaks as often of the 'signs' of God manifested in the natural order as does the Holy Quran, with the possible exception of the Vedas, which are also a direct reflection of the primordial revelation. Moreover, the Quranic references pertaining to nature are concerned

1. 'One of the characteristics of the Quran as the last Revelation is that at times it becomes as it were transparent in order that the first Revelation may shine through its verses; and this first Revelation, namely the Book of Nature, belongs to everyone'. M. Lings, *What is Sufism?*, London, 1975, p. 23. On the relation of the 'two Qurans' mentioned above see S. H. Nasr, *The Encounter of Man and Nature*, p. 95.

mostly with the heavens. This confirmation on the part of the most sacred source of Islam combined with the natural inclination towards the study of the heavens of Arabian nomads, who roamed over vast deserts with the help of the stars, gave a powerful impetus to astronomy from the beginning of Islamic civilization and created for this science and its ancillary disciplines a special position among all 'intellectual sciences', so that even jurisprudents and theologians opposed to some of these sciences respected astronomy while some went so far as to hold it in high esteem.

Of course the cosmic dimension of the Islamic rites, especially the daily prayers, also brought into focus the practical importance of astronomy for the religious community. The times of the daily prayers have to be determined throughout the year for every geographical latitude and longitude where there are faithful, practising Muslims, and the direction for the prayers facing Mecca has to be determined again for every locality where the prayers are performed.

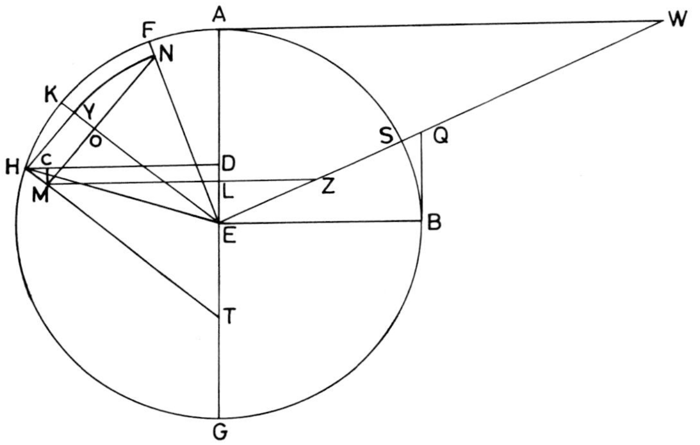

Figure 34a. One of the methods of finding the direction of the *qiblah*, by al-Bīrūnī.

'We transform the direct sine and the versed sine of the longitudinal difference in order to obtain from the ordinary sine the sine of the modified longitude. Further, we multiply the transformed versed sine by the sine of the latitude of our town, and we divide this product by the total sine; then we add the quotient obtained thereby to the versed sine of the sum of Mecca's latitude and the colatitude of our town. We obtain thereby the gauge. If this is less than the total sine, the azimuth of the *qiblah* is south of the east-west line; if the gauge is equal to it, the azimuth coincides with that line, and if the gauge is more than the total sine, then the azimuth is north of the east-west line.

'Further, we square the difference between the gauge and the total sine, and we square the sine of the modified longitude; then we divide the product of the sine of the modified longitude times the total sine by the (square) root of the sum of the two squares. The quotient obtained thereby is the sine of the azimuth displacement from the meridian line.

'Proof of this method: Again, we let the semicircle ABG represent the western horizon of Ghazna, and let us imagine that AKG represents a semicircle of its meridian. We mark off arc AK equal to the colatitude of Ghazna [taken as example by al-Bīrūnī] and arc KH equal to the latitude of Mecca. We join KE and draw HT parallel to it; then we draw HY perpendicular to EK. It is obvious that KE is the line of intersection between the plane of the meridian of Ghazna and the plane of the celestial equator, and that HT is the line of intersection of the plane of the meridian of Ghazna and the plane of the parallel of Mecca, and that HY is the sine of the latitude of Mecca, and EY is the cosine of its latitude. Further, we mark off arc FK equal to the longitudinal difference, and we join FE. With E as centre and with radius EY we draw the arc YN; then we drop NO perpendicular to KE, and we produce NO to meet the line TH at M. It is known that arc YN lies on a circle which is equal to the parallel of Mecca, because it was drawn with a radius equal to the cosine of its latitude, and since YN is similar to arc FK, arc YN is a measure of the longitudinal difference in the parallel (of Mecca). So NO is the sine of the modified longitudinal difference, measured in that circle, and YO is the versed sine of the longitudinal difference, which is also measured in that circle. Hence YO is the transformed amount, and HM is equal to it and is really in an analogous position in the meridian circle of Ghazna.

'We drop both HD and ML perpendicular to AEG. Then HD is the sine of the sum of AK, the colatitude of Ghazna, and KH, the latitude of Mecca. Therefore AD is the versed sine of this sum. Further, we draw MC parallel to AG: then the triangle HMC is similar to the triangle HDT, the triangle of daylight. So the ratio of HM, the transformed versed sine, to MC is as the ratio of the sine of angle HCM, the right angle, to the sine of angle HMC, the colatitude of Ghazna. Hence MC is known. Now, DL is equal to MC, and AL, the gauge, is the sum of AD and DL. (It is called the gauge) because point L is on the line through the foot of the vertical from Mecca parallel to the east-west line. Whenever it falls between the two points A and E, the line that issues from E to the point which is supposed to fall on it, ends up on the southern quadrant AB, but if it falls beyond E, towards G, then that line ends up on the northern quadrant BG.

'Moreover, it is known that the segment between L and the foot of the vertical from Mecca is equal to the sine of the modified longitude, I mean NO. So if we separate LZ, which lies on the prolongation of ML – though it really makes with it a right angle, but if the semicircle AKG is revolved about the axis AEG until it coincides with the eastern half of the horizon, then ML would coincide with the said line and LZ would fall on the prolongation of ML – and if we join EZ and produce it to S, then ES will be the line of the *qiblah*. Now ZE is the hypotenuse of a right triangle with legs ZL and LE; therefore ZE is known. But the ratio of ZE to ZL is as the ratio of the sine of angle ZLE, the right angle, to the sine of angle LEZ whose magnitude is that of arc AS, the displacement of the azimuth line from the meridian line. Therefore the azimuth is known from this proportion, and that is what we wanted to prove.

'Otherwise, if we like, we divide the product of the sine of the modified longitude times the total sine by the difference between the gauge and the total sine. The quotient obtained thereby is a measure of the tangent of the displacement of the azimuth from the meridian line.

'For example, in the last computations for the city of Ghazna, the product of the sine of the modified longitude times the total sine was 1538;17,0. We divided this product by the difference between the gauge and the total sine, which is 8;5 [6,6], and obtained the quotient 172;9,50, which is the tangent of the displacement of the direction of the *qiblah* at Ghazna from the south. The arc (tangent) of this displacement is 70;47, 9°.

'Proof: We draw AW, a tangent line to the circle at A, and we produce ES until it meets the tangent line at W. Then AW is the tangent of arc AS. Further, the ratio of EL, the difference between the gauge and the total sine, to LZ, the sine of the modified longitude, is as the ratio of EA, the total sine, to AW, the tangent. Hence it (the tangent) is known.

'If we wish to find the cotangent function, we multiply the difference between the gauge and the total sine, and we divide the result by the sine of the modified longitude, and what results is the cotangent for the distance of the azimuth from the south point.

'The practical method for the termination of the azimuth of the *qiblah* is evidently as follows: if AHG is the meridian line in a circle whose plane is parallel to the horizon, and if we take arc AK equal to the colatitude of our town, arc KH equal to the latitude of Mecca, arc KF equal to the longitudinal difference between them, and if we join the segments FE and KE, and if we construct HT parallel to KE, and HY perpendicular to KE, and if, with centre E and at a distance EY, we draw the arc YN, and if we construct NO perpendicular to KE and extend NO to meet TH at M, and further, if we construct MLZ perpendicular to AG, and we make LZ equal to NO, and if we produce EZ to meet the circumference of the circle at S, then ES will be the line of prayer.'

That is why, from unknown astronomers to figures such as al-Bīrūnī and Ibn al-Haytham (the Latin Alhazen), Muslims devised means for finding the direction of Mecca (the *qiblah*) and up to recent times (as seen in the treatise of the almost contemporary Persian traditional mathematician Sardār Kābulī) new methods were sought to facilitate the calculation of the direction of the *qiblah*. Practical religious need therefore supplemented profound metaphysical reasons connected with the nature of the Quranic revelation to make astronomy a main concern of Muslim scientists and to enable them to produce a vast corpus which has hardly been studied even now after decades of research by scholars of the East and the West.

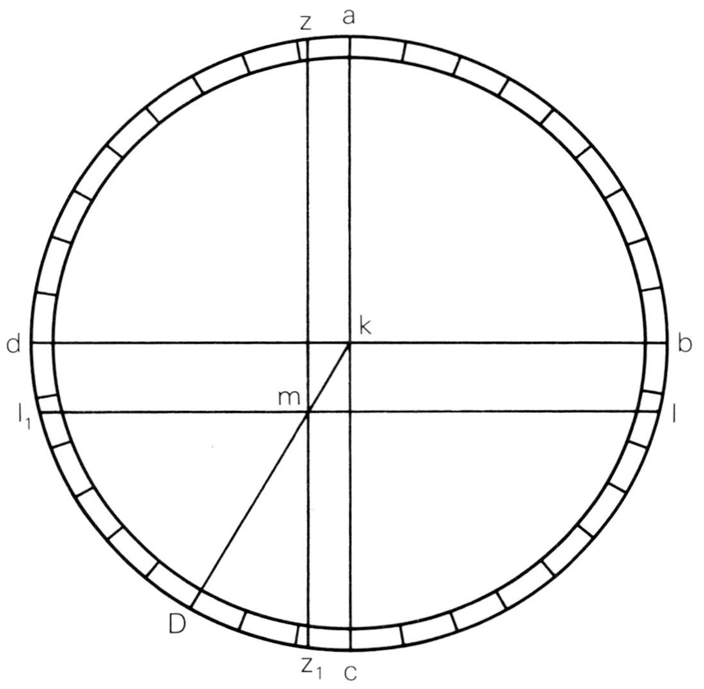

Figure 34b. On finding the direction of the *qiblah* according to Sardār Kābulī.

'Concerning finding the direction of the *qiblah* with the aid of the "Indian circle"* (*dā'ara-yi hindī*).

'Concerning this problem our words are the same as those of Shaykh-i Bahā'ī [Bahā' al-Dīn 'Āmilī] – may God sanctify his inner mystery – at the end of the first chapter of the sixth part of his book Ḥabl al-matin. He first describes how to draw the "Indian circle", to divide it into four parts and each part into 90 degrees. Then he adds that if the longitude of the city in question is more than the longitude of Mecca, mark the difference between the two longitudes from the point of south or north; and if the longitude of the city in question is less than that of Mecca do the same in the direction of the east. From the point found in this way on the circle draw a line parallel to the north-south line. Do the same for the latitude of the city in question and that of Mecca from the point east or west. If the latitude of the city in question is less than the latitude of Mecca mark the difference between the two latitudes from east or west toward the north and if it is more toward the south. From the point thus found on the circumference of the circle draw a line parallel to the east-west line. These two lines, one of which is parallel to the longitudinal line and the other to the east-west line, intersect each other at some point. Connect a line from the centre of the circle to this point of intersection. This line will point in the direction of the *qiblah*. [Of course from the point of view of astronomers this method gives only an approximate answer! But the jurisprudents (*fuqahā'*) consider its accuracy to be sufficient.] As an example let us try to determine the direction of the *qiblah* for the city of Kermanshah [a city in Western Persia which was the city from which the author of this treatise hailed].

Longitude of Kermanshah	46° 59′
Longitude of Mecca	39° 50′
Difference between the two longitudes	7° 9′
Latitude of Kermanshah	34° 19′
Latitude of Mecca	21° 25′
Difference between the two latitudes	12° 54′

'Now we draw the "Indian circle", divide it into four quarters and each quarter into ninety equal parts. Then from the point north, i.e., *a* we mark 7° 9′ towards the west *d* and from the point south *c* we also mark 7° 9′ towards the west and then draw the line zz_1 parallel to the longitudinal line. Then we mark from each of the two points east and west (*b* and *d*) 12° 54′ to the south and draw the line ll_1 parallel to the east-west line. These two lines intersect each other at the point *m*. From the centre of the circle *k* we connect a line to *m* and continue it until it intersects the circumference of the circle at *D*. The line *kD* is in the direction of the *qiblah* and the deviation of the direction of the *qiblah* from the south towards the west is equal to the arc z_1D.'

*The 'Indian circle' is one in which a gnomon is placed at the centre and according to the change of the shadow of the gnomon before and after noon the longitude and the east-west line perpendicular to it are found.

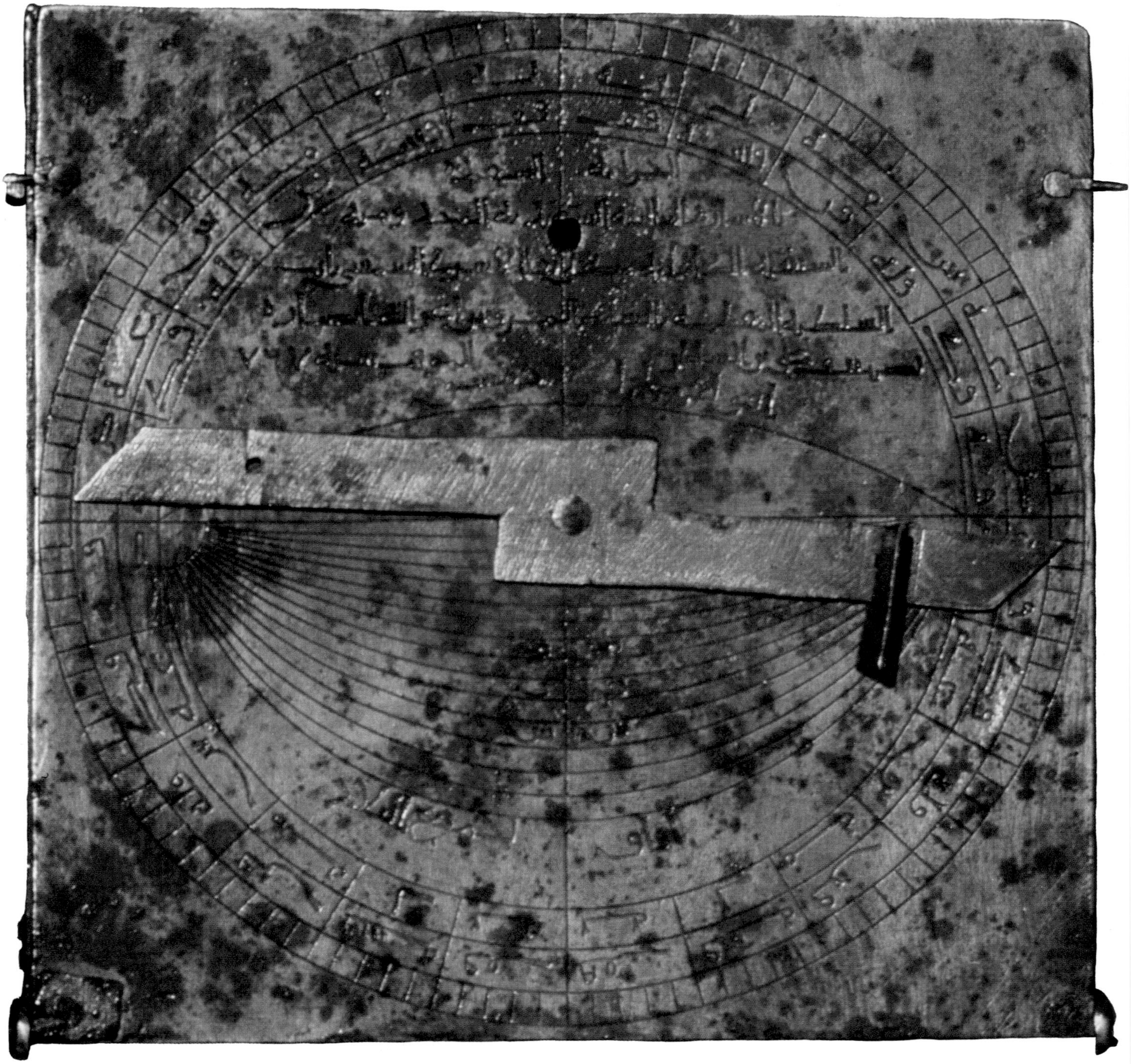

Plate 46. An instrument for finding the direction of the *qiblah*; also used as a sundial.

Astronomy in its traditional Islamic setting is referred to either as *'ilm al-hay'ah*, *'ilm al-nujūm* or *'ilm al-falak* and is concerned with observation of the fixed stars and planets, calculation of planetary motion and construction and use of astronomical instruments but, following Aristotle, not such phenomena as comets and shooting stars, which were relegated to the sublunar region. Muslims also developed the science of 'fixed moments' (for prayers), *'ilm al-mīqāt*, as well as finding the direction of the *qiblah* which as mentioned formed part of astronomy as understood by Muslims.[2]

It is also important to note that as in Greek where for the most part *astronomia* and *astrologia* were used interchangeably and almost synonymously, in Arabic and Persian there was no clear distinction between the two terms, although some philosophers classified astronomy as a branch of mathematics and astrology as part of natural philosophy or occasionally the 'occult sciences' (*al-'ulūm al-khafiyyah* or *gharībah*). For example, when reference is made in classical texts to the *munajjimūn* it is difficult to determine whether it means astronomers or astrologers. In most cases it means both. Although there *were* some authorities who accepted astronomy and condemned astrology, by and large the two intermingled and there was never in Islam the clear distinction that exists in the West today between astronomy considered as a science and astrology as a pseudo-science (with the embarrassing consequence that the supposedly pseudo-science seems to be attracting more Westerners than the science of astronomy itself in this supposedly most rational age of human history).

Sources of Islamic Astronomy

In astronomy as in the other sciences the main sources were Greek, Indian and Persian, except that in this field some Arabic influence of the pre-Islamic period is also to be observed. The pre-Islamic Arabs had had a long tradition of observing the heavens and to this day the nomads of Arabia as well as other parts of the Islamic world know more about the stars and various constellations than most modern educated city dwellers.

The Arabs had divided the trajectory of the moon into twenty-eight stations (*manāzil al-qamar*), a system which was later adopted in both Muslim astronomy and astrology. Moreover, they developed a whole 'science' related to the mansions of the moon and the first appearance of the light of each mansion and each lunar month, a 'science' with the help of which they predicted meteorological phenomena as well as terrestrial events. This 'science', which is called *'ilm al-anwā' – naw'* being the appearance of the first light of the moon as it enters each mansion – survived into the Islamic period and in fact was elaborated by Muslim scientists such as Ibn Qutaybah al-Dīnawarī, whose *Kitāb al-anwā'* is the best known source on the subject in Arabic.

Islam also adopted the Arabic lunar calendar, which determines the rhythm of religious life for Muslims to this day. Moreover, some form of solar calendar has also been in use throughout Islamic history for agricultural and administrative matters.[3] But the Holy Quran forbade the intercalation of the lunar year into the solar one according to the well-known verse:[4] 'Postponement (of a sacred month) (*al-nasī'* – meaning also intercalation) is only an excess of disbelief whereby those who disbelieve are misled . . .' (IX; 37).

This injunction is itself an explicit proof of the non-human origin of the Holy Quran, if proof be needed, for it means that the Holy Book foresaw long before the problem arose that the only way to preserve justice among Muslims was to forbid intercalation. The major Muslim

2. See Anawati, 'Science', in *Cambridge History of Islam*, vol. 2, pp. 757–765; also A. I. Sabra, '*'ilm al-hay'a*' in the *Encyclopaedia of Islam* (new edition).

3. To this day the Arab world uses a form of the Julian calendar with ancient Syriac names for the months which have survived into Arabic, while Persia uses the Jalālī calendar with names of the months derived from Mazdaean angelology. In Afghanistan the Jalālī calendar is also used but the names of the months are those of the twelve Zodiacal signs.

4. On the question of intercalation see C. A. Nallino, *'Ilm al-falak 'ind al-'arab*, Cairo, 1911, pp. 87ff.

rites, such as the daily prayers and fasting, are related to the times of sunrise and sunset. Moreover, Islam is a world-wide religion with adherents living in various geographical locations where the length of day and climactic conditions differ greatly. Had the lunar year been fixed within the solar year – as some modernized Muslims unaware of the consequences of their proposals suggest it should be – a grave injustice would be incurred in that some people would have to fast longer days or perform other religious rites under more difficult conditions throughout their lives. Only the forbidding of intercalation could ensure divine justice for all believers. In this verse the Holy Quran took into consideration the future state of the Islamic community far beyond the geographical confines of that small community in Arabia to which the message was originally addressed.

In any case concern with the calendar continued as a major pre-occupation of Muslim astronomers until with the Jalālī calendar the Seljuq scientists – including Khayyām – who were responsible for its creation produced the most exact and perfect solar calendar to be used widely to this day. Muslim astronomers also devised more popular calendars used by farmers of which the best known in the West is the calendar of Cordova. These calendars served as models for the Western farmers' almanac. In fact the word almanac itself, from the Arabic *al-munākh* (meaning climate), reveals the influence of Islamic works in this field in the West.[5]

Returning to the sources of Islamic astronomy, it must be mentioned that Muslims first became acquainted with Indian and Persian sources and only later with Greek ones. Because of their interest in determining the times of day and the direction for prayers Muslims became attracted early to foreign sources of astronomy and in fact the first extant scientific texts in Arabic are concerned with astronomy and astrology. Already in the 2nd/8th century Sassanid works had been translated into Arabic. Sassanid astro-

Figure 35. Miniature depicting the Holy Prophet preaching against intercalation.

5. Ephemerides of the sun and the moon as functions of annual dates were discovered by Muslims in the 7th/13th century and were the origin of the almanacs used later for navigation across the oceans by Western sailors.

nomy and astrology were themselves deeply influenced by Greek and Indian sources[6] and there is some disagreement among authorities of the subject, such as van der Waerden and Pingree, as to the degree of originality of Sassanid works. This matter is complicated by the fact that Indian astronomy and astrology had themselves been influenced earlier by Greek theories and that there was an extensive exchange of ideas in this field between Greece and India with Persia standing in between.[7] In any case there are certain Sassanid theories such as the use of the flood as the beginning of cosmic cycles, emphasis upon the Jupiter-Saturn conjunction, beginning the day at midnight and of course the Yazdigird calendar,[8] which can be distinguished as distinct Persian elements.

Besides several Pahlavi treatises on astrology, most of which were themselves translated from the Greek and based largely on the popular treatise of Dorotheus of Sidon,[9] the capital work of Sassanid astronomy was the *Royal Astronomical Tables*, *Zīj-ī shāh* or *Zīj-ī shahriyār*, assembled in the 6th century (A.D.) during the rule of Anūshīrawān but itself based on earlier tables. This *Zīj*, the original of which is lost, is quoted extensively by such later astronomers as Māshā'allāh, Abū Ma'shar al-Balkhī and al-Khwārazmī and influenced Islamic astronomy greatly through them. In fact even after it was supplanted by Ptolemy in the eastern lands of Islam it continued to exercise influence in Andalusia for several centuries. Research in the last decade has revealed much more about Sassanid astronomy and its role in Baghdad during the early days of Islamic astronomy[10] and it is now recognized that this influence was greater than earlier scholars had suspected.

As for the Indian sources, such works as the *Khaṇḍakhādyaka* of Brahmagupta, the *Āryabhaṭīya* of Āryabhaṭa and the *Mahasiddhanta* based mostly on the *Brāhmasputasiddhanta*, most of them already noted for their role in the rise of mathematics among Muslims, were also fundamental for the spread of Indian astronomy. Again as early as the 2nd/8th century Muslims became thoroughly acquainted with Indian astronomy thanks to the translations of Ibrāhīm al-Fazārī and Ya'qūb ibn al-Ṭāriq. Al-Fazārī himself composed a work entitled *al-Sindhind al-kabīr* (*The Great Sindhind*) which was based on Indian parameters and means of calculation. The *Sindhind* tradition thus became dominant for a few decades until the translations of Ptolemy became known, but even then it continued to influence certain astronomers, as for example the Andalusian al-Zarqālī.

The appearance of works by Ptolemy in the 3rd/9th century added a basic new element and laid a solid foundation for Islamic astronomy as a distinct school. The major astronomical opus of Ptolemy the *Megalé syntaxis mathematiké* (**μεγάλη σύνταξις μαθηματικὴ**) was translated several times into Arabic by such masters as Ḥunayn ibn Isḥāq and Thābit ibn Qurrah and is known to this day in the West in its Arabic form as *Almagest*. Moreover, other works of Ptolemy such as the *Geography* (containing elements pertaining to astronomy), *Tabulae manuales*, *Hypotheses planetarum*, *Planispherium* and the astrological work the *Tetrabiblos* were also rendered into Arabic. As for other Greek astronomers, the writings of Hipparchus, Aristarchus, Geminius, Antolycus, Theodosius, Hypicles, Theon and many others also became known to Muslims either in part or as a whole. As a result by the 3rd/9th century Muslims became thoroughly acquainted with the astronomical traditions of the Indians, Persians and Greeks and of course, through them, with those of the ancient Babylonians and Egyptians. The ground was thus well prepared for the remarkably intense activity in the field of astronomy which Muslims undertook from the 3rd/9th century onward and which they

6. See D. Pingree 'Astronomy and Astrology in India and Iran', *Isis*, vol. 54, 1963, pp. 229–246; also Pingree, 'Māshā'allāh: Some Sasanian and Syriac Sources', in G. Hourani (ed.), *Essays on Islamic Philosophy and Science*, Albany, 1975, pp. 5–14.

7. See also Pingree, 'On the Greek Origin of the Indian Planetary Model Employing a Double Epicycle', *Journal for the History of Astronomy*, vol. 2, 1971, pp. 80–85.

8. On the old Persian calendars and their historic importance see S. H. Taqizadeh, *Old Iranian Calendars*, London, 1938.

9. The astrological ideas of Dorotheus had a wide dissemination from India to Europe and appeared in numerous languages. D. Pingree is now preparing a basic work on the original text of Dorotheus and its various recensions.

10. See for example the recent works of Pingree, Kennedy and van der Waerden.

continued on a high level until the time of Tycho Brahe and Johannes Kepler and on a more subdued level even during the centuries which followed.

Islamic Works on Astronomy

The works in Arabic and Persian and even other Muslim languages, such as Turkish, on astronomy and allied subjects are of such great quantity that, despite two centuries of study by Western scholars, much of the material has remained nearly untouched while a great many works have been only partially analyzed. This vast corpus consists of works of several different types. Some are treatises devoted to a single facet of the science, such as the fixed stars or a particular instrument. Some are descriptive accounts of astronomy without mathematical treatment of the subject. These range from simple descriptions given often in general works on philosophy to the *Tadhkirah* (*Memorial of Astronomy*) of Naṣīr al-Dīn al-Ṭūsī, which is one of the major works in the field of astronomy but without recourse to mathematics. Yet another genre consists of calendrical works of one kind or another which are concerned with chronology, length of days of the year, etc. Then there are the *zījes* or tables which are numerous in the annals of Islam[11] and usually include results of observations in tabular form with extensive mathematical analysis and even occasionally discussion of mathematics itself. Some of the greatest Islamic works on astronomy such as the Ḥākimite, Īl-Khānid and Ulugh-Beg tables are in this form. Finally, mention must be made of astronomical compendia which try to embrace the whole of the field in an encyclopaedic but at the same time thoroughly analytical manner. To this class also belong some of the major works of Islamic astronomy such as the *Qānūn al-mas'ūdī* (*Mas'ūdic Canon*) of al-Bīrūnī and the *Nihāyat al-idrāk* (*The Limit of Comprehension*) of Quṭb al-Dīn al-Shīrāzī.

To gain full knowledge of Islamic astronomy it would be necessary to study all these types of writing thoroughly. But unfortunately today even some of the most basic works, such as those of al-Bīrūnī and al-Shīrāzī, have been only partially studied, not to speak of many which remain forgotten in manuscript form in various libraries. That is why almost every day there are still important and sometimes major discoveries made in this field, and what can be given as a history of Islamic astronomy today is incomplete to an extent even surpassing most of the other fields of Islamic science, which also suffer from the same fate to some degree or other.

The Major Figures of Islamic Astronomy

Upon foundations laid in the 2nd/8th century major astronomical figures began to appear in the 3rd/9th century associated mostly with the city of Baghdad, but also including Ḥarrānians, some of whom remained Sabaeans while others converted to Islam only later in life. The leader of the group of astronomers responsible for observation, measurement and correction of earlier tables or *zījes*, which for this reason were called 'tested' (*mumtaḥan* in Arabic and *probati* in Latin), was Ḥabash al-Ḥāsib, whose figure dominates the early 3rd/9th century at the court of al-Ma'mūn and who spent forty years observing various astronomical phenomena including lunar and solar eclipses. Ḥabash wandered from place to place in order to take maximum advantage of each site for observation. In this he was followed by the Banū Mūsā, who also began their observations in Baghdad but travelled extensively. Altogether the astronomers of al-Ma'mūn made many original observations, one of the most outstanding being the measurement of the meridian near Mosul, which they found to be 111,814 metres.[12] At the same time Abū Ma'shar al-Balkhī was spreading the study of both astrology and astronomy relying heavily upon Sassanid materials and the famous *Kitāb al-ulūf*

11. The word *zīj* entered into Arabic from Pahlavi and into Pahlavi from Sanskrit. It means originally 'straight lines' and is connected with the lines created on a field when the field is ploughed with the help of a cow or a bull. Most likely it came to be used in conjunction with astronomical tables because of the lines drawn in such works to tabulate the results of observation. There are numerous Muslim *zījes*, some of great significance and others of only local interest. They have been surveyed by E. S. Kennedy in his *A Survey of Islamic Astronomical Tables,* Philadelphia, 1956.

12. The actual value is 110,938 metres. See J. Vernet, 'Mathematics, Astronomy, Optics', *Legacy of Islam,* p. 479.

(*The Book of Thousands*), which had deep repercussions in certain circles in the Islamic world.[13]

Muḥammad ibn Mūsā al-Khwārazmī, already mentioned for his contributions to geography and mathematics, was also of importance in astronomy. He left behind two *zījes*, the greater and the lesser.[14] The lesser *zīj* was adopted by Maslamah al-Majrīṭī for the meridian of Cordova and translated by Adelard of Bath into Latin and thus exercised much influence in both Muslim and Christian Spain. Other astronomers of the period were also to be influential in the West. Al-Farghānī (the Latin Alfraganus) composed the important *Kitāb fi'l-ḥarakat al-samāwiyyah wa jawāmi' 'ilm al-nujūm* (*Principles of Astronomy*), which marked a new phase in the study of Islamic astronomy. Al-Nayrīzī, his near contemporary, also known to the West (as Anaritius), composed a commentary upon the *Almagest* showing special interest in the use of spherical trigonometry in the solution of astronomical problems. The Ḥarrānian Thābit ibn Qurrah, who became a Muslim and who is among the most outstanding scientists of his day, wrote several works on astronomy and was especially concerned with the question of the movement of the solar perigee and the exact measurement of the precession of the equinox. Finally, his contemporary Abū 'Abdallāh al-Battānī (Albategnius) composed the *Zīj al-ṣābī* (*The Sabaean Tables*), which marks a peak of both observational and mathematical astronomy in Islam.[15] Al-Battānī was a careful observer who discovered the amount by which the sun's apogee had increased since Ptolemy. He determined the inclination of the ecliptic with accuracy at $23^\circ\ 35'$ and made a careful study of lunar and solar eclipses which was used in Europe as late as the 18th century.

In the 4th/10th century extensive activity in astronomy continued with such figures as Abū Sahl al-Kūhī, who was the chief astronomer of the Persian ruler Sharaf al-Dawlah, and 'Abd al-Raḥmān al-Ṣūfī, an acute observer who determined the exact length of day in Shiraz and whose *Ṣuwar al-kawākib* (*Figures of the Stars*) is considered one of the masterpieces of observational astronomy. It became rapidly the most authoritative source on the subject in the Islamic world and the most often illustrated text of astronomy. Its pages brought together the inspiration of many artists and the science of many astronomers in a perfect blend of art and science so characteristic of Islamic civilization. Through the *Libros del saber de astronomía* of Alfonso X el Sabio it also exercised much influence upon stellar toponymy in the West.

Another Persian mathematician of note in this period, Abu'l-Wafā' al-Buzjānī, was also a noteworthy astronomer. His study of the evection of the moon was studied by L. A. Sédillot in the 19th century and interpreted as the third inequality of the moon, a discovery which has always been attributed to Tycho Brahe. This led to one of the most heated controversies in the annals of modern research on Islamic astronomy, and finally the views of Sédillot were rejected, without this detracting from the importance of Abu'l-Wafā' for 4th/10th century astronomy.

Other contemporaries of Abu'l-Wafā' continued to produce major astronomical works. In Persia and the East in general several astronomers were active, such as Abū Maḥmūd al-Khujandī, who made the largest mural sextant known (the Fakhrī sextant) to observe the meridian transits of the sun. But the foremost among these figures was again al-Bīrūnī, whose *al-Qānūn al-mas'ūdī* (*Mas'ūdic Canon*) is to astronomy what the *Canon* of Ibn Sīnā is to medicine. Unfortunately even today this work of al-Bīrūnī, which is a compendium of Islamic astronomy up to his day and which contains a wealth of material concerning earlier schools of astronomy as well, has never been fully studied. Al-Bīrūnī also wrote numerous treatises on special problems of astronomy and chronology and a general introduction to both astronomy and astrology, the *Kitāb al-tafhīm*

13. See D. Pingree, *The Thousands of Abū Ma'shar*, London, 1968, where an 'astrological history of science' by Abū Ma'shar is also discussed. It is of interest to note that the West first became acquainted with Aristotelian physics, not though some Peripatetic text, but with the help of the *Introduction to Astrology* of Abū Ma'shar (Albumasar), which became very popular in the Latin world in the 5th/11th century. See R. Lemay, *Abu Ma'shar and Latin Aristotelianism in the Twelfth Century*, Beirut, 1962.

14. The greater *zīj* is lost and survives only as part of the extant Hebrew and Latin versions of the commentary of Ibn al-Muthannā upon it. See R. Goldstein, *Ibn al-Muthannā's Commentary on the Astronomical Tables of al-Khwārizmī*, New Haven and London, 1967.

15. No Islamic astronomical work has received as careful an analysis in modern times as this *zīj*, which was thoroughly studied and translated into Latin by C. A. Nallino in his *al-Zīj al-Ṣābī*, 3 vols., Paris, 1893.

Figure 36. The constellation 'The Dragon'.

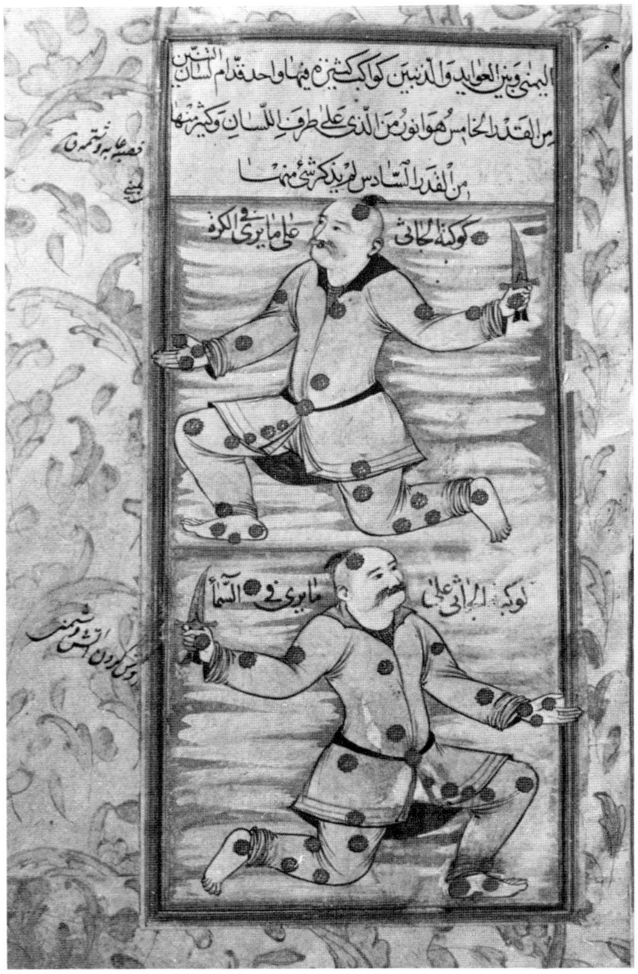

Figure 37. The constellation 'Hercules'.

Figure 38. The constellation 'The Dragon'.

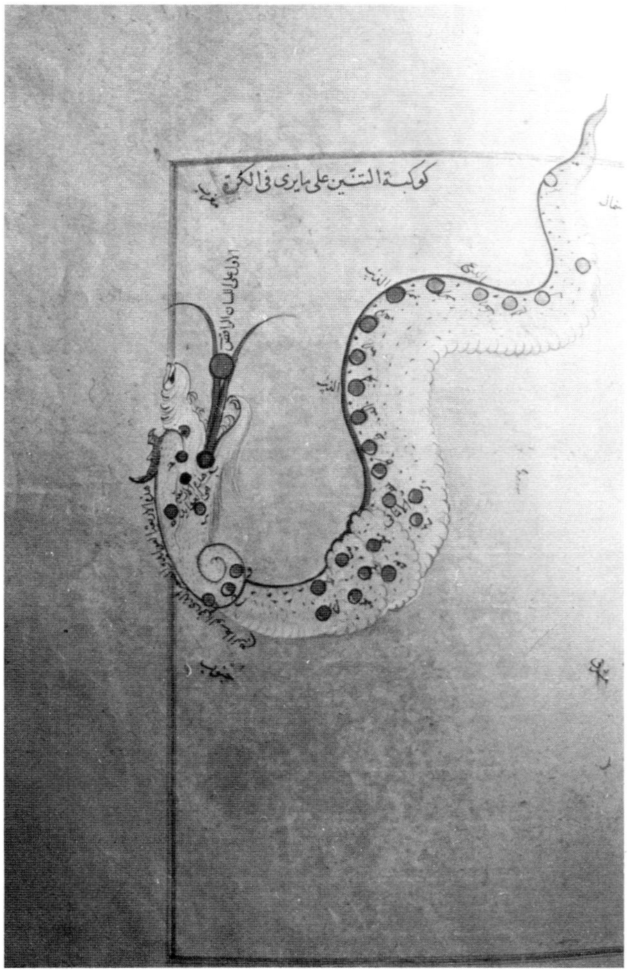

Figure 39. The constellation 'Cassiopeia'.

(*Elements of Astrology*), which is especially important in that al-Bīrūnī wrote it in both Arabic and Persian. This was the first major work on the mathematical sciences in Persian and marks the beginning of a long tradition of works in this language which rely upon the model established by al-Bīrūnī.[16]

During this period Cairo was also a major centre of astronomical activity. It was in this city that Ibn Yūnus composed his *al-Zīj al-ḥākimī* (*The Ḥākimite Tables*)[17] in 397/1007. This work again is a masterpiece of observational astronomy in which many constants have been measured anew and in which extensive use is made of trigonometry for the solution of astronomical problems. Ibn Yūnus was also the first person to make a serious study of the oscillatory motion of a pendulum, which finally led to the invention of the mechanical clock. Ibn Yūnus's contemporary in Cairo, Ibn al-Haytham (the Latin Alhazen), although known primarily as a physicist and specialist in optics, is also important for the domain of astronomy both because of his study of the nature of the heavens and the measurement of the thickness of the atmosphere and the study of the effect of the atmosphere upon astronomical observations.

Plate 47

Plate 48

Plate 47. The constellations 'The Little Bear', 'The Great Bear' and 'The Dragon'.

Plate 48. The constellation 'Perseus'.

16. This work was translated from a faulty Arabic manuscript by R. Ramsay Wright as al-Bīrūnī, *The Book of Instruction in the Elements of the Art of Astrology*, London, 1934. There is a masterly edition of the Persian text and a study of its significance in Islamic astronomy by J. Homā'ī, *Kitāb al-tafhīm li awā'il ṣinā'at al-tanjīm*, Tehran, 1353 (A.H. solar). As an example of another of al-Bīrūnī's astronomical-astrological works available in English see *Al-Bīrūnī on Transits*, trans. by M. Saffouri and A. Ifram with a commentary by E. S. Kennedy, Beirut, 1959; complemented by G. J. Toomer, 'Notes on al-Bīrūnī on Transits', *Orientalia*, vol. 34, fasc. 1, 1965, pp. 45–72. This work is also especially important for the question of the transmission of Indian astronomy to Islam.

17. Studied and partially translated by Caussin de Perceval, 'Le livre de la grande table Hakémite', *Notices et extraits des manuscrits*, vol. 7, 1804, pp. 16–240.

The twelve signs of the Zodiac.

Plate 57. Sagittarius.

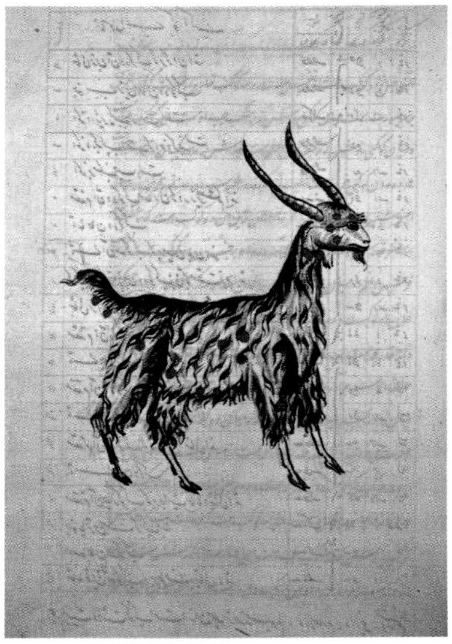

Plate 58. Capricorn.

Plate 56. Scorpio.

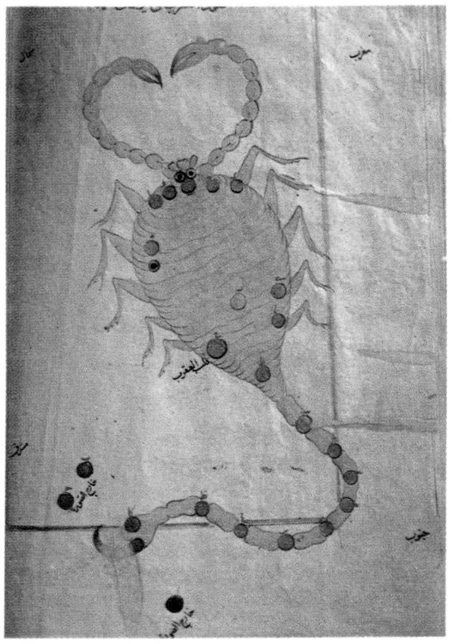

Plate 55. Libra.

Plate 54. Virgo.

Plate 53. Leo.

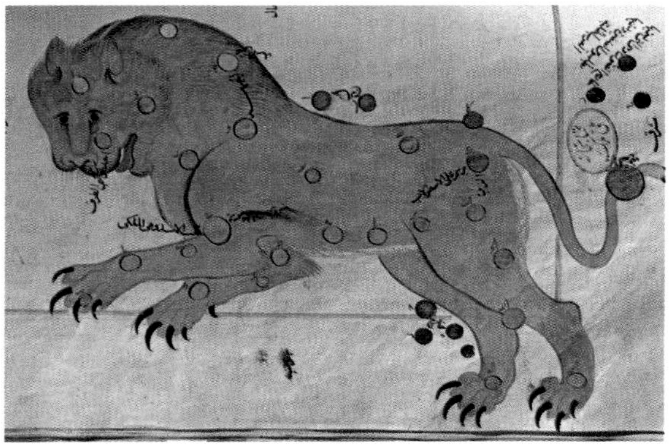

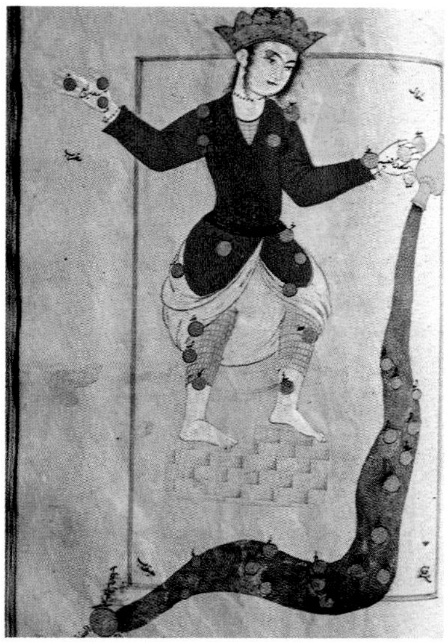

Plate 59. Aquarius.

Plate 52. Cancer.

Plate 60. Pisces.

Plate 51. Gemini.

Plate 49. Aries.

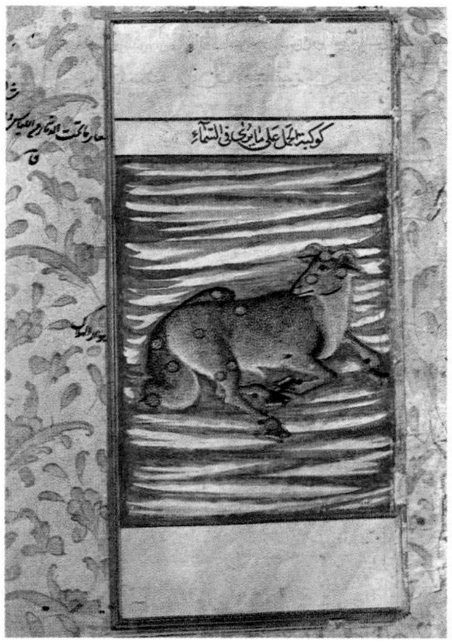

Plate 50. Taurus.

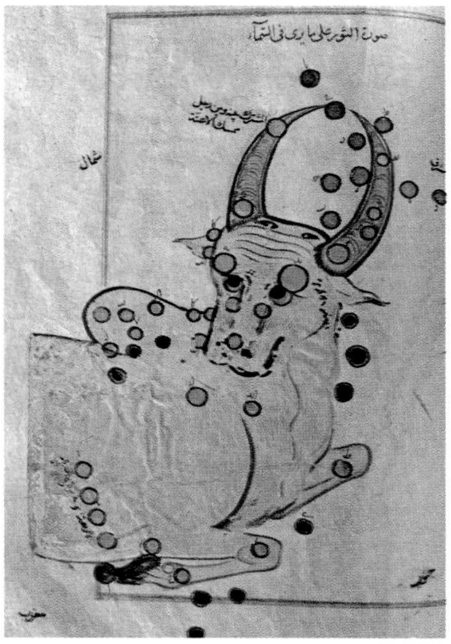

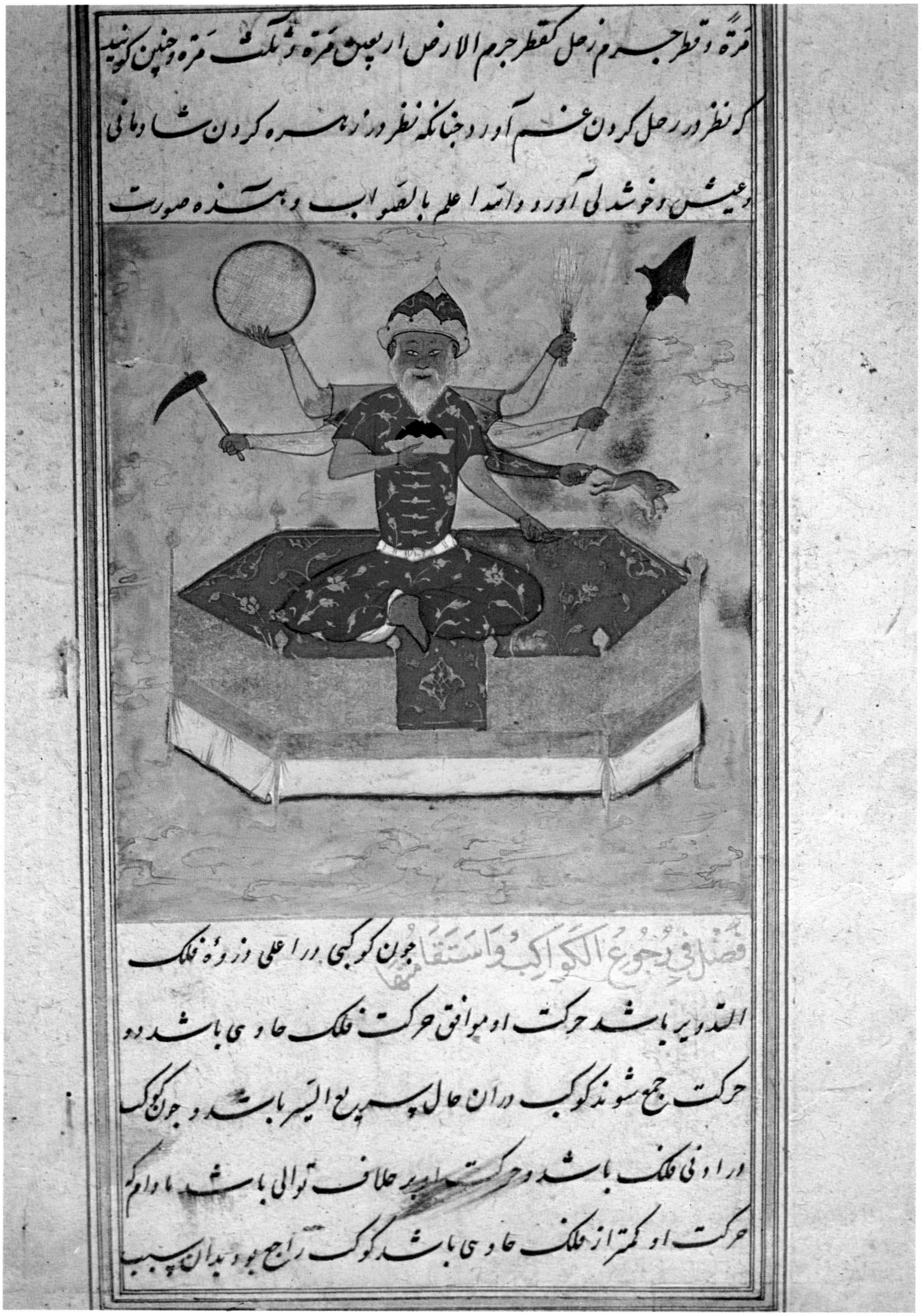

Plate 61. A figure with many arms representing the power of one of the planets.

In the later part of the 5th/11th and the 6th/12th centuries activity in astronomy, as in most of the other 'intellectual sciences', diminished in the eastern lands of Islam, while the Maghrib, especially Andalusia, became the theatre of new activity in these fields. In the East the only really noteworthy astronomical work of this period was the *Zīj-i sanjarī* (*The Sanjarī Tables*), assembled by 'Abd al-Raḥmān al-Khāzinī along with the work done on the Jalālī calendar. But in the Maghrib important astronomers appear, such as al-Zarqālī (Azarquiel in the West), who proved the motion of the apogee of the sun with respect to the fixed stars and who edited the *Toledan Tables*.[18] Meanwhile there developed among the philosophers of Spain a special dislike for Ptolemaic planetary theory and a defence of the Aristotelian homocentric system. This trend led through Abū Bakr Ibn Ṭufayl to his student Nūr al-Dīn al-Biṭrūjī (Alpetragius), who is responsible for the 'theory of spiral motion' and the most developed criticism against Ptolemaic astronomy to appear in the Western lands of Islam.

A major renaissance of Islamic astronomy took place in Persia in the 7th/13th century with the establishment of the famous observatory of Maraghah by Naṣīr al-Dīn al-Ṭūsī and the bringing together of a number of outstanding scientists such as Quṭb al-Dīn al-Shīrāzī, Mu'ayyid al-Dīn al-'Urḍī, Muḥyī al-Dīn al-Maghribī and even a Chinese astronomer named Fao-Mun-Ji. The school of Maraghah marked a new chapter in Islamic astronomy. Besides producing the *Zīj-i īlkhānī* (*The Īl-Khānid Tables*), written first in Persian and then translated into Arabic, it made possible numerous works which, as will be mentioned later, deeply affected planetary theory. It also made possible the construction of new instruments and cooperation on a scale never attempted before by a group of astronomers to create an observatory in which both observation and computation were carried out by teams of scientists.

In the 8th/14th and 9th/15th centuries the aura of Maraghah still lingered on the horizons. While certain individual scholars such as Ibn al-Shāṭir of Damascus continued to study the implications of the new planetary theories of Ṭūsī and Shīrāzī, in Samarqand a major new observatory was established on the model of Maraghah by Ulugh Beg, himself both ruler and astronomer. But the leading light of the group in Samarqand was Ghiyāth al-Dīn Jamshīd al-Kāshānī, the already mentioned mathematician, who had composed the *Zīj-i khāqānī*. While in Samarqand he cooperated with Ulugh Beg, Qāḍī-zādah Rūmī and several other astronomers to compose the *Zīj-i Ulugh Beg*, which is again one of the masterpieces of observational astronomy and noted for its new observation of fixed stars.

After Samarqand Islamic astronomy gradually began to recede into the background. Despite a short period of activity by Taqī al-Dīn in the 10th/16th century in Istanbul and individual efforts in Persia as well as the Maghrib, no major new works comparable to those of the early centuries appeared. In fact it seems that the Islamic astronomers, after having studied all the intricacies of the closed Ptolemaic-Aristotelian universe, remained content with seeking the Infinite in the beyond instead of breaking the bounds of the cosmos.[19] It needed a revolt against Heaven to rend asunder the bounds of the mediaeval finite Universe. This act, however, did not result in making the Infinite more accessible to man but had the ultimate consequence of profaning an esoteric truth and thereby shattering the 'iconic' aspect of the cosmos, which alone permitted the vast majority of men to gaze upon the sky as the roof of the world and therefore to be aware of the Infinite beyond and above the closed world depicted by traditional astronomy.

18. A major study has been devoted to various aspects of al-Zarqālī's astronomical works by J. M. Millás Vallicrosa. See his *Estudios sobre Azarchiel*, Madrid-Granada, 1943–50.

19. On the process whereby the bounds of the cosmos were broken in the West see A. Koyré, *From the Closed World to the Infinite Universe*, New York, 1958. Anyone acquainted with the structure of Islamic thought can see why such a process could not have taken place in Islam despite all the available scientific tools and techniques, which were put to quite different use in the West.

The Development of Planetary Theory

Until the 4th/10th century Muslims followed Indian and Persian planetary models, while from the time of al-Battānī the Ptolemaic theory became completely dominant. For the next two to three centuries Islamic astronomers occupied themselves with refining the intricacies of Ptolemaic planetary theory, with which they became ever more dissatisfied as they improved various constants and made more accurate calculations. This finally led to two types of criticism of the Ptolemaic system, which came in the 6th/12th and 7th/13th centuries at the two ends of the Islamic world. As already mentioned, partly as a result of a domination of a purer form of Aristotelianism than was prevalent in the East, a wave of criticism arose in Spain in the 6th/12th century against Ptolemy and in favour of the Aristotelian spheres, which had in fact also been well-known to the eastern Peripatetics such as Ibn Sīnā, who describes them fully in his *Shifā'*. But in Spain attempts were made to create astronomically meaningful models based on the Aristotelian system and to do away with the epicycle-deferent system of Ptolemy, which moreover displaced the earth from the centre of the Universe. Al-Biṭrūjī marks the peak of this movement which, however, remained more of philosophical than astronomical significance, although this attempt to criticize Ptolemy was of some importance in the later attacks made against him during the Renaissance in the West.

Plate 62. Diagram by al-Bīrūnī showing eclipses of the moon.

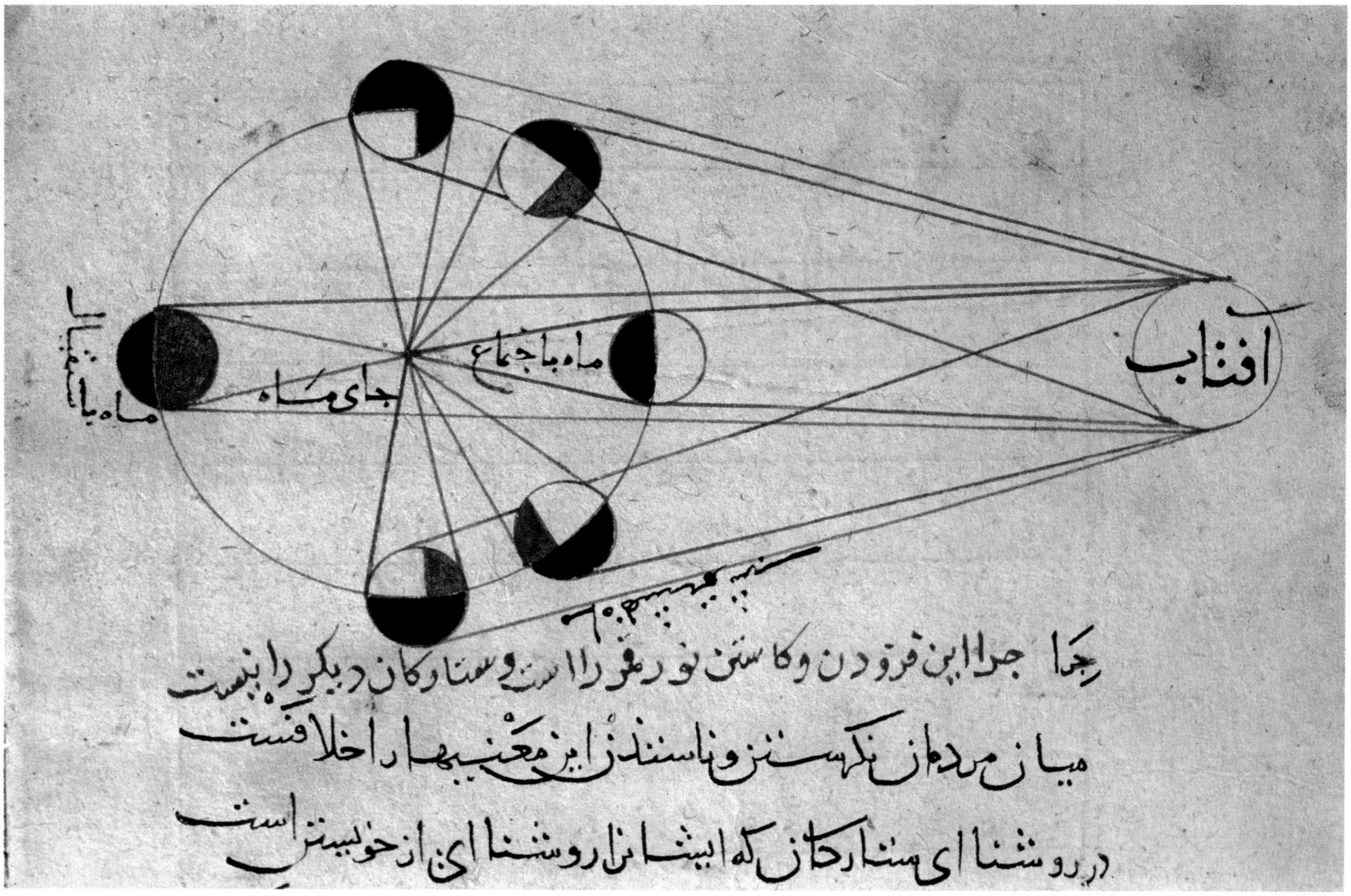

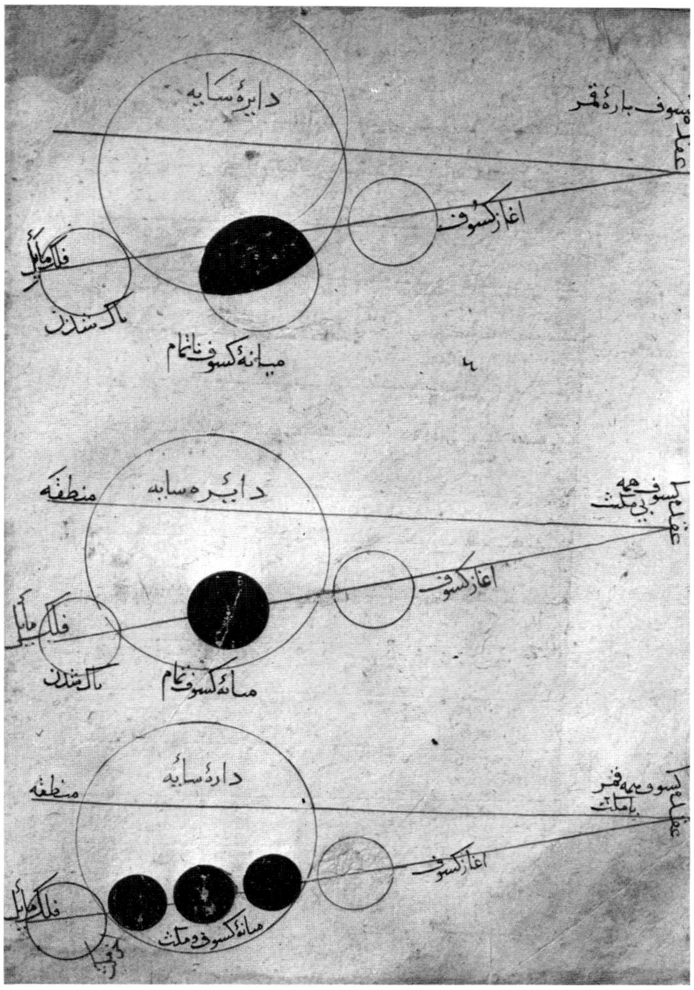

Figures 40 and 41. Diagrams by al-Bīrūnī and al-Ṭūsī showing eclipses of the sun and the moon.

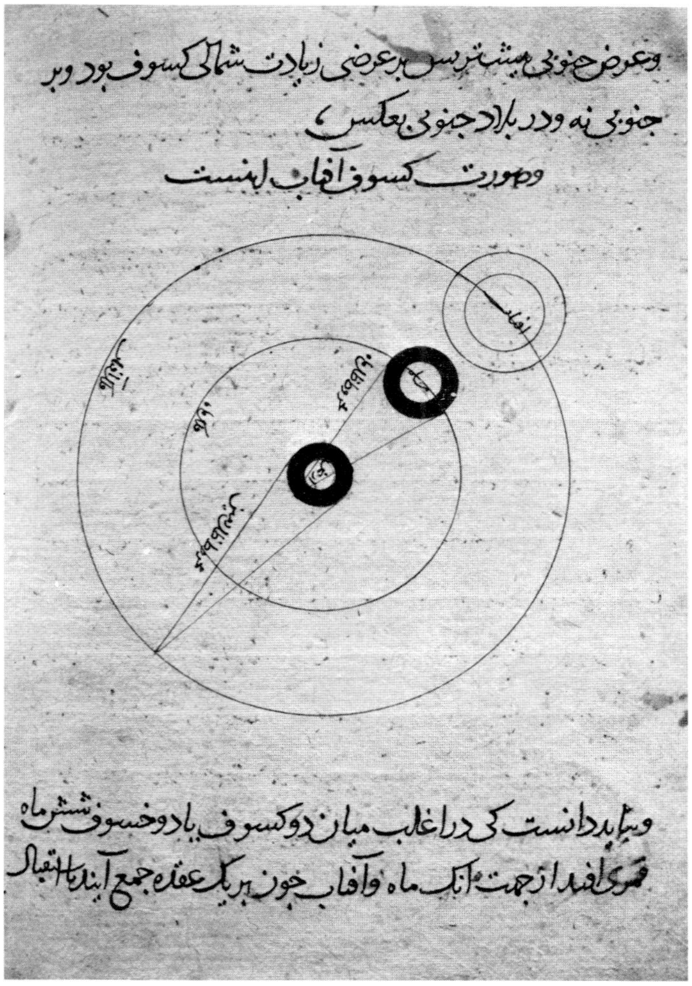

Figure 41

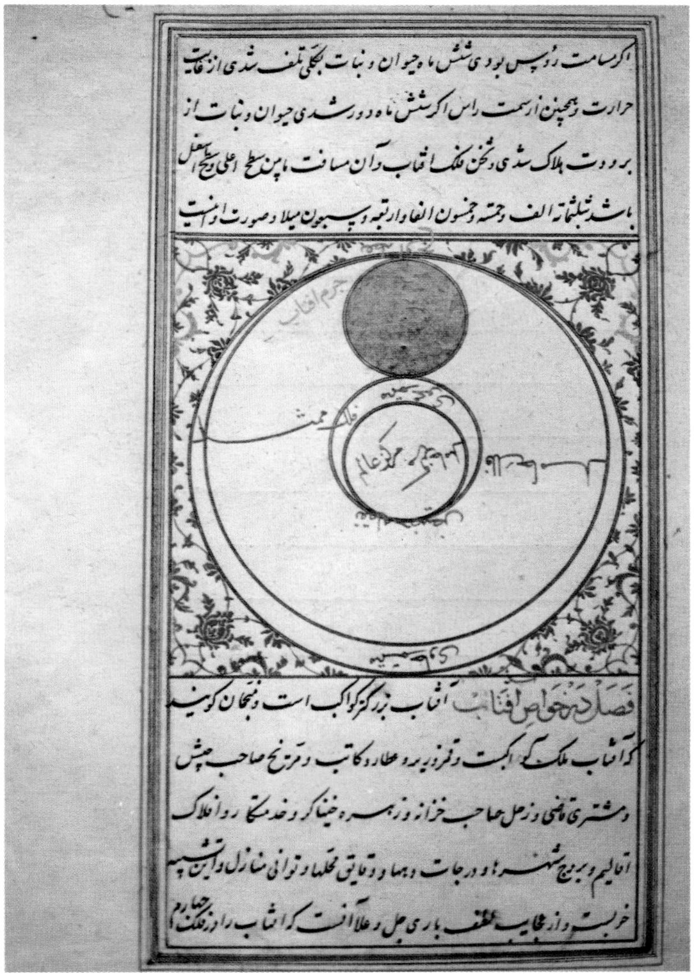

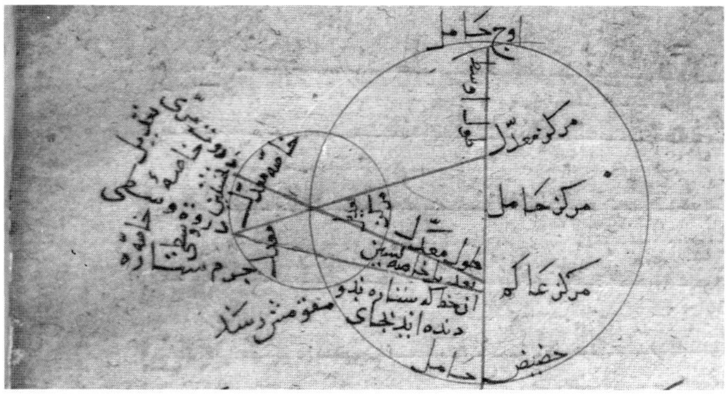

Figure 42. Planetary model by al-Bīrūnī.

Plate 63. The deferent and the ecliptic.

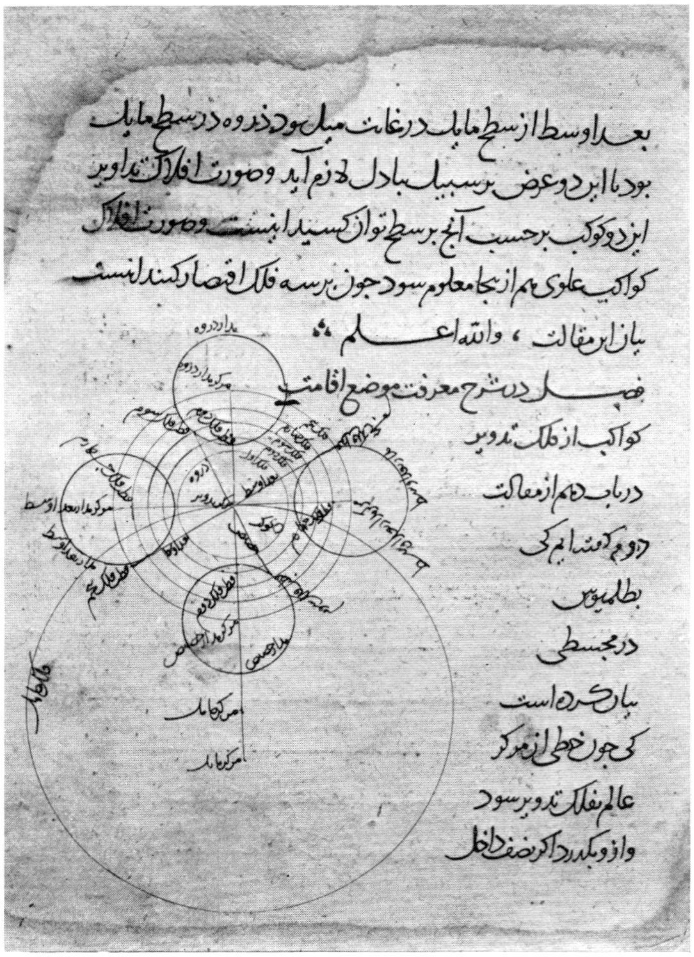

Figure 43

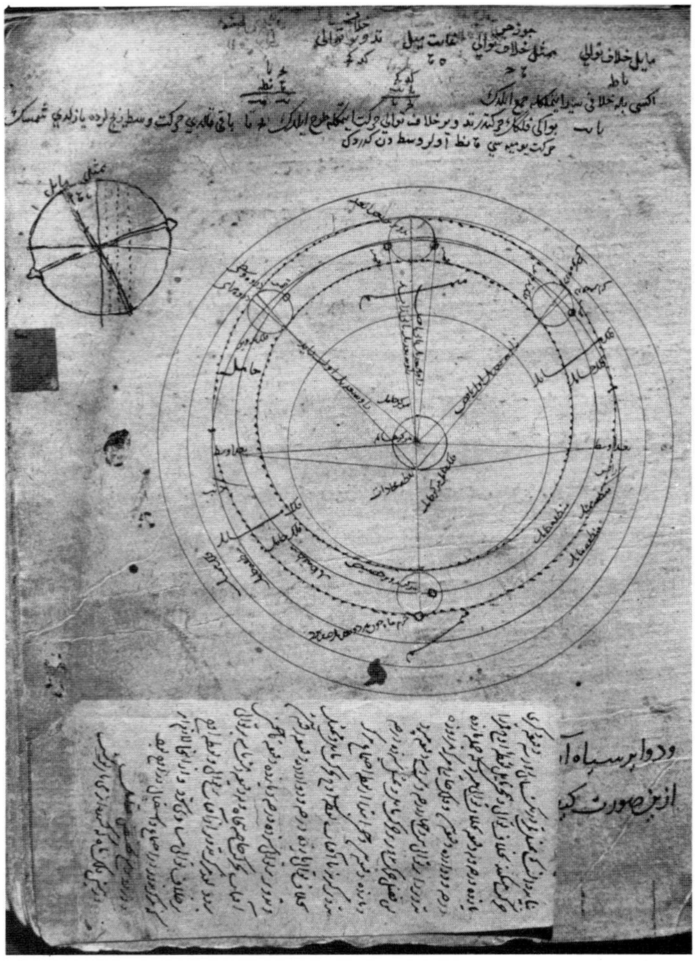

Figure 44

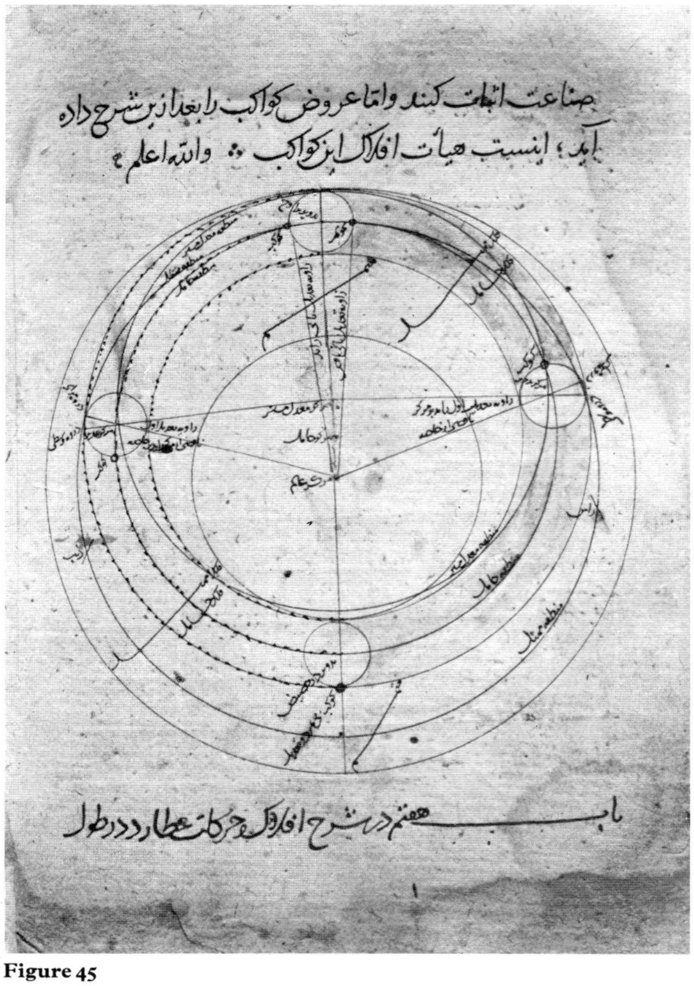

Figure 45

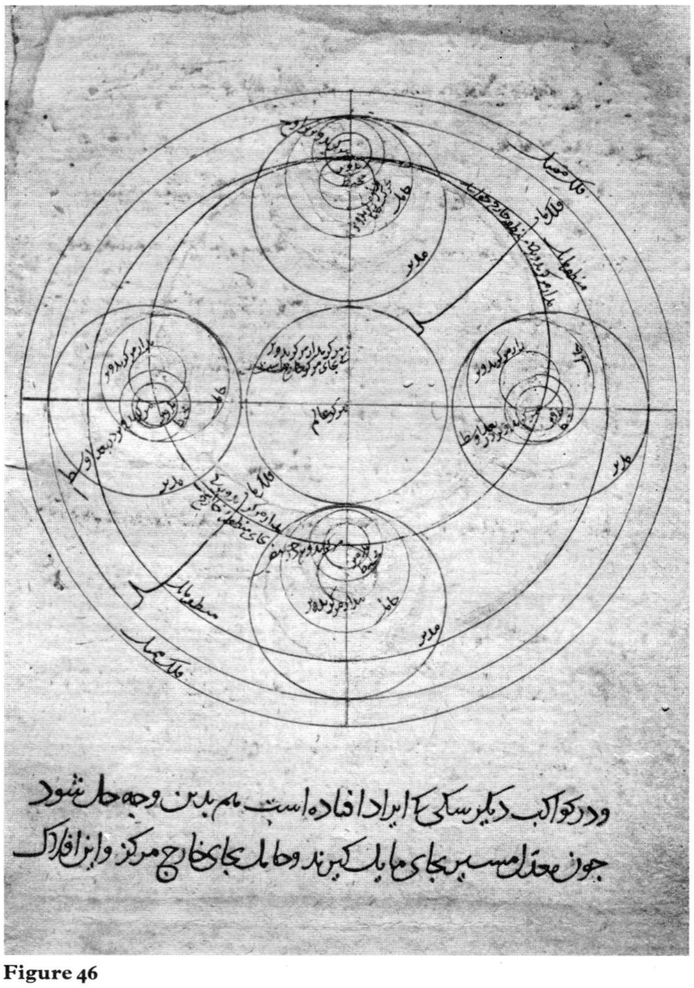

Figure 46

In Persia the criticism of Ptolemaic planetary theory was of much greater astronomical importance. In his astronomical masterpiece, the *Tadhkirah* (*Memorial of Astronomy*), Naṣīr al-Dīn al-Ṭūsī criticized severely the shortcomings of the Ptolemaic planetary model. His associate Quṭb al-Dīn al-Shīrāzī in his *Nihāyat al-idrāk* (*The Limit of Comprehension*) followed the suggestions of his teacher and applied the *Ṭūsī-couple* to Mercury, while the Damascene Ibn al-Shāṭir applied the new theory to the motion of the moon and produced a lunar model identical with that of Copernicus. The new planetary model applied mathematically by Quṭb al-Dīn and Ibn al-Shāṭir was proposed originally by Naṣīr al-Dīn and has for this reason been called by its discoverer E. S. Kennedy the *Ṭūsī-couple.* It is a model which uses only uniform circular motion and is based, to use modern language, on one vector moving at the end of another. To quote Kennedy's own words:

'He [Ṭūsī] seems to have been the first to notice that if one circle rolls around inside the circumference of another, the second circle having twice the radius of the first, then any point on the periphery of the first circle describes a diameter of the second. This rolling device can also be regarded as a linkage of two equal and constant length vectors rotating at constant speed (one twice as fast as the other), and hence has been called a *Ṭūsī-couple.* Naṣīr al-Dīn, by properly placing such a couple on the end of a vector emanating from the Ptolemaic equant centre, caused the vector periodically to expand and contract. The period of its expansion being equal to that of the epicycle's rotation about the earth, the end-point of the couple carries the epicycle centre with it and traces out a deferent which fulfils all the conditions imposed upon it by Ptolemy's observations. At the same time, the whole assemblage is a combination of uniform circular motions, hence unobjectionable, and it preserves the equant property, also demanded by the phenomenon itself.'[20]

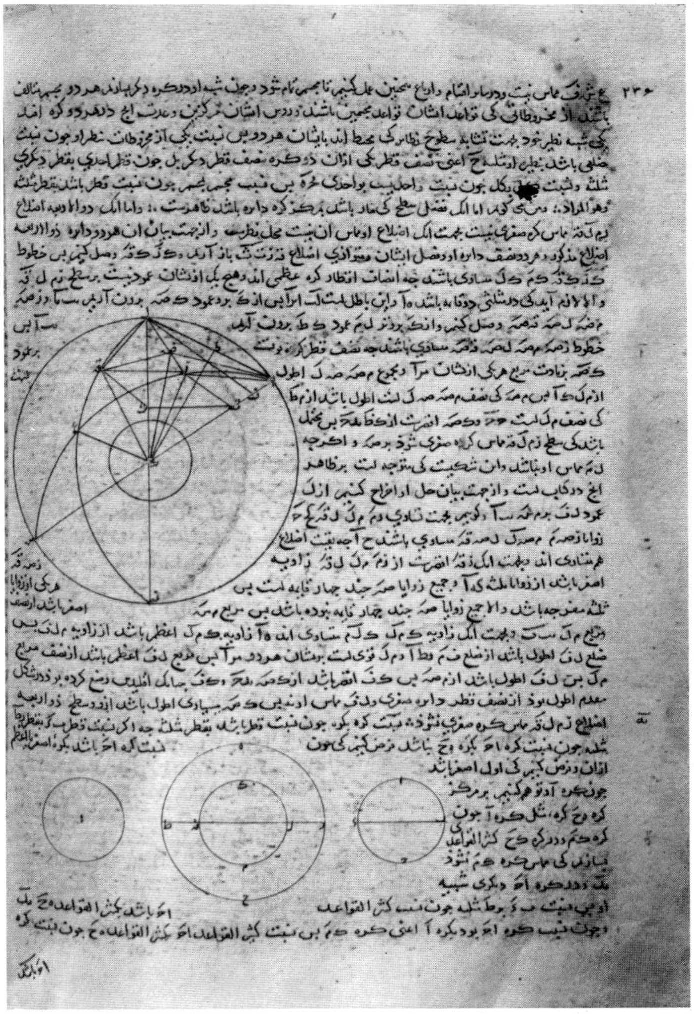

Figure 47. A page from the astronomical section of the Persian encyclopaedia *Durrat al-tāj* of Quṭb al-Dīn al-Shīrāzī.

Figures 43, 44, 45 and 46. Various models for planetary motion by Naṣīr al-Dīn al-Ṭūsī.

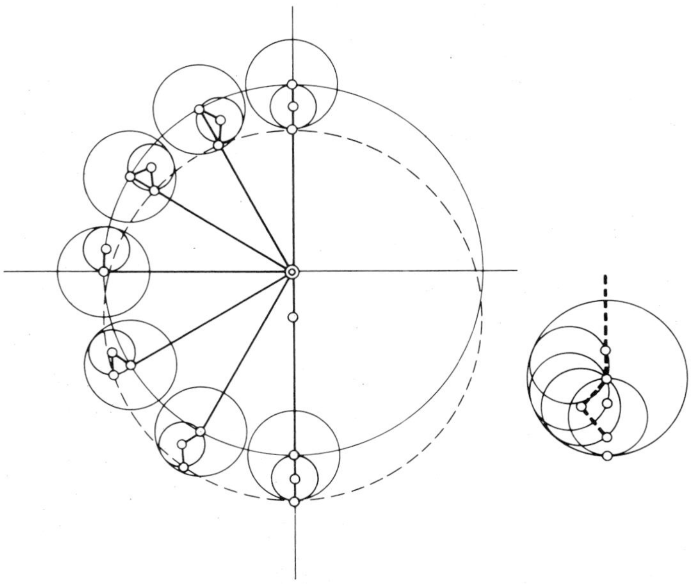

Figure 48a

20. E. S. Kennedy, 'The Exact Sciences in Iran under the Saljuqs and Mongols', *Cambridge History of Iran*, vol. 5, p. 669; see also E. S. Kennedy, 'Late medieval Planetary Theory', *Isis*, vol. 57, 1966, pp. 365–378.

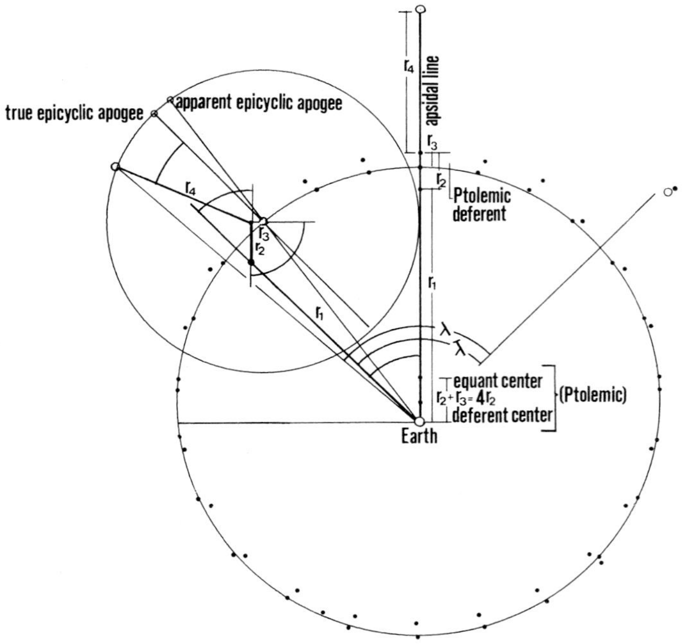

Figure 48b

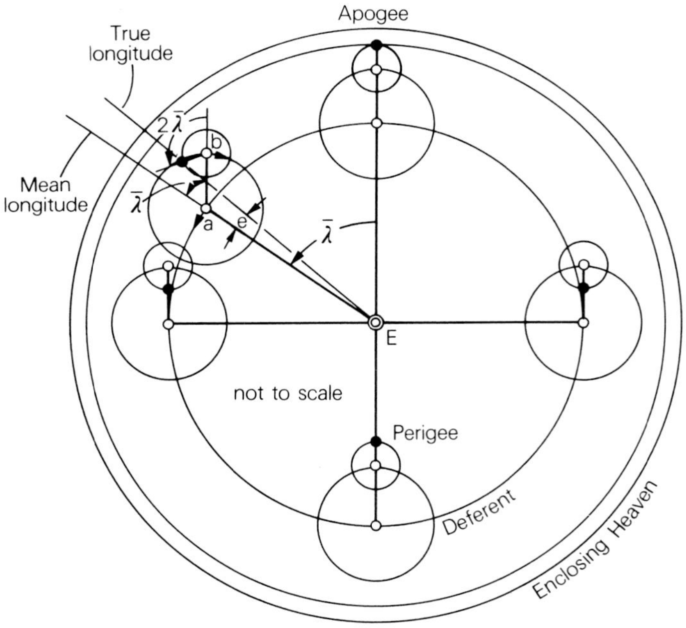

Figure 48c

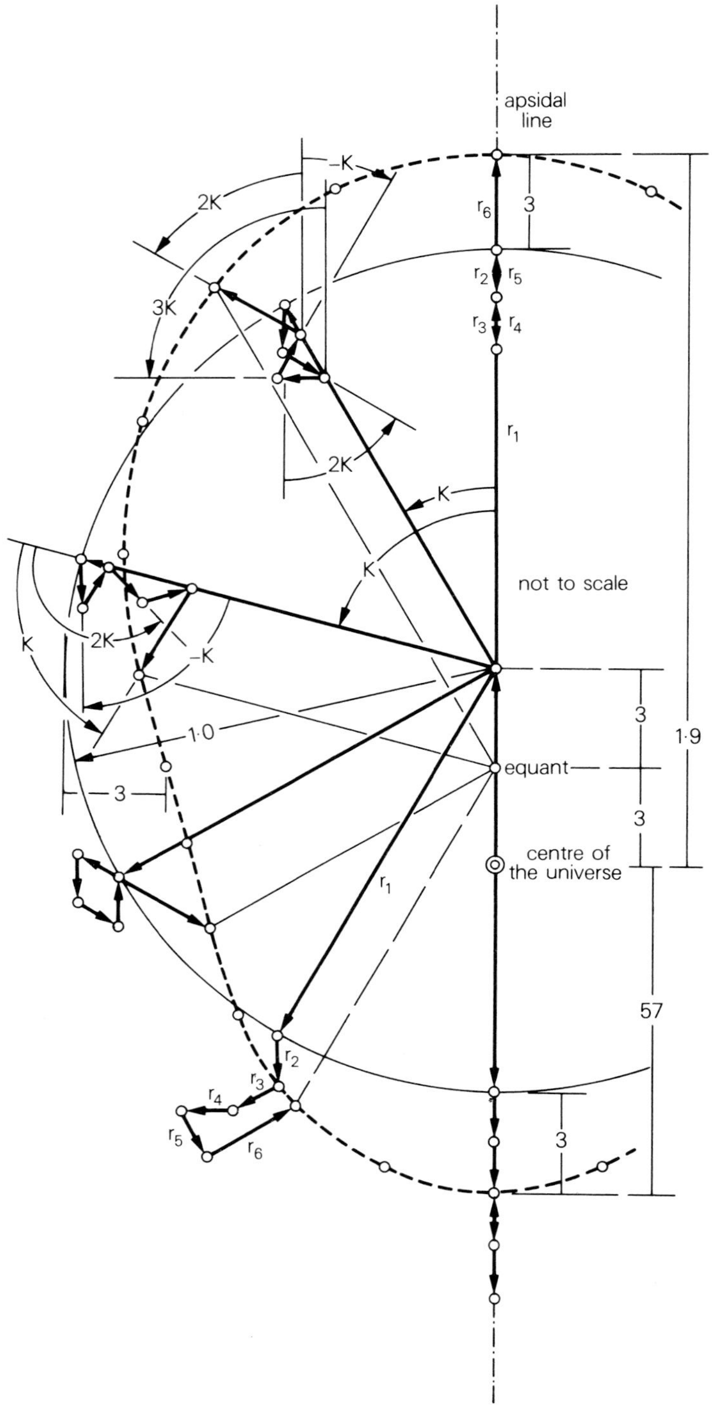

Figure 48d

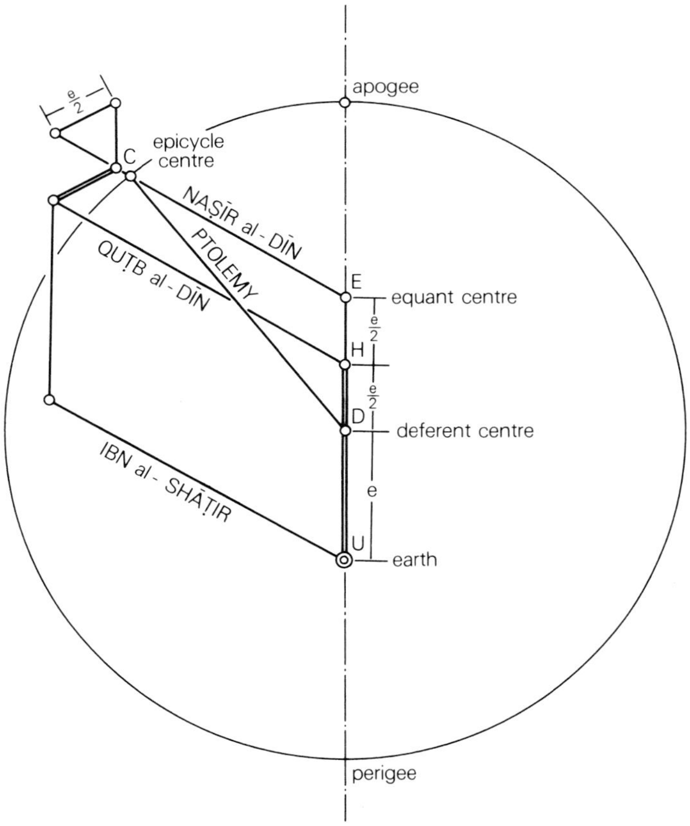

Figure 48e

Without doubt this new planetary theory as applied by the entourage of Ṭūsī at Maraghah and later Islamic astronomers is the most important transformation brought about in this aspect of astronomy by Muslims. Through channels which are not completely clear – although it is known that Byzantine scholars translated some works of Islamic scientists into Greek during the Īl-Khānid period – the fruit of the planetary theory of the school of Maraghah reached Copernicus and later European astronomers, who used it in the new heliocentric world-picture which became dominant in the West after the 16th century, while the Muslims, who were completely aware of the possibility of the heliocentric system, remained content with the geocentric one. They realized, as al-Bīrūnī stated explicitly, that the decision in this matter was more a metaphysical and theological question than an astronomical one,[21] and they shunned that step, which could not but contribute to the loss of equilibrium for humanity whose dire consequences parade before the eyes of the modern world today.

Figures 48a, b, c, d and e. The later development of planetary theory by Naṣīr al-Dīn, Quṭb al-Dīn and Ibn al-Shāṭir.

21. See Nasr, *An Introduction to Islamic Cosmological Doctrines*, pp. 135–136.

Observatories and Astronomical Instruments

The earliest record of an astronomical observation in the Islamic world dates back to 184/800 when Aḥmad al-Nahāwandī observed the motion of the sun in Jundishapur in Persia. But it took several centuries for the observatory to be brought into being as a distinct scientific institution.[22] The earlier astronomers, such as 'Abbās ibn Firnās of Cordova, worked in their own houses or on nearby hills or even used minarets as in the case of the Giralda tower in Seville, which is said to have been used for this purpose by Jābir ibn Aflaḥ. Occasionally also observatories were built for individual astronomers, such as that of Ibn Yūnus on the Muqaṭṭam hill on the outskirts of Cairo. Altogether most Muslim cities had an observatory in one form or another which usually fell into disuse and ruin with the death or falling out of favour of the astronomer who built it, or the disappearance from the scene of his patron.

With the establishment of the observatory at Maraghah in 657/1259 the history of the observatory entered a new stage.[23] Naṣīr al-Dīn was able to turn the observatory from an individual concern to a scientific institution in which a noteworthy group worked together and which did not depend for its survival upon an individual. Recent excavations by the Azarabadegan University of Tabriz in Maraghah have unearthed the foundations of this observatory and made known many aspects of its construction. There is no doubt that the Maraghah observatory is the first in the history of science as such institutions are understood today.

Moreover, Maraghah had a direct link with the early Western observatories. About a century after Maraghah the observatory of Samarqand was established on a grandiose scale based in every way upon Maraghah. In fact Ulugh Beg tried consciously to re-create at Samarqand the ambience and the instruments which had enabled the Maraghah scientists to achieve what they did. For this reason the Samarqand observatory, of which more survives than that of Maraghah, is a key to an understanding of the earlier observatory established by Naṣīr al-Dīn.

A third major observatory of this kind was established in Istanbul in 983/1575 by Taqī al-Dīn. Although it was short-lived and its

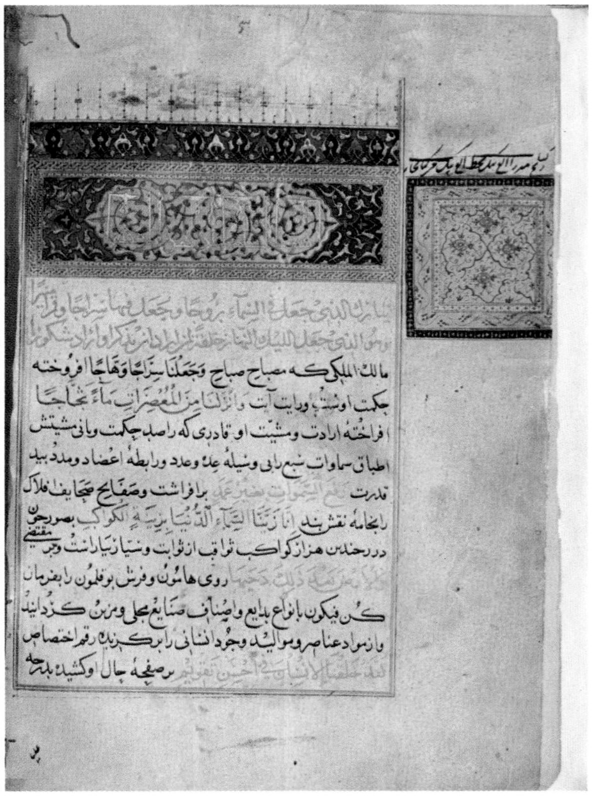

Plate 64. The opening page of the *Zīj* of Ulugh Beg.

Figure 49. A painting of the reconstruction of the Samarqand Observatory.

22. The definitive work on the history of the astronomical observatory in Islam is still A. Sayılı, *The Observatory in Islam*, Ankara, 1960. As for the general history of astronomy among Muslims, including observatories and astronomical instruments, see E. Wiedemann, 'Zu der Astronomie bei den Araben', *Aufsätze zur arabischen Wissenschaftsgeschichte*, vol. 1, pp. 258–271; and Wiedemann, 'Astronomische Instrumente', *Aufsätze . . .*, pp. 544–564.

23. For the details concerning this observatory see Sayılı, *op. cit.* Of course excavations of the last few years have added a great deal of information to that assembled by Sayılı.

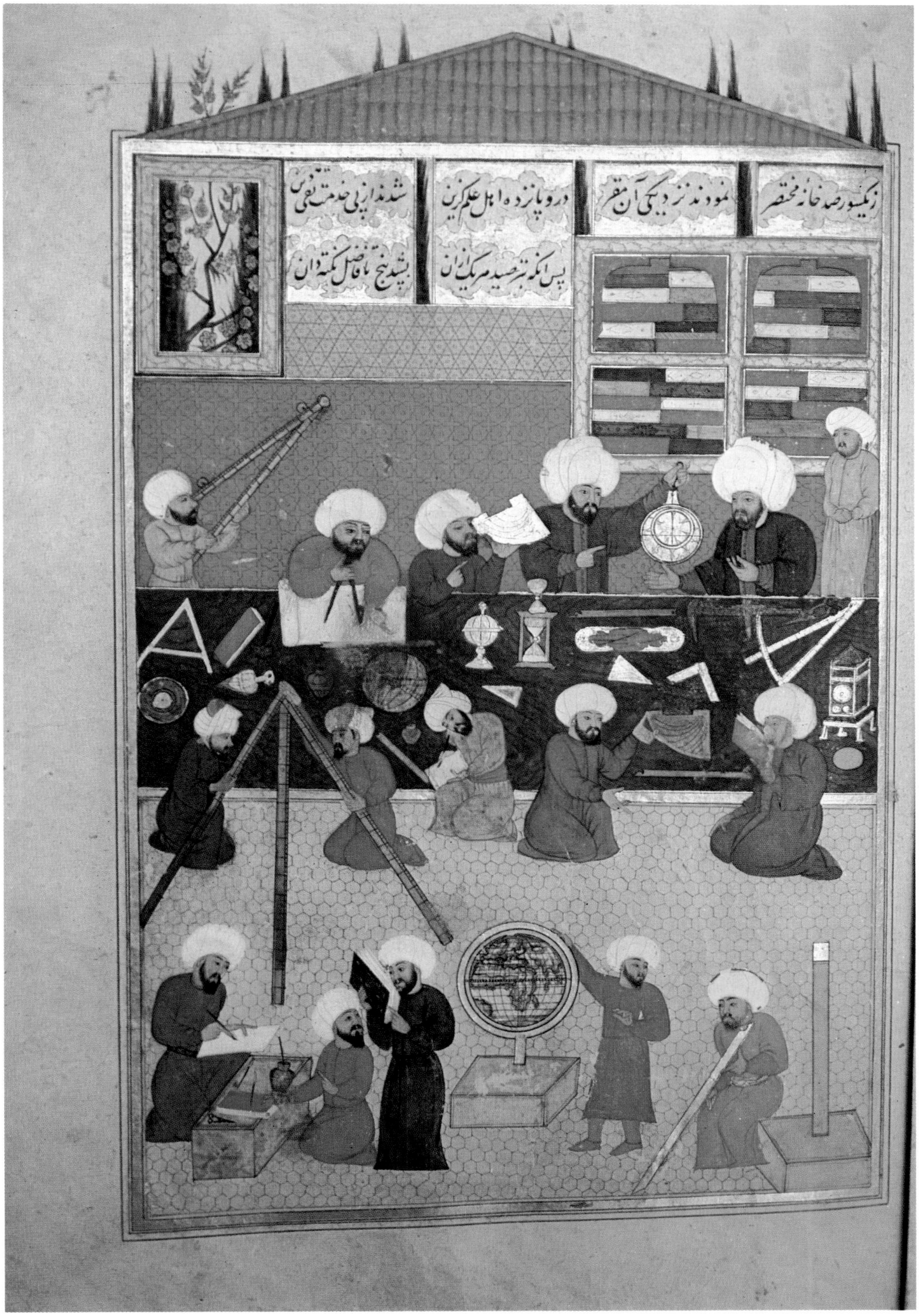

Plate 65. Taqī al-Dīn and other astronomers working in Istanbul.

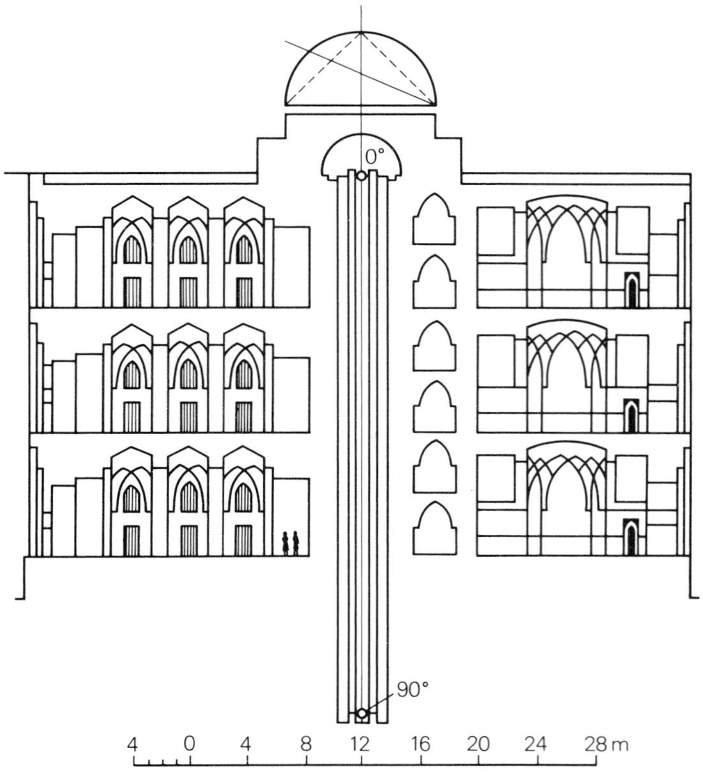

Figure 50. A sketch of the Samarqand Observatory.

Figure 51

destruction was ordered by the caliph angered by certain predictions of the astrologers, it is of great importance in that most likely it is to some extent on the basis of the Istanbul observatory as well as the earlier ones of Samarqand and Maraghah that the first major observatories of the West such as those of Brahe and Kepler were constructed and supplied with similar instruments. The observatory as a scientific institution is one of the important achievements of Islamic science.

In the East, meanwhile, no major observatories were built after Istanbul except in the sub-continent of India, where in the 12th/18th century the Indian Prince Jai Singh constructed major observatories in several cities including Delhi, Jaipur and Ujjain. These observatories, although containing some elements of Hindu astronomy, are essentially continuations of the Islamic observatories and therefore represent the most precious remains of the long tradition of observatory building in the Islamic world. As for the Islamic countries themselves, until a century or two ago in many cities such as Yazd in Persia or Fez in Morocco there were still observational towers and the like, and the present century marks curiously enough the first time in a millennium that most of the Islamic countries are devoid of observatories.[24]

As far as astronomical instruments are concerned, Muslims had a special love for instrument building, into which they poured their artistic gifts, creating works of art which in the characteristic Islamic manner combined beauty and utility. The love for astronomy and astronomical instruments even caused Muslim architects to decorate buildings with them, the earliest example being the Quṣayr ʿAmrah Umayyad palace of the early 2nd/8th century where the constellations are represented; later fine examples are found from the Safavid, Zand and Qajar periods in such Persian cities as Isfahan and Shiraz. Mosques also throughout the Islamic world have almost always been embellished with sundials of various degrees of perfection, accuracy and beauty.

Figure 51. Remnants of the Samarqand Observatory discovered in recent excavations.

24. It is a sad state of affairs when most Western-educated Muslims who criticize their own culture for not having produced 'science' in the modern Western sense are not even aware of this and many other pertinent facts related to the domain of the traditional sciences.

Plate 66

Figure 52. A sundial from Morocco.

Plates 66 and 67. Two views of the Jai Singh Observatory, Jaipur, India.

Plates 68 and 69. Two views of the Jai Singh Observatory, Delhi, India.

Plate 70. A man determining the time from a sundial in Morocco.

Plate 71. A water clock from Morocco.

Figure 53

The most important Islamic astronomical instrument is of course the astrolabe, which consists of the stereographic projection of the celestial sphere on the plane of the equator taking the pole as the viewpoint. The circle of declination and the azimuthal co-ordinates appear on the plates of the astrolabe, while the asterisms are on the spider or net. This multi-functional instrument can determine the altitude of the stars, the sun, the moon and other planets in much the same way as the sextant or quadrant. The astrolabe can also be used to tell time, and to measure the height of mountains and the depth of wells.[25]

Figure 53. A sundial from Old Cairo, Egypt.

Plate 72. A sundial from Persia.

Figures 54, 55 and 56. Description of the astrolabe according to al-Bīrūnī.

25. On the astrolabe and ways of using it the best work is still that of W. Hartner, 'The Principle and Use of the Astrolabe', chapter 57 of A.U. Pope and P. Ackerman (eds.), *A Survey of Persian Art,* vol. VI, Tokyo, n.d., pp. 2530–2554; also in W. Hartner, *Oriens – Occidens,* Hildesheim, 1968, pp. 287–311. On the Islamic astrolabes see L. A. Mayer, *Islamic Astrolabists and their Works*, Geneva, 1956.

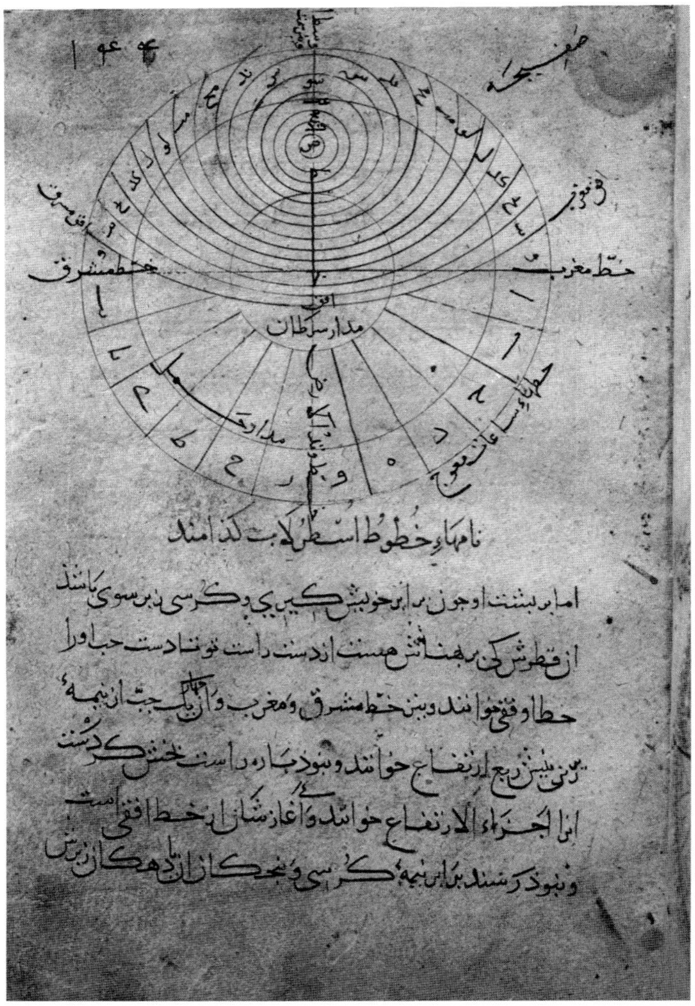

Figure 54

Plate 72

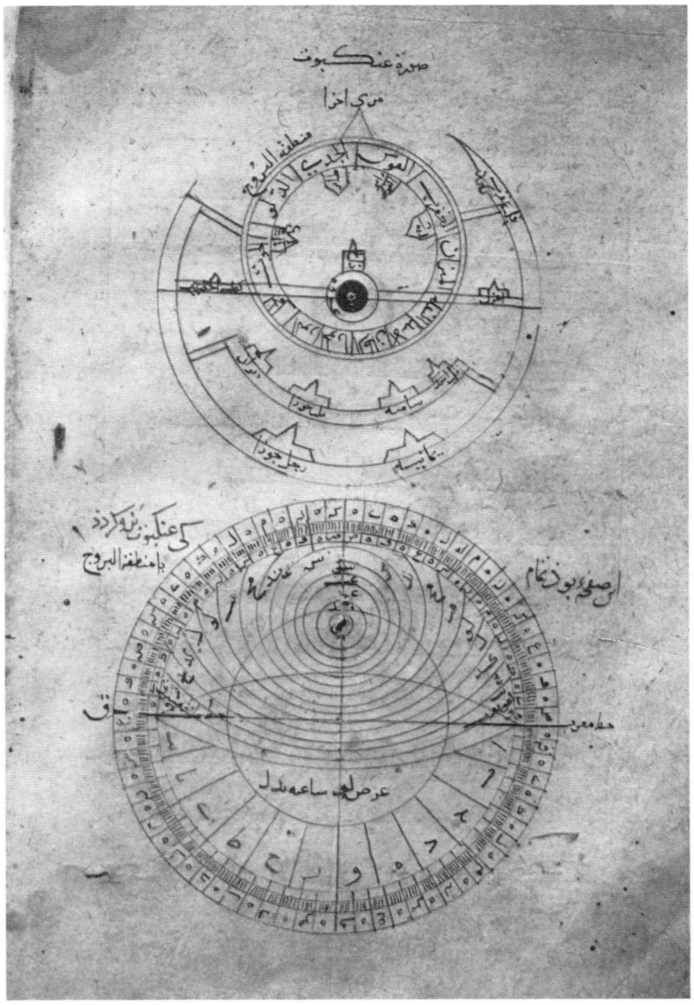

Figure 55

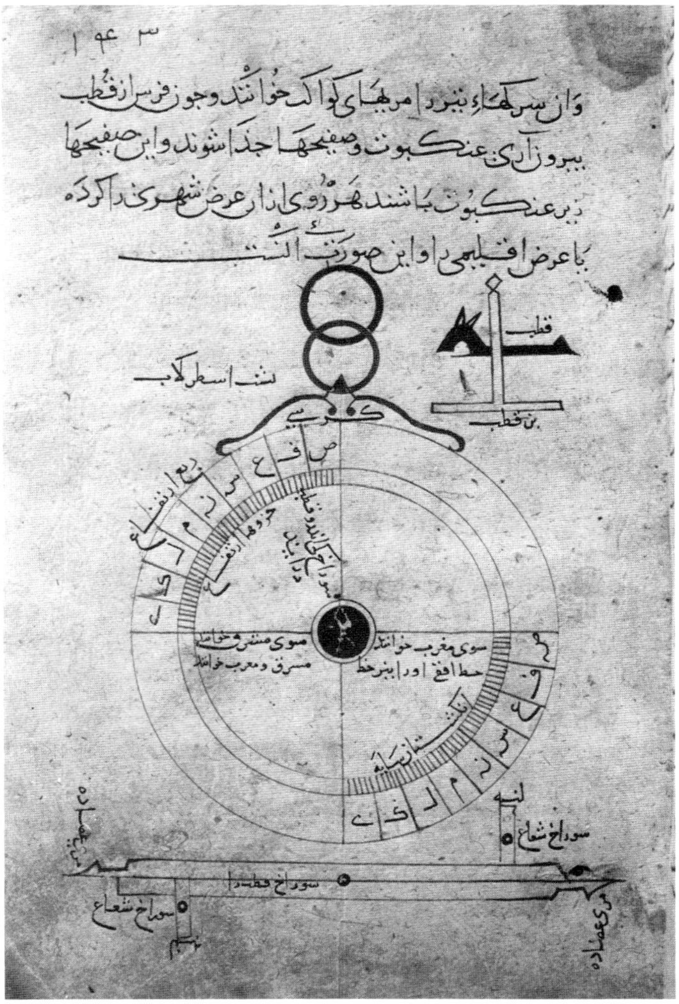

Figure 56

The astrolabe owes its origin to the pre-Islamic period. The Christian philosopher Johannes Philoponus wrote a treatise on it in Greek and the Christian bishop of Kennesrin, Severus Sebokht of Nisibis, also wrote a description of the astrolabe in Syriac. The earliest treatise in Arabic on the astrolabe dates from the 3rd/9th century and is by Māshā'allāh, the Messahalla who influenced Chaucer in his treatise *The Conclusions of the Astrolabie*. But the original of this treatise is lost and it survives only in its Latin version. The earliest extant manuscript in Arabic on the subject is by 'Alī ibn 'Īsā, followed by numerous later works in Arabic, Persian and other languages, some by relatively unknown authors, others by such masters as al-Bīrūnī and Naṣīr al-Dīn al-Ṭūsī. As for the astrolabe itself, the earliest one extant is from 4th/10th century Isfahan, while numerous other examples survive from later centuries from India to Morocco. Some, like that of Shāh Sulṭān Ḥusayn, the last Safavid king, are of unparalleled finesse and delicacy. Altogether some of the astrolabes are outstanding examples of Islamic art. Perhaps that is why they caught the eyes of Europeans in the 19th century and today most of the fine ones are housed in European and American museums.

Plates 73, 74, 75, 76, 77 and 78. Astrolabes from various parts of the Islamic world.

Plate 74

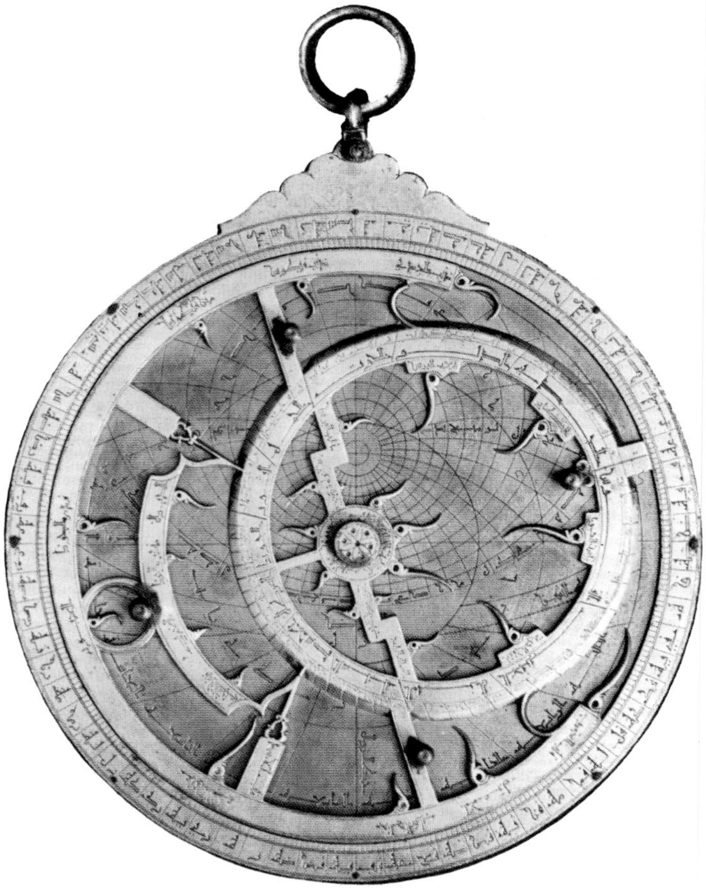

Plate 75

Plate 76

Plate 77

Plate 78

Plate 79. A contemporary master astrolabe maker of Isfahan.

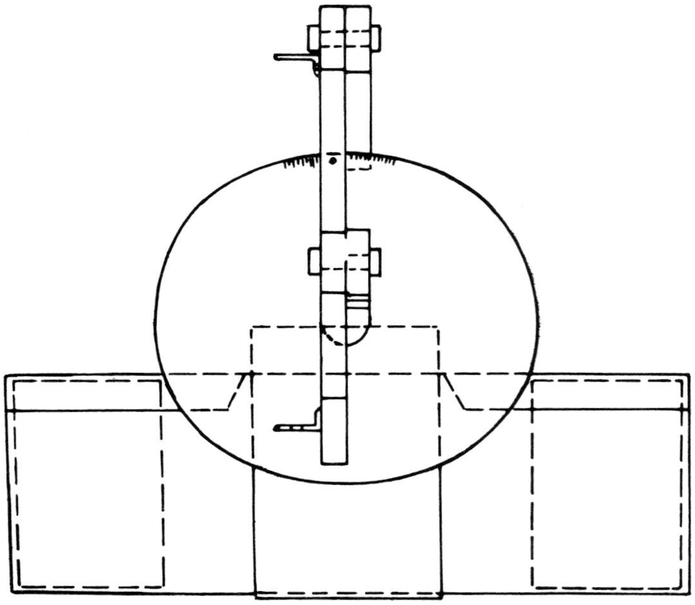

Figure 57

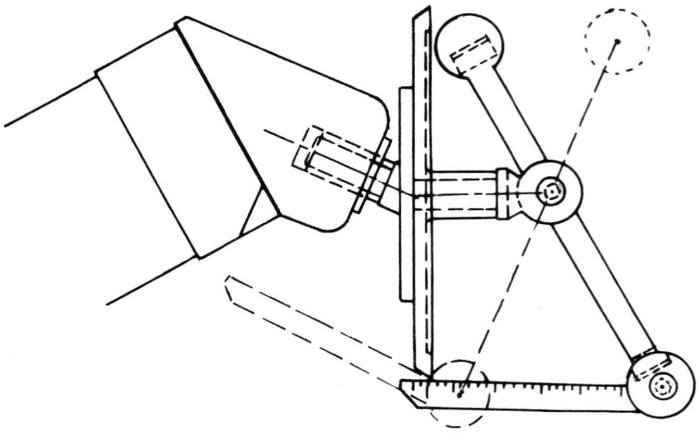

Figures 57 and 58. The universal instrument of Jābir ibn Aflaḥ.

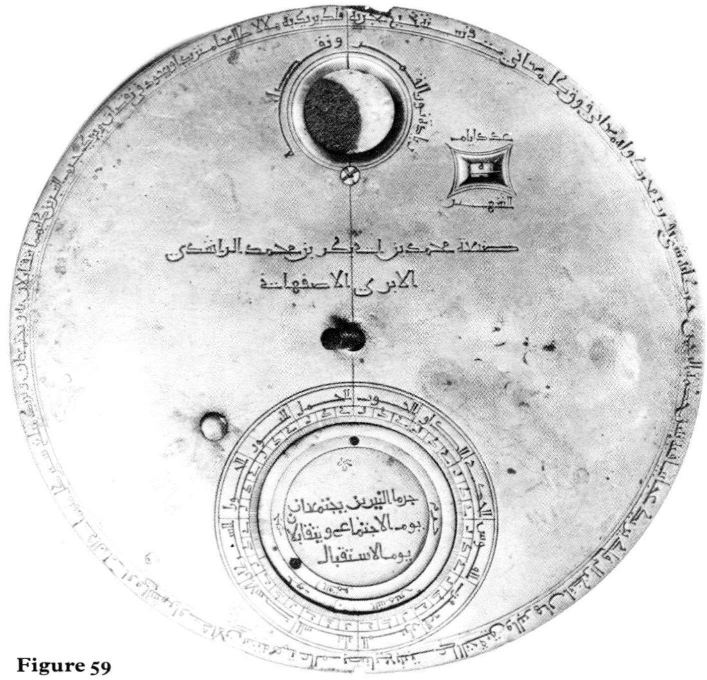

Figure 59

Figure 60

Figure 61

Figures 59 and 60. Front and back of an astrolabe with gears.

Figure 61. Front of a Persian nocturnal, a mechanical instrument to show the direction of the stars.

Since the astrolabe needs as many plates as the number of latitudes employed, it usually becomes heavy and cumbersome to carry about. As a result attempts were made to improve upon it. Thus 'Alī ibn Khalaf in the 4th/10th century invented the 'universal plate' which was the stereographic projection of the sphere on a plane perpendicular to the ecliptic and cutting it according to the solstitial line of Cancer-Capricorn. Al-Zarqālī followed with his famous instrument *al-ṣafīḥah*, which was an astrolabe in which the two stereographic projections of the circles of the equator and the ecliptic were presented on the same surface.[26] His compatriot Jābir ibn Aflaḥ had also invented a 'universal instrument' to be used for astronomy as well as mathematics and physics, an instrument which many consider as the fore-runner of the European *torquetum*. Following them Muẓaffar Sharaf al-Dīn al-Ṭūsī invented the linear astrolabe to simplify the instrument.

Certain Muslim astronomers had also made mechanical astrolabes by which the positions of planets and stars were determined with the help of a gear mechanism. Al-Bīrūnī had already possessed such an instrument and it was later perfected by the Andalusian astronomer Ibn al-Samḥ with his 'plates of the seven planets' and by al-Zarqālī. This instrument spread later into Europe and was the forerunner of the mechanical clock. Altogether the Muslims developed three kinds of astrolabes: the flat ones which are the most common, the linear one called also the 'staff of Ṭūsī' after its inventor Muẓaffar Sharaf al-Dīn al-Ṭūsī, and the spherical one of which some descriptions survive[27] but of which there is but a single complete example known to be extant, the famous one at Oxford.

Muslims also used many other astronomical instruments. For example, the azimuthal quadrant (*dhāt al-rub'ayn*) was known to Ibn Sīnā and perfected by Naṣīr al-Dīn. It was the predecessor of the theodolite used by Tycho Brahe to determine altitudes and azimuths. Muslims also made numerous zodiacal armillaries (*dhāt al-ḥilaq*) and celestial globes, some of which still survive, and equatoria to predict planetary longitudes.[28] Altogether the art of making astronomical devices reached its peak at Maraghah where Mu'ayyid al-Dīn al-'Urḍī was responsible for the construction of the instruments.[29]

Plate 80. Spherical astrolabe.

26. See J. Vernet, 'Mathematics, Astronomy, Optics', pp. 475–476.

27. See for example, C. Pellat, 'L'astrolabe sphérique d'al-Rūdānī', *Bulletin d'Etudes Orientales*, vol. XXVI, 1973, pp. 7–83, where the Arabic text of *al-Nāfi'ah 'ala'l-'ālat al-jāmi'ah* of the Moroccan scientist and Sufi is given and analyzed. The text describes an instrument which is both a spherical astrolabe and an armillary sphere. The instrument itself has not, however, been as yet discovered.

28. See E. S. Kennedy, 'The Equatorium of Abū al-Ṣalt', in *Physis-Rivista internazionale di storia della scienza*, vol. XII, fasc. 1, 1970, pp. 73–81; and E. S. Kennedy, *The Planetary Equatorium of Jamshīd al-Kāshī*, Princeton, 1960.

29. On the instruments at Maraghah see H. J. Seemann, 'Die Instrumente der Sternwarte zu Marāgha nach den Mitteilungen von al-'Urḍī', in *Sitzungsberichte der Physikalisch-medizinischen Sozietät*, Erlangen, vol. 60, 1928, pp. 15–126.

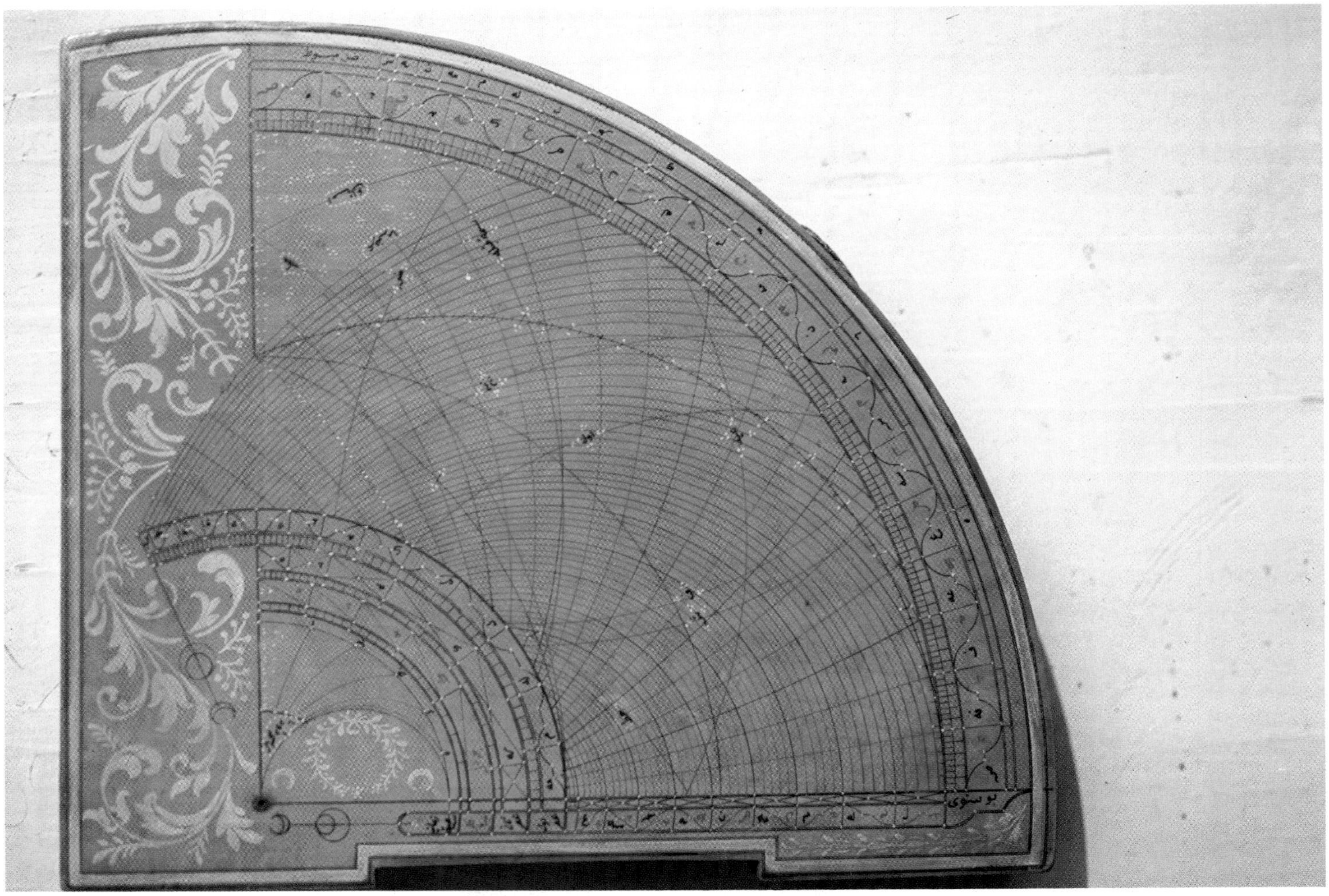

Plates 81 and 82. Wooden Turkish quadrants.

Plate 82

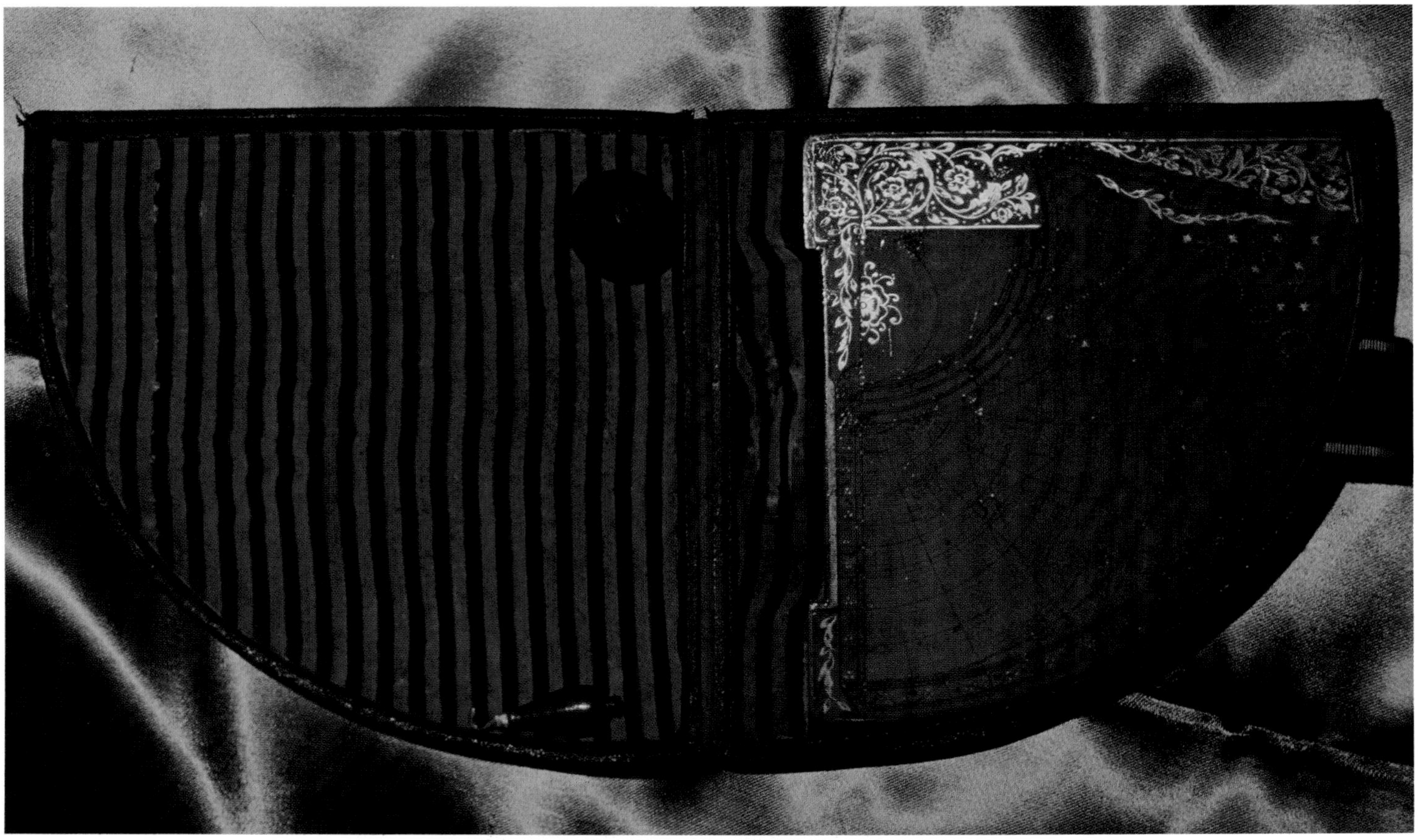

Plate 83

Plate 84

Plate 83. An astronomer observing a meteor with a quadrant.

Plate 84. Astronomers working with an armillary sphere.

A point of much interest is the remarkable similarity between the instruments described by al-'Urḍī, those described by Taqī al-Dīn in his work on the Istanbul observatory, and those found in Tycho Brahe's *Astronomiae instauratae mechanica*. A comparative study[30] reveals the strong influence of Islamic instruments upon those used by Tycho and other European astronomers. For example, the mural quadrant in which Tycho took great pride and which he called Tichonicus was also built by Taqī al-Dīn and called by him *libnah*.[31] The same is true of many of the other instruments described by Taqī al-Dīn and going back ultimately to the Maraghah observatory. Altogether a close study of later Islamic astronomical instruments reveals the astonishing degree to which early European observatories followed Islamic models, although inasmuch as they breathed in an already secularized cosmos the European astronomers reached very different conclusions from those of their Muslim predecessors while making use of both their ideas and their instruments.

Astrology

Astrology as a systematized art originated in Ptolemaic Egypt while its cosmological symbolism recedes into the dawn of human history and antedates all historical records of various human civilizations.[32] It was in fact the profound symbolism inherent in astrology which made its integration into Islamic civilization and especially into certain aspects of Islamic esotericism possible, despite the obvious external differences between the astrological attempt to predict future events and the Islamic emphasis upon the omnipotent character of the Divine Will. Throughout Islamic history theologians and jurisprudents continued to oppose astrology and with the same persistence astrology continued to be cultivated on the popular level as well as by outstanding astronomers and even masters of gnosis.[33] The loss of the metaphysical foundations upon which all traditional sciences including astrology are based has made of this art today a real superstition according to the very etymology of this term. But in the traditional universe of Islam it was possible for a single person to be a rigorous mathematician of the level of al-Bīrūnī or Naṣīr al-Dīn al-Ṭūsī and at the same time compose treatises on astrology without the least contradiction or hypocrisy. It would be a grave error to read back into history the fragmented vision of reality in which modern man – including modernized Muslims – takes pride.[34] The world in which the traditional Muslim found himself was vast enough to enable both the mathematical aspects of astronomy and the symbolic aspects of astrology to survive together, often in the mind of a single astronomer or philosopher.

30. See S. Tekeli, 'Ālāt-i raṣadiye li zic-i şehinşahiye', *Araştirma*, 1964, pp. 71–122, containing the text of the treatise on the instruments of the Istanbul observatory; and S. Tekeli, 'Nasirüddin, Takiyüddin ve Tycho Brah'nin Rasat aletlerinin mukayesesi', *Ankara Üniversitesi Dil ve Tarih-Coğrafya Fakultesi Dergisi*, vol. XVI, No. 304, 1958, pp. 302–393, where a careful comparison is made between the instruments of Maraghah, those of the Istanbul observatory as described in Taqī al-Dīn's *Sidrat al-muntahā* and *Ālāt al-raṣadiyyah li zīj shāhanshāhiyyah* and the instruments of Tycho.

31. S. Tekeli, *op. cit.*, p. 329. S. Tekeli is of the view that the *torquetum* so popular in the West did not come from Turkey but from the equatorial armillae (*dā'irat al-mu'addil*) so common in the eastern lands of Islam up to the 9th/15th century.

32. See G. Di Santillana and E. von Dechend, *Hamlet's Mill*.

33. Hermeticism and along with it both astrology and alchemy were integrated on the highest level into certain schools of Sufism because of the contemplative quality of the symbolism inherent in the Hermetic cosmological sciences. For a unique analysis of the integration of astrology into Sufism see T. Burckhardt, *Clé spirituelle de l'astrologie musulmane*, Paris, 1950. On the question of the attitude of various Muslim savants to astrology as well as a thorough discussion of the sources and history of Islamic astrology see M. Ullmann, *Natur- und Geheimwissenschaft im Islam*, chapter 5. See also C. A. Nallino, *Raccolti di scritti editi e inediti*, vol. 5, Rome, 1944.

34. Few facts can be more embarrassing for modernized men, who take pride in the gradual 'evolution' of humanity away from superstition toward rationalistic 'enlightenment', than to witness that the number of works published today in many of the cities of the most industrialized countries of the West, which are citadels of rationalism, on the 'occult sciences', including astrology, is greater than those written on the official sciences.

The sources of Islamic astrology are the well-known Greek works such as those of Dorotheus of Sidon, Ptolemy, Antiochus, Vettius Valens and Teukros along with Sassanid writings which were often Pahlavi translations of the same Greek texts, and Indian astrological writings. The Muslim astrologers had greater information at their disposal and were more exact in assembling their material than their predecessors. But the branches of astrology among Muslims are the same as among the Greeks or ancient Persians. They include judicial astrology, dealing with the prediction of the future of events or institutions, genethliac astrology, dealing with the horoscopes of individuals, and the cosmological aspect of astrology. Many Muslim thinkers were attracted only to the cosmological symbolism of astrology, while the astronomers who were also devoted to astrology often shied away from casting horoscopes and foretelling the futures of individuals.[35] Of course horoscopes *were* made, especially for important historical personages such as kings and viziers; even astrological histories of mankind were attempted, the best known being those of Māshā'allāh and Abū Ma'shar al-Balkhī, who was the most famous of mediaeval astrologers in both the Islamic world and the West.[36] Muslim astronomers also took special advantage of the interest of rulers in astrology to advance the cause of astronomy, as seen so clearly in the roles of al-Bīrūnī and Naṣīr al-Dīn *vis-à-vis* Maḥmūd of Ghazna and Hulāgū, respectively.

At one extreme, astrological symbolism based on the wedding between heaven and earth and a study of the angelic aspect of cosmic reality in determining the course of events in the terrestrial domain became an organic aspect of Islamic metaphysics and cosmology. This aspect of astrology appears in works of authors as diverse as Ibn Sīnā, Suhrawardī and even the Ash'arite theologian Fakhr al-Dīn al-Rāzī. At the other extreme, popular astrology combined with other 'predictive' arts to provide a means for certain people to alleviate their anxieties about the future. In this respect astrology was divided into three branches: questions (*masā'il*) concerning the life and activities of someone who is absent; selecting propitious moments for undertaking an important event in life (*ikhtiyārāt*); and finally foretelling the future of a particular individual.

Plate 85. The horoscope of the Persian Qajar king Fatḥ 'Alī Shāh.

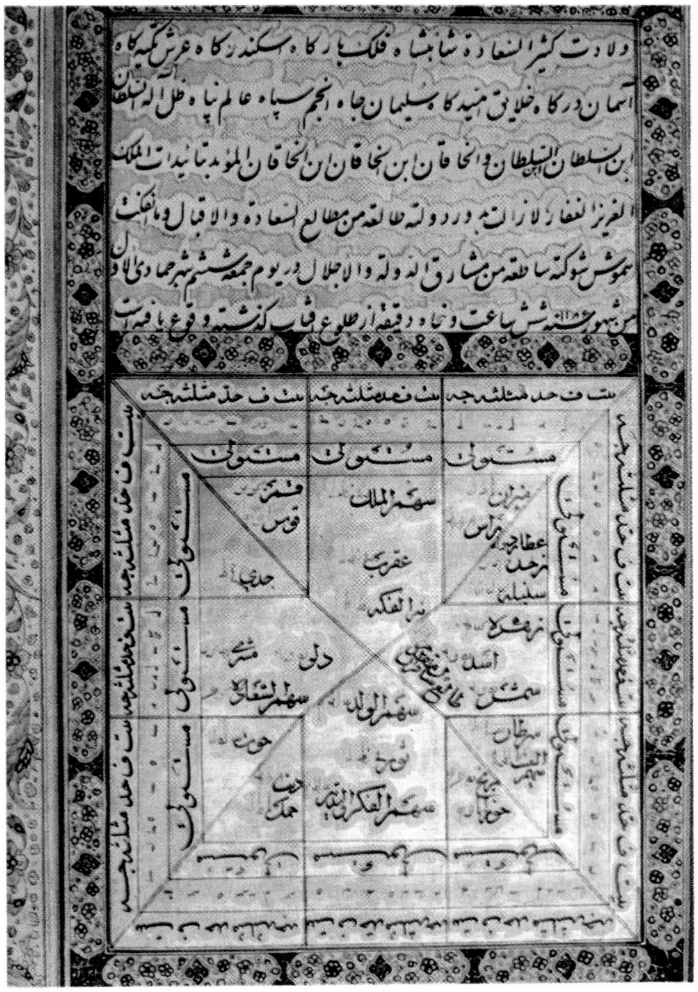

35. Al-Bīrūnī in fact gives detailed astrological reasons why exact predictions cannot be made. On al-Bīrūnī's astrological views see Nasr, *An Introduction to Islamic Cosmological Doctrines*, chapter 9.

36. See Kennedy and Pingree, *The Astrological History of Māshā'allāh*, Cambridge (U.S.A.), 1971; and Pingree, *The Thousands of Abū Ma'shar*.

Plate 86. Page from an astrological treatise describing the influences of the various houses.

ماه چون در عقرب اید نیک باشد کمینه سر
چون زدن داروو قی گردن طعام وعبر ختن
هم جراحت قبت شاید نیم معاجین ساختن
نیم شد ان که ماه هستم برحذم برون ناند
اسب را با در باندن ان دادن باش نکند
لیک دیگر کارها هرکز باشد سود مند

ماه چون در قوس پس ها بند نیک باسه جا کار
اوشش روع وتعلیم اهرش فصادوشکار
هرکه بیع جوهر وجیوان کند نبود دخل
خاصه نوبوشاد برقاضی رود پارد سخل
قرض دادن مستردن یکم کشن بود
ورکسی مسهل جوزد بی شک عدوی خود بود

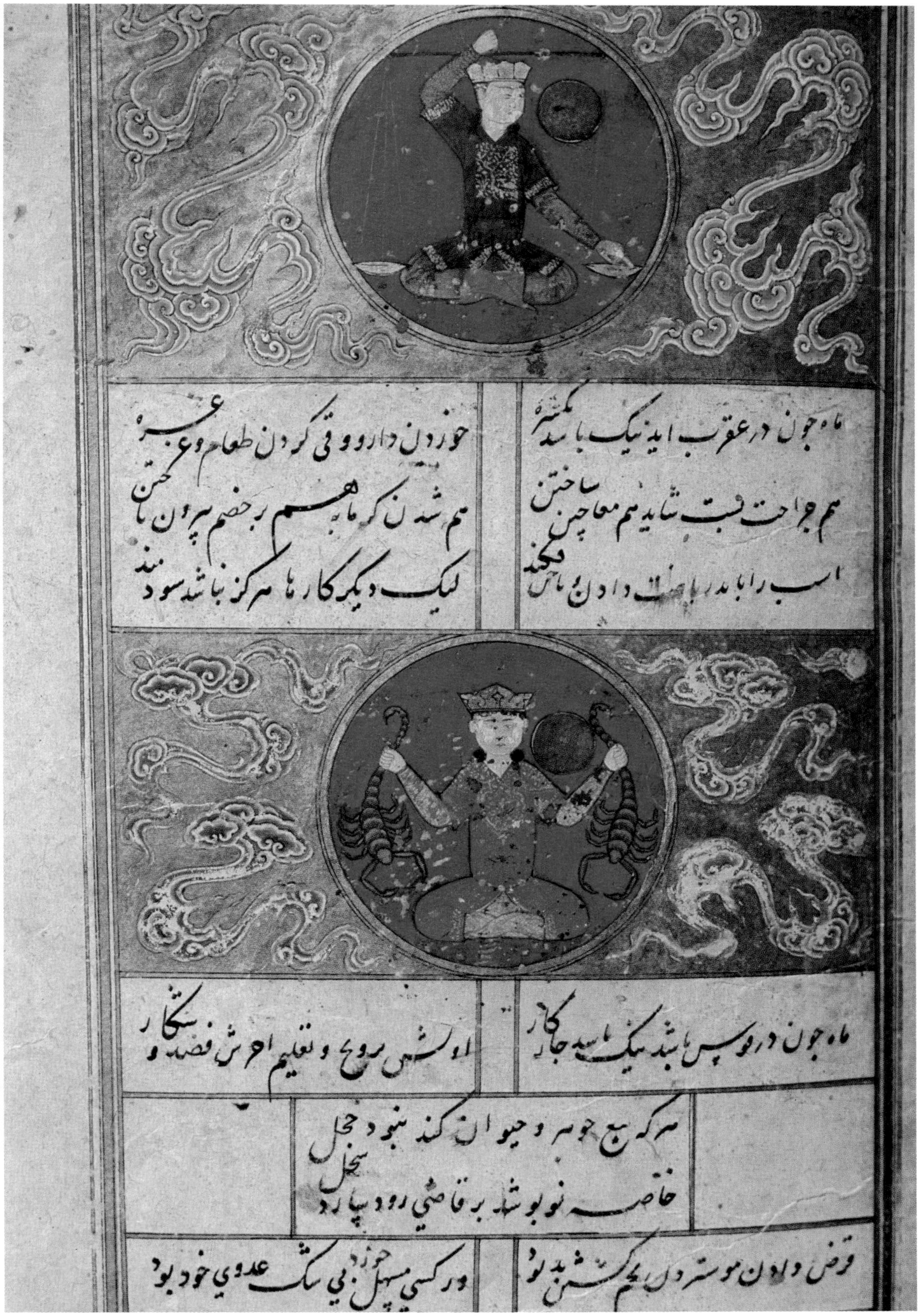

Plate 87. Page from an astrological treatise describing the influence of the various houses.

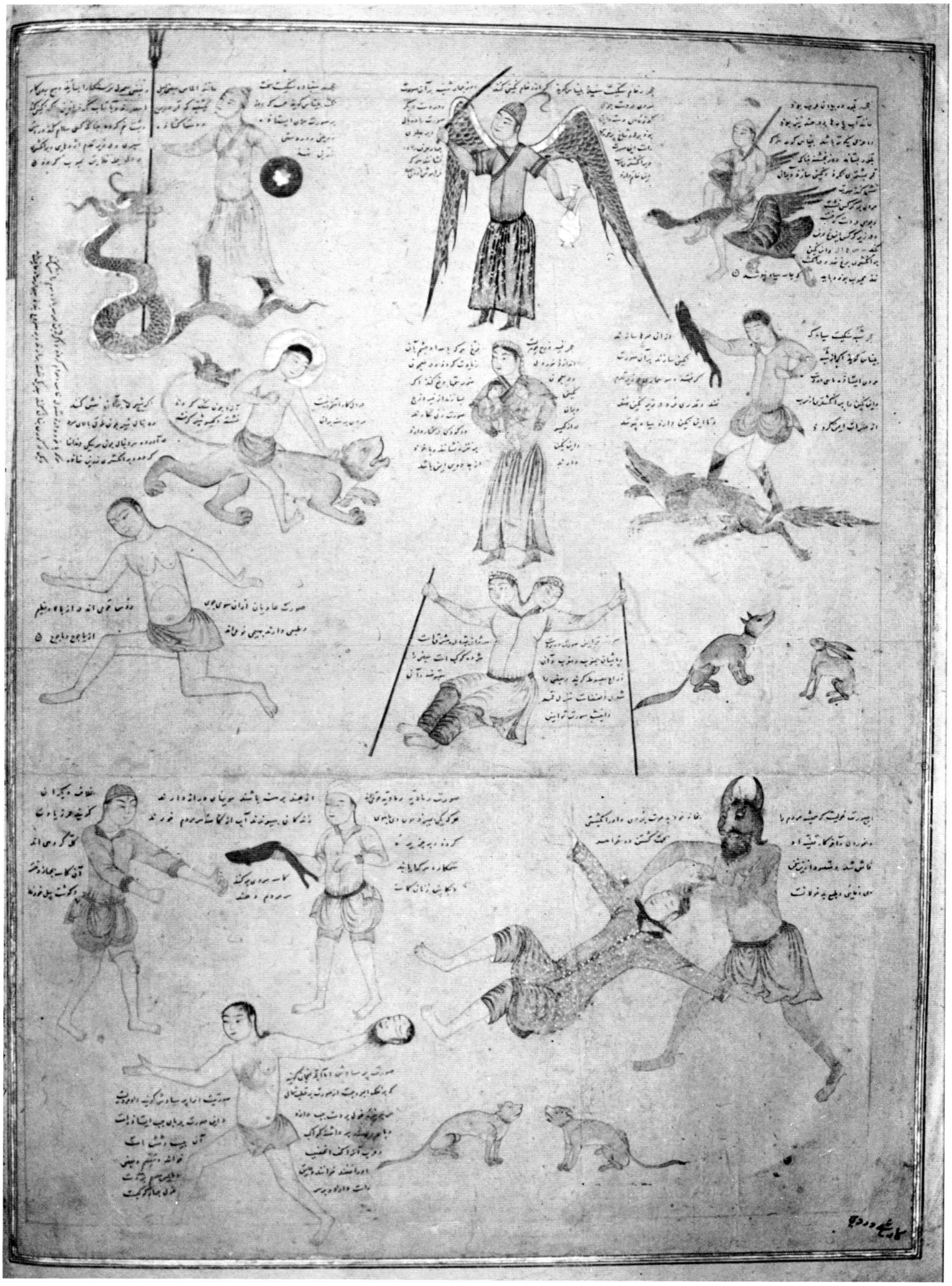

Figure 62

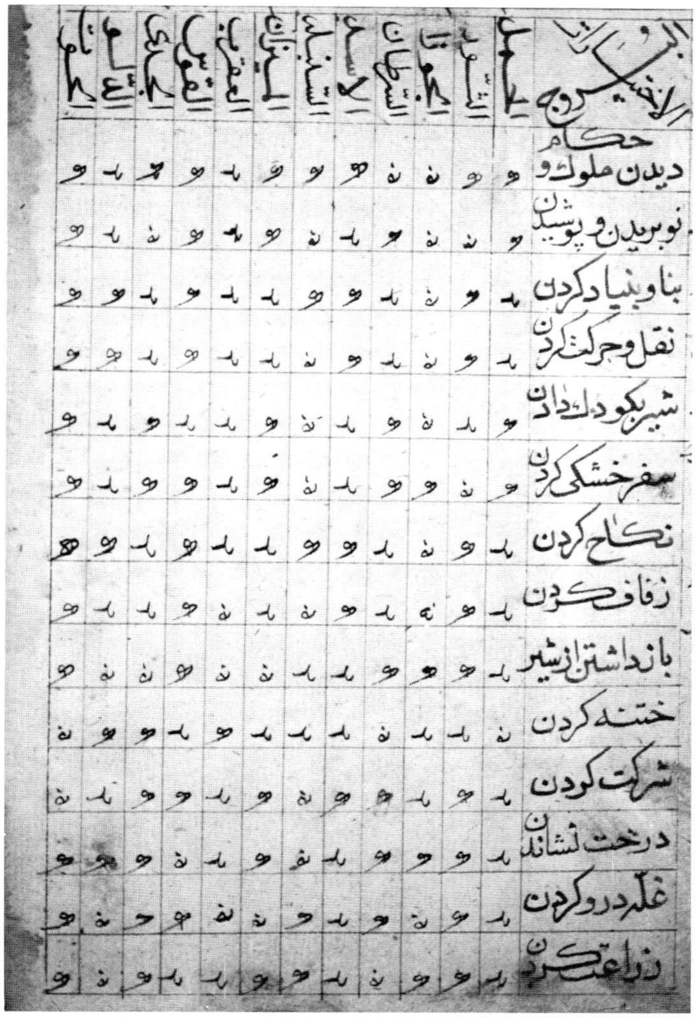

Figure 63. A chart determining astrological influences on various daily actions.

Figure 62. A page from an astrological treatise.

Despite the opposition of religious authorities to the predictive aspect of astrology, its practice has continued far and wide in Islamic civilization over the centuries. Many notable astronomical treatises have astrological sections attached to them and numerous pages of Arabic, Persian, Turkish and other literatures of the Islamic peoples are concerned with the interrelation between man's terrestrial life and celestial influences. But on the highest level, namely in metaphysical and gnostic works, the powerful symbolism of astrology has been integrated perfectly into Islamic esotericism. In these works astrology is revealed to be in its symbolic aspect a means whereby man rediscovers his own cosmic dimension and becomes aware of his own angelic and archetypal reality and the influence of this reality upon his terrestrial existence. This was achieved without in any way destroying or weakening the direct relation which man possesses *vis-à-vis* the metacosmic Reality, which lies at once beyond the Universe and at the centre of his own being.

The Achievements of Islamic Astronomy

It is not easy to evaluate more than a thousand years of activity in the field of astronomy ranging from Spain to India, especially when numerous works remain neglected in various libraries, and writings of even such major figures as Quṭb al-Dīn al-Shīrāzī have not as yet been printed. Nevertheless, as already mentioned, as a result of nearly two centuries of research on Islamic astronomy by Western and Muslim scholars, there have appeared numerous books and articles which reveal at least the main contours of Islamic astronomy although without doubt libraries in various countries still hold many surprises for future scholars.

The first notable feature of Islamic astronomy is of course the vast amount of actual observation that was made of the heavens, far more than was undertaken by the Greeks. The observations of Muslim astronomers dealt with all aspects of astronomical phenomena. Old constants were improved, new star catalogues composed and many new stars discovered,[37] the inclination of the ecliptic was remeasured, the

37. The Islamic contribution to this branch of astronomy is revealed by the number of stars still bearing Arabic names in European languages.

motion of the solar apogee was observed and tied to the movement of the fixed stars (i.e., the gradual precession of the equinox), and other important discoveries concerning the movement of various planets were made.

Another important feature of Islamic astronomy was the new methods of applying mathematics to astronomy. As already mentioned Muslim scientists used the calculus of sines and trigonometry instead of the calculus of chords and were therefore able to achieve much greater precision in their measurements. They also perfected computation techniques dealing with the motion of the planets far beyond anything achieved before.

Islamic astronomy attempted essentially to refine and at the same time criticize Ptolemaic astronomy. It added a ninth heaven to account for diurnal motion and deleted the sphere which Ptolemy had placed at each heaven to communicate diurnal motion. But this criticism went far beyond astronomical intricacies. It involved, as already seen, one type of criticism emanating from the point of view of Aristotelian cosmology and another which was also essentially of a philosophical nature associated with Ṭūsī and his collaborators, who saw as the greatest fault of the Ptolemaic system that the earth was not actually at the centre of the Universe. As a matter of fact the first type of criticism did not produce a

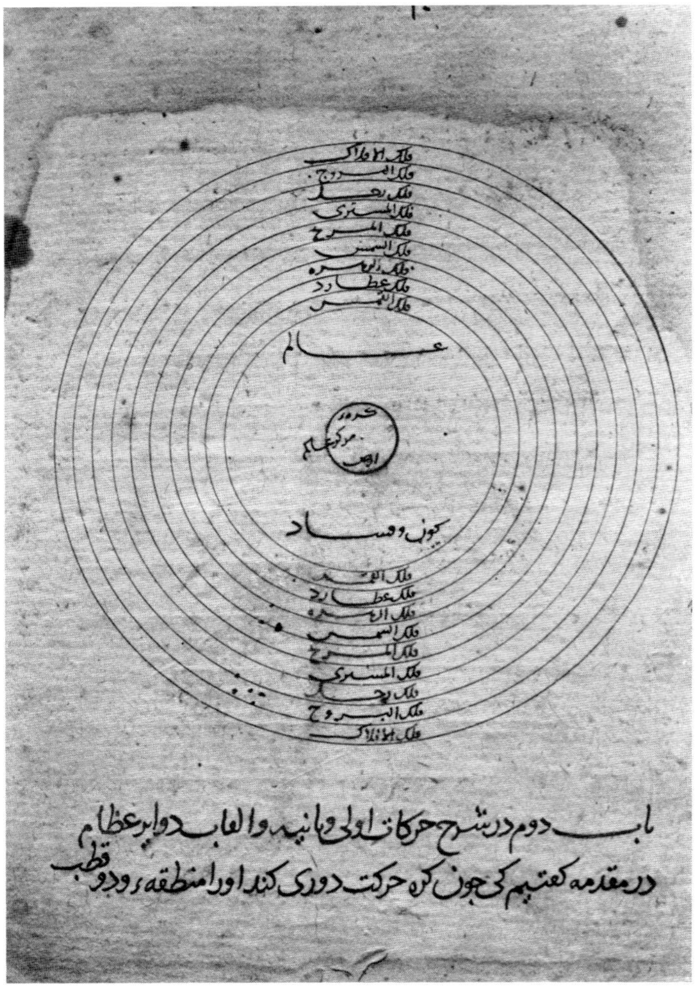

Figure 64. The nine heavens of Islamic astronomy.

Plate 88. The nine heavens of Islamic astronomy.

new mathematical model while the second did; but from the point of view of the history of astronomy, and especially 16th century debates about geocentric astronomy in the West, both are of great importance. The major lesson to learn from this aspect of Islamic astronomy is that Muslims had all the technical knowledge necessary to overthrow the Ptolemaic system, including knowledge of the heliocentric system, but they did not do so because they had not as yet become forgetful of the symbolic content of traditional astronomy nor of the fact that the best way to remind most men of the presence of God is to remind them of the limited character of the created world.

The concern of Muslim astronomers with measuring the size of the Universe was related to this deep insight. Using the principle that there is no 'waste' in the cosmos and that therefore the outer limit of each sphere had to be tangent to the inner limit of the next, and also benefiting from the measurements of Greek astronomers like Hipparchus, Eranosthenes and Ptolemy, they gave tables for distances of planets and the fixed stars.[38] Those of al-Farghānī and al-Bīrūnī were especially famous and those of al-Farghānī in addition influenced Western thinkers for several centuries.

But perhaps the most enduring contribution of Muslims to the history of astronomy was their transforming the Ptolemaic spheres from merely mathematical models to 'physical' realities. It is known that the Greek mathematicians and astronomers spoke of 'saving the phenomena' and saw the role of science as devising models which help to 'save the phenomena' studied.[39] Aristotle was of course opposed to this view but then he did not devise any mathematical models. Already during the Islamic period Thābit ibn Qurrah believed in the 'solidity' of the heavens, while in his very important *Resumé of Astronomy*, which survives today only in Latin and Hebrew translations, Ibn al-Haytham gave actual 'physical' models for the heavens.[40] He was followed in this by Ṭūsī and other eminent astronomers in the East as well as by Western scientists to the extent that in the late Middle Ages and the Renaissance everyone quite naturally thought that the goal of science was to discover some aspect of reality. Even when Galileo and Newton were overthrowing Ptolemaic astronomy and Aristotelian physics they did not think for one moment that they were merely 'saving phenomena'. They believed firmly that they were discovering aspects of physical reality. Their science still had an ontological aspect. It is necessary to study the debates of modern philosophers of science such as Émile Meyerson and Henri Poincaré on the very nature of science to realize how profound was the actual transformation brought about by Muslim astronomers, and especially Ibn al-Haytham, a transformation which changed the role of the mathematically orientated sciences from 'saving the phenomena' to discovering an aspect of reality.

As far as Islamic civilization itself is concerned the achievement of Islamic astronomy was to provide at one extreme for the practical needs of the community by devising calendars, almanacs, treatises to find the direction of the *qiblah* and the like, and at the other extreme a mathematical astronomy of remarkable accuracy. It provided a science which influenced the West

38. On the dimensions of the Universe among Muslims see W. Hartner, 'Mediaeval Views on Cosmic Dimensions and Ptolemy's *'Kitāb al-Manshūrāt'*, *Oriens-Occidens*, pp. 319–348. See also Nasr, *Science and Civilization in Islam*, pp. 182–183. The outer limit of the visible cosmos is given by al-Farghānī as 80.2 million English miles.

39. In his *Hypotheses of the Planets*, Ptolemy speaks of the 'reality' of the heavens, but this is an exception. The main thrust of his other and better known writings as well as those of other Greek mathematical astronomers was to consider the complicated astronomical models no more than mathematical models which helped to compute the motion of the planets and which did not in themselves have any 'reality'.

40. See P. Duhem, *Le système du monde*, vol. II, Paris, 1914, pp. 119ff., where this treatise in its Latin version is analyzed; also Nasr, *Science and Civilization in Islam*, pp. 175–178. As these words were being written one of the scientific journals in the Soviet Union reported the discovery of a treatise by Ibn al-Haytham in Arabic on the nature of the heavens. Perhaps after several centuries the original of this important work has been discovered.

profoundly, which transformed astronomy in India[41] and even added a new chapter to Chinese astronomy.[42] But more than all this it provided a science vast enough to embrace the mathematical genius of a Naṣīr al-Dīn al-Ṭūsī and the poetic vision of a Sanā'ī or an 'Aṭṭār, a science able to depict a cosmos in which eclipses and motions of planets were calculated with all the accuracy needed by a normal human civilization and in which at the same time the sacred horse *al-Burāq* could raise the Holy Prophet in his ascension or *al-mi'rāj* to the Divine Throne (*al-'arsh*), a cosmos where every contemplative following the example of the Holy Prophet could ascend through the power of the Spirit to the heavens and participate in that Divine force which Dante describes as the love that moves the heavens and the stars, *L'Amor che muove il sole e l'altre stelle.*

41. Long before Jai Singh Islamic astronomy had entered into India and had many followers especially during the Mogul period when important works such as the *Zīj-i shāhjahān* by Farīd al-Dīn al-Dihlawī were composed.

42. On the influence of Islamic astronomy and other sciences in China, an influence which took place mostly during the Mongol period, see J. Needham, *Science and Civilization in China*, Vol. 1, Cambridge, 1954, pp. 150ff.

Chapter VII
Physics

The word physics as understood today is of course of relatively recent usage. Sir Isaac Newton still referred to himself as a natural philosopher and in this sense shared a world view common with the Muslim scientists. In the Islamic sciences also there was no separate discipline corresponding to physics in its modern sense. There was natural philosophy (*ṭabīʿiyyāt*) which included the life and the earth sciences as well as physics; and there were certain sciences such as optics which although understood today as branches of physics, were classified by Muslims among the mathematical sciences. It is, therefore, mostly for the sake of the modern reader that such disciplines as optics and the study of machines and automata are discussed in this section rather than elsewhere, so that the reader may gain some inkling of the manner in which Islamic science dealt with what are now called the physical sciences and the range of subjects in this domain with which Muslim scientists were primarily concerned.

The General Principles of Physics

As far as the principles or philosophy of physics and also the philosophy of nature are concerned, numerous Muslim scientists and philosophers dealt extensively with the subject and in fact produced a treasury of thought containing the profoundest philosophy and also theology of nature which is of great pertinence even – and indeed especially – today.[1] The principles of natural philosophy were usually discussed, following Ibn Sīnā, under the heading of *fann al-samāʿ al-ṭabīʿī* (literally 'section dealing with what is "heard" concerning natural philosophy')[2] and the most extensive discussion of the subject in Islam is in fact given by Ibn Sīnā in his *Shifāʾ*.[3] Nearly every major Muslim philosopher, whether specifically interested in physics or not, from al-Kindī to Mullā Ṣadrā and Sabziwārī devoted a section of his writings to it, since in traditional doctrines physics is an application of metaphysics and the principles of physics

1. See Nasr, *The Encounter of Man and Nature*, chap. III.

2. Scholars cannot agree why such a name has been given to this section of natural philosophy. One explanation is that it concerns what the student 'hears' before everything else when studying natural philosophy, hence the term *samāʿ*.

3. We have analyzed this work extensively in our *An Introduction to Islamic Cosmological Doctrines*, chap. 13, 'Principles of Natural Philosophy'.

are to be found solely in metaphysics and nowhere else. Moreover, scientists, theologians and even gnostics were interested in the principles of natural philosophy, in such questions as the nature of time, space, matter and motion. As a result several different schools of thought developed concerning the principles of physics and natural philosophy itself, schools which ranged from those interested in experimenting with natural forces to those which sought to provide a purely symbolical science of the natural world and to aid man in the contemplation of nature as the theophany of the Divine Names and Qualities, of realities which stand above and beyond nature.[4]

The most widespread Muslim school of thought dealing with the principles of natural philosophy is without doubt the Peripatetic, which in this as in other domains saw Aristotle mostly through the eyes of his Alexandrian commentators and in fact followed Aristotle more closely in this field than in other branches of philosophy. The doctrine of hylomorphism, the definition of space as the inner surface of the body which is tangential to the outer surface of the body in question, and the consideration of time as the measure of motion were taken over from Aristotle and given their most extensive treatment by Ibn Sīnā in his *Shifā'* and Naṣīr al-Dīn al-Ṭūsī in his *Sharḥ al-ishārāt wa'l-tanbīhāt* (*Commentary upon the Book of Directives and Remarks*) (of Ibn Sīnā). It was only in the question of motion, and even there in the special problem of projectile motion, that, as we shall shortly observe, even the Muslim Peripatetics criticized Aristotle and developed ideas which had major consequences for the later history of physics.

A second group of Muslim thinkers who produced ideas of great importance in this field were the anti-Peripatetic philosophers and scientists such as Muḥammad ibn Zakariyyā' al-Rāzī (the Latin Rhazes), al-Bīrūnī and Abu'l-Barakāt al-Baghdādī.[5] Each of these men followed an independent line of thought but shared this one feature with the others in the group: he was critical of the prevalent Peripatetic natural philosophy. Al-Rāzī developed an independent cosmology based upon 'the five eternals' (*al-qudamā' al-khamsah*) which included time and space and drew mainly from Manichaean sources as well as from Plato's *Timaeus*. He also developed a special form of atomism which some have considered to have originated in India.[6]

As for al-Bīrūnī, he provided what is perhaps the most devastating criticism of Aristotelian physics of the mediaeval period in the questions and answers he exchanged with Ibn Sīnā on problems of natural philosophy.[7] Al-Bīrūnī criticized many of the fundamental premisses of Aristotelian physics such as hylomorphism, the natural place of objects in the sub-lunary region, the denial of the vacuum, etc., appealing to both reason and observation of the natural phenomena and even to experiment. These questions and answers which contain in fact two sets of questions by al-Bīrūnī and two sets of answers, the first by Ibn Sīnā and the second by his student al-Ma'ṣūmī, are one of the highlights of this aspect of Islamic thought and reveal the profundity with which the basic concepts of the physics of the day were discussed and analyzed.

Al-Baghdādī, the Jewish philosopher who towards the end of his life embraced Islam, was a powerful, original thinker in the domain of natural philosophy. His *Kitāb al-mu'tabar* (*The Book of*

4. On the various perspectives concerning nature in Islam see S. H. Nasr, 'The Meaning of Nature in Various Intellectual Perspectives in Islam', *Islamic Quarterly*, vol. 9, 1965, pp. 25–29.

5. See S. Pines 'Quelques tendences antipéripateticiennes de la pensée scientifique islamique', *Thalès*, vol. 3–4, 1937–1939, pp. 210–220; S. Pines, 'What was New in Islamic Science?' in A. Crombie, (ed.) *Scientific Change*, London, 1963, pp. 181–205. See also H. A. Wolfson, *Crescas' Critique of Aristotle: Problems of Aristotle's Physics in Jewish and Arabic Philosophy*, Cambridge (U.S.A.), 1929, especially chap. III, where anti-Aristotelian ideas in physics among Islamic as well as Jewish philosophers are discussed thoroughly.

6. See S. Pines, *Beiträge zur islamischen Atomenlehre*, Berlin, 1936 (translated into Arabic with extensive new notes by Muḥammad Abū Riḍah, as *Madhhab al-dharrah 'ind al-muslimīn*, Cairo, 1946). This classical work also contains, in addition to an analysis of the atomism of Rāzī, sections on the views of Īrānshahrī, Nāṣir-i Khusraw and other less-studied Islamic philosophers.

7. The Arabic text of this important exchange was edited critically for the first time by S. H. Nasr and M. Mohaghegh as, *al-As'ilah wa'l-ajwibah*, Tehran, 1973. Many of these questions have been translated and analyzed in Nasr, *An Introduction to Islamic Cosmological Doctrines*, pp. 167ff.

What has been Established by Personal Reflection) contains many ideas of interest in physics.[8] He not only continued the criticism against the Aristotelian theory of projectile motion, but also studied the question of acceleration of falling bodies and dealt with time in a new manner, considering it as being related to the very process of becoming rather than to translational motion alone. His speculations on accelerated motion are also amazing for he was perhaps the first person to have rejected the Aristotelian theory that a constant force causes uniform motion with a velocity proportional to the force.

A third and major school of thought directly concerned with the principles of natural philosophy is, strangely enough, that of the theologians (*mutakallimūn*). The theologians, Sunnī and Shī'ite alike, were not especially interested in problems of physics, but each group was drawn into this subject through the implications of its theological studies. The Shī'ite schools, both Ismā'īlī and Twelve-Imām, developed 'philosophies of nature' similar to those found in the philosophical and theosophical schools associated with them. But Sunnī theology, both Mu'tazilite and Ash'arite, developed a distinct atomism which left an indelible mark upon their discussion of the principles of natural philosophy.[9]

Some of the theologians such as the Mu'tazilite al-Naẓẓām and the Ash'arite al-Bāqillānī were more directly interested in questions of physics and others less so. But altogether, the writings of these theological schools contain numerous pages devoted to a 'philosophy of nature' based upon the atomistic point of view. In order to 'safeguard' the Divine Omnipotence these theologians segmented reality in such a way that the only remaining nexus between things was the 'vertical' or Divine Cause, the horizontal cause being totally obliterated.[10] They first of all believed that bodies are composed not of the form and matter of the Peripatetics, but of atoms (in Arabic *juz' lā yatajazzā'*) which are, however, unlike the atoms of Democritus, dimensionless. They also believed that time consists of separate moments and space of discontinuous points. As for projectile motion, they propounded a curious theory called *i'timād* or 'support', according to which the motion of one object by nature engenders the motion of another after it.[11] Altogether, they conceived of a totally atomized world in which only the Divine Will reigns, and where the relation between various objects and events which appear to man to be of a causal nature is seen in fact to be the result of what has been called occasionalism. Fire does not burn because it is in its nature to do so, but because God has willed it. It is only the habit of man's mind to see the burning as an effect of fire. Hence miracles are called events which literally 'break the habit' (*khāriq al-'ādah*) of the mind in its perception of external reality.

The Muslim philosophers and theosophers of nearly all schools rose against this view and defended causality as did most of the Shī'ite theologians. A severe debate took place, the best known chapter of which is that between al-Ghazzālī and Ibn Rushd. The debate involved the whole of philosophy and theology but interestingly enough a central theme that ran throughout concerned physics and especially the nature of causality.[12]

The theologians conceived of atomism in order to assert the Divine Will in the very matrix

8. S. Pines has devoted numerous studies to him. See especially his 'Études sur Awḥad al-Zamān Abu'l-Barakāt al-Baghdādī', *La Revue des Études Juives*, vol. 3, 1938, pp. 3–64, and vol. 4, 1938, pp. 1–33; and also his *Nouvelles études sur Awḥad al-Zamān Abu'l-Barakāt al-Baghdādī*, Paris 1955; also Pines, 'Un précurseur Bagdadien de la théorie de l'impetus', *Isis*, vol. 44, 1953, pp. 247–251.

9. Numerous works have been devoted since the 19th century by Western orientalists to the problem of *Kalām*, in which many of them in fact sought erroneously the equivalent of Christian theology. See for example, L. Gardet and M. M. Anawati: *Introduction à la théologie musulmane*, Paris, 1948; M. Horten, *Die Religiöse Gedankwelt des Volkes in Heutigen Islam*, 2 vols., Halle, 1917–1918; M. Fakhry, *Islamic Occasionalism and its Critique by Averroes and Aquinas*, London 1958; and the numerous studies of H. A. Wolfson, especially his *Crescas' Critique of Aristotle* and *The Philosophy of the Kalam*, Cambridge (U.S.A.), 1974.

10. On the question of causality among Ash'arites, see J. Obermann, 'Das Problem der Kausalität bei den Arabern', in *Festschrift Joseph R. von Karabaček*, Vienna, 1916, pp. 15–42, as well as the already cited works of Wolfson.

11. See S. Pines, 'Études sur Awḥad al-Zamān ...'

12. The arguments of al-Ghazzālī's *Tafāhut al-falāsifah* and Ibn Rushd's *Tahāfut al-tahāfut* are summarized in Nasr, *Science and Civilization in Islam*, pp. 307–321.

of the world which surrounds man and in conformity with a certain 'atomism' associated with the Semitic mentality. Today a great deal of interest is being shown in their ideas because of quite different reasons. David Hume offered nearly the same arguments and in fact gave some of the same examples as the Muslim theologians in his attack upon the notion of causality and began a phase in European thought which, combined with the developments within physics since the beginning of this century, is mostly responsible for the current interest in Ash'arite natural philosophy. But it must be remembered that the Muslim theologians sought to assert the primacy of the Divine Will while Hume and the empiricists wanted to destroy the very power of human reason to perceive causality and refused to have recourse to any higher principle. The results of the two schools stand therefore at the very opposite poles of the intellectual spectrum and should never be confused with each other. Empiricism is closely wedded to modern science while in Islam most of the outstanding scientists were philosophers or Sufis and not theologians. The theologians who negated causality only contributed to the field of science by providing criticism which forced the Muslim philosophers and scientists to develop their own teachings to provide answers for them. They thus played a role of some importance in the Islamic sciences, and especially physics, without, however, providing the background for the development of the sciences in any way comparable to the role of empiricism *vis à vis* modern science in the West.

Yet another school which developed a distinct physics of its own is that of the Illuminationists (*ishrāqīs*). Suhrawardī, the founder of the school, gave the basis for a 'physics of light' in his *Ḥikmat al-ishrāq* (*Theosophy of the Orient of Light*) followed by his commentators, such as Muḥammad al-Shahrazūrī and Quṭb al-Dīn al-Shīrāzī, the latter one of the most outstanding of Muslim physicists. In this school, the Aristotelian theory of hylomorphism is rejected in favour of one in which the very substance of the world is considered to be light, and 'matter' no more than 'darkness' (*ghasaq*) or the absence of light. Suhrawardī also removed the barrier between the sublunar world and the planets and considered the whole region from the fixed stars below to be dominated by the same forces and laws. For him the heavenly part or the 'orient' of the cosmos begins with the region beyond the fixed stars.[13] But more than anything else Suhrawardī developed a symbolic science of the cosmos including of course the natural world which is described with great beauty in his visionary recitals.[14]

Finally, mention must be made of the physics developed by Ṣadr al-Dīn Shīrāzī (Mullā Ṣadrā), the outstanding Safavid theosopher, in his various works, especially the *Asfār al-arba'ah* (*The Four Journeys*) which set the foundation for the school of 'transcendent theosophy' (*al-ḥikmat al-muta'āliyah*). This school, which is still dominant in Persia today, draws heavily upon the Sufism of Ibn 'Arabī as well as earlier schools of Islamic philosophy and theology. Although many works have been devoted to Mullā Ṣadrā during the past two decades, a period which has witnessed a veritable revival of his teachings in Persia and a growing interest in him in the West, still not enough research has been carried out on his specifically cosmological and physical doctrines and theories.[15] Here, suffice it to say that Mullā Ṣadrā developed the idea of trans-substantial motion (*al-ḥarakat al-jawhariyyah*) which in contrast to Aristotelian physics made motion a property of the substance of physical objects and not only of their accidents. Hence, the whole question of motion and time as well as mechanics and

13. Concerning the doctrines of Suhrawardī, see H. Corbin's two prolegomenas to his edition of Suhrawardī, *Opera Metaphysica et Mystica*, vols. I and II, Istanbul, 1945 and Tehran-Paris, 1952; his *En Islam iranien*, Vol. II, Paris 1971; S. H. Nasr, *Three Muslim Sages*, chapter II; and Nasr, 'Suhrawardi', in M. M. Sharif (ed.), *A History of Muslim Philosophy*, Vol. I, pp. 372–388.

14. The original text edited by S. H. Nasr as *Opera Metaphysica et Mystica*, vol. III, Tehran–Paris, 1970. A French translation of the whole series by H. Corbin and an English translation by L. Bakhtiyar are to be published soon.

15. On Mullā Ṣadrā see Corbin, *En Islam iranien*, vol. IV, pp. 54–122; S. H. Nasr, 'Ṣadr al-Dīn Shīrāzī' in Ṣharif (ed.), *A History of Muslim Philosophy*, Vol. II, pp. 932–961, and the numerous works of Sayyid Jalāl al-Dīn Āshtiyānī on him in Persian. Also one work of some value in Persian has been devoted to his natural philosophy by A. Mishkāt al-dīnī, *Ta'thīr wa mabādī-yi ān yā kulliyāt-i falsafa-yi tabī'ī-yi Ṣadr al-Dīn Shīrāzī*, Mashhad, 1347 (A.H. solar), Tehran, 1349 (A.H. solar), but without serious consideration of the development of physics in either East or West. Two extensive works on Mullā Ṣadrā in English are now being completed by F. Rahman and S. H. Nasr.

dynamics was seen in a new perspective. He even spoke of the three dimensions of space and time as the four dimensions determining physical existence. He also divorced the arguments of traditional metaphysics from their reliance upon Ptolemaic astronomy and in this way safeguarded this perennial wisdom from the types of attack made upon it in the West by those who had rejected the Ptolemaic cosmos for astronomical reasons and did not have the perspicacity to understand its symbolic significance beyond purely astronomical considerations. The 'natural philosophy' developed by Mullā Ṣadrā is one of the last monuments of Islamic thought in this domain, and of great import in the present-day impasse which modern science faces precisely because of the lack of a natural philosophy which would do justice to the reality and fullness of the natural world.

Mechanics and Dynamics

From the point of view of the later development of physics the contribution of Muslims to the whole question of force and motion is of great importance and has come to occupy a central position in the concerns of Western historians of science. Ever since the pioneering works of P. Duhem and E. Mach, followed by the research of such scholars as A. Meier, E. J. Dijksterhuis, J. Murdoch and others, have made known the importance of late Scholastic works in the criticism of Aristotelian physics and in providing the roots for many of the ideas of Galileo and Newton, an even greater degree of interest has been shown in the works of Islamic authors who in turn influenced the late Scholastics.

The Muslim philosophers and scientists developed several concepts of major importance concerning the problem of motion. Following the criticism by the Christian philosopher John Philoponos of Aristotle's theory of motion, Ibn Sīnā developed the concept of *mayl* (literally inclination, the Latin *inclinatio*) to explain projectile motion, this weakest link in Aristotelian physics. John Philoponos had asserted that the force which causes projectile motion imparts to the moving body a motive force which the Latins called *impetus*, a force which is gradually spent when a body moves in a void so that the movement comes to an end, contrary to Aristotle's assertion that there would be no way to stop projectile motion in a void. Ibn Sīnā developed this idea for projectile motion encountering resistance such as air and is responsible for the *inclinatio* theory which was further elaborated by Abu'l-Barakāt al-Baghdādī and which also became known to the Scholastics. In his *Pisan Dialogue* Galileo makes use of the impetus theory which goes back originally to John Philoponos and which owes its development to several Muslim figures, especially those already mentioned.

A second important concept which was developed by the Muslims is that of momentum, described by Ibn al-Haytham in his *Kitāb al-manāẓir* (*Optical Thesaurus*) and called *quwwat al-ḥarakah*.[16] Considering the significance of this concept and its persistence throughout all the cycles of the history of physics even to the modern period, the contribution of Ibn al-Haytham and other Muslim physicists who developed this concept becomes clear.

Yet another Muslim contribution of note is what has become known in the West as 'Avempacean dynamics' since it is associated with the name of the Andalusian philosopher Ibn Bājjah (the Latin Avempace). Again in his *Pisan Dialogue*, in criticizing the Aristotelian theory according to which if V = velocity, P = motive power and M = the resisting medium, then $V = P/M$, Galileo asserts that $V = P - M$ so that in a vacuum where $M = 0$ the velocity does not become infinite.[17] Actually Galileo was basing himself upon Ibn Bājjah who became known to the West through Ibn Rushd's quotation of his views while the latter was commenting upon Book IV of the *Physics* of Aristotle.

The Muslims also made extensive studies of gravity and such men as Ibn Sīnā, Ibn al-Haytham, Abu'l-Barakāt, Fakhr al-Dīn al-Rāzī and Ibn Bājjah presented ideas of great interest on the subject. The Muslims knew that the

16. See Jalāl Shawqī, *Turāth al-'arab fi'l-mīkānīkā*, Cairo, 1973, p. 51. Ibn al-Haytham also made other important contributions to physics. He studied the laws of motion, knew the principle of inertia, and conceived of the void and space in a manner reminiscent of the 17th century physicists who developed classical mechanics and dynamics. The work of Shawqī summarizes most of these discussions in the writings of Ibn al-Haytham, Ibn Sīnā and other Muslim scientists. See also Nasr, *Science and Civilization in Islam*, pp. 313–316.

17. See E. A. Moody, 'Galileo and Avempace', *Journal of the History of Ideas*, vol. XII, no. 2, 1951, pp. 163–193; no. 3. 1951, pp. 375–422.

acceleration of a body falling under the force of gravity did not depend upon its mass and also qualitatively that the power of attraction between two bodies increased as their distance decreased and as their mass increased.[18] Moreover, Ibn Bājjah conceived of gravitation as an inner form which moved bodies from within in the same way that the intelligences moved the heavens. His arguments again found their echoes in Galileo.

Altogether the Muslims made important contributions to various branches of mechanics and dynamics, departing in many ways from Aristotelian physics and even developing such cardinal concepts as momentum. They, however, never quantified physics completely nor ignored the symbolic nature of the natural world. Even their quantitative studies moved within the orbit of a cosmos which remained hierarchic, with each level of existence symbolizing the states above. They were moreover able to achieve what they did from the point of view of the history of physics without bringing about the calamities caused directly or indirectly by Galileo and his followers because the science developed by these Muslim figures always remained bound within the hierarchy of knowledge. The greatest of Muslim physicists like al-Bīrūnī, Ibn al-Haytham and Quṭb al-Dīn al-Shīrāzī accepted willingly this hierarchy and never attempted to make a quantitative science of the Universe central or relegate to the periphery the qualitative science of things which is the most essential precisely because at its highest level it alone can deal with the essences of things.[19]

Optics

One of the fields of physics to which Muslims made important contributions is optics, and that mostly thanks to Ibn al-Haytham who in the 4th/10th century established this science upon new foundations and made of it an organized discipline, hence gaining the title of 'father of optics'. Before Ibn al-Haytham, several Muslim scientists had been concerned with optics, but following mostly the Greek sources such as Aristotle, Euclid, Heron, Archimedes, Ptolemy and Theon with which they were well acquainted. Already al-Kindī had written a work on optics based upon Euclid which in its Latin translation as *De Aspectus* first introduced Euclid's *Optics* to the West. Al-Kindī also wrote a treatise explaining the reason for the blueness of the sky.

Others after al-Kindī such as al-Nayrīzī who studied atmospheric phenomena and Ibn Sīnā and al-Bīrūnī who discussed the finiteness of the speed of light contributed to optics while such physicians as Ḥunayn ibn Isḥāq and al-Rāzī studied the anatomy and physiology of the eye. But it was Ibn al-Haytham who brought about a major transformation in the whole of this science and who made so many discoveries that he has been called the most important student of optics between Euclid and Kepler. Some have also considered him the greatest of the Muslim physicists, taking the latter term in its modern sense. Ibn al-Haytham wrote numerous works on optics and related subjects such as atmospheric phenomena, some of these, like the treatise on twilight, having also been translated into Latin.[20] But his major opus on the subject, which is also the most important mediaeval work on optics, is the *Kitāb al-manāẓir* (*Optical Thesaurus*), first published in Basle in 1572. Not only did this work influence earlier authors such as Witelo, Roger Bacon and Peckham, but its effect is even to be seen in the optical works of Kepler and Newton. His Latin name, Alhazen, was as familiar to students of optics in the West as that of Euclid.

The *Kitāb al-manāẓir*, in which Ibn al-Haytham reveals his competence in medicine as well as physics, begins by studying the anatomy and physiology of the eye. He traces the functioning of the eye from the optic nerve originating in the brain to the eye itself, whose various parts, such as the conjunctive, iris, cornea and lens, he describes in a masterly fashion, pointing out the

18. See Shawqī, *op. cit.*, pp. 75ff.

19. On this question, see Nasr, *op. cit.*, pp. 144–145.

20. Many studies exist on Ibn al-Haytham and his optics in European languages. See M. Schramm, *Ibn al-Haitam, Zur Weg der Physik*, Wiesbaden, 1963; also A. I. Sabra, 'Explanation of Optical Reflection and Refraction: Ibn al-Haytham, Descartes, Newton', in *International Congress on the History of Science*, Ithaca, vol. 26, 1962, pp. 551–554; H. J. J. Winter and W. 'Arafat, 'A Discourse on the Concave Spherical Mirror by Ibn al-Haitham', *Journal of the Royal Asiatic Society of Bengal*, vol. XVI, no. 1, 1950, pp. 1–16; Hakim Muhammad Said (ed.), *Ibn al-Haitham*, Karachi, 1970; and the still-valuable Arabic work of Muṣṭafā Naẓīf Bey, *al-Ḥasan ibn al-Haytham wa buḥūthuh*, 2 vols., Cairo, 1942–1943.

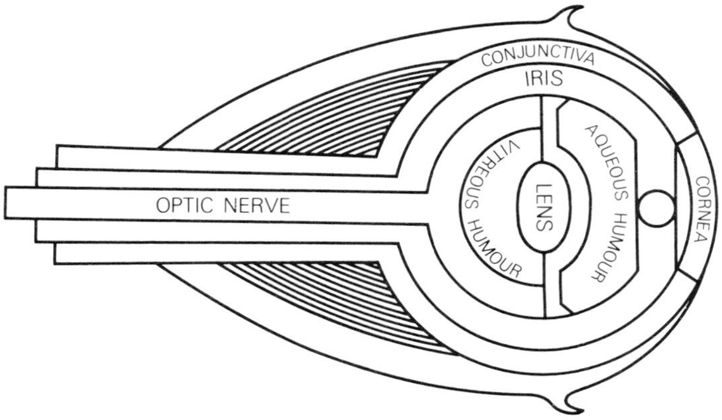

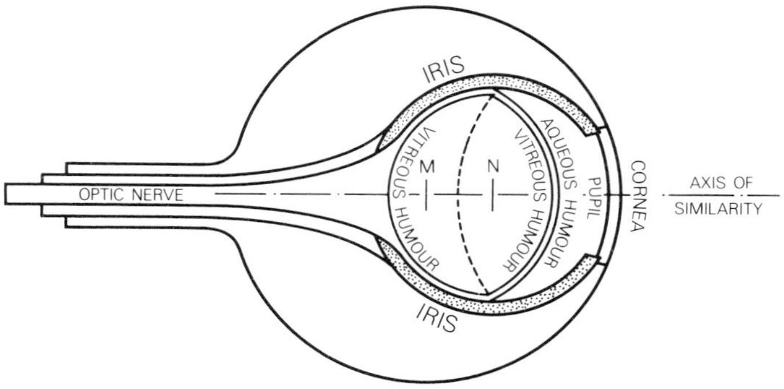

Figures 65a and 65b. The anatomy of the eye according to Ibn al-Haytham.

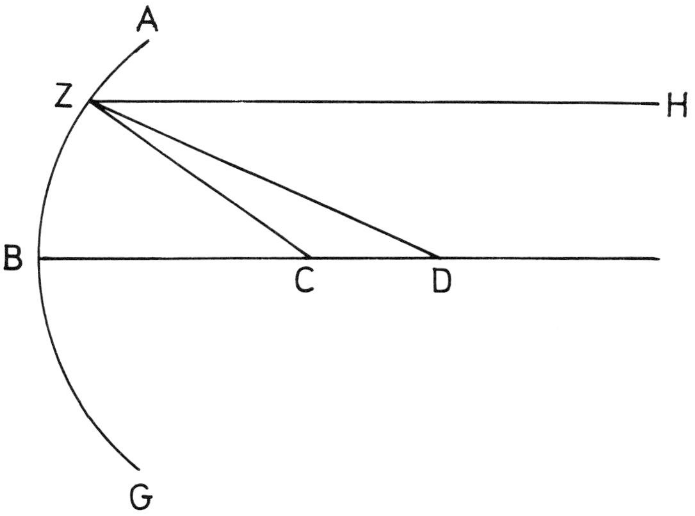

Figure 66. Alhazen's problem.

role of each in vision. He also shows the interrelation between the various parts of the eye and how the eye acts as a unitary organ and dioptric system during the process of vision. Ibn al-Haytham, like Ibn Sīnā and several other Muslim scientists, did not hold that rays issue from the eye but believed that during the process of vision rays of light reach the eye from the object which is seen.

Ibn al-Haytham made contributions to catoptrics and dioptrics as well as to the study of atmospheric phenomena. As far as catoptrics is concerned, during the period from Euclid to Theon numerous mathematicians and physicists had made notable contributions to the subject. Ibn al-Haytham continued their studies but concentrated his efforts especially in the study of parabolical and spherical mirrors, including their aberration. The problem which in fact has come to be known by his name to this day – Alhazen's problem – concerns a spherical mirror: given a spherical mirror with an object and its image reflected in the mirror, find the point of reflection. The solution of this problem leads to a fourth degree equation which Ibn al-Haytham solved by geometric means. The same problem was solved several centuries later by Huygens algebraically. In the field of catoptrics Ibn al-Haytham was the first to demonstrate the second law of reflection, namely that the incident ray, the normal and the reflected rays are in the same plane.

As far as the study of refraction is concerned, Ibn al-Haytham made many more original contributions. Perhaps the most important of these is that a ray of light takes the easier and quicker path, a thesis which enunciates the principle of 'least time' associated with the name of Fermat. Ibn al-Haytham also applied the rectangle of velocities at the surface of refraction long before Newton and only failed to discover Snell's Law because he was used to calculating by means of chords rather than sine functions. Ibn al-Haytham also made numerous experiments with glass cylinders immersed in water to study refraction and also sought to determine the magnifying power of lenses.

As far as atmospheric phenomena are concerned, as mentioned in the chapter on astronomy, Ibn al-Haytham's studies were of major importance for both astronomical observations and meteorology. He determined the thickness of the atmosphere, the effect of the atmosphere upon observation of celestial phenomena, the beginning and end of twilight (it begins and ends when the sun is 19° below the horizon), the reason why the sun and the moon are larger on the horizon than in the middle of the sky and many other optical effects of the atmosphere and related phenomena. His contributions to this domain are of no less interest than those in pure optics.

Ibn al-Haytham was at once philosopher, mathematician and experimentalist. He devised a lathe with the help of which he made lenses for his experiments. He studied the *camera obscura* mathematically for the first time and made an experiment which also for the first time made possible the experimental demonstration that light travels in a straight line. He was able to plan experiments carefully and at the same time analyze problems mathematically. That is why he is considered such an outstanding physicist by contemporary historians of science. Yet, even Ibn al-Haytham moved within the matrix of the Islamic intellectual universe. He was also a philosopher of note, a man who, while performing experiments on light, never forgot that 'God is the light of the heavens and the earth.'

Strangely enough, during the period immediately following Ibn al-Haytham, no work comparable to his in stature appeared in the realm of optics. Even the great Naṣīr al-Dīn al-Ṭūsī in his commentary upon Euclid's *Optics* ignored all that Ibn al-Haytham had done. But probably because of the spread, at that time, in Persia, of the school of Illumination (*ishrāq*), which is based upon light, a renewal of interest in optics is to be observed in the 7th/13th century leading to major new discoveries. Quṭb al-Dīn al-Shīrāzī, Naṣīr al-Dīn's associate at Maraghah, discussed Ibn al-Haytham's views in his treatment of optics in his *Nihāyat al-idrāk*. Moreover, Quṭb al-Dīn himself made a special study of the rainbow and was the first to give a qualitatively correct explanation of it.

In Antiquity, Aristotle and Seneca had tried to explain the rainbow, but unsuccessfully. Quṭb al-Dīn, aware of this as well as earlier Muslim scientists' efforts, applied the optics of Ibn al-Haytham to explain the cause of the rainbow as a combination of reflection and refraction through drops of water. His own student, Kamāl al-Dīn al-Fārsī, who wrote the most important commentary upon Ibn al-Haytham entitled *Tanqīḥ al-manāẓir* (*The Revision of the Optics*), followed Quṭb al-Dīn's ideas and made an experiment based upon them. He suspended a spherical glass in a dark room and studied the effect of rays of light cast upon the sphere through a hole. He discovered that the primary rainbow is caused by two refractions and one reflection and the secondary rainbow by two refractions and two reflections.[21] Meanwhile in the Occident Theodore of Freibourg was also applying the fruits of Ibn al-Haytham's discoveries to the problem of the rainbow and making the same discoveries as Kamāl al-Dīn.

21. See E. S. Kennedy, 'The Exact Sciences', in *The Cambridge History of Iran*, vol. 5, p. 676; and the several studies of Wiedemann in the *Aufsätze . . .*, especially 'Über die Brechung des Lichtes in Kugeln nach Ibn al-Haitam und Kamâl al Dîn al Fârisî, *Aufsätze . . .*, vol. I, pp. 597–640. It is of interest to note also the original work done on the physics of the rainbow by Shihāb al-Dīn al-Qarāfī in his *Kitāb al-istibṣār fī mā tudrikuhu'l-abṣār* (*The Scrutinization of what the Eyes Perceive*). See A. Sayīlī, 'Al-Qarāfī and his Explanation of the Rainbow', *Isis*, vol. 32, 1940, pp. 16–26. For the history of the discovery of the cause of the rainbow, see C. B. Boyer, *The Rainbow from Myth to Mathematics*, New York, 1959.

The Balance and the Measurement of Specific Densities

As a major civilization concerned with trade and daily transactions in all their different facets, the Muslims naturally devoted a great deal of attention to the question of weights and measures (*al-awzān wa'l-maqādīr*), to which in fact a special branch of the Sacred Law (*Sharī'ah*) is devoted. In the traditional Muslim city, a person is chosen with the specific duty of controlling the correct use of various units in commercial transactions, the title given to such a person being in Arabic *muḥtasib*, literally 'he who reckons'. Numerous means for measuring different commodities were invented or adopted from earlier civilizations, some of them surviving to this day in certain parts of the Islamic world.[22] But this whole question is perhaps of greater concern to the student of economic and commercial aspects of Islamic civilization than to the sciences as such, although the determination of various units of measurement is of course also basic to any study of the sciences making use of these measurements.

There is one aspect of this question, however, to which Muslims devoted a great deal of attention beyond everyday commercial needs, and that is the development of the balance (*al-mīzān*) as a scientific instrument to measure the specific weight of various metals, minerals and alloys. The writings of Archimedes, as already mentioned, were well known to Muslims and therefore they were fully aware of the Archimedes principle. From the time of al-Ma'mūn, the balance was developed to make use of this principle to measure specific weights. Al-Bīrūnī is noted for his careful measurements of the specific weights of several metals and minerals in his *Kitāb al-jawāhir*.[23] Khayyām wrote a treatise on the subject as did Abū Ḥātim al-Isfazārī. But the most famous treatise on the subject is the *Kitāb mīzān al-ḥikmah* (*The Book of the Balance of Wisdom*) of 'Abd al-Raḥmān al-Khāzinī, a book whose very title evokes the idea of the cosmic balance of Jābir ibn Ḥayyān. Al-Khāzinī made use of the works of Archimedes as well as his Muslim predecessors such as al-Nayrīzī and especially al-Bīrūnī to develop the balance as a refined instrument for the measurement of specific weights.[24] He was even aware of the role of heat in affecting the density of objects.

The famous *eureka* story of Archimedes is mentioned by al-Khāzinī and, basing himself on the Archimedes principle, he developed a formula for determining the respective weights of gold and silver in an alloy made of the two metals. If $X=$ the weight of the silver in the alloy; $A=$ the absolute weight of the alloy; $S=$ the specific gravity of the alloy; $d_1=$ the specific gravity of gold; and $d_2=$ the specific gravity of the silver, then:[25]

$$X=A\frac{\frac{1}{d_1}-\frac{1}{S}}{\frac{1}{d_1}-\frac{1}{d_2}}$$

The treatise of al-Khāzinī shows that the Muslim physicists could make careful measurements of the specific weight as well as the absolute weight of any body composed of either one or two simple substances. Little further refinement was made upon al-Khāzinī's treatise in later centuries, but fine balances both accurate and of artistic beauty have continued to be made almost to the present day throughout the Islamic world.

22. The whole question of weights and measures in Islam has been treated by numerous authors. As far as the history of Islamic science is concerned, those of Wiedemann in the *Aufsätze* . . . are of particular importance. See also W. Hinz, *Islamische Masse und Gewichte umgechnet ins metrische System*, Leiden, 1970.

23. See Wiedemann, 'Über die Waage des Wechselns von al Châzini und über die Lehre von den Proportionen nach al Bîrûnî', *Aufsätze* . . ., vol. II, pp. 215–229; Wiedemann, 'Über die Kenntnisse der Muslime auf dem Gebiet der Mechanik und Hydrostatik', *Archiv für Geschichte der Naturwissenschaften*, 1910, vol. II, pp. 394–398; and several other studies on the subject in the *Aufsätze*. . . . For a comparison of the values attained by al-Bīrūnī and al-Khāzinī with modern ones see Nasr, *Science and Civilization in Islam*, p. 140.

24. This important treatise on statics and especially hydrostatics was made known to the West in the 19th century through the translation of N. Khanikoff, 'The Book of the Balance of Wisdom', *Journal of the American Oriental Society*, 1860, pp. 1–128. See also E. Wiedemann, '*al-Mīzān*' in the old *Encyclopaedia of Islam*.

25. See Nasr, *Science and Civilization in Islam*, pp. 143–144; M. Clagett, *The Science of Mechanics in the Middle Ages*, Madison (Wisconsin), 1959, p. 65.

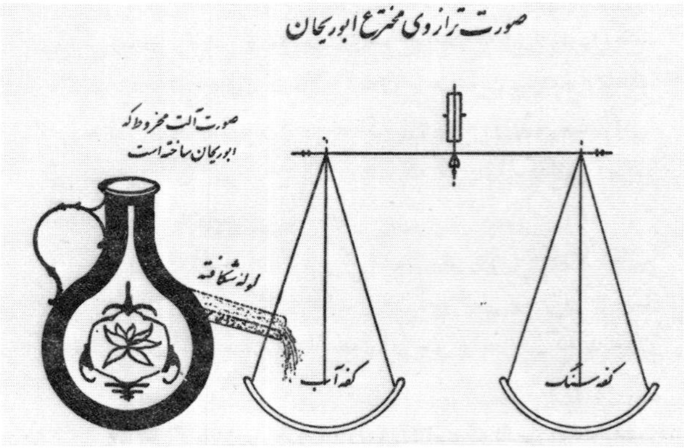

Figure 67a

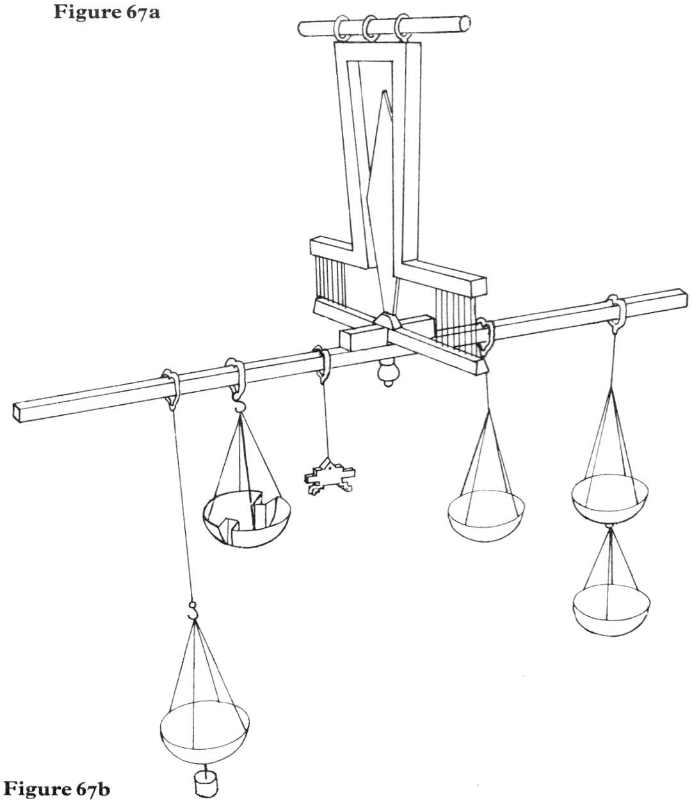

Figure 67b

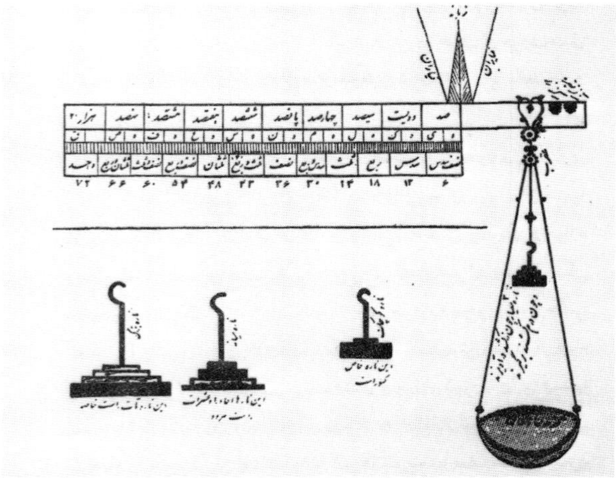

Figure 68

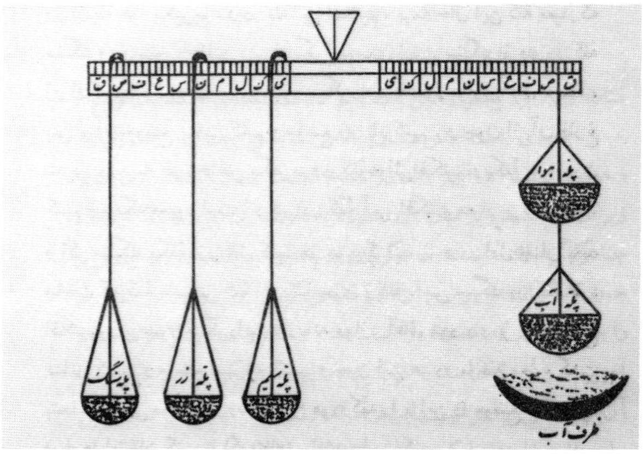

Figures 68 and 69. The balance of al-Khāzinī.

Figures 67a and 67b. Sketch of the balance made by al-Bīrūnī.

Simple Machines and Mechanical Gadgets

Many of the Muslim scientists also devoted themselves to the study of the laws of simple machines, basing themselves on both the Archimedean and the pseudo-Aristotelian schools, the latter associated with the *Mechanica*.[26] They also knew the *Mechanica* of Hero of Alexandria and the *Pneumatica* of Philo of Byzantium. These and other Greek and Alexandrian works served as the basis for their research in this domain.

As far as laws of simple machines are concerned, as early as the 3rd/9th century Thābit ibn Qurrah wrote his famous work on the lever which has come to be known in the West as *Liber Karatonis* and in which he sought to derive the law of the lever from the principles of dynamics following the pseudo-Aristotelian tradition rather than Archimedes. In Baghdad the same interests were pursued by the Banū Mūsā and other mathematicians and from that period onward numerous works appeared dealing with the subject. Even al-Khāzinī's already cited work on the

26. On this subject, see Wiedemann, 'Zur Mechanik und Technik bie den Arabern', *Aufsätze . . .*, vol. I, pp. 173–228. Wiedemann has devoted numerous other studies to this subject in the collection of the *Aufsätze. . . .*

balance is as important for the study of centres of gravity of various bodies as it is for hydrostatics.

Besides works concerned with physical laws of levers, wheels, etc., there also appeared a series of writings on various mechanical devices, gadgets, automata, etc., again following the Alexandrian school. This branch of science is called *'ilm al-ḥiyal* in Arabic and has always been related in the Muslim mind with the occult sciences and magic, as the word itself whose root means stratagem or ruse, shows. From the treatise of the Banū Mūsā on the balance (*qarasṭūn*), those attributed to Ibn Sīnā such as the *Mi'yār al 'uqūl* (*The Standard of the Intelligences*) (but written by his students), to the work of the 7th/13th century author Ibn al-Sā'ātī who described the clock of Damascus, there appeared a series of works describing complicated machines and gadgets which caught the imagination of Muslims as being concerned with the unusual and in fact with what lies for the most part outside the normal preoccupations of men. This type of work culminated in the well-known work of Badī' al-Zamān Ismā'īl ibn Razzāz Abu'l-'Izz al-Jazarī *Kitāb fī ma'rifat al-ḥiyal al-handasiyyah* (*The Book of Knowledge of Ingenious Mechanical Devices*) which, because of the variety of its content and its beautifully illustrated manuscripts found in relative profusion, has become the best-known work of its kind in the West.[27] In this work, which consists of six parts, fifty complicated mechanical devices such as clepsydras and fountains, some of practical use and others more for amusement, are described, following again the tradition of the Alexandrians. Even after al-Jazarī, interest in such problems continued, some scientists like Qayṣar al-Ḥanafī writing works of a more practical concern, for example his treatise on the water wheel;[28] others, like some of the Safavid and Ottoman authors, writing on automata and the like which were a source of wonder and served as pastimes for princes and rulers. Al-Jazarī's own treatise was translated from Arabic into Persian as late as the 13th/19th century.

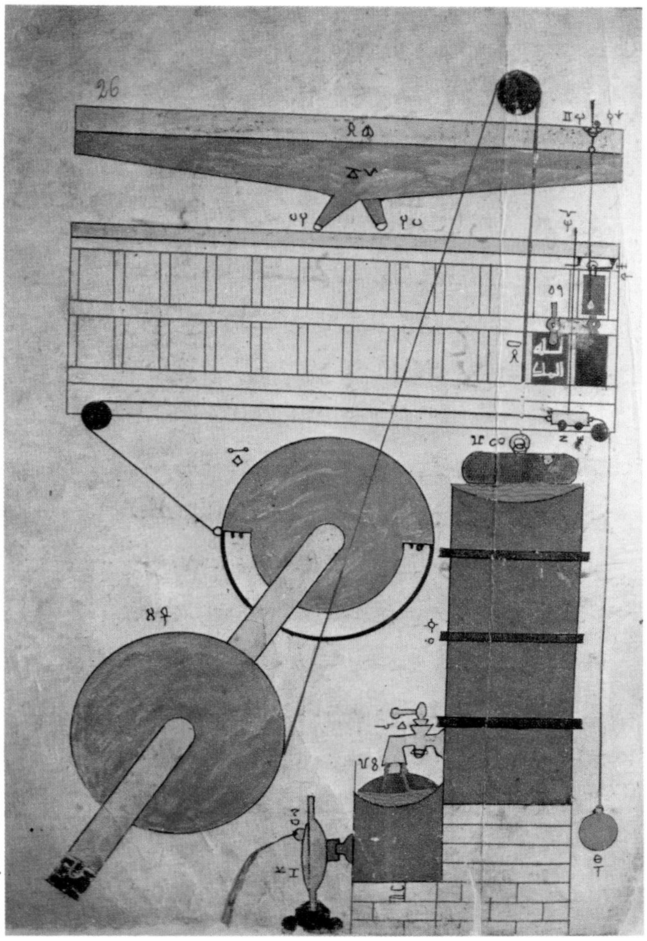

Plate 89. A mechanical device from al-Jazarī.

27. See A. K. Coomaraswamy *The Treatise of al-Jazarī on Automata*, Boston, 1924; and D. Hill, *The Book of Knowledge of Ingenious Mechanical Devices*, Dordrecht–Boston, 1974. The work has also been translated and analyzed in German by E. Wiedemann in the *Nova Acta* and several other journals. See Sarton, *Introduction* . . ., vol. II, part II, p. 633.

28. Al-Ḥanafī is also responsible for the famous celestial globe which is now to be found in the Naples Museum.

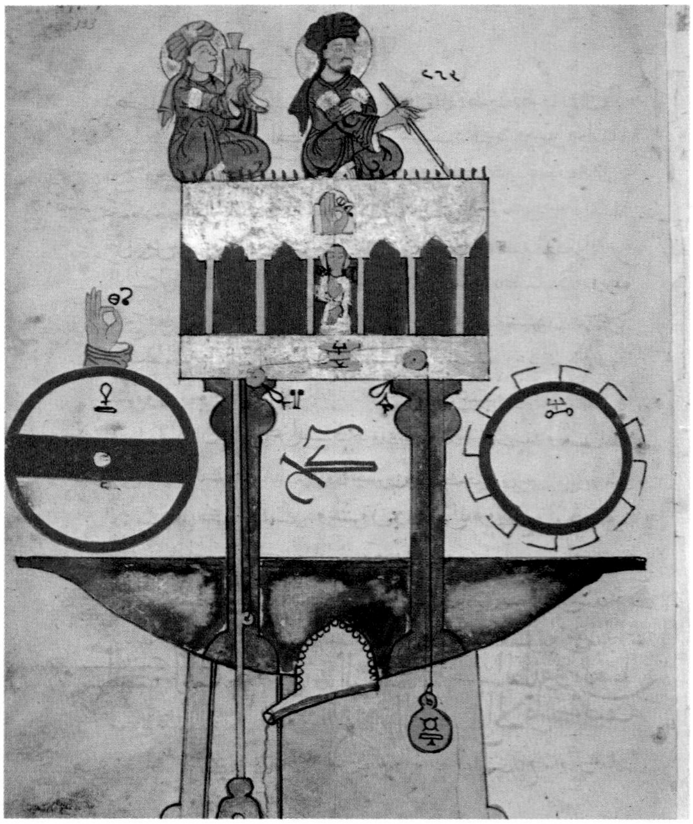

Plate 90

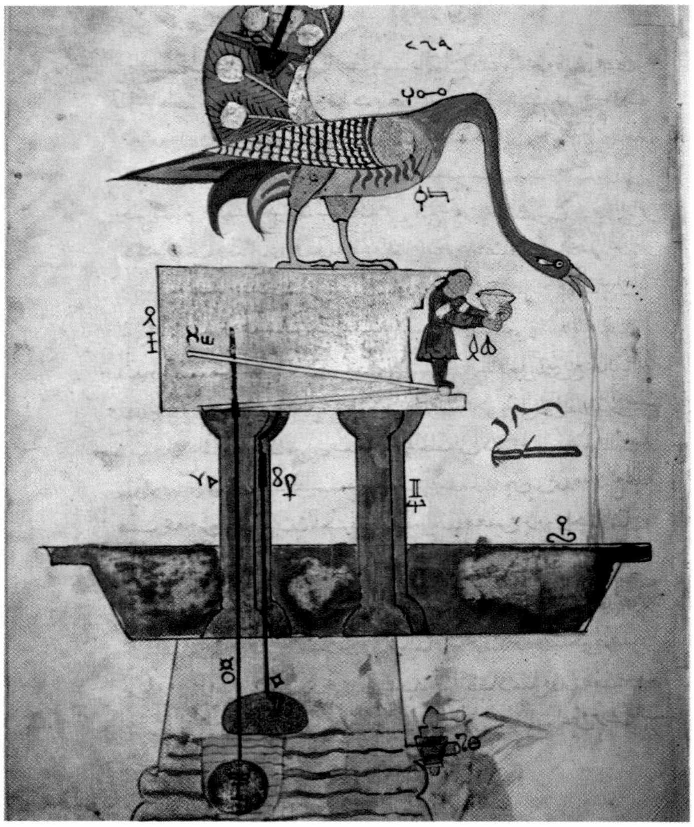

Plate 91

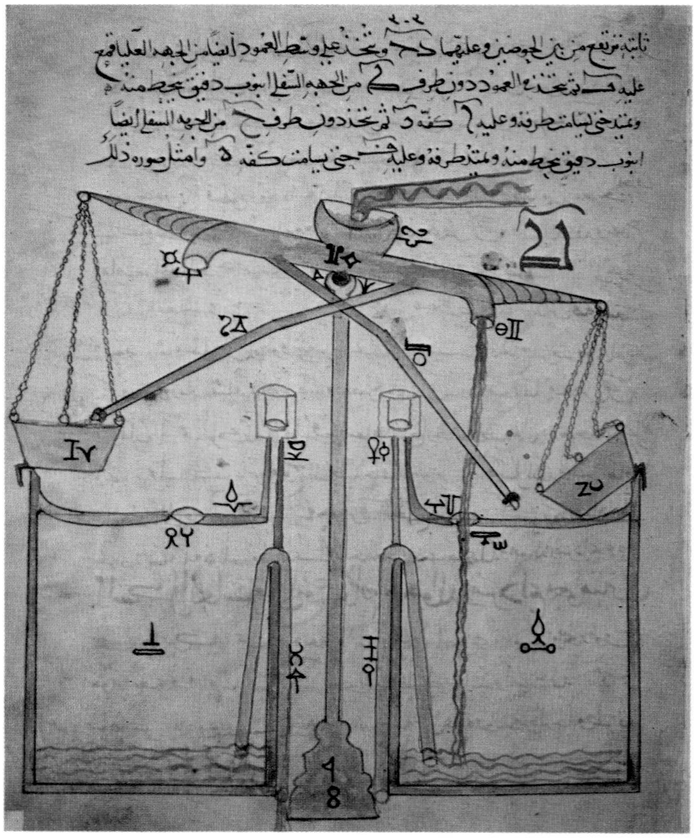

Plate 92

Plates 90, 91, 92 and 93. Various mechanical devices from al-Jazari.

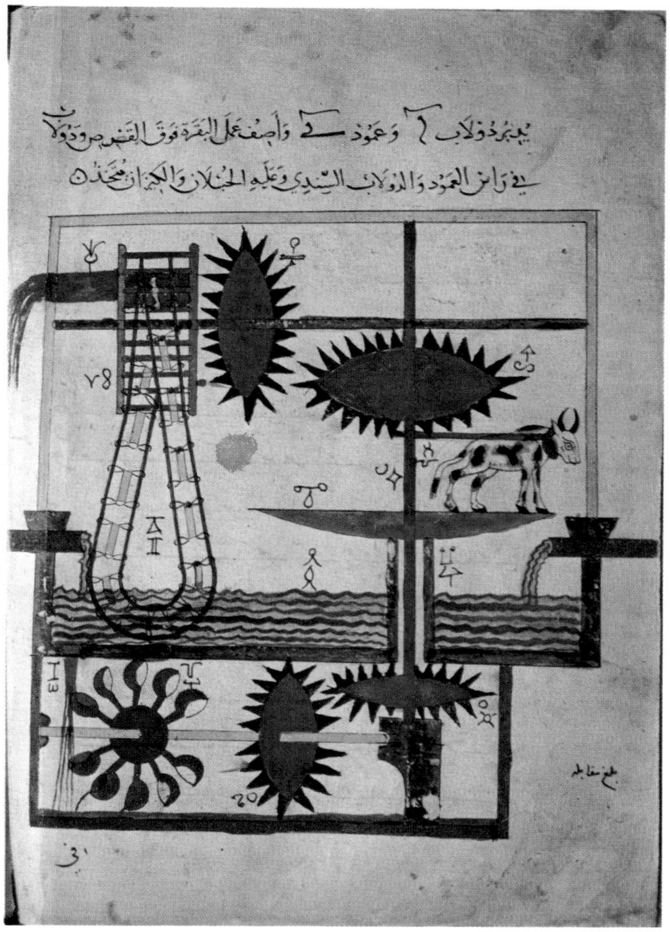

Plate 93

Plate 94. A mechanical device from a Persian encyclopaedia of the sciences.

It is of great importance for an understanding of Islamic science as well as technology and their difference from modern science and technology to study the role in Islamic civilization of these treatises and the complicated machines they describe. Of course many of these treatises were concerned with practical technology, describing wind-mills, water-mills, architectural elements, irrigation problems, distilling and other chemical processes, military equipment, etc. What is of basic interest to note here is that the technology they dealt with was one which utilized natural forces within the environment in question, making the maximum use of human skills and causing the minimum amount of disturbance within the natural environment. Certain of the other treatises described complicated machines which are most like what modern technology has developed during the past two centuries. But it was precisely this kind of technology which the Muslims never took seriously as a possible way of changing their economic life and means of production. The fruit of these treatises was the making of complicated clocks and gadgets as if the Muslims wanted to show that the only safe kind of complicated machine is a toy. For them these machines always recalled the strange inventions of the Alexandrians who made temple doors which opened when the light of the sun shone upon them and achieved other amazing feats that passed into Muslim folklore as well as science.[29]

29. Even the great Andalusian Sufi and seer Ibn 'Arabī described in his *Futūḥāt al-makkiyyah* his own vision of one of these Alexandrian temples.

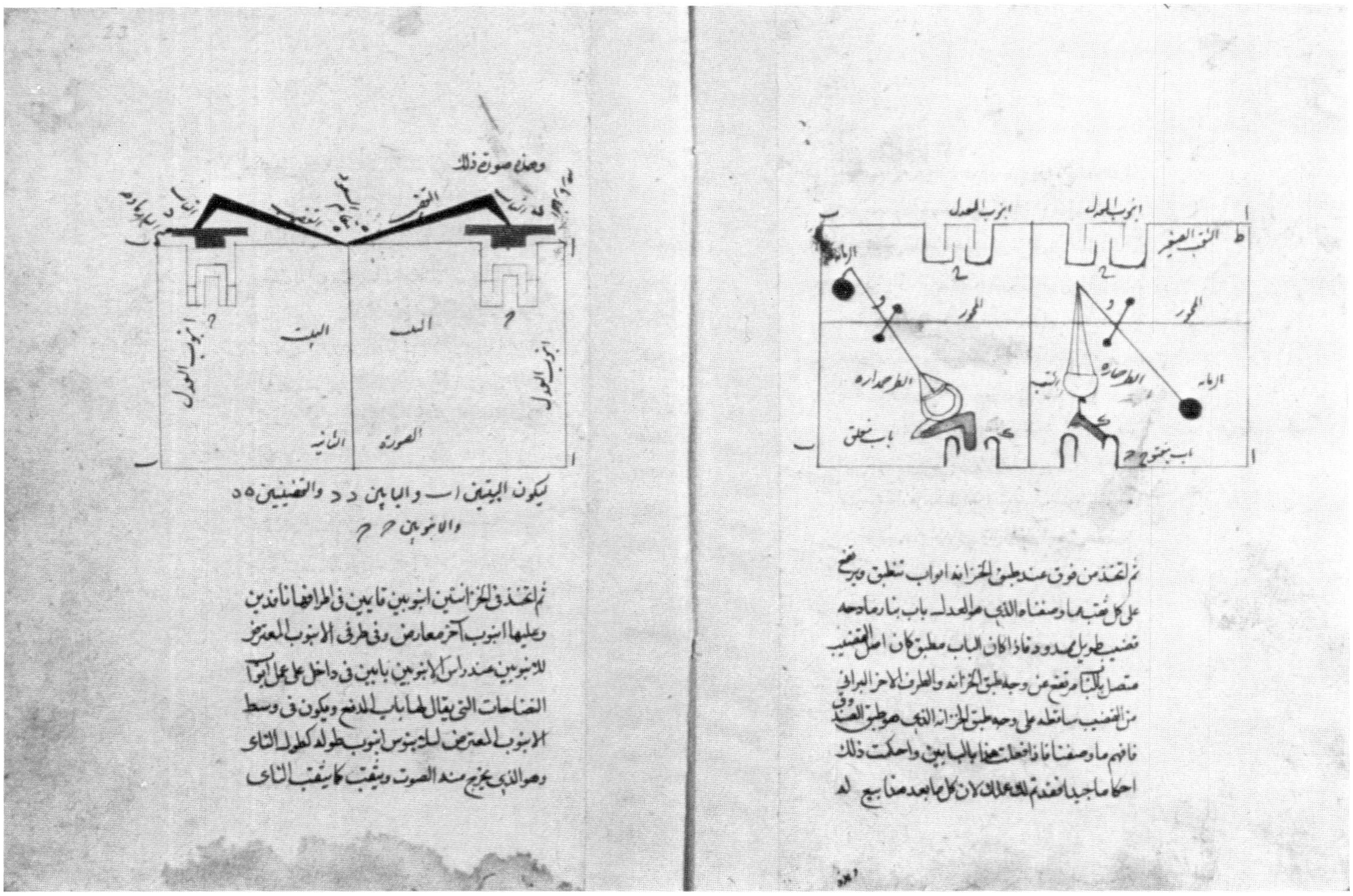

Figure 70. A page from a manuscript on mechanical devices.

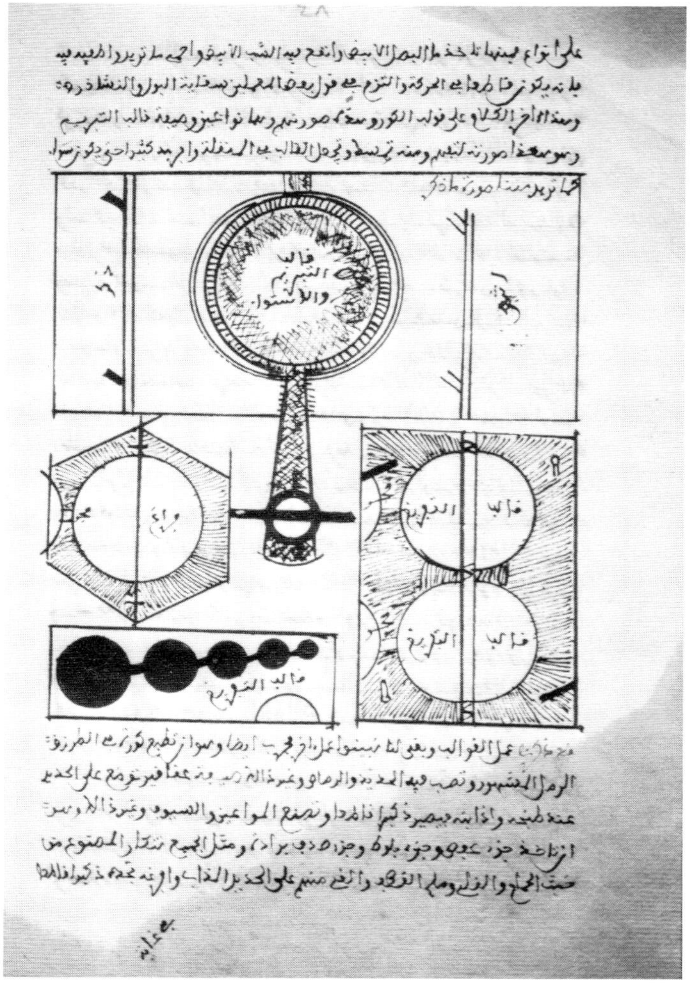

Figures 71 and 72. From a Maghribi work on making canons.

Figure 72

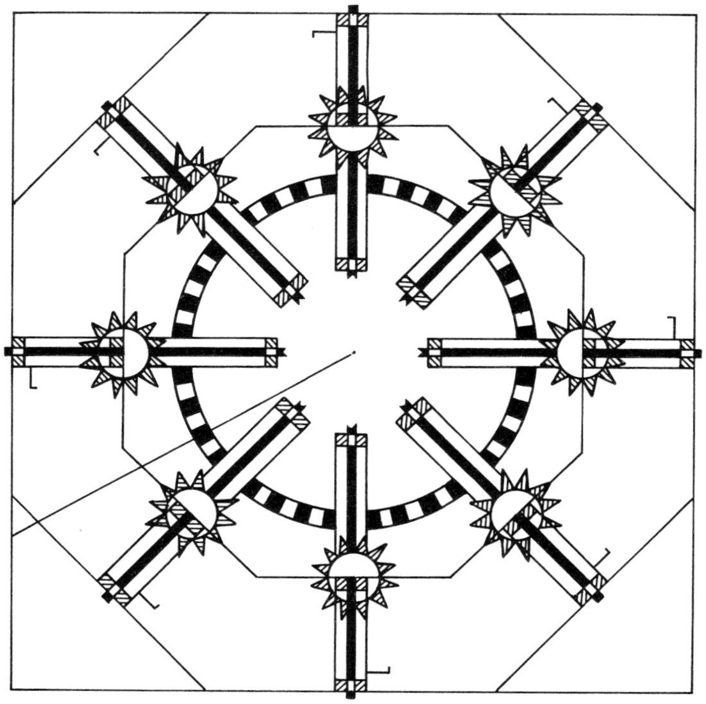

Figures 73a and 73b. A device to make a canon, from Mogul India.

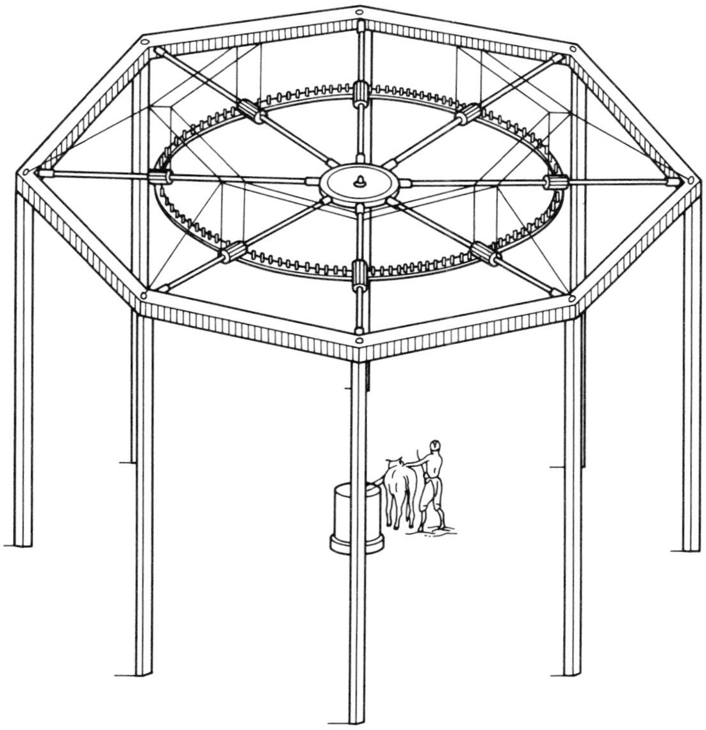

Figure 73b

Islamic civilization had the means to make complicated machines and apply them to the problems of the daily life of the Islamic community. But like the Chinese who had gunpowder but never made guns, the Muslims never took that step which would mean the creation of a technology out of harmony with the natural environment. Their works on machines dealt with a variety of subjects all the way from agricultural and transportational devices which were actually used in everyday life to complicated clocks which were the joy of caliphs and princes, to other complicated gadgets and devices which at their extreme became combined with magic and magical practices. They did not make practical use of all they knew in this domain, feeling instinctively the danger of the development of a technology which makes use of metals and fire, both elements alien to the natural environment, and which therefore ultimately results in the loss of that equilibrium *vis à vis* nature which is so central to the Islamic perspective and whose destruction is such a danger for modern man.

In physics itself, as seen in the above pages, Muslims made major contributions to various branches of the sciences and would need to be considered in any thorough history of the subject from the Western point of view. But the significance of their studies from the Islamic point of view becomes clear only when considered in the light of the total structure of Islam and its civilization. The Muslim physicists studied various phenomena with the exactness of a physicist in the modern sense but did not secularize the cosmos they were studying because they never lost sight of the totality in order to gain knowledge of the part. They knew that the higher can never be sacrificed for the lower except at the cost of intellectual and spiritual suicide, and they were aware that a certain amount – and *only* a certain amount – of science in the modern sense can be developed within the traditional cosmos provided this science knows its limit and does not expect to 'progress' indefinitely in a domain which is by nature finite.

The 9th/15th century Persian Sufi poet 'Abd al-Raḥmān Jāmī seemed to have a presentiment of the present day predicament of man, who in his attempt to gain knowledge of the atom has lost sight of the spiritual empyrean. In one of his quatrains, he says,

I lost my intellect, soul, religion and heart,
In order to know an atom in perfection.
But no one can know the essence of the atom
completely.
How often must I repeat that no one shall know it;
then farewell!

Part Four
The Applied Sciences

Chapter VIII
Medicine and Pharmacology

'Abū Dardā once said: "O Prophet of God (Muḥammad), if I am cured of my sickness and am thankful for it, is it better than if I were sick and bore it patiently? And the Holy Prophet replied: Verily, the Prophet of God loves sound health just as you do.'

(prophetic *ḥadīth*)

Islamic medicine and its allied subjects such as pharmacology, surgery and the like drew their spiritual sustenance from the message of Islam and received their nourishment from the rich soil of Graeco-Alexandrian, Indian and Persian medicine. The result was the creation of an extensive field embracing nearly every branch of the medical sciences, some fourteen centuries of history and a vast geographical area stretching from southern Spain to Bengal, for in this particular field nearly all the regions of the Islamic world made some contributions. This fact, added to the nature of Islamic medicine which is at once an applied science, an art and in fact an aspect of the whole of life touching upon activities ranging from eating to bathing, has caused many scholars to separate medicine from the other sciences and to treat its history as a discipline distinct from the history of the other Islamic sciences. In fact to do justice to all the branches of Islamic medicine it would really be necessary to devote a separate study to it. If it is nevertheless treated here, albeit in summary fashion, as a chapter within a general work on Islamic science, it is because no picture of Islamic science itself can be complete even in a relative sense without a glimpse at least of the vast horizons of Islamic medicine. Otherwise, from the point of view of medicine itself, its summary treatment given here of necessity cannot but do injustice to its remarkable richness and variety.

Islam and Islamic Medicine

In the same way that in mathematics the central Islamic doctrine of unity (*al-tawḥīd*) and its applications accorded with the Pythagorean philosophy of numbers and made the integration of Greek mathematics into the Islamic perspective possible, another basic Islamic doctrine, namely that of harmony and balance, made the philosophy underlying the Hippocratic and Galenic traditions easily digestible by Muslims. The principle of the balance between the natures and the humours became easily a part of the Islamic view of nature because it was but a particular instance of a universal principle enunciated by Islam and forming one of the cardinal aspects of its view of the cosmos and of man's situation within it. From the metaphysical and cosmological points of view, the principles of Islamic medicine are deeply rooted in the Islamic tradition, although this medicine itself came into being as a result of the integration by Muslims of several older traditions of medicine of which the most important was the Greek.

The whole of Islamic medicine is also related to Islam through the injunctions contained in the Quran and the *Ḥadīth* concerning health and various questions related in one way or another to medicine. The aspects of the Divine Law (*Sharīʿah*) concerning personal hygiene, dietary habits, ablutions, and many other elements affecting the body are again related to medicine. Finally, esoteric teachings concerning the soul in its relation to the body and the body as the 'temple of the spirit' again create a link between medicine and various aspects of the teachings of Islam. The result is that, whatever historians may say of the Greek, Syriac, Indian or old Persian origins of this or that medical idea or practice, Islamic medicine has always been seen by Muslims as closely related to religion. Certain jurists to be sure have attacked Galen or other medical authorities but then they have supported 'prophetic medicine' in one form or another. Moreover, even among the jurists there have been those who have pointed out that of the 'foreign' sciences only medicine was studied by even one or two of the Companions of the Holy Prophet, and that medical practices which would lead to the regaining of health of body and soul were encouraged from the earliest period of Islam. In any case, to this day within the Islamic world what survives of the traditional medicine in the way of traditional drug stores, baths and the like are closely associated by the mass of the people with the actual practice of religion and are even enfolded within an aura of piety.

The Practice of Islamic Medicine

As far as the practice of medicine is concerned, again Islamic civilization created certain institutions and norms closely related to its own general structure in order to make the teaching and practice of medicine possible. Gradually, the figure of the physician who had originally been usually of Christian, Jewish or even Zoroastrian background or actually a member of these communities, became totally Muslimized and there came into being the Islamic figure of the *ḥakīm* (literally wise-man or sage) who was at once physician and philosopher as well as master of most of the other traditional sciences.[1] Most of the early Islamic philosophers from al-Kindī to Ibn Sīnā and Ibn Rushd were in fact accomplished physicians, and some like Muḥammad ibn Zakariyyā' al-Rāzī and Ibn Sīnā were unrivalled authorities on medicine.[2] As a result, the practice and teaching of medicine was inseparable from the other disciplines and especially from philosophy. Medical knowledge usually reached the student through a figure who stood for the unity of the Islamic sciences and who presented various branches of knowledge to him as grades within a hierarchy rather than as compartmentalized and disparate forms of science.

As far as the actual teaching of medicine is concerned, although its general principles were taught in *madrasahs*, most of the clinical aspects as well as surgery, pharmacology and the like were taught in the hospitals to which usually a medical school was added. Some outstanding physicians also taught their students in private circles at their homes or other places specially designated for such meetings. A great deal of instruction also took place in family circles or in private dispensaries or apothecaries, especially as far as pharmacology was concerned, for the tradition of generations of one family practising medicine was strong in Islamic civilization for both Muslims and oriental Christians and Jews living among Mus-

1. On the centrality of the role and function of the *ḥakīm*, see our *Science and Civilization in Islam*, pp. 41–42.

2. According to traditional authorities, since Muslim philosophers considered it below the dignity of philosophy to receive payment for teaching it, they usually practised medicine to earn their living. In the later period of Islamic history, especially in Persia, the role of medicine in this context was often replaced by jurisprudence, although men who were both physicians and philosophers of note have continued to appear up to modern times.

lims. Some of the best-known medical families such as that of Ibn Zuhr in Spain and of Bukhtīshū' in Persia and Iraq produced well-known physicians for several centuries.[3]

The institution of the hospital was inherited by Muslims from both the Persians and the Byzantines. Already, before the rise of Islam, the hospital at Jundishapur, near the present Persian city of Ahvaz, was a major medical institution in which, in addition to the care of patients, medical instruction was carried out on an extensive basis. In fact, this hospital and medical school complex was the main link of transmission of Graeco-Alexandrian as well as Indian and Persian medicine to Islam.[4] There were also hospitals established by Byzantines in their eastern provinces such as Syria which became rapidly integrated into the Islamic world.

Benefiting from the existence of these institutions, the Muslims soon created their own hospitals.[5] Although al-Walīd I is said to have created the first hospital in Islam in the 1st/7th century, the first real hospital with all the required facilities of that day was established by Hārūn al-Rashīd in Baghdad, during the 2nd/8th century, and the Christian physician Jibra'īl ibn Bukhtīshū' was called from Jundishapur to head it. It was this hospital which became the pivot of medical activity and the centre for the rise of Islamic medicine. The Baghdad hospital was later headed by such famous physicians as Yuḥannā ibn Māsawayh and it served as model for numerous other hospitals in Baghdad, the most famous being the 'Aḍudī founded by the Persian ruler 'Aḍud al-Dawlah in the 4th/10th century. Hospitals were also established in other Muslim cities such as the one in Rayy which was headed by Muḥammad ibn Zakariyyā' al-Rāzī before his coming to Baghdad.[6]

Another major hospital was the one established by Nūr al-Dīn al-Zanjī in Damascus in the 6th/12th century, said to have been built from the money received as ransom for one of the Frankish kings. A similar Nūrī hospital was also built in Aleppo. Soon afterwards Ṣalāḥ al-Dīn al-Ayyūbī constructed the Nāṣirī hospital in Cairo and from then on for several centuries a close link existed between the medical centres of Syria and Egypt. The most notable hospital in Egypt was, however, the Manṣūrī hospital built by al-Manṣūr Qalā'ūn in the 7th/13th century from an old Fāṭimid palace. The hospital had beds for several thousand patients with different wards specified for various illnesses and separate sections devoted to each of the sexes. It also possessed lecture halls, a library, a mosque and separate administrative quarters.

A century earlier, the Almohad king Ya'qūb al-Manṣūr built the first large hospital of the Maghrib in Marrakesh and attracted notable physicians such as Ibn Ṭufayl and Ibn Rushd to his court. From then on hospitals continued to be built in the Maghrib, some, like the 7th/13th century one at Salé, built by Mawlay 'Abd al-Raḥmān, being still in use. Likewise in Tunis, Algeria and Andalusia itself, many hospitals were built whose descriptions remain in various literary sources, and the word *bīmāristān* (a Persian word meaning 'the place of the sick'), which has always been used in Arabic as the word for hospital, entered into the Spanish language in the form of *malastan* or *marastān*.

In the Ottoman empire, hospital building continued to follow the earlier Seljuk and Abbassid models. The first Ottoman hospital was the *Dār al-shifā'* in Bursa built in the 8th/14th century followed by that of Mehmet II built in the 9th/15th century as part of his *Külliye*. During

3. Even now in certain parts of the Middle East, there are Christian and Jewish pharmacists and firms dealing in pharmaceuticals which have been carrying out both the science and the business of administering and dealing in medicaments for several centuries.

4. Jundishapur was a cosmopolitan centre where, in addition to Persians themselves, there were a large number of Syriac-speaking Christians, who formed the main body of the medical faculty and most of whom had emigrated from the cities of Syria such as Edessa, and also a number of Indian physicians well acquainted with Sanskrit medical sources.

5. On the history of hospitals in the Islamic world, see the still valuable classical work of Aḥmad 'Īsā Bey, *Histoire des bimaristans (hôpitaux) à l'époque islamique*; also his *Ta'rīkh al-bīmāristānāt fi'l-islām*, Damascus, 1939; A. Khayrallāh, *Outline of Arabic Contributions to Medicine and the Allied Sciences*, Beirut, 1946, pp. 59–73; C. Elgood, *A Medical History of Persia and the Eastern Caliphate*; *idem.*, *Safavid Medical Practice*, London, 1970. See also the article *'bīmāristān'* in the new *Encyclopaedia of Islam*, by D. M. Dunlop *et al.*

6. Al-Rāzī also wrote a book on the necessary characteristics of a hospital entitled *Kitāb fī ṣifāt al-bīmāristān (Book on the Characteristics of the Hospital)* cited by Ibn Abī Uṣaybi'ah and others.

Plate 95. The interior of a Seljuk hospital.

the same century under the order of Bāyazīd II there was created a set of institutions including a hospital, some of which still stands. As for Istanbul, the great hospitals in that city began to be built from the 10th/16th century onwards, leading directly to the modern hospitals of the 13th/19th century, influenced greatly by the practice of Western medicine.

As for Persia and India, there also accounts of travellers reveal flourishing hospitals in many cities, but there is little doubt that during the last centuries the hospitals built by the Muslims of India were usually on a grander scale than those of Persia. To this day, in fact, the only remnants of large-scale hospitals and dispensaries where Islamic medicine is practised are to be found in the sub-continent, some of the outstanding examples being the Osmania hospital in Hyderabad, Deccan, and the Hamdard Institutes of Delhi and Karachi.

Supported usually by religious endowment (*waqf*) and also by help from living persons or the state, the hospital became a major scientific institution in the Islamic world. It developed into various types, ranging from general hospitals catering for all kinds of diseases to those specializing in the treatment of lepers or the insane and even animals. The teaching and the practice of Islamic medicine is inseparable from the institution of the hospital which at its height in fact contained, in addition to wards, major libraries, lecture halls and other facilities necessary for the training of medical students.

The practice of Islamic medicine has always been closely connected with the dispensaries and chemists' shops either adjoining a hospital or functioning independently. The druggist (usually called *al-'aṭṭār*) has, however, always been more involved in the intimate life of the people than the official physician. To this day the traditional druggist himself caters for many of the daily needs of his customers and proposes various drugs for maladies which have not as yet become very serious. His knowledge of various drugs, especially herbs, which comprise most of the traditional medicaments, is often extensive, and

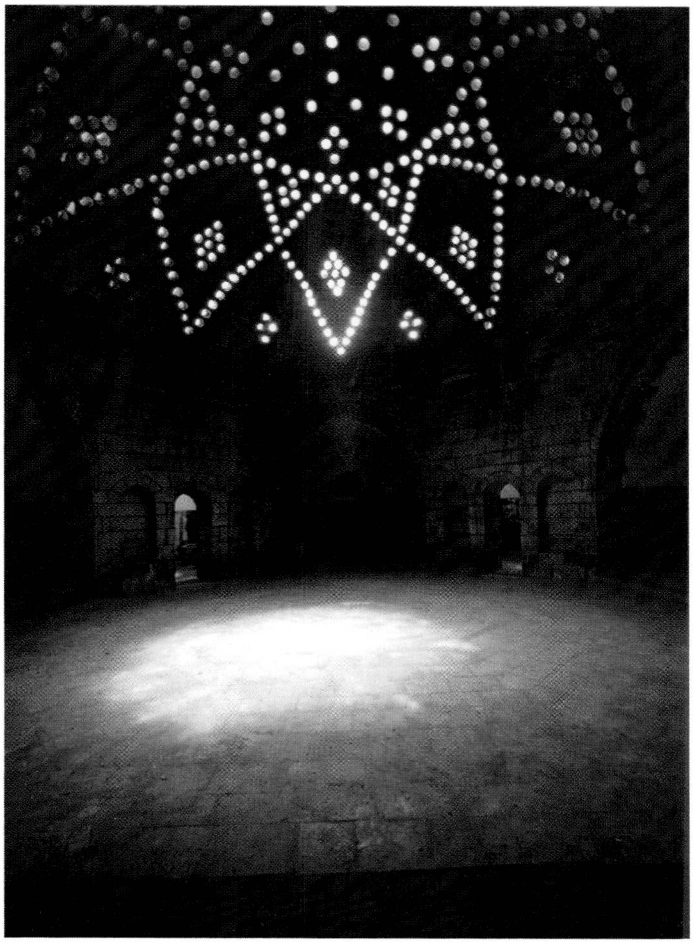

Plate 96. Inside a bath-house in Aleppo.

Plate 97. Inside a traditional bath-house.

his role from both the medical and the economic points of view is of importance.

Also significant for its medical uses is the traditional bath (*ḥammām*) which is to be found in one form or another throughout the Islamic world. Because of various forms of bodily purification required by Islamic Law, baths were built from the earliest times and to this day there is no small village without a public bath which is attended regularly for ritual as well as hygienic reasons. But in addition the use of hot and cold air and water and the rub-down or massage which is administered by a professional class trained in this art[7] have been used by Muslim physicians for medical purposes and numerous treatises have been written on the subject such as that of Qusṭā ibn Lūqā. Ibn Sīnā also discusses the medical uses of the bath and he as well as Rāzī are said to have treated some patients in the bath itself.[8]

The traditional use of the Muslim bath is almost a rite of its own. It usually takes several hours. Besides the washing of the body, the rub-down and ritual purification, special liquids are drunk and specified periods spent either in the steam room or the cool waiting-room outside. Physicians have used the bath for all kinds of cures ranging from overcoming headaches to reviving sexual energy. The Turkish bath which is so celebrated in the West is the last chapter in a long history of the bath as both a social and medical institution stretching over the whole of Islamic history. To this day, traditional baths function

7. Some philologists even believe that the word massage itself has its origin in the Arabic *massa*, whose root means to rub or to touch with one's hand.

8. It is necessary here to mention the Roman baths which preceded the baths built by Muslims. There is a difference between the two, however. The Roman bath was an important social institution with a minor medical role; the Muslim bath, although also important socially, possesses a much greater medical, as well as religious, significance than its predecessors.

Plate 98. The interior of a Persian bath-house in Kerman.

Figure 74. Vapour rising from a Turkish bath-house in Istanbul.

from Morocco to Persia and Afghanistan, and, although used less medically than before, continue to fulfil medical as well as religious and hygienic functions for those who still wish to be treated according to the teachings of Islamic medicine.

The Theory of Islamic Medicine

The theory of Islamic medicine is related inextricably to the whole of Islamic metaphysics, cosmology and philosophy, because the object of medicine, namely man, is a microcosm who recapitulates within himself the whole of existence and is in fact the key to an understanding of existence, for according to the Arabic dictum *al-insān ramz al-wujūd* (man is the symbol of existence). Islamic physicians saw the body of man as but an extension of his soul and closely related to both the spirit and the soul. Moreover, it was specially concerned with the interpenetration and interrelation of cosmic forces and the effect of these forces upon man. Muslim physicians remained also fully aware of the 'sympathy' between all orders of existence and the mutual action and reaction of one creature upon the other. They, therefore, envisaged the subject of medicine, namely man, to be related both inwardly through the soul and the spirit and 'outwardly' through the grades of the macrocosmic hierarchy to the Principle of cosmic manifestation itself. Likewise they sought the principles of medicine in the sciences dealing with the Principle and its manifestations, namely metaphysics and cosmology. Whatever may have been the historical origins of Islamic medicine, its principles cannot be understood save in the light of Islamic metaphysics and cosmological sciences.[9]

The Muslims did adopt much of Greek medicine, especially its theory, but this adoption was possible only because of the traditional nature of this medicine and its concordance with the Islamic conception of the Universe. It must not be forgotten that here as in the domain of philosophy the Muslims considered the origin of this science to be prophetic and sacred and in fact related to the Abrahamic prophetic chain which the Muslims considered to be their own.[10] The rapid assimilation of Greek medical theory into the Islamic perspective is due most of all to this latent possibility within the Islamic perspective itself and the close relation between the idea of the harmony of parts in Hippocratic and Galenic medicine and the concept of balance and harmony so central to Islam. It is not accidental that the theoretical background of Greek medicine belongs to the same schools of Greek philosophy which were easily assimilated into the Islamic perspective and not to those which the Muslims rejected. The reasons for the 'Muslimization' of a Hippocrates or Galen are nearly the same as those of a Plato or an Aristotle and are also related to the reasons for the rejection of other schools of Greek thought, such as the Epicurean or the Sophist. Had Greek medicine possessed a theoretical background related to the anti-metaphysical schools of late Antiquity, it is very doubtful whether it would have been integrated so perfectly within the Islamic intellectual universe.

As far as the general theory of Islamic medicine is concerned, its basis rests upon the two cardinal doctrines of all traditional cosmologies, namely the hierarchic structure of the cosmos and the correspondence between the microcosm and the macrocosm alluded to earlier in this book.[11] As for the specific field of medicine itself, it is with the four elements and the four natures that it usually begins its theoretical discussion, leaving the relation between the natures and the elements,

9. The same holds true for all traditional schools of medicine, whether they be those which influenced the Muslims, such as the Greek, or those which did not, such as the Tibetan and the Chinese. In fact, the very existence of several schools of medicine, all of which are successful in treating illnesses, but are different in their methods, proves that there is not simply one valid system of medicine based upon simple observation of different phenomena. Rather, besides the official modern medicine there are several systems derived from various cosmological principles which meet solely at the level of unity of metaphysical doctrine.

10. See 'Hermes and Hermetic Writings in the Islamic World', in S. H. Nasr, *Islamic Studies*, Beirut, 1966, pp. 63–89; also Nasr, *An Introduction to Islamic Cosmological Doctrines*, Prologue.

11. See also Nasr, *ibid.*, where both these doctrines in their Islamic setting are dealt with thoroughly.

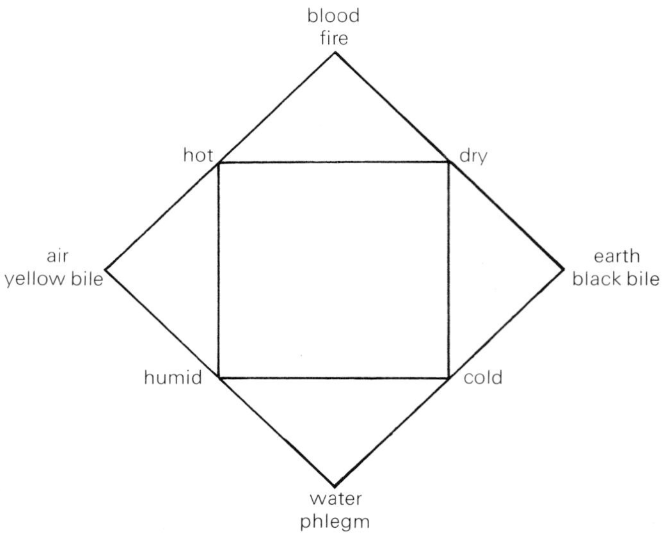

Figure 75a. The four natures and humours.

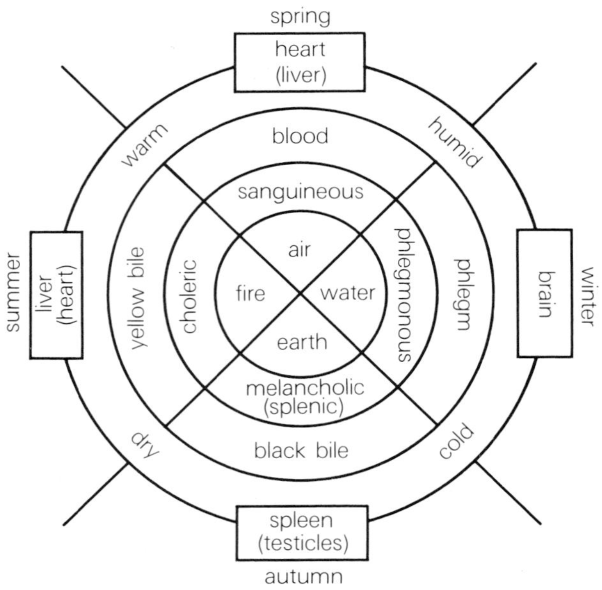

Figure 75b. The basic organs of the body in relation to the humours, qualities, natures and seasons according to the Jābirean corpus.

the *materia prima* and form and the imposition of form upon matter to general works on natural philosophy. Concerning the elements and the natures, it must be remembered that in medicine as in physics and alchemy, they must not be thought of as simply the fire, air, water and earth found in nature, nor the cold, heat, dryness and humidity man feels during the various seasons of the year. Rather are they the principles of the gross elements and qualities called by the same names in daily language.[12]

The four humours, that is blood, phlegm, yellow bile and black bile are composed of the elements and natures according to the above diagram (Figure 75a). Each humour is related to two natures and two elements and possesses qualities which are at once the same and different from other humours. The humours form the foundation of animal activity and the body of all animals including man is comprised of them. They mix together to form the temperament of each individual. In fact each person possesses a unique temperament as do the organs of his body based upon the particular combination of the humours comprising his constitution. Moreover, the harmony of the humours tends in each case towards a particular type of imbalance; hence some tend to be phlegmatic, others melancholic, etc. Also, each temperament possesses its own heat in addition to the innate heat which everything possesses.

But neither the humours nor their mixture is the cause of life. They are only the vehicle which make possible the manifestation of life. The Muslim physicians believe in the spirit (*rūḥ*)[13] which descends upon this mixture of the humours and which is the subtle body standing intermediate between the physical body comprised of the humours and the force of life which comes from the world above. It is worth drawing attention to the similarity between the words *rūḥ* and *rīḥ* (the wind or air) in Arabic and to the Galenic doctrine that through the air breathed by the organism the life-force enters the body. It is also of significance to note that in Arabic as in many other languages the words for breath (*nafas*)

12. On the theory of Islamic medicine relatively few serious works have appeared in the West where, until quite recently, any view of nature other than that of modern Western science was laughed at and ridiculed. For the works which give a positive exposition of the theories of Islamic medicine see O. C. Gruner, *A Treatise on the Canon of Medicine, Incorporating a Translation of the First Book*, London, 1930; and Hamdard Institute, *Theories and Philosophies of Medicine*, New Delhi, 1962; see also F. E. Peters, *Allah's Commonwealth*, pp. 173ff.; and M. Ullmann, *Die Medizin im Islam*, Leiden, 1970, pp. 97–100.

13. The medical use of the term *rūḥ* must not be confused with the metaphysical and theological use of this term as the spirit which stands above the soul and belongs to the purely angelic world.

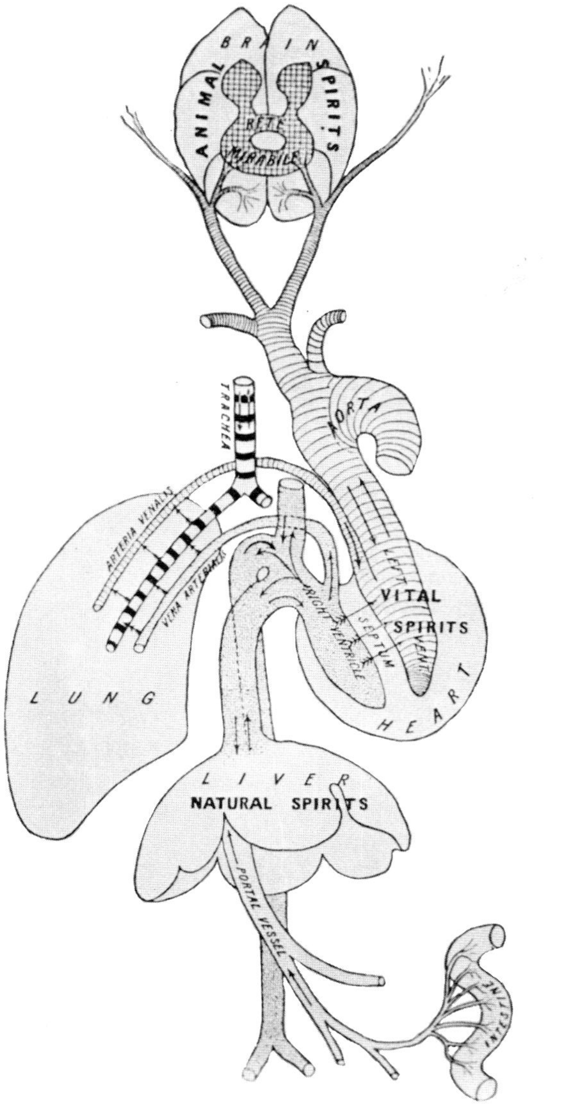

Figure 76. Illustration depicting Galen's ideas concerning the spirits.

and soul (*nafs*) are related. Therein lies a profound cosmological principle which is also related to the invocation of the Name of God (*dhikr*) as the central technique of Sufism for spiritual realization.

The spirit or *rūḥ* in its medical sense is, according to Muslim physiologists, and following Galen, of three kinds:

1. The vital spirit which is hot and dry, has its centre in the left ventricle of the heart, preserves life, causes the body to grow, move and reproduce, and travels within the arteries.
2. The psychic spirit which is cold and wet, has its centre in the brain, causes sensation and movement and moves within the nerves.
3. The natural spirit which is hot and wet, has its centre in the liver, is concerned with the reception of food, growth and reproduction and travels within the veins.

Each of the spirits produces a series of faculties which carry out its functions. For example, each physical sense has its faculty, the heartbeat its faculty, etc.

In addition to these factors, there operate of course within man the three souls, namely the vegetable, animal and rational, all of which descend from the world above and each of which possesses its own faculties.[14] The more refined the mixture of the humours the greater the perfection and the more complete and perfect the possibility of receiving the soul. Moreover, in each man, health means the harmony of the humours and illness the disruption of the balance of the constitution.[15] Of course the harmony is never perfect in any person,[16] but relative to his own constitution, health means the re-establishment of the balance of the humours. Diagnosis for such disorders as fever are in fact based on searching for the way in which the balance of the humours has been upset. But for diseases which show overt signs, the most notable sign or signs are made use of for diagnostic purposes and often the disease receives the name of the leading sign connected with it. Even in English to this day people speak of having a fit or a stroke.

14. This is the subject of the well-known 'faculty psychology' developed by so many Muslim philosophers and physicians such as Ibn Sīnā and referred to earlier in Chapter IV.

15. Modern medicine cannot define the meaning of health in its own terms, whereas for traditional Greek and Islamic medicine the definition of both health and sickness is quite clear.

16. Many traditional sources believed that only the Prophet of Islam as the most perfect of God's creatures possessed a perfectly balanced temperament, both medically and psychologically.

Beside the internal causes of health, Muslim physicians believed that six external factors are essential and must be present to guarantee the health of the patient. These were usually called the '*Six Necessities*' (*sittah ḍarūriyyah*)[17] and are as follows:

1. Air (including the effects of various climates, soils, etc.).
2. Food (including times of meals, what should be eaten and drunk and their amount, etc.).
3. Bodily rest and movement (including exercise).
4. Sleep.
5. Emotional rest (including the question of which emotional states help or harm health).
6. Excretion and retention (including the effects of sexual intercourse).[18]

The traditional physician who usually knew his patient well sought to restore health not only by examining internal problems but by studying all the different external factors listed here so as to discover the one or several causes which had disrupted the harmony of the humours within the body and *vis à vis* the environment, causes which can range from having eaten the wrong food to emotional strain.

Since the external world of man is also comprised of the elements possessing various natures, there is a constant action and reaction between the total external environment of man and the humours. First of all, each climate causes the people living within it to have a different type of temperament from people of another climate. Likewise, racial heredity, age, sex, and many other factors influence the temperament. Moreover, all the food and drugs that man consumes possess various natures in different degrees. Hence they too affect the temperament. Health is then a question of living in harmony within oneself and with the environment, taking into full consideration what one eats and drinks in view of each person's particular inner constitution. There is a vast cycle comprising the individual, the air, water, soil, etc. about him, the food and water he eats and drinks and even cosmic forces further removed from him, including the stars. Even the substances surrounding man, such as wood, brick or metal, influence his health to some degree. It is for him at first and secondly for his physician to discover the nature of his temperament, the tendencies within his constitution to move away from the state of harmony, and the means necessary through diet, medicament, exercise or other factors to re-establish the harmony which is synonymous with health.[19]

Different Branches of Islamic Medicine

Anatomy and Physiology

Anatomy and physiology formed an inseparable unit in Islamic medicine and in fact served as preludium for all the branches of medicine. Moreover, the study of the anatomy and physiology of the human body remained of the greatest interest to Sufis, theologians and philosophers as well as to physicians, and students of most other traditional disciplines acquired some knowledge of it. In accordance with the Islamic perspective which sees creation as 'signs' (*āyāt*) of God, Muslims considered the study of the human body as of prime importance for an understanding of the wisdom of God so manifest in man, his supreme creation. That is why the Ikhwān al-Ṣafā' in their *Epistles* paid so much attention to the numerical symbolism of the parts of the human body and their correspondence with various parts of the cosmos, or Sufis such as al-Ghazzālī and Ibn 'Arabī dealt so extensively with the symbolism of human anatomy, or a philosopher and theosopher such as Mullā Ṣadrā

17. There was, in fact, a treatise written in the 10th/16th century under that very title by an anonymous author and dedicated to the Indian prince Burhān Niẓām Shāh.

18. The all-embracing nature of Islamic medicine which considers both environmental and psychological factors in health can be seen from this aspect of medicine alone.

19. It is paradoxical that in the highly individualistic modern civilization there is a crass uniformity in medicine which assumes that the reaction of all bodies to a drug is the same or nearly so, whereas in traditional medicine belonging to a civilization in which the individual order is always subservient to the universal order each patient is treated individually and his temperament taken to be a unique blend of the humours never to be found in exactly the same balance in another individual.

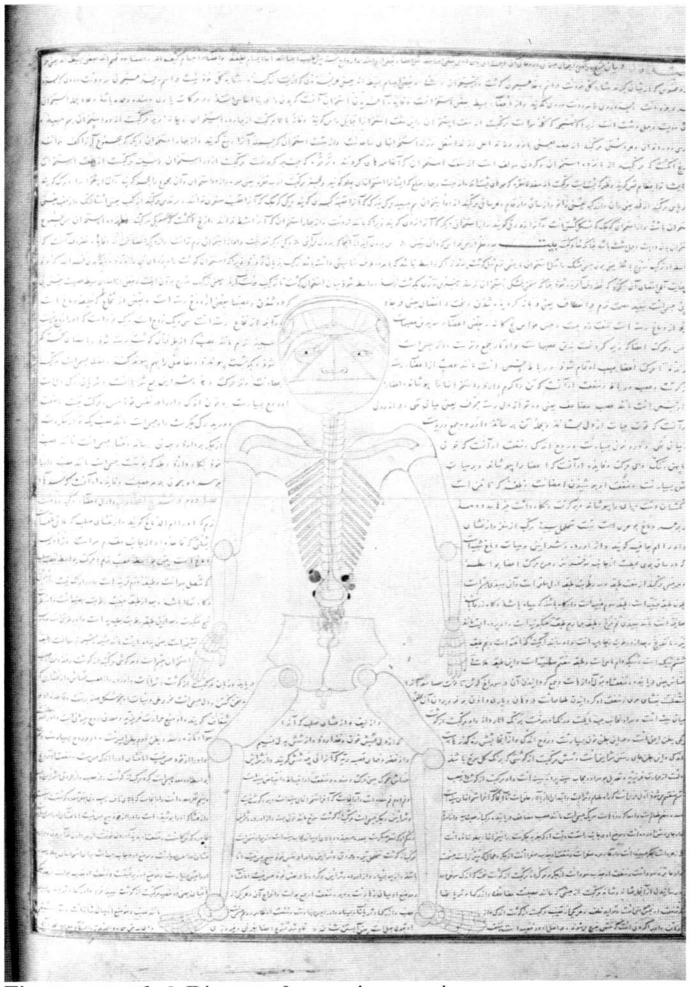

Figures 77 and 78. Diagrams from various treatises on anatomy.

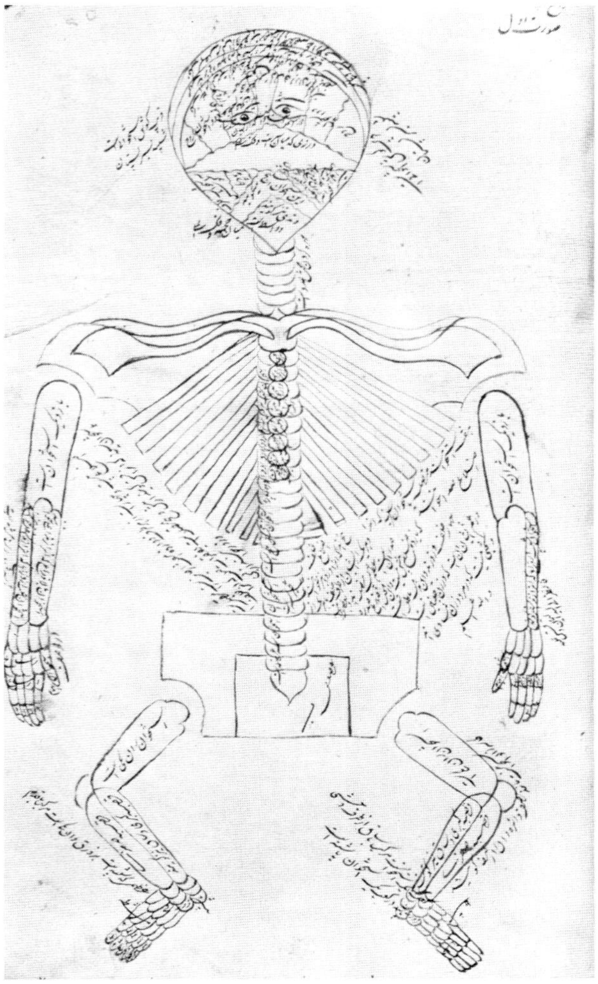

Figure 78

turned to an extensive discussion of this subject in his masterly opus, the *Mafātīḥ al-ghayb* (*Keys to the Unseen*).[20] Even Islamic political thinkers such as al-Fārābī explained their theory of human society by appealing to the symbolism of human anatomy.

Islamic Law did not permit the dissection of the human body, although its strict prohibition has been debated by some of the jurists over the ages. Whatever the technical legal status might be, the religious climate in any case opposed an act which appeared as a violation of the respect which is due to God's most noble creation. As a result, practically no dissections were carried out and Muslims relied heavily upon Galenic anatomy and physiology and its theory of the circulation of the blood and the spirits which are reflected clearly in such famous Islamic texts of anatomy as the *Mukhtaṣar dar 'ilm-i tashrīḥ* (*A Brief Manual of Anatomy*) of 'Abd al-Majīd al-Bayḍāwī and the *Tashrīḥ-i manṣūrī* (*Manṣūr's Anatomy*) by Manṣūr ibn Muḥammad ibn Faqīh Ilyās, written during the 7th/13th and 9th/15th centuries respectively. The major departure of Muslims from Galenic anatomy and physiology came with the discovery of the lesser circulation of the blood by Ibn al-Nafīs to which we shall turn soon.

20. As an example of this type of use of anatomy see 'The Microcosm and Its Relation to the Universe' in our *An Introduction to Islamic Cosmological Doctrines*, pp. 96 ff. See also al-Ghazzālī, *Alchemy of Happiness*, trans. by H. Homes, Albany, 1873, pp. 38–39, as well as the pages devoted to the study of the body as the 'temple' of the spirit by Ibn 'Arabī, al-Jīlī, Nasafī and others. The title of one of Ibn 'Arabī's famous works, *Kitāb al-tadbīrāt al-ilāhiyyah fi'l-mamlakat al-insāniyyah* (*The Book of Divine Regimens Concerning the Human Dominion*), where dominion (*mamlakah*) is directly related to the symbolism of the human body, is specially significant from this point of view.

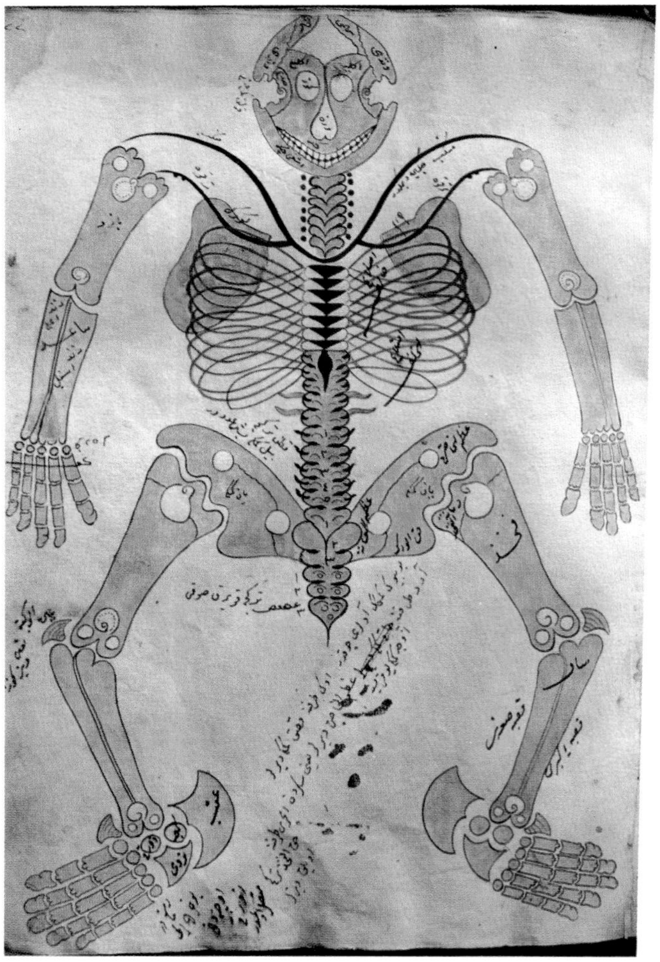

Plates 99, 100, 101, 102, 103 and Figure 79. Diagrams from various treatises on anatomy.

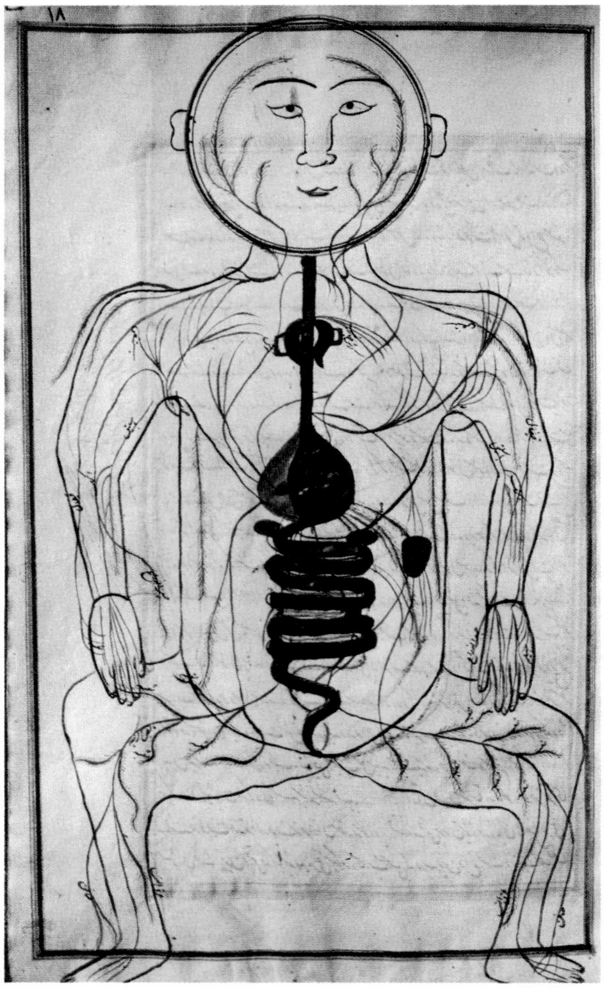

Plate 100

The Islamic works on these subjects were usually concerned with the description and enumeration of various parts of the body, especially the bones, the nerves and the muscles. The bones were usually considered to be 248 in number and a fairly exact description of some of them was given. The nerves were generally the most exactly described parts of the body while the anatomy and physiology of muscles remained scanty. Much attention was also paid to the relation between organs, some being 'masters' of others which were then called 'servile'. For example, the lung is 'servile' in relation to the heart and the heart 'master' *vis-à-vis* the lungs. Moreover, some organs were considered to give, others to receive and yet a third group to be neither donor nor recipient. Altogether the greatest concern of Muslims was with the overall functioning of the body and the inter-relation of the organs within the total unity of the body.

Hygiene and Public Health

Islamic medicine is more concerned with the prevention of illness than with its cure; therefore the question of hygiene and also preventive medicine plays a major part in both its theoretical and practical considerations. Westerners travelling to some of the big cities of the Islamic world where poverty and overpopulation combined with a certain degree of decadence within traditional Islamic civilization provide plenty of evidence for unhealthy conditions and unsanitary practices might protest against the assertion that cleanliness is a basic aspect of Islam. They also compare these unhealthy conditions with the machine-produced cleanliness of industrial societies, which comes from quite another order, and forget the conditions prevalent in Europe until only two centuries ago. Older Western travellers did not suffer from this optical illusion and were struck in their travels through the Islamic world with the general cleanliness of the people.

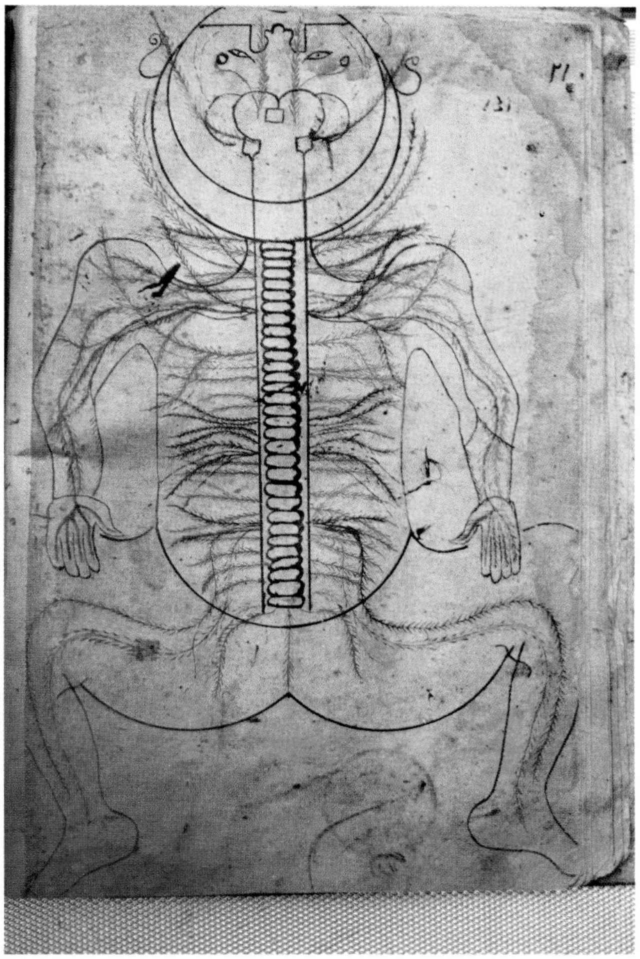

Plate 101

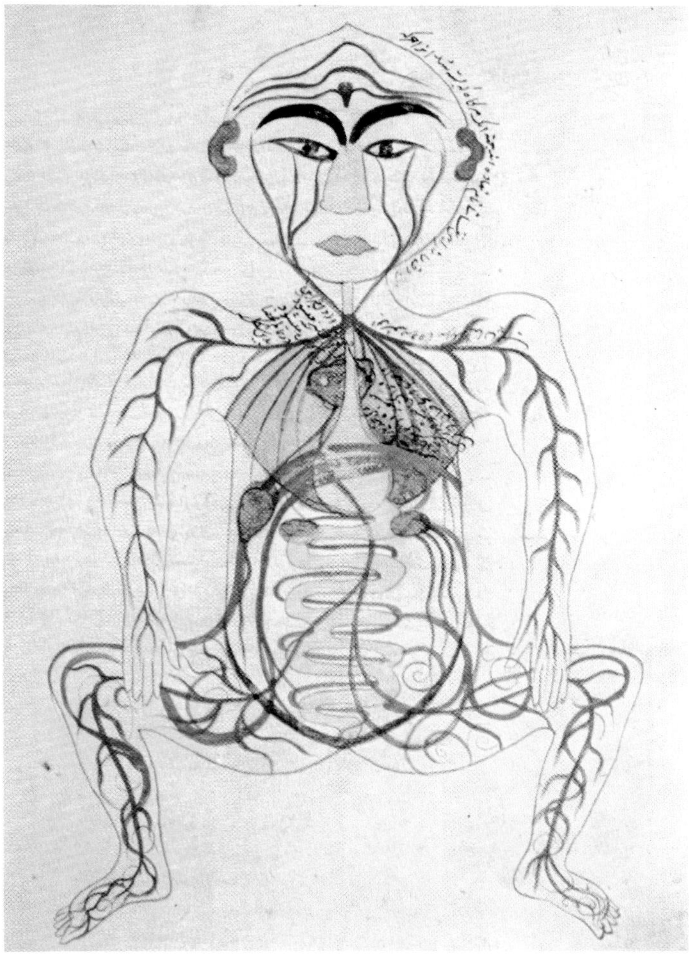

Plate 102

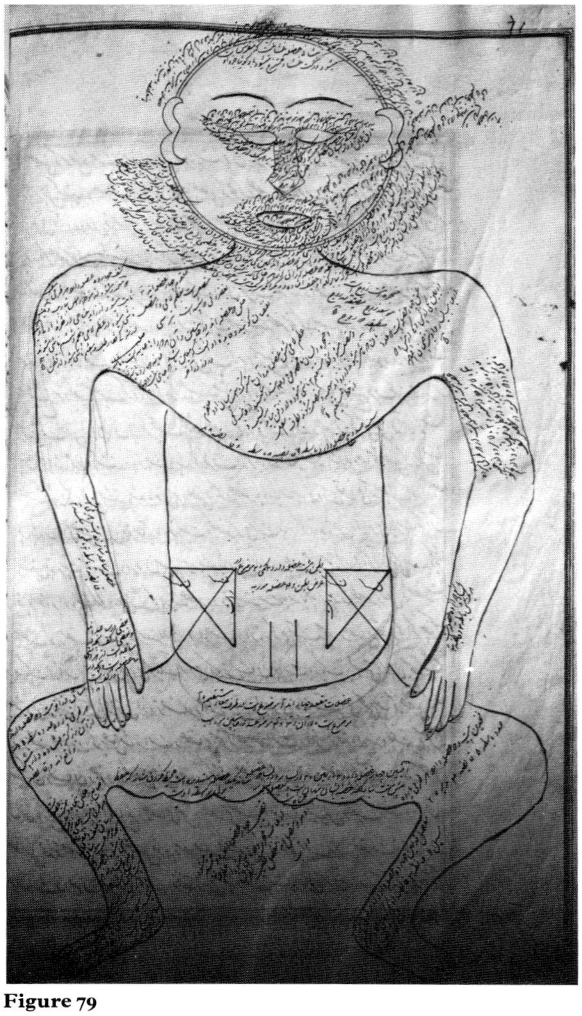

Figure 79

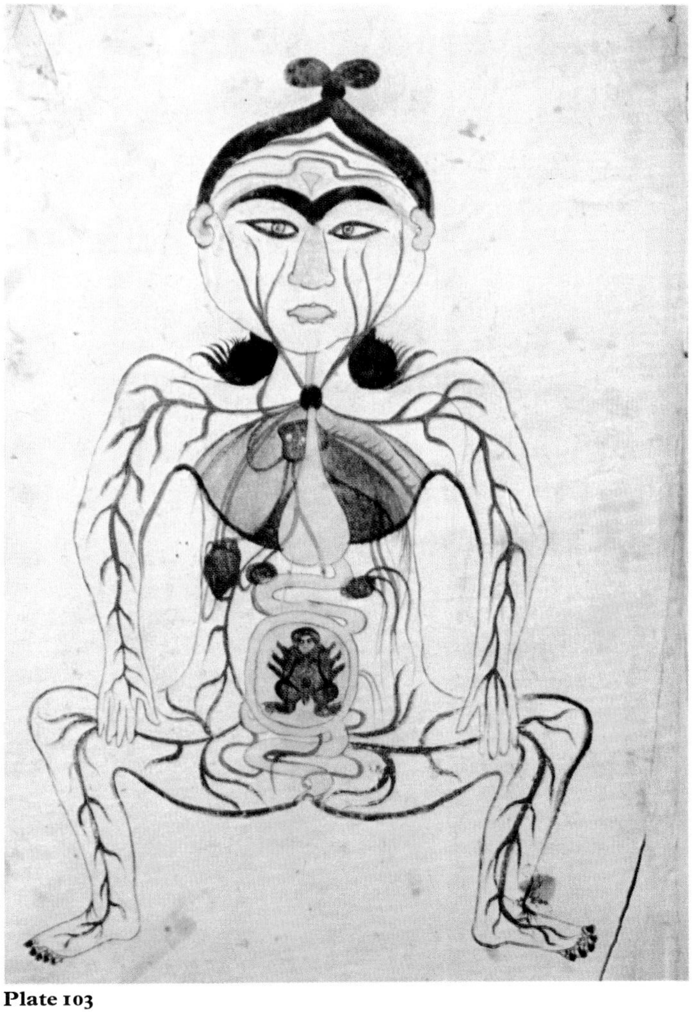

Plate 103

The emphasis upon personal hygiene and cleanliness in Islamic medicine is in fact a direct effect of the teachings of Islam. Ritual cleanliness requires Muslims to wash themselves regularly. The use of the toothbrush goes back to the Holy Prophet and certain strict injunctions concerning private and public hygiene are rooted directly in the teachings of the *Sharī'ah*. The same is true of dietary habits which include not only total abstention from alcoholic drinks and pork, but also fasting, eating less than one's full appetite, eating slowly and numerous other injuctions with direct medical effects. The aspects of Islamic medicine concerning hygiene and public health include both these religious teachings[21] and purely medical ones inherited through millennia of experience and science. The major compendia of medicine usually devoted a section to it and numerous separate treatises were written with the title hygiene and public health (*ḥifẓ al-ṣiḥḥah*), the most famous being those of Isḥāq ibn 'Imrān, Ibn al-Jazzār, Ibn al-Muṭrān, Fakhr al-Dīn al-Rāzī and Ibn al-Quff, not to speak of the treatises of Muḥammad ibn Zakariyyā' al-Rāzī and Ibn Sīnā bearing on this subject.[22]

As far as hygiene is concerned, it is important to emphasize the importance of diet from the point of view of Islamic medicine. It plays a much more important role than does diet in modern medicine. The Muslims considered the kind of food and the manner in which it is consumed to be so directly connected to health that the effect of diet was considered by them as being perhaps more powerful than that even of drugs on both health and illness. It is not accidental that the Andalusian physician Abū Marwān ibn Zuhr in the 6th/12th century wrote the first scientific work on diet ever composed, the *Kitāb al-aghdhiyah (The Book of Diet)*, and that food plays such an important therapeutic role to this day in the Islamic world.

Internal Medicine

Most of Islamic medicine is concerned with internal medicine compared to which surgery plays a secondary role. Muslim physicians have always believed that health rather than illness is the natural state of the body and therefore the body possesses a natural force to bring any disequilibrium back to the state of equilibrium characterizing the state of health. Great emphasis is placed upon the ability of the body to recover and the use of all external factors such as medicaments is seen as an aid to this innate power within the body to repel whatever has caused ill health. These external factors are not seen as the direct cause of the cure of sickness.

Muslim physicians relied, of course, a great deal upon external symptoms such as the pulse and complexion and possessed remarkable powers to diagnose a disease through these factors. As far as ordinary diseases are concerned, they were especially aware of the importance of the digestive system in internal disorders and had recourse to a range of purgatives to re-establish the orderly function of the digestive organs. They also relied upon blood-letting, either to remove poisons within the body or to bring the body into harmony with new climatic conditions such as change of seasons. They were able to distinguish a large number of diseases, some of which they learned from ancient medical sources and others, like small-pox, meningitis, whooping cough, hay fever, etc., which they were the first to distinguish and describe correctly in the history of medicine. Their treatment of these and other diseases depended, of course, upon the humoural pathology and the theory of the correspondence between the natures within the humours and in external factors such as climate, food and drugs which forms the foundation of the whole of Islamic medicine.

Ophthalmology

A branch of medicine which received special attention in Islamic medicine was ophthalmology and throughout the Islamic world the ophthalmologist (*kaḥḥāl*) had a distinct personality among the various classes of physicians. The Muslims inherited the whole of Greek and Alexandrian knowledge on the subject which is reflected in the earliest Arabic treatises on it such as those of Ḥunayn ibn Isḥāq. To this was gradually added the experience and knowledge of various

21. As a proof of the importance of the religious element in hygiene, we must point to the central place it occupies in 'prophetic medicine' and also to the fact that 'Alī ibn Mūsa'l-Riḍā, the eighth Shī'ite Imām, wrote a treatise on health and hygiene entitled *al-Risālat al-dhahabiyyah* (*The Golden Treatise*).

22. See Ullmann, *Die Medizin im Islam*, chap. 5, pp. 190 ff.

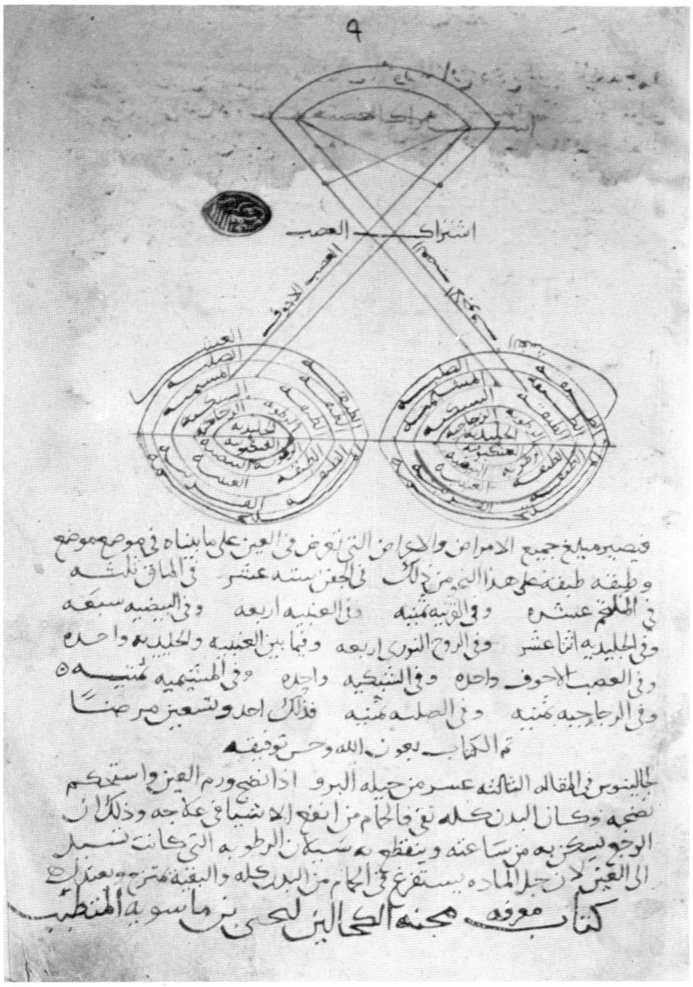

Figure 80. Anatomy of the eye.

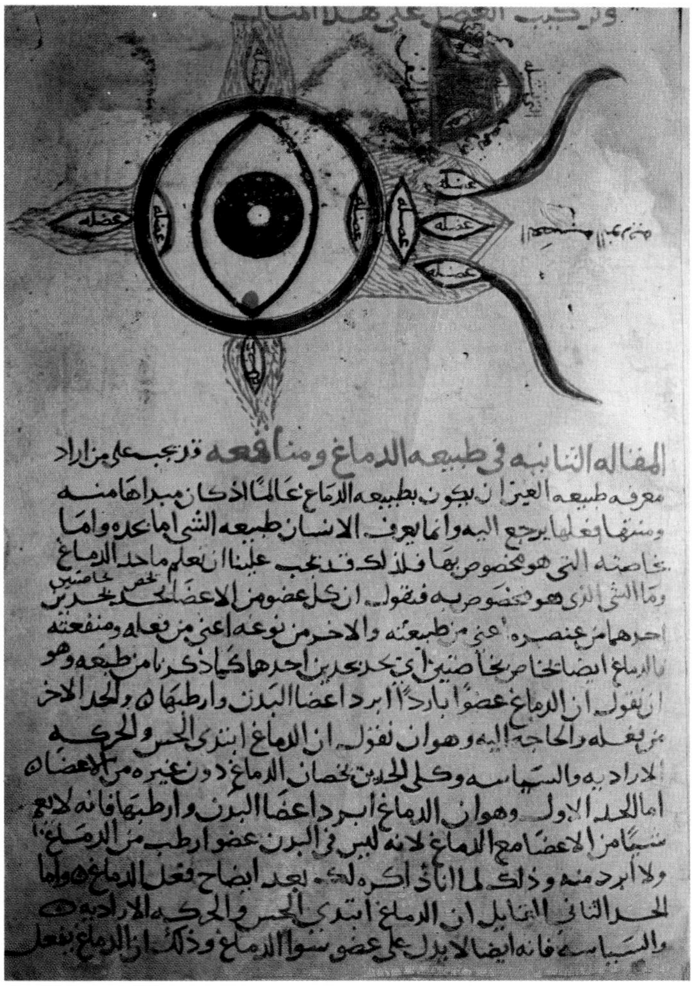

Plate 104. Anatomy of the eye.

Muslim ophthalmologists and oculists leading to the work of the outstanding figures of this branch of Islamic medicine such as the Christian oculist 'Alī ibn 'Īsā, the author of the most famous Arabic treatise on ophthalmology, the *Tadhkirat al-kaḥḥālīn* (*Treasury for Ophthalmologists*), and Abū Rūḥ Muḥammad al-Jurjānī entitled 'Zarrīndast' (The Golden Hand), the greatest of the Persian oculists whose *Nūr al-'ayn* (*The Light of the Eye*) has served the practitioners of the art for centuries.

Ophthalmology was specially pursued in Egypt as a result probably of the prevalence of eye diseases in that land due to the dust brought by the winds from the desert. Even during the pre-Islamic period, Alexandrian physicians were particularly noted for their works on ophthalmology. But this does not mean that it was not practised on a high level elsewhere. In both the eastern lands, especially Persia, and the Maghrib there appeared also notable treatises on the subject, while 'Alī ibn 'Īsā was taught everywhere and even translated into Latin as *Tractus de oculis Jesu ben Hali*. Many of the technical terms pertaining to ophthalmology in Latin as well as some modern European languages are of Arabic origin, and attest to the influence of Islamic sources on this subject. Eastward also the works of such men as al-Jurjānī spread into India where practices such as couching for the treatment of cataract have survived to the present day.

Surgery

The Muslim physicians usually disapproved of surgery where it was not considered as absolutely necessary, but nevertheless many surgical operations from the Caesarean section to complicated eye operations are described. Numerous surgical instruments especially various types of scalpels were developed, some quite elaborate and combining as elsewhere utility and beauty, and most have survived relatively unchanged over the ages with only small local variations. Most of the instruments revert back to those described in the work which marks the peak of surgery in Islam, the *Kitāb al-taṣrīf* (*The Book of Concession*) of the Andalusian Abu'l-Qāsim al-Zahrāwī whom the West knew so well as Albucasis.

Surgery in Islam was also concerned greatly with cauterization, which was widely practised as in the mediaeval West, and which also has traditional religious sources to support its practice. Cauterization was used not only for destroying infection around a wound but also for such specific problems as haemorrhoids. It of course also played an important role in the amputation of limbs, the destruction of certain tumours, and the like.[23]

It is of interest to note the treatment given for broken or disjointed parts of the body which forms part of surgery today. In Islamic medicine most such cases were not operated upon but were treated by means of external pressure applied to place the dislocated parts in their original position and even to set broken bones. The mastery of practitioners of this art has been so great that to this day they are able to compete with modern physicians in many parts of the Islamic world and can treat even such difficult fractures as broken shoulders not to speak of disjointed ones. Because of the mastery and practical success of the practitioners of traditional osteology, this branch of Islamic medicine has remained one of the most living until today, even in those parts of the Islamic world where the other branches are no longer practised seriously.[24]

Also in conjunction with surgery it is necessary to say something about oral surgery and dentistry in general. Muslim physicians performed various operations on the mouth as well as treating the teeth themselves. In addition to providing various instructions for keeping healthy teeth,[25] they provided regular service for patients with tooth trouble and even made false teeth from the bones of animals for some of their patients.

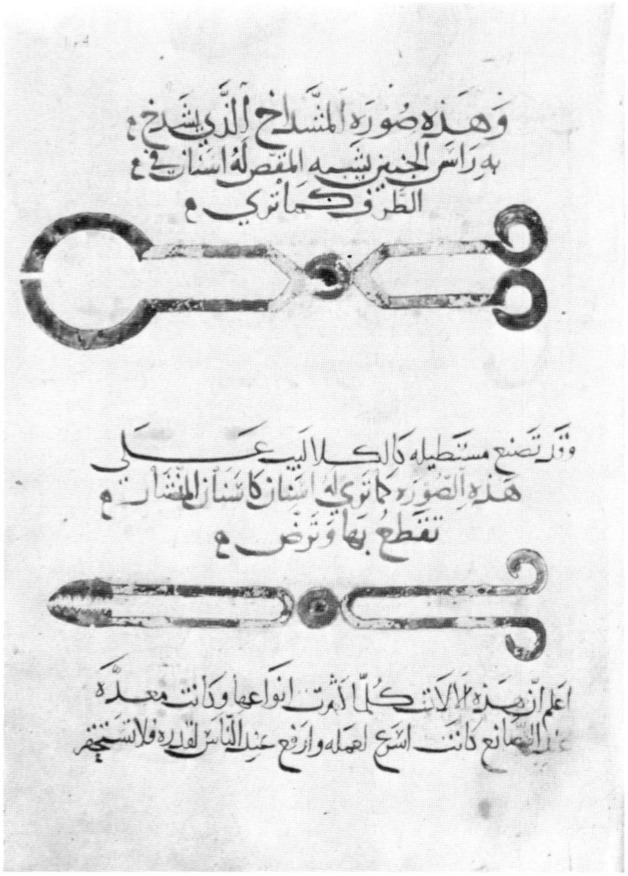

Figure 81. Surgical instruments from al-Zahrāwī.

23. Some of the simpler forms of cauterization as well as other operations were performed in the Islamic world as in the West by barbers. This was especially true of circumcision, which is also a religious rite in Islam and is usually combined with special religious ceremonies in the family.

24. Not the least reason for the success of this class of *ḥakīms* is the various effective ointments which they possess, ointments whose composition they usually keep secret. Some of these ointments have been kept within one family over the centuries.

25. It is remarkable how the quality of teeth deteriorates with the 'advance' of modern civilization, as one can observe among living members of a single family in many Islamic cities today. The more modernized their life style becomes, the more rapidly usually do their teeth and eyes deteriorate. This is not a matter of historical speculation but of actual experience and observation.

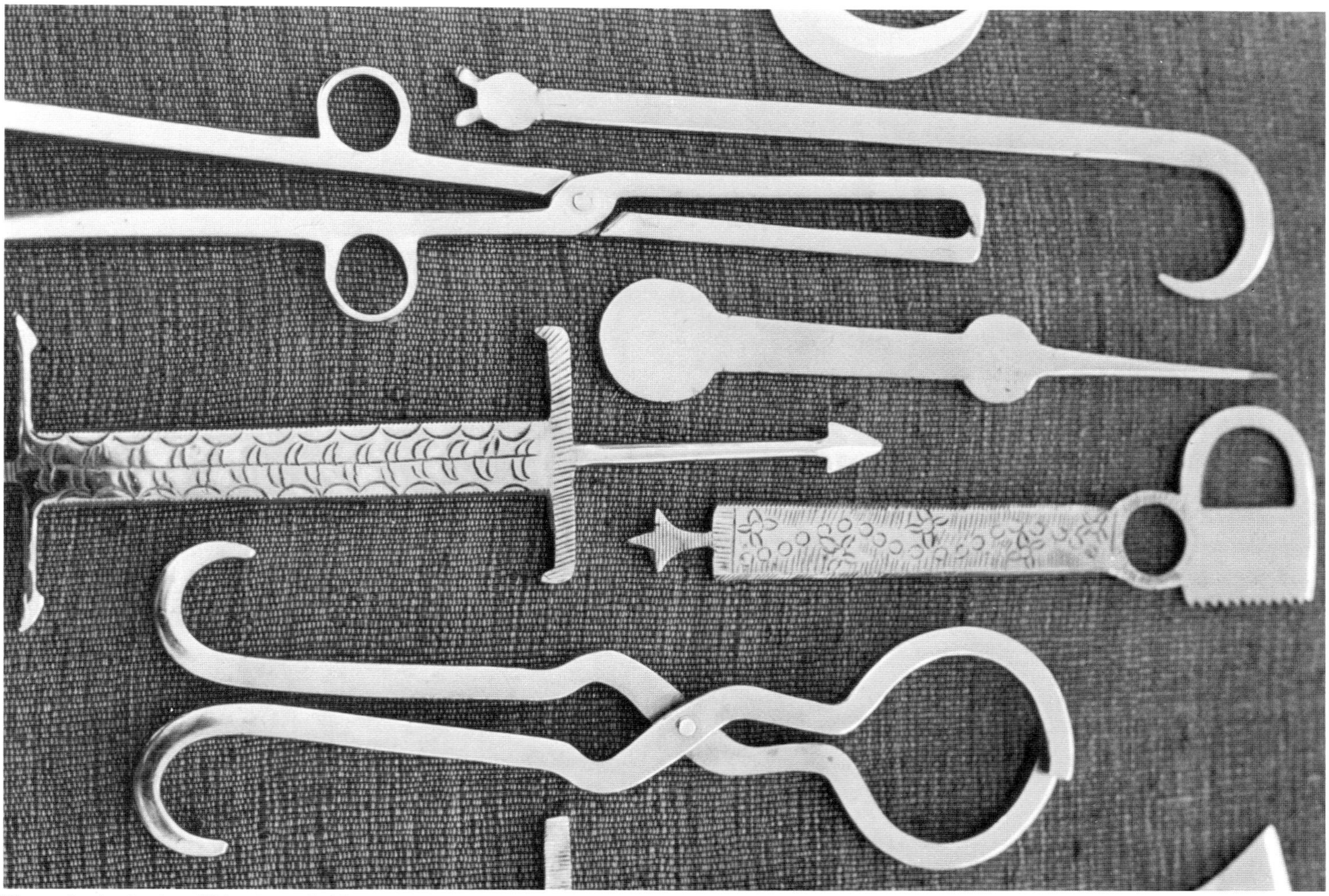

Figure 82. A selection of Islamic surgical instruments.

Figure 83. A Caesarean operation.

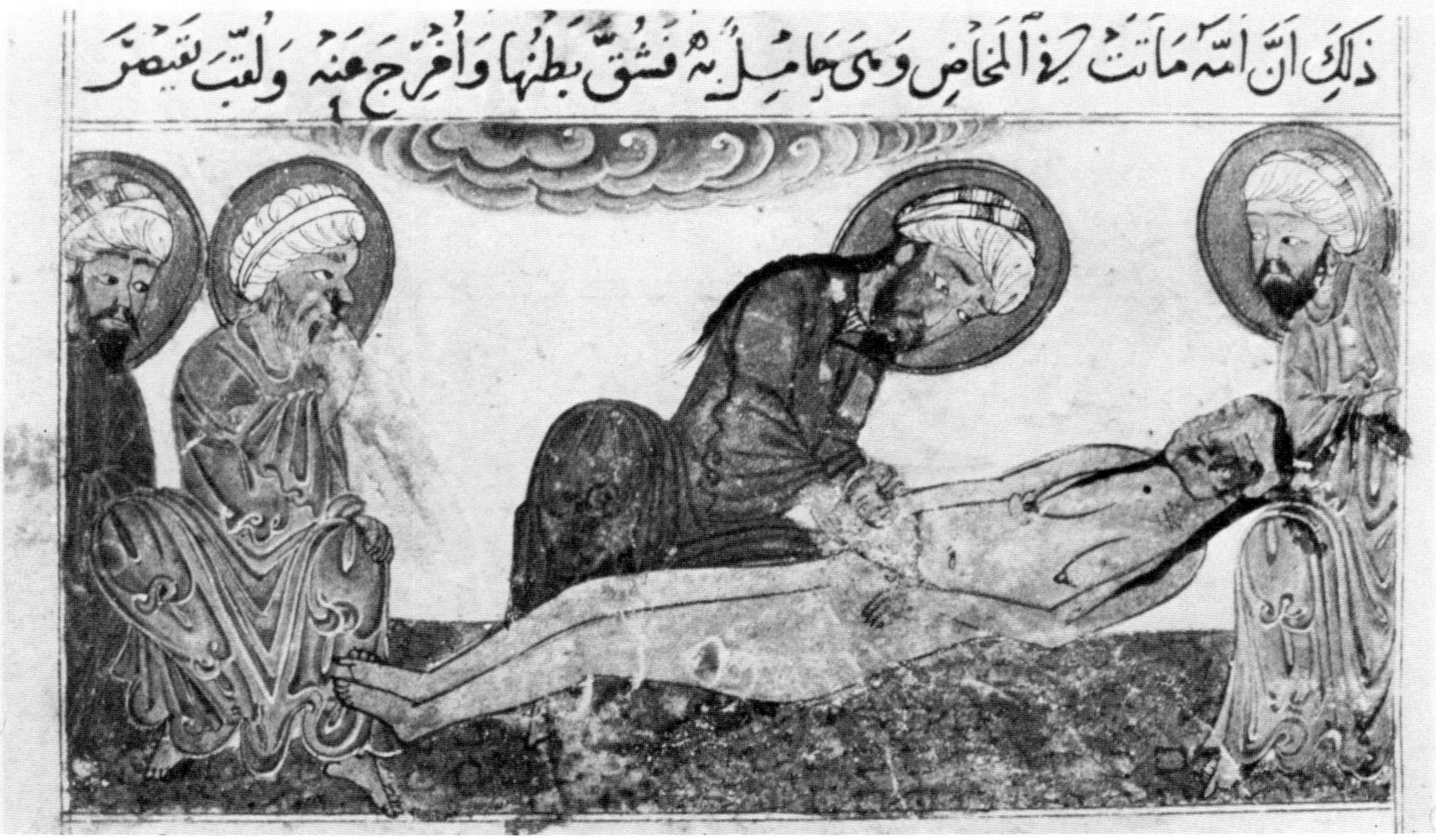

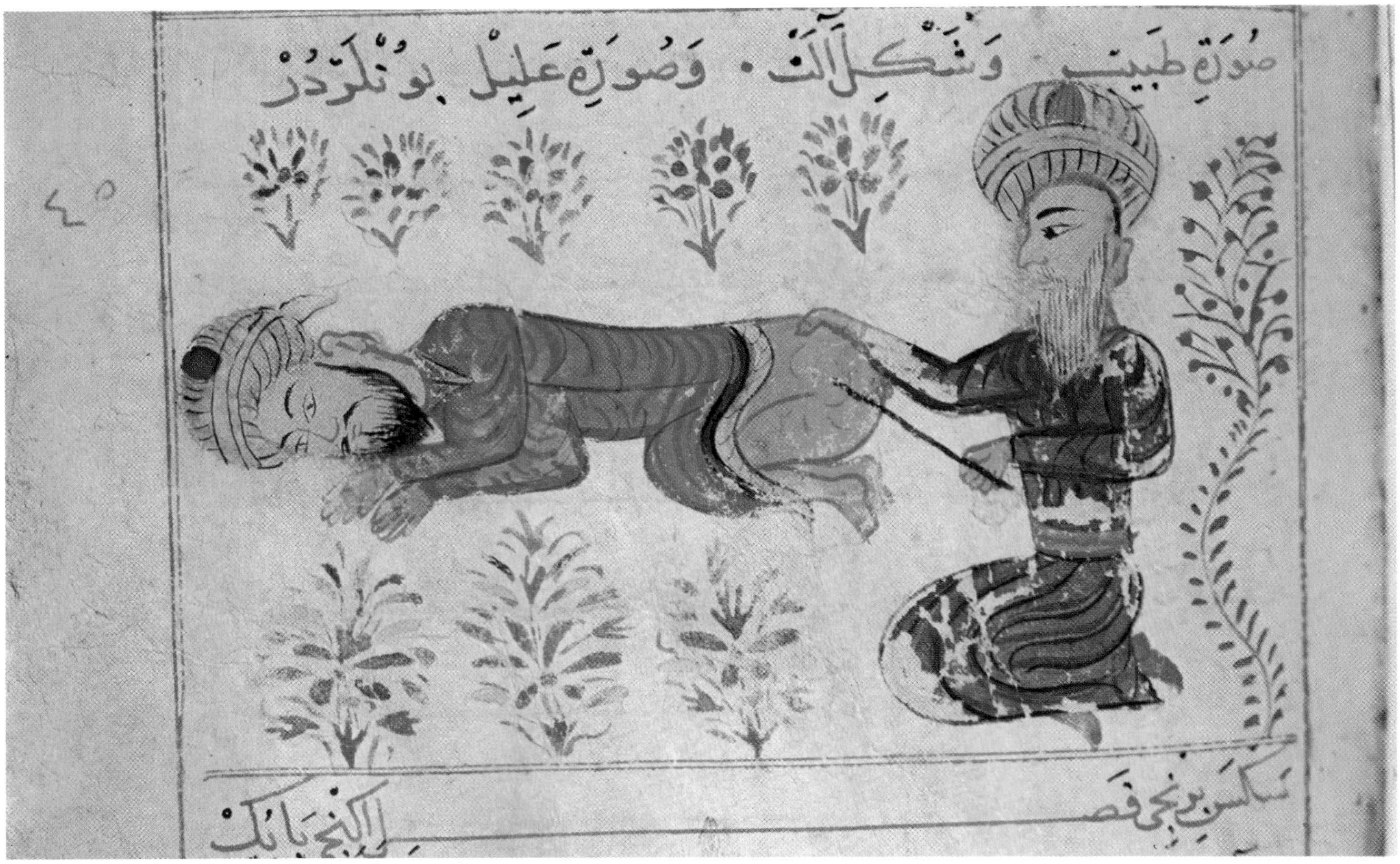

Plate 105. A patient with haemorrhoids being treated.

Plate 106. A dislocated shoulder being set.

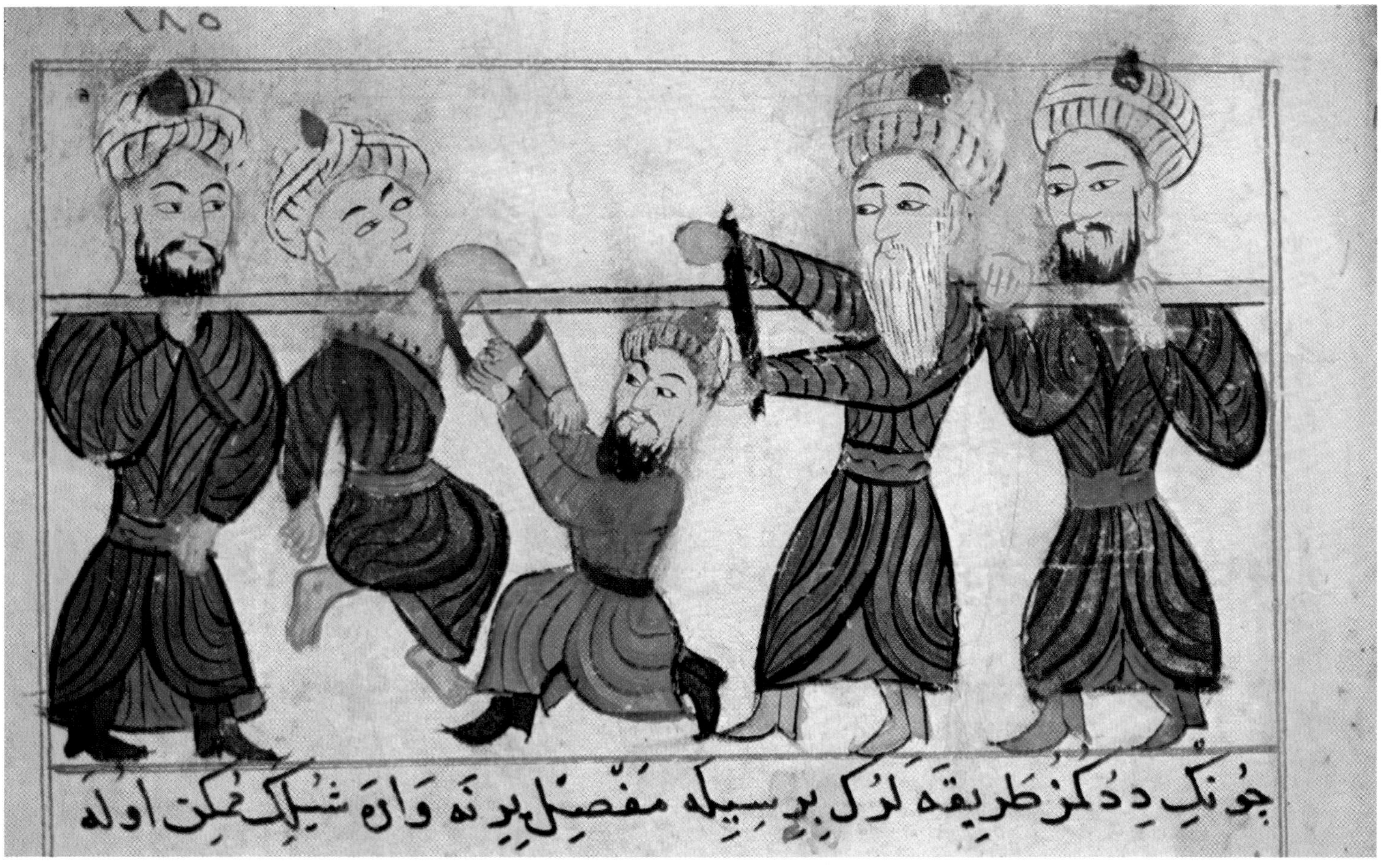

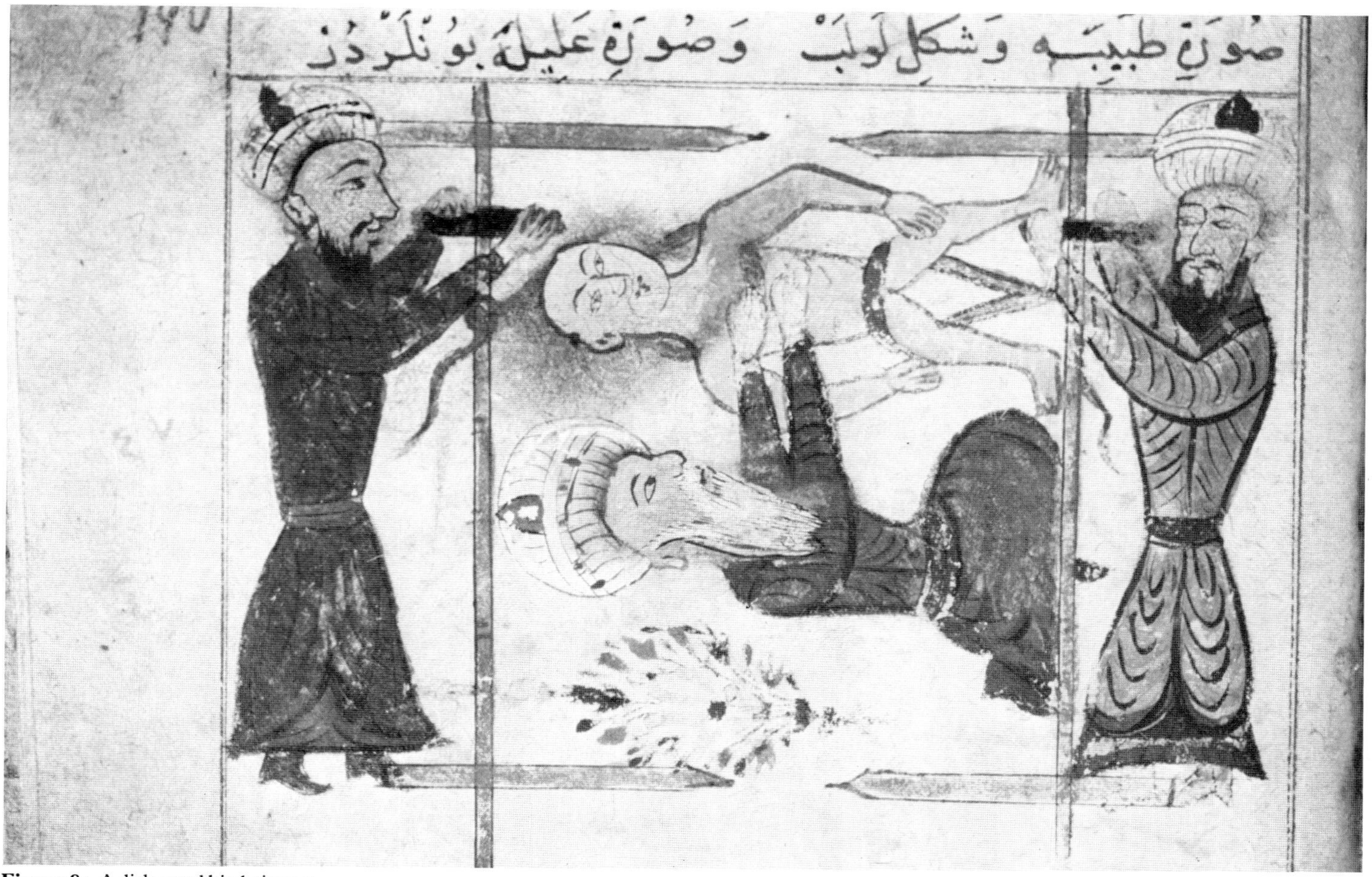

Figure 84. A dislocated hip being set.

Plate 107. A dentist at work.

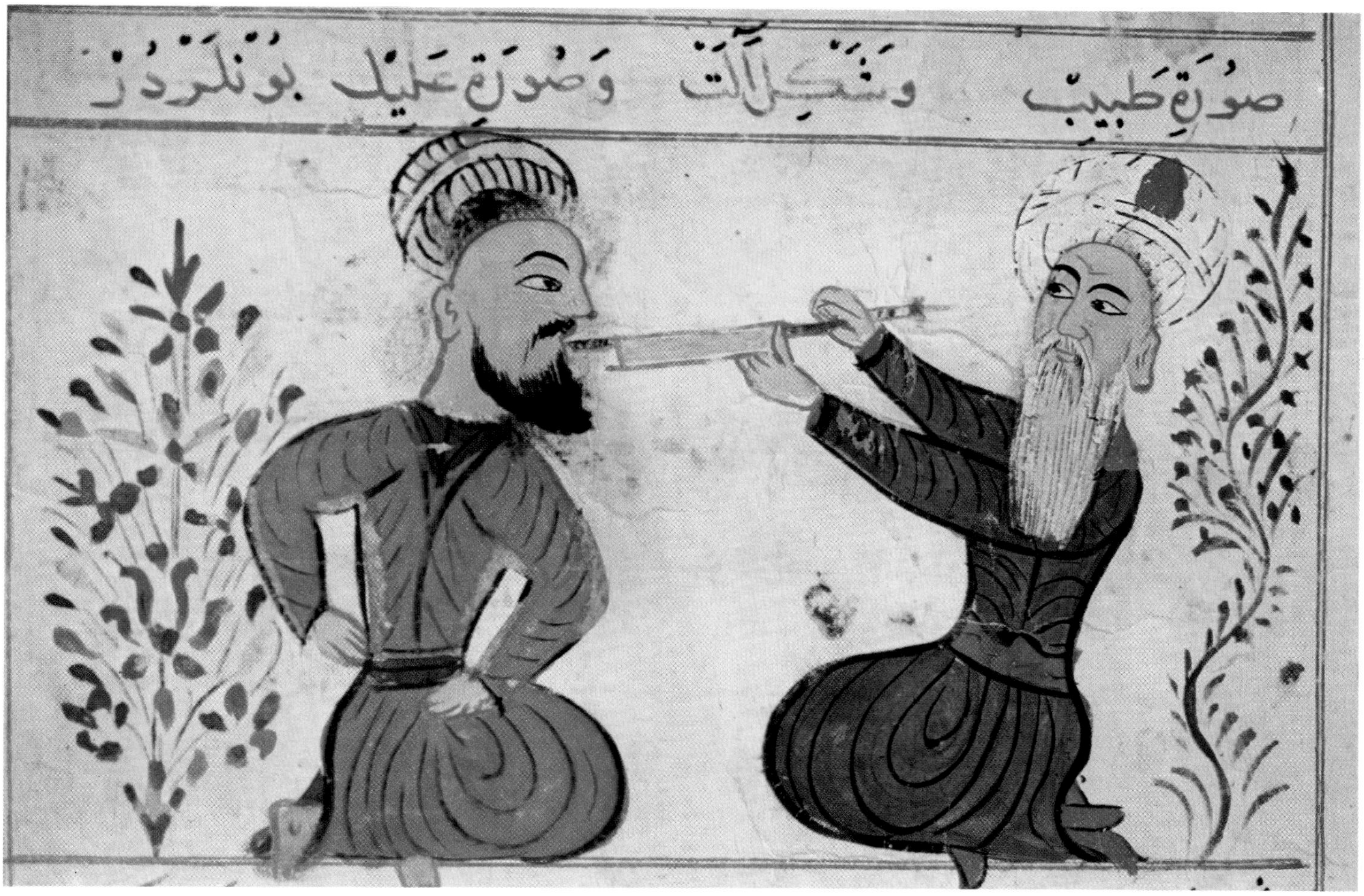

Medicine and the Occult Sciences

Finally in this brief treatment of the various aspects of Islamic medicine a word must be said about the relation of this medicine to such occult sciences as astrology, the 'occult properties of objects' (*khawāṣṣ al-ashyā'*), etc. This is a complicated subject treated in certain medical works and not in others. Most physicians believed in astrological correspondences and took them into consideration in their treatment of both psychological and physical ailments. Some wrote of the special influence of certain minerals or plants upon various physical forces within the body or special ailments and numerous treatises exist where tables are given to show these relations. Likewise the discussion of the medical effects of the occult properties of various minerals and plants is a part and parcel of most lapidaries and works on natural history as mentioned already. This type of treatment is of course distinct from recourse to prayer, fasting, litanies and use of certain traditional sciences connected with the 'therapeutic' power of various formulas of the Holy Book which is also a very common practice among all Muslim peoples today as before. Altogether the relation between medicine and all the forces which belong to the worlds above nature forms an essential aspect of Islamic medicine and no amount of criticism by modern physicians or Muslim apologists can obliterate this fact. Moreover, this aspect of Islamic medicine, if secondary accretions are shorn away from it, is an essential aspect of it, containing a knowledge of the relationship between the microcosm and other orders of reality to which modern medicine is completely alien, but which nevertheless many people are seeking to discover today through whatever means they find at their disposal.

Islamic Medicine in its Historical Development

The Historiography of Islamic Medicine

A great deal of research has been carried out over the past two centuries by Western and Muslim scholars alike to make better known the history of Islamic medicine.[26] But although the task is far from finished because of the vast amount of material involved, the work of these scholars has been facilitated by the historiography of medicine within the Islamic world itself which is the most complete and developed of any traditional civilization.

Scholars working within the Islamic world, at first Christians such as Isḥāq ibn Ḥunayn and then Muslim ones, began to write histories of medicine based on the earlier work of John the Grammarian. By the 4th/10th centuries major histories of philosophers and physicians – these being usually treated together – appeared, such as the well-known histories of Abū Sulaymān al-Manṭiqī al-Sijistānī and his student Abū Ḥayyān al-Tawḥīdī in Baghdad, Ibn Juljul and Qāḍī Ṣā'id al-Andalūsī in the Maghrib. These in turn served as bases for the major works of the 7th/13th century which mark the peak of writings on the history of Islamic medicine, namely the *'Uyūn al-anbā' fī ṭabaqāt al-aṭibbā'* (*Important Informations concerning the Generations of Physicians*) of Ibn Abī Uṣaybi'ah, the *Ta'rīkh al-ḥukamā'* (*The History of Physicians and Philosophers*) of Ibn al-Qifṭī and the *Wafayāt al-a'yān* (*The Demise of Eminent Men*) of Ibn Khallikān. These works complemented the vast amount of information on the history of medicine contained in actual medical treatises such as the *Kāmil al-ṣinā'ah* (*The Perfection of the Art*) of al-Majūsī.

26. Concerning the history of Islamic medicine, see A. Fonahn, *Zur Quellenkunde der persischen Medizin*, Leipzig, 1919; C. Elgood, *A Medical History of Persia and the Eastern Caliphate*; *idem*, *Safavid Medical Practice*; E. G. Browne, *Arabian Medicine*, Cambridge, 1921; D. E. H. Campbell, *Arabian Medicine and Its Influence on the Middle Ages*, London, 1926; L. Leclerc, *Histoire de la médecine arabe*; *exposé complet des traductions du grec*; *les sciences en Orient, leur transmission par les traductions latines*, 2 vols., Paris, 1876, also New York, 1960; F. Sezgin, *Geschichte des arabischen Schrifttums*, vol. III, Leiden, 1970; Ullmann, *Die Medizin im Islam*, pp. 108–189; and M. Najmābādī, *Tārīkh-i ṭibb dar īrān pas az islām*; also A. Dietrich, *Medicinalia Arabica*, Göttingen, 1966. For a general bibliography of works on Islamic medicine, see S. Hamarneh, *Bibliography on Medicine and Pharmacy in Medieval Islam*, Stuttgart, 1964. The numerous studies of M. Meyerhof need especially to be mentioned here, for they cover nearly every field of Islamic medicine.

Together they have enabled the scholars to trace the general historical development of Islamic medicine while the particular features continue to be filled through the study of individual physicians and treatises.[27]

The Sources of Islamic Medicine

Islamic medicine came into being as a result of the integration of the vast heritage of the Graeco-Alexandrian, Near Eastern (Syriac), Persian and Indian traditions into the general perspective of Islam with the orientation and general direction provided by the Holy Quran and prophetic *Ḥadīth*. Muslims considered practically every Greek philosopher including Pythagoras and Plato to be a physician as well, in accordance with their own identifying of the philosopher and the physician in the single figure of the *ḥakīm*. But the most important Graeco-Alexandrian sources were first of all Hippocrates and Galen, and then nearly all the other Greek physicians of note such as Alexander of Tralles and Paul of Aegina, and such famous treatises as the *Pandects* of Ahron and works attributed to Hermes and Asclepius.[28] Hippocrates, known in Arabic as Buqrāṭ – which is a household name in Arabic and Persian – is already cited by Jābir ibn Ḥayyān and was recognized from the earliest period as the father of Greek medicine. Numerous works by him were rendered into Arabic from the beginning of the movement of translation. As for Galen (Jālīnūs in Arabic which is also a very popular name in Islamic languages) more of his works survive in Arabic than in Greek and Muslims especially identified him as much with philosophy as with medicine since it was through him that they received the synopsis of the dialogues of Plato as well as the debates of the Alexandrian commentators of Aristotle. Islamic medicine was particularly fortunate in receiving the Hippocratic and Galenic corpus in the unmatched translation of Ḥunayn ibn Isḥāq who was himself an outstanding physician. He is perhaps responsible more than any other translator for the perfection of the medical vocabulary in Arabic.[29] In both quantity and quality the translations of the treatises of Galen occupy a unique position among the sources of Islamic medicine.[30]

As far as Syriac works are concerned, the works of Sarjīs of Resh'aynā which were taught at Jundishapur influenced Muslim authors as did a few other treatises such as the work of Yarbūqā on poisons.[31] Jundishapur was also the locus of Persian influences upon Islamic medicine. But as far as actual texts are concerned little has survived, the most important being the introduction of Burzōe to the *Kalīlah wa Dimnah*. As for Indian sources the most influential works translated either at Jundishapur or Baghdad were the *Cānakya* (the Arabic *Shānāq*) on poisons, the *Suśruta* (the Arabic *Susrud*) cited by al-Ṭabarī and al-Rāzī, and the *Caraka saṃhitā* of Caraka (*Saharik al-hindī*). Together these works constituted the written record which along with the practical knowledge and the oral tradition were transmitted to Islamic civilization at Jundishapur, Alexandria and elsewhere, making possible the genesis of Islamic medicine in the 2nd/8th century.

27. On the historiography of Islamic medicine, see M. Plessner, 'The Natural Sciences and Medicine', in the *Legacy of Islam*, pp. 456–458; and Ullmann, *Die Medizin im Islam*, pp. 228–233.

28. On these sources, see Sezgin, *op. cit.*, pp. 21 ff.; and Ullmann, *op. cit.*, pp. 25 ff.

29. The technical terminology of Islamic medicine, as well as other sciences, has been a subject of research for many decades in the West and was also always of interest to traditional Islamic philologists and scientists, as seen in the treatment given to such terms in many Arabic, Persian and Turkish lexicons. As far as Western works are concerned, see G. S. Colin and H. P. J. Renaud, *Glossaire sur le Mansuri de Rasès*, Rabat, 1941; A. Fonahn, *Arabic and Latin Anatomical Terminology*, Kristiania, 1922; and also the more general work of A. Siggel, *Arabisch-deutsches Wortbuch der Stoffe aus den drei Naturreichen*, Berlin, 1950.

30. Sezgin cites 163 Arabic works by Galen or attributed to him. See Sezgin, *op. cit.*, pp. 78–140.

31. See M. Levey, *Medieval Arabic Toxicology, the Book of Poisons of Ibn Wahshiya and Its Relation to Early Indian and Greek Texts*, Philadelphia, 1966.

'Prophetic Medicine'

The religious basis of Islamic medicine is to be found in a group of traditions of the Holy Prophet concerning medicine assembled in a special section by the early canonical scholars who brought together the general collections of *Ḥadīth*. Gradually around this nucleus there grew a particular branch of medicine called 'prophetic medicine' (*al-ṭibb al-nabawī* or *ṭibb al-nabī*) which later accepted certain features of the Galenic system but remained always of an overwhelmingly religious character. Throughout the ages, works were composed in this field, the first, according to tradition, being the collection of the prophetic sayings pertaining to medicine assembled by 'Alī al-Riḍā, the eighth Shī'ite Imām, during the caliphate of al-Ma'mūn.[32] Soon this type of writing became a distinct class of its own, so that such later compilers as the Ottoman bibliographer Ḥājjī Khalīfah in his *Kashf al-ẓunūn* (*The Removal of Doubts*) devoted a special section to it.

Such authors as Abū Nu'aym al-Iṣfahānī, the outstanding biographer of early Sufism, the jurisprudent and theologian Ibn al-Jawzī, the historian and traditionalist Abū 'Abdallāh al-Dhahabī, the encyclopaedist Jalāl al-Dīn al-Suyūṭī, the physician-astronomer Maḥmūd ibn 'Umar Chaghmīnī[33] and many others wrote on 'prophetic medicine'. And interest in such works continued in the later centuries with texts appearing in Persian, Turkish and even Urdu as well as Arabic on the subject. Moreover, in Shī'ism, a class of works entitled 'the medicine of the Imāms' (*ṭibb al-a'immah*) associated particularly with the first, sixth and eighth Imāms, was collected and edited as complementary to prophetic medicine and enjoying the same wide popularity. Altogether this branch of Islamic medicine is important not only for an understanding of regulations concerning health, followed by a vast number of believers because of their prophetic origin, but also because it reveals the religious matrix in which the older schools of medicine were received by Muslims. For it was from the integration of the Islamic 'form' with the '*materia*' provided through translation that Islamic medicine as a distinct school came into being.

Islamic Medicine from its Origins to Ibn Sīnā

Nearly all traditional sources mention that the first Muslim physician was a Companion of the Holy Prophet, Ḥārith ibn Kaladah, who had studied at Jundishapur and had carried out a discourse with the Sassanid king Anūshirawān on questions of health. He later returned to Medinah where the Holy Prophet sent to him many patients for treatment. His son al-Nadr is also said to have been a physician. But despite this very early contact of Islam with schools of medicine of foreign origin, during the earliest period Arab Muslims themselves did not pursue this field and nearly all of the early physicians were either Christians, Jews or Persians. It was only after the establishment of Arabic as a major medical language and the penetration of medicine and its lore into the texture of everyday life that Arab Muslims became gradually drawn to this subject.

Since Muslims had conquered both Jundishapur and Alexandria while they were both functioning as centres of medicine, especially the former being in fact at the height of its activity, competent physicians were available to them from the earliest years of the Islamic era. But the first translation of an Arabic treatise did not take place until the Umayyad period during the reign of the Caliph Marwān I when Māsarjawayh, a Jewish physician from Basra, translated the *Pandects* of Ahron into Arabic.

The establishment of Islamic medicine is related, however, to the city of Baghdad and the

32. There is also a treatise in the Jābirean corpus entitled *Kitāb al-ṭibb al-nabawī'alā ra'y ahl al-bayt (The Book of 'Prophetic Medicine' according to the view of the Household of the Prophet)*.

33. The text of al-Suyūṭī entitled simply *Ṭibb al-nabī* is perhaps the most famous of this type of literature in Islam. It has been translated along with the *Ṭibb al-nabī* of Chaghmīnī by C. Elgood, '*Tibb-ul-Nabbi* or Medicine of the Prophet, being a Translation of Two Works of the Same Name', *Osiris*, vol. 14, 1962, pp. 33–192. The text of al-Suyūṭī was also translated into French in the 13th/19th century: see A. Perron, *La médecine du prophète*, Paris-Algiers, 1860.

Plate 108. The physician, 'Abdallāh ibn Bukhtīshū'.

transfer of major medical figures from Jundishapur to that city during the caliphate of al-Manṣūr, Hārūn al-Rashīd and al-Ma'mūn. Chief among these figures were members of the Bukhtīshū' family. Jūrjīs ibn Bukhtīshū' came to Baghdad during the reign of al-Manṣūr albeit not permanently while Jībra'īl Bukhtīshū' migrated to that city and established a medical practice, writing many works on medicine and training students. Aided by the caliphs as well as by the Barmakid family, some of whose members were viziers, the Bukhtīshū' as well as Māsawayh and other families transferred the heart of the medical centre of Jundishapur to Baghdad which henceforth became the most important medical centre in the world of that day.[34]

During the second half of the 2nd/8th century the dominating medical figure of Baghdad was Yuḥannā ibn Māsawayh, whose father had emigrated from Jundishapur and gained fame as an ophthalmologist in Baghdad. Ibn Māsawayh, known in the West as Mesuë Senior was the first Christian author to write independent medical works in Arabic and in fact was a prolific author.[35] He was also a translator of Greek texts and is said to have rendered into Arabic some of the manuscripts brought back by Hārūn al-Rashīd after his battle against the Byzantines in Ancyra and Amorium. He was particularly well known as an ophthalmologist[36] but also wrote in other fields of medicine as well as in pharmacology.[37]

The foremost translator and also medical figure in Baghdad after Ibn Māsawayh during the early decades of the 3rd/9th century was his student Ḥunayn ibn Isḥāq, an Arab Christian with great mastery of Arabic, Greek and Syriac who, as already mentioned, is more than anyone else responsible for the high quality of translation of the work of the Greek masters of medicine, especially Hippocrates and Galen, into Arabic.

It is important to note also that Ḥunayn not only translated individual texts but a whole medical curriculum, as *The Alexandrian Summaries* (*Jawāmi' al-iskandarāniyyīn*) shows. He thus influenced directly not only the practice but also the teaching of medicine. Ḥunayn was also an accomplished physician and was the author of two basic works on ophthalmology: the *Kitāb al-'ashr maqālāt fi'l-'ayn* (*Ten Dissertations on the Eye*) which is the oldest systematic treatment of the subject containing also diagrams of the anatomy of the eye, and the *Kitāb al-masā'il fi'l-ayn* (*The Book of Questions Concerning the Eye*).[38] He also composed other influential works on general

34. Belonging also to this period and of much importance for the theoretical aspect of medicine are the writings of Jābir on medicine. However, they have not, as yet, been seriously studied from the medical point of view. See Sezgin, *op. cit.*, pp. 211–223.

35. Ibn Abī Uṣaybi'ah mentions 42 medical works by him.

36. See M. Meyerhof, 'Die Augenheilkunde des Juḥannā b. Māsawaih', *Der Islam*, vol. 6, 1915, pp. 217–256.

37. See M. Levey, 'Ibn Māsawaih and his Treatise on Simple Aromatic Substances', *Journal of the History of Medicine*, vol. 16, 1961, pp. 394–410.

38. Numerous scholars, especially J. Hirschberg and M. Meyerhof, have studied Ḥunayn's ophthalmology. See especially M. Meyerhof, 'Die Lehre von Sehen bei Ḥunain b. Isḥāq', *Archiv für die Geschichte der Medizin*, vol. 6, 1913, pp. 21–33; and Meyerhof, *The Book of the Ten Treatises on the Eye ascribed to Ḥunain*, Cairo, 1928.
A group of British scholars are now making a systematic study and translation of the Galenic and Hippocratic corpus in Arabic mostly associated with Ḥunayn and his school. See the competent translations of J. N. Mattock, M. C. Lyons and others in the *Arabic Technical and Scientific Texts* series being published by Cambridge University.

medical themes and left an indelible mark on the history of Islamic medicine.

Ḥunayn's contemporary in Baghdad, the philosopher al-Kindī, was also interested in medicine, and especially pharmacology, although he did not devote as much attention to the subject as did the later Peripatetics.[39] Likewise the great astronomer of that period, Thābit ibn Qurrah, dealt to some extent in his writings with medicine and must have been an accomplished physician for in his *Tadhkirah* (*The Treasury*) which was later to become a standard text of medicine he described measles and smallpox before al-Rāzī did.[40]

The first notable Muslim physician appeared also during the first half of the 3rd/9th century. 'Alī ibn Rabban al-Ṭabarī, whose family was converted to Islam, hailed from northern Persia but came to Baghdad. He is responsible for the *Firdaws al-ḥikmah* (*The Paradise of Wisdom*) which is the first systematic Islamic work on medicine. Al-Ṭabarī made full use of Syriac and Greek sources, apparently without the aid of the translations of Ḥunayn, and also of Sanskrit translations. His work contains not only chapters on general cosmological principles and all the branches of medicine, but also a special section devoted to Indian medicine. It is particularly known for its extensive treatment of anatomy.[41]

Contact with original Greek and Syriac medical sources continued during this period, as seen in such a figure as Qusṭā ibn Lūqā, who knew both Greek and Syriac and wrote numerous medical works, most of which have not been studied until now. But by this time the main medical heritage of the ancient world was already translated into Arabic and upon the foundation established by al-Ṭabarī on the one hand and Ḥunayn on the other, Islamic medicine began its golden age. And this occurred almost immediately with the appearance of Muḥammad ibn Zakariyyā' al-Rāzī (Rhazes), considered by many to be the greatest of Muslim physicians, especially in the experimental and clinical aspects of medicine.

He was born in Rayy, received his earliest education in that city, turned to music and alchemy early in life and only later to medicine. He came to Baghdad, where he headed the main hospital in the city and finally returned to Rayy, where he died in 313/925.[42] Nothing is known of his medical education and in fact so much legend has surrounded him that it is difficult to depict a distinct historical image of him.[43] It is known that he had immense clinical experience, trained numerous students, wrote a great deal and had a mastery of many subjects from philosophy and psychology to alchemy and medicine. Although he has attracted many modern scholars with his philosophical works,[44] it is mostly as an alchemist and physician that his name has survived in Islamic history.

The incomparable historian and scientist al-Bīrūnī was so deeply interested in the writings of al-Rāzī that he devoted years to collecting his

39. The degree of al-Kindī's knowledge and mastery of pharmacology can be gauged from his *Aqrābādhīn*. See M. Levey, *The Medical Formulary or Aqrābādhīn of al-Kindī. Translated with a Study of its Materia Medica*, Madison (Wisconsin) and London, 1966. Al-Kindī was also one of the first Muslim authors to write on the relation between astronomy-astrology and medicine, a branch of the subject which became known later as *al-ṭibb al-nujūmī*.

40. See R. Y. Ebied, 'Thābit ibn Qurra: Fresh Light on an Obscure Medical Composition', *Muséon*, vol. 79, 1966, pp. 453–473.

41. See Meyerhof, ''Alī ibn Rabban aṭ-Ṭabarī, ein persischer Arzt des 9. Jahrhunderts n. Chr.', *Zeitschrift der Deutschen Morgenlandischen Gesellschaft*, vol. 85, 1931, pp. 38–68; Meyerhof, 'Alī aṭ-Ṭabarī's "Paradise of Wisdom", one of the oldest Arabic compendiums of medicine', *Isis*, vol. 16, 1931, pp. 6–54; and A. Siggel, 'Die indischen Bucher aus dem Paradies der Weisheit über die Medizin', *Abhandlungen der Geistes-und-Sozialwissenschaftlichen Klasse der Akademie der Wissenschaft, u.d. Literatur*, Nr. 14, 1950, pp. 1097–1152.

42. On his life, see Browne, *Arabian Medicine*, pp. 44–53; Walzer, *Greek into Arabic*, pp. 15–17; Elgood, *A Medical History of Persia and the Eastern Caliphate*, pp. 184ff; M. Mohaghegh, *Filsūf-i rayy*, Tehran, 1349 (A.H. solar); and P. Kraus, 'Raziana I', *Orientalia*, vol. 4, 1935, pp. 300–334.

43. We are of those who believe that the traditional legendary aspects of figures such as Rāzī or Ibn Sīnā reveal as much and sometimes more about them than facts discovered through modern historical research relying solely upon texts concerning them.

44. The pioneering work in this domain was accomplished by P. Kraus, followed by R. Walzer and A. Badawi and more recently M. Mohaghegh, L. Goodman and several other younger scholars.

works and then wrote a catalogue of them in which, of the 184 works listed, 56 are devoted to medicine and allied subjects.[45] Of these, the most important is the immense encyclopaedia *al-Ḥāwī* (*Continens*) which was so celebrated in the Latin West.[46] It is based upon al-Rāzī's own daily clinical observations and is rich from the observational and experimental point of view rather than for its contribution to theory. A shorter and also famous work is the *Kitāb al-manṣūrī* (*The Book of Manṣūr*), again well known in the West as *Liber medicinalis ad Almansorem*. Other famous writings of al-Rāzī include the *Kitāb taqsīm al-ʿilal* (*The Book on the Division of the Causes of Disease* – known in Latin as *Liber divisionum*), the *Kitāb al-fakhrī* (*The Splendid Book – Liber pretiosus*) and, perhaps his most famous work in the West, the *Kitāb al-jadarī wa'l-ḥaṣbah* (*Treatise on Smallpox and Measles*, famous in Latin as *Liber de pestilentia*).[47]

The works of al-Rāzī cover nearly every aspect of medicine. The man who considered himself as the equal of Plato and Aristotle combined the medical heritage of Antiquity and his own powers of observation and deduction to discover many new maladies, propose new cures and point to new paths in the field of traditional medicine. He marks a major peak in Islamic medicine and his influence in the Islamic world and the West in nearly all branches of medicine is practically beyond measure.[48] His fame throughout the past millennium is sufficient proof of his role in the history of Islamic and even Western medicine.

Al-Rāzī's successor on the philosophic scene, Abū Naṣr al-Fārābī, was of much greater influence in the field of philosophy than al-Rāzī but not at all as much concerned with medicine. Al-Fārābī did, however, show some interest in medicine, especially in its methods and principles and its place in the hierarchy of the sciences.[49] He is also purported to have practised medicine especially when he was in Aleppo and Damascus.

The most notable medical figure following al-Rāzī was another Persian, ʿAlī ibn al-ʿAbbās al-Majūsī from Ahvaz, known in the West as Haly Abbas. Al-Majūsī is known particularly for his masterly compendium written in the 4th/10th century, the *Kāmil al-ṣināʿah* known also as *Kitāb al-malikī* (*The Perfection of the Art* or *The Royal Book*), famous in Latin as *Liber regius*. This work stands in both size and content between al-Rāzī's *al-Ḥāwī* and the *Kitāb al-manṣūrī* and is known both for its clear and logical treatment of the subject and its study of the history of medicine. Al-Majūsī was the director of the famous ʿAḍūd al-Dawlah hospital in Baghdad and the book reflects a knowledge which comes not only from book learning but also from extensive personal experience.[50]

The 4th/10th and 5th/11th centuries were the age of numerous medical authorities of the highest rank. While al-Majūsī was dominating the field of internal medicine in the East, Andalusia produced the first of its great medical figures, Abu'l-Qāsim al-Zahrāwī (from Madīnat al-Zahrā' of Cordova) whose name in its Latin form of Albucasis is practically as famous as in its Arabic form. Al-Zahrāwī was the greatest of Muslim

45. See al-Bīrūnī, *Epître de Beruni contenant le répertoire des ouvrages de Muḥammad b. Zakariya al-Razi*, Paris, 1936; re-issued with a new introduction by M. Mohaghegh, Tehran, 1974. On the writings of Rāzī, see also M. Najmābādī, *Mu'allafāt wa muṣannafāt-i Abū Bakr Muḥammad ibn Zakariyā-yi Rāzī ḥakīm-i buzurg-i īrānī*, Tehran, 1339 (A.H. solar).

46. As the research of A. Z. Iskandar, reflected in his doctoral thesis at Oxford University, shows, there are two versions of this work. Iskandar has also revealed the great influence of this vast encyclopaedia upon Ibn Sīnā.

47. Translated as late as the 12th/18th century and published by J. Channing as *Rhazes de Variolis et Morbillis*, London, 1766.

48. On various aspects of Rāzī's medicine, see O. Temkin, 'Texts and Documents, a Medieval Translation of Rhazes' Clinical Observations', *Bulletin of the History of Medicine*, vol. 12, 1942, pp. 102–117; Meyerhof, 'Thirty-three Clinical Observations by Rhazes (circa 900 A.D.)', *Isis*, vol. 23, 1935, pp. 321–356; P. de Koning, *Trois traités d'anatomie arabe*, Leiden, 1903, pp. 2–89 (containing the anatomical section of the *Kitāb al-manṣūrī*); and A. J. Arberry, *The Spiritual Physik of Rhazes*, London, 1950.

49. On al-Fārābī's medical interests, see M. Plessner, 'Al-Fārābī über Medizin, eine übersehene und seine neuentdeckte Quelle', *XXI Congress Internazionale di Storia Medicina*, 1970, pp. 1533–1539. Al-Fārābī was also particularly interested in the therapeutic effects of music and wrote a treatise on the subject.

50. On al-Majūsī and his work, see de Koning, *Trois traités d'anatomie arabe*, pp. 90–431; B. Ben Yahia, 'Constantin l'Africain et l'école de Salerne', *Cahiers de Tunisie*, vol. 3, 1955, pp. 54–55; Ullmann, *Die Medizin im Islam*, pp. 140–147, where the content of the work is analyzed.

surgeons and the thirtieth section of his *Kitāb al-taṣrīf* (*The Book of Concessions*) or *Concessio*, which is a medical encyclopaedia, was the definitive guide for surgeons over the centuries. It gives the most systematic treatment of surgery in Islamic medicine, the text being accompanied with illustrations of the instruments used by al-Zahrāwī.[51] The surgical part of *al-Taṣrīf*, which is the first illustrated surgical treatise, consists of three parts: the first on cauterization advised by prophetic tradition and suggested by al-Zahrāwī for apoplexy; the second on operations performed with a scalpel and also operations of the eye as well as oral surgery; and the third on various forms of bone fractures and dislocations, as well as on child delivery. The work of al-Zahrāwī was also widely disseminated in the West thanks to the Latin translation of Gerard of Cremona and exercised much influence upon Italian and French surgeons and interest in it survived into the modern period.[52]

This was likewise the period of major works on ophthalmology, the age of the most famous authority in Islam, 'Alī ibn 'Īsā whose *Tadhkirat al-kaḥḥālīn* (*The Treasury of Ophthalmologists*) occupied the same position in its field as that of al-Zahrāwī did in surgery.[53] He was also the first person to propose the use of anaesthesia for surgery. There appeared at this time another celebrated oculist, 'Ammār al-Mawṣilī (Canamusali), who was born in Mosul but flourished in Egypt and like 'Alī ibn 'Īsā also gained fame in the Occident.[54] Further west in Tunis, Isḥāq ibn Sulaymān al-Isrā'īlī (Isaac Judaeus) also practised ophthalmology in Qayrawān, and like his contemporaries was translated into Latin and in his case also into Hebrew. Likewise it was at this time that Ibn al-Haytham was carrying out his important optical studies including ophthalmology to which reference has been made already.

The most illustrious figure of this period and Islam's most famous physician was Abū 'Alī ibn Sīnā, the 'prince of physicians', the Avicenna of Western Scholastics and physicians and one by whose name many people in the East call Islamic medicine to this day. Ibn Sīnā lived throughout his life in Persia. Born near Bukhara he wandered throughout his life over Persia going from one city to another, until he died of colic in Hamadan in 428/1037.[55] He was self-taught in medicine and was already a famous physician by the age of 18. Access to the royal library of the Samanids, vast clinical experience and an intellectual power which has made of him the most influential and well known of all Muslim philosopher-scientists permitted Ibn Sīnā to systematize medicine in such a definitive manner that his works became dominant authorities in East and West for centuries to come and are still the main reference for the practitioners of Islamic medicine wherever they may be.

Ibn Sīnā's most famous medical work is *al-Qānūn fi'l-ṭibb* (*The Canon of Medicine*) which is perhaps the most influential single work in the whole history of medicine, even including the writings of Hippocrates and Galen. Written in Arabic, it was translated later into Persian, Turkish, Urdu and other Islamic languages as well as into Hebrew, Catalan and Latin, the Latin translation being one of the most often printed works in the 10th/16th century. It consists of five books as follows:

1. General principles of medicine (*al-kulliyyāt* in Arabic and *Colliget* in Latin) which includes the philosophy of medicine, anatomy and physiology, hygiene and the treatment of diseases.
2. Simple drugs.

51. See K. Sudhoff, *Beiträge zur Geschichte der Chirurgie im Mittelalter*, vol. II, Leipzig, 1918, pp. 16–84; P. de Koning, *Traité sur le calcul dans les reins et dans la véssie*, Leiden, 1896; and the recent but somewhat less-than-perfect edition and translation of the text of al-Zahrāwī by M. S. Spink and G. Lewis, *Albucasis on Surgery and Instruments, A Definitive Edition of the Arabic Text with English Translation and Commentary*, London, 1973. There is an earlier French translation by L. Leclerc, *La Chirurgie d'Albucasis*, Paris, 1861.

52. The first modern edition goes back to the 1778 Oxford edition of the Arabic text with a Latin translation.

53. Studied and translated by J. Hirschberg, J. Lippert and E. Mittwoch, *Die Arabischen Augenärzte nach den Quellen bearbeitet*, vol. I, Leipzig, 1904; and C. A. Wood, *Memorandum of a Tenth-Century Oculist, for the Use of Modern Ophthalmologists*, Chicago, 1936.

54. Hirschberg, *et al.*, *ibid.*, vol. II, Leipzig, 1905.

55. A vast number of writings have been devoted to the life and works of Ibn Sīnā. For a synopsis and also a bibliography of the subject, see Nasr, *An Introduction to Islamic Cosmological Doctrines*, chapter 11 and bibliography; Nasr, *Three Muslim Sages*, chap. I; also S. Afnan, *Avicenna, His Life and Works*, London, 1958.

3. Disorders of each internal and external organ of the body.
4. Illnesses which affect the body in general and are not limited to a single organ or limb.
5. Compound drugs.

Besides making extensive use of all the medical experience and knowledge of both Islamic and non-Islamic sources available to him, Ibn Sīnā also made many new observations of his own, including the discovery of meningitis, the manner of spread of epidemics, the contagious nature of tuberculosis, etc. He also made many discoveries in what is called psychosomatic medicine today. The *Canon*, as well as *al-Ḥāwī* and some of the other works of al-Rāzī, have in fact still much to reveal as far as their new contributions to the discovery and cure of various ailments are concerned.

Ibn Sīnā also wrote numerous other works dealing with specific medical subjects, some in Arabic and others in Persian. But perhaps the most widespread of his other medical works was his *al-Urjūzah fi'l-ṭibb* (*Medical Poem*) in which the principles of medicine are summarized in poetic form to facilitate their being memorized by medical students.[56] But this work does not of course compete with the *Canon* which has been studied and commented upon by generations of physicians in both East and West.[57]

Islamic Medicine after Ibn Sīnā

After Ibn Sīnā, Islamic medicine gradually underwent a regional development while preserving its basic unity. Of course ideas still travelled the width and breadth of the Islamic world but medicine came to possess enough of a local and regional character to make it possible to discuss its history in regions without doing injustice to its nature. This is possible, however, only if the underlying unity which binds the various parts of the Islamic world during the later centuries, despite external political divisions, is kept constantly in mind. For the sake of convenience the main regions where medicine developed from the middle of the 5th/11th century onward may be summarized as Iraq, Syria, Egypt and the adjacent areas; the Maghrib; Persia and India; and the Turkish part of the Ottoman world.

Iraq, Syria, Egypt and adjacent lands

In the Eastern Arab countries Baghdad continued to produce important physicians up to the 6th/12th century although even until this date many of the most famous names belong to Christians such as Ibn Buṭlān and Ibn Tilmīdh. In Egypt, serious study of medicine began with the Fāṭimids, and the famous physicians al-Tamīmī and al-Baladī were personal physicians to Ibn Killīs, the Fāṭimid vizier. Also during the reign of al-Ḥākim bi'llāh, 'Alī ibn Riḍwān flourished in Cairo and from there carried out his famous correspondence and debate with Ibn Buṭlān which marks a highlight of medical controversy between two leading physicians in the Islamic world.[58]

56. See H. C. Krueger, *Avicenna's Poem on Medicine*, Springfield, Illinois, 1963; H. Jahier and Abdelkader Noureddine, *Avicenne, Poème de la médecine, cantica Avicennae*, Paris, 1956, which also contains the original Arabic text; also K. Opitz, 'Avicenna Das Lehrgedicht über die Heilkunde (*Canticum de Medicina*)', *Quellen und Studien zur Geschichte der Naturwissenschaften und der Medizin*, vol. 7, 1940, pp. 304–374.
As for the *Canon*, and the other medical works of Ibn Sīnā in general, the most important exposition is still that of O. Gruner already cited (note 12). There are also numerous more specialized studies dealing with specific areas such as anatomy, gynaecology, etc. See Ullmann, *op. cit.*, p. 153.

57. There is unfortunately no complete translation of the *Canon* in any European language except Russian (by V. N. Ternovskii, *et al.*). But two translations are now being made simultaneously into English, that of M. H. Shah, which began earlier, and the one by a group of scholars under the direction of Ḥakīm Muḥammad Sa'īd. See Shah, *The General Principles of Avicenna's Canon of Medicine*, Karachi, 1966.

58. See J. Schacht and M. Meyerhof, *The Medico-Philosophical Controversy between Ibn Buṭlān of Baghdad and Ibn Riḍwān of Cairo*, Cairo, 1937.

With the building of new hospitals in Damascus and Cairo in the 6th/12th century these cities and especially Cairo became centres of attraction for physicians from everywhere including Maimonides who journeyed all the way from Andalusia to settle in Cairo. Likewise, ʻAbd al-Laṭīf al-Baghdādī, the 7th/13th century polymath who also wrote on medicine and commented upon the *Aphorisms* of Hippocrates, left Baghdad to live in Cairo.

Medical activity in Syria and Egypt became so closely interrelated in the 6th/12th and 7th/13th centuries that ʻAbd al-Raḥīm al-Dakhwār became the superintendent of the medical departments of both provinces. His student Ibn ʻAbī Uṣaybiʻah has been already cited for his contribution to the history of medicine. But his most important disciple from a purely medical point of view was ʻAlāʼ al-Dīn ibn Nafīs, at once philosopher, theologian and physician, who was entitled ʻthe second Ibn Sīnāʼ and who worked in both Damascus and Cairo.[59] Although Ibn al-Nafīs has been celebrated throughout the Islamic world including Persia and India since his death in 687/1288, it was only in 1924 that an Egyptian doctor, Muḥyī al-Dīn al-Ṭaṭāwī discovered that centuries before Servetus and Colombo, Ibn al-Nafīs had explained correctly the minor circulation of the blood. This was one of the most important discoveries in the history of medicine and made the name of Ibn al-Nafīs celebrated in the West as the real predecessor of William Harvey rather than Servetus and Colombo who had been credited until then with the discovery of the minor circulation.[60] Although the line of transmission is not clear, Servetus, Colombo and other Western writers may in fact have come to know of Ibn al-Nafīs's views through the translations of Andrea Alpago.

Ibn al-Nafīs wrote a major compendium entitled *al-Shāmil fiʼl-ṣināʻat al-ṭibbiyyah* (*The Comprehensive Work on the Art of Medicine*) which included a treatment of surgery, and which seems to have remained incomplete. He also wrote

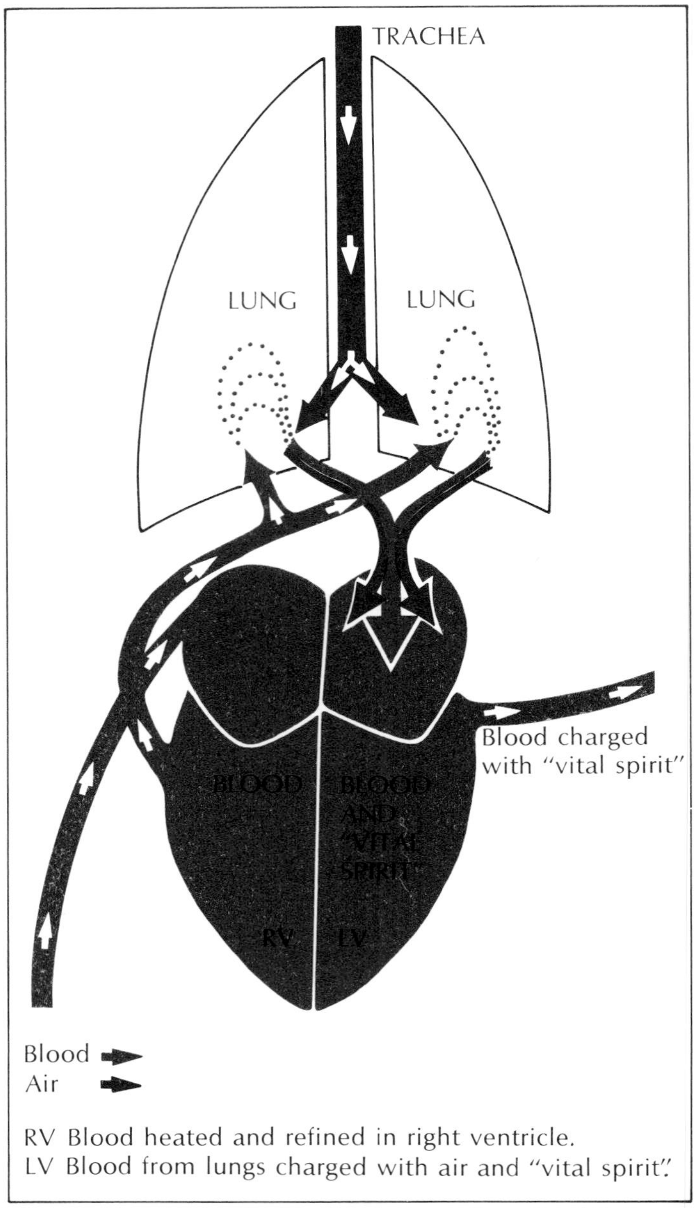

Plate 109. The minor circulation of the blood according to Ibn al-Nafīs.

59. For his most famous theological work see Meyerhof and Schacht, *The Theologus Autodidactus of ibn al-Nafīs*, Oxford, 1968.

60. On the minor circulation of the blood, see Meyerhof, ʻLa découverte de la circulation pulmonaire par Ibn al-Nafīs, médecin arabe au Caire (XIIIe siècle)ʼ, *Bulletin de l'Institut d'Egypte*, vol. 16, 1934, pp. 33–46; Meyerhof, ʻIbn al-Nafīs (XIIIth cent.) and his Theory of the Lesser Circulationʼ, *Isis*, vol. 23, 1935, pp. 100–120; A. A. Khairallah and S. I. Haddad, ʻA Forgotten Chapter in the History of the Circulation of the Bloodʼ, *Annals of Surgery*, vol. 104, 1936, pp. 1–8; and J. Schacht, ʻIbn al-Nafīs, Servetus and Colomboʼ, *Al-Andalus*, vol. XXII, 1957, pp. 317–336. For a general study of Ibn al-Nafīs, see A. Iskandar, ʻIbn al-Nafīsʼ, in Ch. Gillespie (ed.), *Dictionary of Scientific Biography*, New York, 1969 on.

commentaries upon Hippocrates and Ibn Sīnā. As far as Ibn Sīnā is concerned, Ibn al-Nafīs wrote the *Kitāb mūjiz al-qānūn* (*The Summary of the Canon*) which became a very popular introduction to Ibn Sīnā and which was translated into Turkish and Hebrew. In this commentary he follows Ibn Sīnā's views without proposing any new ideas on anatomy and physiology. He also wrote the *Sharḥ tashrīḥ al-qānūn* (*Commentary upon the Anatomy of the Canon*) and *Sharḥ al-qānūn* (*Commentary upon the Canon*), and it is in these two works that he describes for the first time the minor circulation of the blood.[61] He also wrote a work on ophthalmology which has not as yet been studied.

After Ibn al-Nafīs his student Ibn al-Quff gained fame as a surgeon and wrote the *Kitāb al-'umdah fī ṣinā'at al-jirāḥah* (*The Basic Work concerning the Art of Surgery*) in twenty articles. He is also the first person to have pointed out clearly the existence of capillaries which were seen under a microscope for the first time by Malpighi in 1661. At the same time Shams al-Dīn al-Akfānī was also flourishing in Egypt. He is responsible for a novel work on first aid entitled *Kitāb ghunyat al-labīb 'ind ghaybat al-ṭabīb* (*The Refuge of the Intelligent during the Absence of the Physician*). He also wrote on ophthalmology. But by now the main centres of activity in the field of medicine had moved east and north and it is mostly in the Turkish part of the Ottoman empire along with Persia and India where the most important scenes of the final chapter of the history of Islamic medicine were enacted.

The Maghrib

As far as the Maghrib is concerned the high level of medical practice and science established in Cordova by the 4th/10th century continued for the next few hundred years. In the 5th/11th and 6th/12th centuries the Ibn Zuhr (Avenzoar) family established itself as a leading medical family and the most famous among its members, Abū Marwān ibn Zuhr, composed the *Kitāb al-taysīr fi'l-mudāwāt wa'l-tadbīr* (*The Book Facilitating the Study of Therapy and Diet*) which is among the most celebrated products of Islamic medicine in Andalusia and which was translated into both Hebrew and Latin. Another of his well-known works is the *Kitāb al-aghdhiyah* (*The Book of Diet*) which again is among the best of its kind dealing with a subject which is so much emphasized in Islamic medicine.

In the 6th/12th century there appeared in Spain a group of men who were at once eminent philosophers and physicians. Ibn Ṭufayl, the author of the well-known *Ḥayy ibn Yaqẓān* (*Living Son of the Awake*), was a practising physician, and Ibn Rushd (Averroës), the most celebrated Islamic philosopher of Andalusia, also practised medicine and wrote commentaries upon Galen. He also composed an independent work on medicine, the *Kitāb al-kulliyyāt* (*The Book of General Principles – Colliget* in Latin) which became famous in the West along with his philosophical works.[62]

The Jewish physician and philosopher Abū 'Imrān Mūsā ibn Maymūn (Maimonides) was a student of both Ibn Rushd and Ibn Ṭufayl and like them accomplished in both philosophy and medicine. In fact he was such a competent practitioner of the healing art that after emigrating to Egypt he became physician to Salāḥ al-Dīn al-Ayyūbī (Saladin) and his family. Maimonides is the author of, among other medical works, the *Kitāb al-fuṣūl* (*The Book of Aphorisms*) as well as a work on hygiene dedicated to Afḍal Nūr al-Dīn 'Alī, the oldest son of Salāḥ al-Dīn, and entitled *Kitāb tadbīr al-ṣiḥḥah* (*The Regimen of Health*).[63] Like Ibn Rushd, Maimonides also wrote commentaries upon Galen.

After these celebrated figures, medicine gradually declined in Andalusia but survived in Morocco where it continues in certain quarters to this day. But perhaps the most outstanding contribution of the Maghrib to Islamic medicine was in the field of pharmacology to which we shall turn shortly.

61. Some people think that Ibn al-Nafīs's discovery was completely ignored by later Muslim writers. Such, however, is not the case. Although some later anatomists ignored it and reverted back to the Galenic and Avicennian conceptions, others, like Sadīd al-Dīn al-Kāzirūnī and 'Alī ibn 'Abdallāh al-Maṣrī, both in the 8th/14th century, were aware of it. See Iskandar, *op. cit.*

62. See M. Alonso Alonso, 'Averroes observador de la naturaleza', *Al-Andalus*, vol. V, 1940, pp. 215–230.

63. See Meyerhof, 'L'oeuvre médicale de Maimonide', *Archivio di storia della scienza* (*Archeiòn*), vol. XI, 1929, pp. 136–155; and Moses Maimonides, *Two Treatises on the Regimen of Health, Fī Tadbīr al-Ṣiḥḥa and Maqāla fi Bayān Ba'ḍ al-A'rāḍ*, trans. and ed. by A. Bar-Sela, H. E. Hoff, *et al.*, Philadelphia, 1964.

Persia and India

The later medical history of Persia and India, even more than that of other regions, is dominated by Ibn Sīnā. A century after him, his virulent critic in the field of philosophy, the Ash'arite theologian, Fakhr al-Dīn al-Rāzī, commented upon the *Canon* and explained many of its difficulties. Al-Rāzī, who was probably the most learned of the theologians (*mutakallimūn*) in the domain of the 'intellectual sciences', devoted a section to medicine in his scientific encyclopaedia, *Kitāb al-sittīnī* (*The Book of Sixty Sciences*), and also began a large independent work on medicine entitled *al-Ṭibb al-kabīr* (*The Great Medicine*) which was apparently never completed. He also wrote a Persian treatise on hygiene, the *Kitāb ḥifẓ al-badan* (*Treatise on Preserving Bodily Health*).[64]

Likewise, in the 6th/12th century, there appeared the first extensive medical encyclopaedia in Persian modelled upon the *Canon*, the *Dhakhīra-yi khwārazmshāhī* (*Treasury dedicated to the King of Khwārazm*) by Sayyid Zayn al-Dīn Ismā'īl al-Ḥusaynī al-Jurjānī.[65] The work is without doubt the most important of its kind in the Persian language and second in influence only to the *Canon* in the Persian and Indian worlds. Besides its significance for technical medical terminology in Persian, it is one of the most systematic treatments of Avicennan medicine including pharmacology. Al-Jurjānī also wrote other well-known medical works such as the *Yādigār-i ṭibb* (*Medical Memoranda*) and *Aghrāḍ al-ṭibb* (*The Aims of Medicine*). Altogether, he is perhaps responsible more than any other figure for the perpetuation of the medical teachings of the early masters and especially Ibn Sīnā during the later centuries wherever Persian has been spoken.

After the Mongol invasion, despite the destruction of many centres of learning, medicine continued to be studied and taught. Quṭb al-Dīn al-Shīrāzī, already noted for his major contributions to astronomy and physics, spent a lifetime in studying earlier commentaries upon the *Canon* and travelled as far away as Cairo to see manuscripts of such works before writing his own *al-Tuḥfat al-sa'diyyah* (*The Present to Sa'd*) which many consider to be the most thorough and profound commentary upon the *Canon*.[66] Abū Ḥāmid Muḥammad al-Samarqandī composed at the same time the *Kitāb al-asbāb wa'l-'alāmāt* (*The Book of Causes and Symptoms*) in which he discussed various diseases according to their causes and symptoms and proposed cures for each. He also wrote a treatise describing arthritis and its treatment. Major efforts to revise medical learning were also carried out at this time by Rashīd al-Dīn Faḍlallāh, the powerful but ill-fated vizier and physician of the Īl-Khānids, who created a major university centre near Tabriz (the Rab'-i rashīdī) with special emphasis upon medicine, encouraged the writing of works on medicine by offering outstanding prizes to the best works and himself composed a medical encyclopaedia and even caused to be written the only known work on Chinese medicine in Islam, the Persian treatise *Tanksūkhnāma-yi Īlkhānī dar 'ulūm wa funūn-i khatā'ī* (*The Īl-Khānid Compendium Concerning the Sciences and the Arts of the Chinese*) which is yet one more example of the great cultural and scientific exchange between Islam and China following the Mongol invasion.[67]

64. Despite recent interest in this altogether neglected figure, most works composed concerning him during the past few years have involved his theology while his medical writings have been nearly completely neglected. On Fakhr al-Dīn al-Rāzī in general, see Nasr, 'Fakhr al-Dīn al-Rāzi', in *A History of Muslim Philosophy*, vol. 1, pp. 642–656.

65. The Persian text of this large compendium is being edited in Tehran in two different versions, the first by I. Afshar and M. Danechepazhuh and the second by J. Mostafavi. The first is a more critical edition from the literary point of view, while the second is, perhaps, of greater medical interest, being edited by a scholar who is himself a physician well acquainted with both traditional and modern medicine. For a study of this work, see A. Naficy, *Les Fondements théoriques de la médecine persane, d'après l'encyclopédie médicale de Gorgani, avec un aperçu sommaire sur l'histoire de la médecine en Perse*, Paris, 1933.

66. See Nasr, 'Quṭb al-Dīn al-Shīrāzī', in the *Dictionary of Scientific Biography*.

67. On Rashīd al-Dīn, who was also the author of the first world history *Jāmi' al-tawārīkh*, see the numerous works of J. A. Boyle and K. Jahn, as well as the *Cambridge History of Iran*, vol. 5, where his cultural significance is mentioned in many chapters. As for his work concerning Chinese medicine, see A. Adnan, 'Sur le Tanksukname-i Ilkhani der Ulum-u-Funun-i-Khatai', *Isis*, vol. 32, 1940, pp. 44–47; and A. Suheyl Ünver and A. B. Golpinarli, *Tansūknāmei Ilhān der funūnu ulūmu Hatai mukaddimesi* (Université d'Istanbul, T.T.F. n. 14), Istanbul, 1939. The edition of the Persian text has been made by M. Minovi as *Ṭibb-i ahl-i Khatā*, Tehran, 1350 (A.H. solar).

During the Īl-Khānid and Timurid periods, other medical authors continued to appear in Persian. Najm al-Dīn Maḥmūd al-Shīrāzī produced his *al-Ḥāwī al-ṣaghīr* (*The Small Ḥāwī*) following the model of al-Rāzī in the 8th/14th century. During the following centuries, medical education in Persia and Turkey developed close ties so that a person such as Ghiyāth al-Dīn Muḥammad al-Iṣfahānī studied in both lands. He wrote his *Mir'āt al-ṣiḥḥah* (*The Mirror of Health*) in Persian but dedicated it to the Ottoman sultan.

There was a revival of medical activity in the Safavid period with the re-establishment of political order and the encouragement to establish schools and dispensaries.[68] The foremost medical figure of the whole age, who lived in fact mostly before the Safavid period but survived into the reign of Shāh Ismā'īl, was Muḥammad Ḥusaynī Nūrbakhsh, known usually by his title of Bahā' al-Dawlah. He is the author of the *Khulāṣat al-tajārib* (*The Quintessence of Experience*) based on the style of al-Rāzī's *al-Ḥāwī*. Bahā' al-Dawlah was himself an acute clinical observer and is credited with the first clear description of whooping cough and hay fever. Among other notable Safavid physicians may be mentioned Ḥakīm Muḥammad (11th/17th century), earlier an officer in the Ottoman army who wrote the *Dhakhīra-yi kāmilah* (*The Perfect Treasury*), which is the only Safavid work devoted solely to surgery. It is also necessary to mention the *Dastūr al-'ilāj* (*Rules of Treatment*) of Sulṭān 'Alī Gunādī, the *Risālah dar tiryāq* (*Treatise on Theriaca*) of Kamāl al-Dīn Ḥusaynī who hailed from Mahan and the famous and still popular 11th/17th century work, the *Tuḥfat al-mu'minīn* of Mīr Muḥammad Zamān and his son which is concerned with pharmacy as well as medicine. As far as the spread of syphilis into Persia at this time is concerned, it is important to note the treatise of 'Imād al-Dīn on the disease, which the Persians called 'Frankish fire' (*ātishak-i farangī*). The disease was first observed by Bahā' al-Dawlah, but the treatise of 'Imād al-Dīn is the first to deal with it thoroughly. His authority in medicine was, in fact, so great that his treatise continued to be used in Persia and India until modern times.

From the reign of Nādir Shāh onward, modern European medicine was introduced into Persia and the process became more accelerated during the Qajar period with the establishment of a new university (*Dār al-funūn*) in Tehran where modern medicine was taught. But in Persia, as in Egypt, Turkey and other lands of Western Islam, the traditional system has continued, although receding continuously before the spread of Western medicine, and survives today mostly in such particular branches as bone setting, pharmacology and the like.

As far as India is concerned, the history of Islamic medicine in that land is hardly separable from that of Persia because of the flow of a large number of Persian physicians, especially from Shiraz and Isfahan, to India from the 9th/15th to the 12th/18th century, as well as the common use of Persian as the primary scientific language, especially in medicine, in the two regions. There had been a gradual spread of the Islamic sciences including medicine into India from the 7th/13th century and even earlier in certain areas, such as the Punjab and Sindh, but the establishment of Islamic medicine on a large scale coincides with both the emigration of Persian physicians competent in this form of medicine, the availability of medical texts in Persian and, to a certain extent, the translations of medical works from Sanskrit into Persian, such as *Ṭibb-i sikandarī* (*The Medicine of Sikandar*) dedicated to Sikandar Shāh Lodi of Delhi. It was also at this time that Manṣūr ibn Faqīh Ilyās wrote the already mentioned famous anatomical treatise in Persian, the *Tashrīḥ-i manṣūrī* (*The Anatomy of Manṣūr*), dedicated to the Muslim prince Pīr Muḥammad Bahādur Khān.[69]

During the Mogul period, especially from the time of Akbar onwards, the migration of notable Persian medical figures into India increased for a complex set of reasons of which the most important was the remarkable opportunities,

68. On the history of medicine during this period, see Elgood, *Safavid Medicine*; also M. Laignel-Lavastine and J. Vinchon, 'La médecine en Perse en XVIIe siècle', *Mélanges Iorga*, Paris, 1933, pp. 465–485.

69. See K. Sudhoff, 'Ein Beitrag zur Geschichte der Anatomie in Mittelalter speziell der anatomischen Graphik nach Hdschr. des 9. bis 15. Jhdts.', in D. Puschmann (ed.), *Studien zur Geschichte der Medizin*, vol. IV, Leipzig, 1908, pp. 52–73.

both economic and political, that existed for such figures in India.[70] Some of the most famous among these figures are 'Ayn al-Mulk, Amīr Fatḥ al-Dīn, Ḥakīm Ṣadrā and Fatḥallāh Gīlānī who dominated the medical scene at Delhi and elsewhere within the Mogul empire. But the greatest of the Persian physicians at the Mogul court was probably Nūr al-Dīn Muḥammad Shīrāzī, author of the immense *Ṭibb-i Dārā Shukūhī* (*The Medicine of Dārā Shukūh*), whose manuscripts are usually richly illustrated. Even in the 12th/18th century there were famous physicians who migrated from Persia to India, such as Muḥammad Hāshim Shīrāzī known as 'Alawī Khān who accompanied Nādir Shāh back from India to Persia, but returned at the end of his life to die in India.

There were, of course, also eminent teachers and physicians of completely Indian background, such as Mīr Ḥājjī Muḥammad Muqīm of Bengal and especially his son Muḥammad Akbar Arzānī, who was the author of *Ṭibb-i akbar* (*The Great Work on Medicine*), as well as a commentary upon the *Qānūnchah* (*The Small Canon*) of Chaghmīnī. But it was especially after the 12th/18th century that Muslim and even Hindu physicians from India itself came to the fore to continue the cultivation of Islamic medicine and to add a new chapter to its history.[71] During the 13th/19th century, works on medicine began to be translated into or written in Urdu along with Persian, and to this day, Islamic medicine has been kept alive as a living tradition in India as well as Pakistan and Bangladesh. In fact, it is in these regions that Islamic medicine is most alive today.

The Ottoman World

Medical activity in the Turkish part of the Ottoman world was closely related to that of Persia until the 9th/15th century, after which it developed its own distinct features, although works continued to be written mostly in Arabic and Persian and the classical texts were taught throughout the many hospitals and schools established by the Ottoman sultans.[72] In the 9th/15th century, there appeared the first important Ottoman physician, Ḥājjī Bāshā Khiḍr al-Āyidīnī who lived, however, in Cairo. He wrote the *Kitāb shifā' al-asqām wa dawā' al-ālām* (*The Book of the Cure of Sicknesses and Remedy of Pains*) with a summary which has been attributed by mistake by some to Ibn Sīnā.

Another famous Turkish physician, Muḥammad al-Qawṣūnī, was physician to Sulṭān Sulaymān I and Selim II and wrote a treatise on haemorrhoids, the *Kitāb zād al-masīr fī 'ilāj al-bawāsīr* (*The Book of the Provision of the Way on the Cure of Haemorrhoids*). The 10th/16th century also was witness to the activities of one of the foremost of the later figures in Islamic science, Dā'ūd al-Anṭākī, originally from Antioch, who knew Greek and lived mostly in Damascus and Cairo. His *Tadhkirah ūlu'l-albāb wa'l-jāmi' li'l-'ajab al-'ujāb* (*The Treasury of the People of Understanding and Compendium of the Wonder of Wonders*) deals with medicine and pharmacology and is among the most important of later Islamic medical works.

From the 11th/17th century onward the influence of European medicine began to make itself felt in Turkish sources. This is seen for the first time in the *Ghāyat al-itqān fī tadbīr badan al-insān* (*The End of Perfection concerning the Regimen of the Body of Man*) by Ṣāliḥ ibn Sallūm, physician of Sulṭān Mehmet IV. The fourth part of this work is entitled *'al-Ṭibb al-jadīd al-kīmiyā'ī alladhī ikhtara'ahū Barākalsūs* (*The New

70. On the question of the general history of Islamic medicine in India see Elgood, *Safavid Medical Practice*, chap. 5, 'The Emigrés'; M. Z. Siddiqi, *Arabic and Persian Medical Literature*, Calcutta, 1959; Chanpuri, H. K., 'Medical developments in the Mughal period', *Hamdard Medical Digest*, vol. 3, nos. 1–2, 1959, pp. 177–190; and M. Z. Siddiqi, 'The unani ṭibb (Greek Medicine) in India', *Islamic Culture*, vol. 42, 1968, pp. 161–172.

71. In general, the history of Islamic science in India has been sadly neglected until now. This is especially unfortunate in the case of medicine and pharmacology because of the vast amount of activity that has been carried out in that region in this field during the past five centuries.

72. On the history of medicine in Ottoman Turkey, see A. Suheyl Ünver, *Umumi Tib Tarihi: Bazi Resimler ve Vesikalar (Allgemeine Geschichte der Medizin; einiger Bilder und Dokumente)* (Turkish and German), Istanbul, 1943; also his 'The Origins of the History of Turkish Medicine', *Hamdard Medical Digest*, vol. 3, nos. 1–2, 1959, pp. 121–138.

Alchemical Medicine which was Invented by Paracelsus)' where the European mediçine of the Renaissance is described based mostly on Paracelsus who is called 'the chief of masters of this art' (*ra'īs arbāb hādhihi'l-ṣinā'ah*).[73] The influence of Paracelsus was further spread by Ḥasan Efendi and 'Alī Efendi within the Ottoman world, and this marked the beginning of the influence of Western medicine which, after a lull during the 12th/18th century, increased to full force in the 13th/19th century, leading to the nearly total replacement of traditional medicine by the modern European system, a system that had, by now, moved completely away from the traditional principles still found in Paracelsus.

Pharmacology

Theory and Sources

The sources of pharmacology, concerning both simple and compound drugs, are hardly separable from those of medicine and, as seen already, many medical works contain sections devoted to drugs.[74] The theory underlying pharmacology is also inseparable from that of medicine. Each drug possesses natures with various degrees of intensity and is prescribed for a particular malady in the light of the type of nature and the degree of intensity of that nature needed to re-establish the equilibrium of the humours. The use of drugs is, therefore, related both to the nature of the drug in question and the temperament of the patient. Moreover, the administration of drugs is based on long experience and observation. Islamic pharmacology is the depository of the experience and observation of countless generations of human beings extending over aeons of prehistory. It seems even from the empirical point of view absurd that such a wealth of knowledge acquired through experience and observation should be so easily discarded by many, even when there is a clear choice, in favour of drugs the ill-effects of many of which have not even been tested and which are often forced upon the public without a close study of their long-term consequences for the human body as a whole.

Putting aside the question of the theory of the natures and humours and degrees of intensity of the natures included in the properties of each drug, all of which are closely related to the Galenic medical theories, the actual knowledge of medicaments inherited by Muslims from earlier sources is much more dependent upon Persian and Indian sources than is the case in other branches of medicine. The Sassanids already possessed an extensive knowledge of various drugs, especially herbs, and there are even Pahlavi pharmacological terms in Greek. Likewise, Indian medicine had had access to a very rich world of herbs as well as minerals used for medicaments very different from that of the Greeks. Indian medicine made special use of various poisons and perfumes as drugs in addition to the usual herbal and mineral substances.[75] Islamic pharmacology was heir to this rich ancient Persian and Indian tradition as well as to the tradition of the Graeco-Alexandrian school. Throughout its phases of later development also the Islamic pharmacopoeias continued to list many drugs such as camphor and tamarind not seen in the Greek sources, if for no other reason than that Muslims had access to other sources and also lived in regions whose flora and fauna were not known to the classical Greek sources.

Nevertheless, the most important source for Islamic pharmacology is without doubt Dioscorides, whose manuscripts in Arabic, like the Greek, were among the first to be illustrated. His *Materia Medica* was translated into Arabic in the 3rd/9th century by Iṣṭafān ibn Bāsīl and Ḥunayn ibn Isḥāq under the title of *Kitāb*

73. See P. Richter, 'Paracelsus im Lichte des Orients', in *Archiv für die Geschichte der Naturwissenschaften und der Technik*, vol. 6, 1913, pp. 294–304.

74. Of course, pharmacology is also closely related to botany since most of the drugs used in Islamic medicine are of a herbal nature. It is also related to alchemy in many ways, and, as far as the use of animal derivatives as medicament is concerned, even to zoology.

75. The pre-Islamic Arabs also made use of poisons in the treatment of illnesses, but the importance of both poisons and perfumes in Islamic medicine is related most of all to Indian medicine – particularly the famous *Kitāb al-shānāq* – and in the case of perfumes also to a certain extent to ancient Egypt. See Ullmann, *Die Medizin im Islam*, pp. 313–342; also Wiedemann, 'Über Parfüms und Drogen bei dem Arabern', *Aufsätze . . .*, vol. II, pp. 415–430.

Plate 110. Dioscorides handing over the fabulous mandragora to one of his disciples.

al-ḥashā'ish fī hayūlā'l-ṭibb and rapidly became the main reference for pharmacologists.[76] Its influence is already to be seen in the *Firdaws al-ḥikmah* of al-Ṭabarī and is quoted in *al-Ḥāwī*. It was translated into Persian as early as the 4th/10th century by Ḥusayn ibn Ibrāhīm al-Nātilī and translated again into Arabic by Mihrān ibn Manṣūr al-Masīḥī in the 6th/12th century. Besides the dominating influence of Dioscorides, the pharmacological treatises of Galen, Paul of Aegina and other Graeco-Alexandrian authors were also known to Muslims and translated into Arabic along with Sanskrit and Pahlavi texts, thus setting up the background for the rise of Islamic pharmacology as an independent school.

Pharmacognosy

Islamic sources always distinguish between simples and compounds, the *mufradāt* and *murakkabāt* of the classical Islamic sources, the first dealing with drugs in their natural and simple state, or pharmacognosy in contemporary terms, and the second with drugs as they are usually understood today, and which were, in most cases, discussed under the heading of *aqrābādhīn*. In the light of this traditional division, these two parts of pharmacology will be also treated here separately, starting with pharmacognosy. The first Arabic work on pharmacognosy actually preceded the translation of Dioscorides, for already in the 2nd/8th century Māsarjīs had written the *Kitāb quwa'l-'aqāqīr wa manāfi'ihā wa maḍārrihā* (*Treatise on the Power of Drugs, their Benefits and Ill-Effects*) followed early in the 3rd/9th century by 'Īsā ibn Siḥārbakht, a student of Jurjīs ibn Bukhtīshū', who wrote the *Kitāb quwa'l-adwiyat al-mufradah* (*The Book of the Powers of Simple Drugs*). A treatise by the title of *Kitāb al-adwiyat al-mufradah* (*The Book of Simple Drugs*) exists in the Jābirean corpus and a work of the same title by Ḥunayn ibn Isḥāq includes a set of questions and answers on simples. Moreover, general medical and agricultural works which appeared during the 3rd/9th century, such as the writings of Ibn Waḥshiyyah, al-Ṭabarī and al-Rāzī include extensive sections on drugs. The *al-Ḥāwī* mentions 829 drugs and their properties arranged alphabetically, while al-Rāzī also wrote other independent works on this subject.

The first treatise in the Persian language on medicaments, noted for its philological rather than medical importance, is the *Kitāb al-abniyah 'an ḥaqā'iq al-adwiyah* (*The Book of the Fundamentals of the Properties of Remedies*) of Abū Manṣūr Muwaffaq written in the 4th/10th century.[77] It marks the beginning of a long tradition of pharmacological works in Persian which has spanned a millennium to the present day. During the 4th/10th century, also, important works continued to be composed in Arabic, including the first treatises on the subject to appear in Spain, the *Kitāb al-jāmi' bi aqwāl al-qudamā' wa'l-muḥaddithīn min al-aṭibbā' wa'l-mutafalsafīn fi'l-adwiyat al-mufradah* (*The Comprehensive Book on the Views of the Ancients and the Moderns among Physicians and Philosophers concerning Simple Drugs*) by Abū Bakr ibn Samghūn of Cordova in which drugs are alphabetically arranged, and the commentary of Ibn Juljul upon Dioscorides as well as his treatise on those drugs which are not mentioned by Dioscorides. Al-Zahrāwī also devoted a good part of his *al-Taṣrīf* to plants and drugs.

As for the East, during this same period there appeared the well-known work of the Palestinian Abū 'Abdallāh al-Tamīmī, the *Kitāb al-murshid fī jamāhir al-aghdhiyah wa quwa'l-mufradāt min al-adwiyah* (*The Book of Guidance on the Precious Substances of Diet and the Powers of Simple Drugs*), important both for diet and pharmacology, and the *Kitāb al-i'timād fi'l-*

76. See the monumental study of C. Emilio Dubler and E. Terés, *La 'Materia Médica' de Dioscórides. Transmisión medieval y renacentista, vol. II: La versión árabe de la 'Materia Médica' des Dioscórides (texts, varientes é indices)*, Tetuan and Barcelona, 1952–1957; also Meyerhof, 'Die Materia Medica des Dioskorides bei den Arabern', *Quellen und Studien zur Geschichte der Naturwissenschaften und der Medizin*, vol. 3, 1933, pp. 280–292. There have appeared a series of works by S. Hamarneh on the influence of Dioscorides and, in fact, the whole history of Islamic pharmacology. See, for example, his 'Sources and Development of Arabic Medical Therapy and Pharmacology', *Sudhoffs Archiv*, vol. 54, 1970, pp. 30–48; and his 'Origins of Arabic Drug and Diet Therapy', *Physis*, vol. II, 1969, pp. 267–286. On Islamic pharmacology and its roots see also Wiedemann, 'Über von dem Arabern benutzte Drogen', *Aufsätze . . .*, vol. II, pp. 230–274.

77. See Abu Mansur, *Die pharmakologische Grundsätze des Abu Mansur Muwaffak bin Ali Harawi übersetzt von Abdul-Chalig Achundow aus Baku*, Halle, 1893.

adwiyat al-mufradah (*The Book of Confidence concerning Simple Drugs*) in which Syriac, Persian and Arabic equivalents are given for drug names and where emphasis is placed upon the 'occult' properties of drugs. This work was translated by Stephanus of Saragossa into Latin and was influential in the West. There were also, of course, at this time the major medical compendia, especially those of al-Majūsī and Ibn Sīnā with sections concerning drugs. As already mentioned, the second book of the *Canon* is devoted to a detailed discussion of simples, and the powers and qualities of drugs are listed in charts.[78]

Perhaps the most valuable Islamic work on pharmacology is again, as in so many other fields, written by al-Bīrūnī, in this case his *Kitāb al-ṣaydalah* (*The Book of Drugs*), which he wrote in Arabic and which was translated into Persian by Abū Bakr al-Kāshānī. This work, which is a fruit of the last years of al-Bīrūnī's life, is a vast compilation of pharmacological knowledge concerning 850 drugs drawn from every conceivable source with names of drugs given in several languages including Greek, Syriac, Sanskrit, Arabic, Persian and occasionally Khwārazmian, Soghdian and the like. It has always been a veritable challenge to scholars and perhaps for this reason neither the Arabic nor the Persian text has been, as yet, printed in a critical edition.[79]

Al-Bīrūnī set the model for later works of pharmacology. A century later Ibn Jazlah was to compose a similar work arranged alphabetically, but not as extensive as that of al-Bīrūnī. Meanwhile, the centre of activity in this field shifted to the Maghrib, which has produced some of the greatest Islamic pharmacologists. In the 6th/12th century, the Jewish druggist Yūsuf ibn Isḥāq ibn Biklārish from Almeria wrote the *Kitāb al-musta'īnī* (*The Book of Seeking Assistance*), which contains a theoretical discussion of pharmacology as well as synonyms of names for plants in Arabic, Persian, Greek, Syriac, Latin and Spanish.[80] Nearly at the same time, Abu'l-Ṣalt and Ibrāhīm al-Maghribī al-'Alā'ī, again from the Maghrib, wrote on simple drugs. Also the celebrated Andalusian philosopher Ibn Bājjah (Avempace) wrote in collaboration with Abu'l-Ḥasan al-Andalūsī the *Kitāb al-tajribatayn 'alā adwiyat ibn Wāfid*, (*The Book of the Two Experiences concerning the Drugs of Ibn Wāfid*) which is itself lost, but which is known through citations by Ibn al-Bayṭār.

The 6th/12th century also witnessed the appearance of the *Kitāb al-adwiyat al-mufradah* (*The Book of Simple Drugs*) of Abū Ja'far al-Ghāfiqī, which is exceptional for its accurate descriptions and richness of information and is considered by many as the most notable Islamic work on simples, especially as far as herbals are concerned.[81] This work exercised a deep influence upon the works of Ibn al-Bayṭār, the foremost of Islamic botanists, and at the same time the great systematizer of pharmacological knowledge. Ḍiyā' al-Dīn ibn al-Bayṭār was born in Malaga and spent his early life in Andalusia, but, like so many of his compatriots of that day, set out for the East and finally settled in Damascus where he died in 646/1248. Besides writing a commentary upon Dioscorides, Ibn al-Bayṭār composed the *Kitāb al-mughnī fi'l-adwiyat al-mufradah* (*The Independent Treatise concerning Simple Drugs*) which lists some 1400 drugs of

78. This part of the *Canon* was translated and commented upon separately by Vopisco Fortunato Plempio in the 11th/17th century.

79. See Meyerhof, 'Études de pharmacologie arabe tirées de manuscrits inédits. I. Le livre de la diagnosie d'Abu'r-Rayḥān al-Bērūnī', *Bulletin de l'Institut d'Egypte*, vol. 22, 1940, pp. 133–152; Meyerhof, 'Das Vorwort zur Drogenkunde des Bērūnī', *Quellen und Studien zur Geschichte der Naturwissenschaften und der Medizin*, vol. 3, 1932, pp. 1–47; F. Krenkow, 'The Drug Book of Bērūnī', *Islamic Culture*, vol. 20, 1946, pp. 109 ff. Recently a translation of the work into English has been made by a group under the direction of Ḥakīm Muḥammad Sa'īd as *Al-Biruni's Book on Pharmacy and Materia Medica*, Karachi, 1973. The second volume of this work is to contain the commentary by S. Hamarneh upon the text.

80. Several studies have been devoted to him by H. P. J. Renaud, including, 'Trois études d'histoire de la médecine arabe en Occident', *Hespéris*, vol. 10, 1930–1931, pp. 135–150.

81. See Meyerhof, 'Über die Pharmakologie und Botanik des Aḥmad al-Ghāfiqī', *Archiv für Geschichte der Mathematik, der Naturwissenschaften und der Technik*, vol. 13, 1931, pp. 65–74; also Meyerhof and G. P. Sobhy, *The Abridged Version of the 'Book of Simple Drugs' of Ahmad ibn Muhammad al-Ghāfiqī by Gregorius Abu'l-Farag (Barhebreus), edited from the Only Two Known Manuscripts*, The Egyptian University, The Faculty of Medicine Publication No. 4, Fasc. 1–3, Cairo, 1932, 1933, 1938.

animal, plant and mineral origin. The work marks a summit in its own field and is the most influential Islamic work on the subject, both within and outside the Islamic world, its influence having even reached Armenia.[82] Like so many other works in the field, it is a basic work on botany as well and also pertains directly to the question of diet.

From the 7th/13th century onward, works on pharmacology continued to appear in both the Ottoman and the Persian-Indian worlds based mostly on the earlier masters. As far as the Ottoman world is concerned, in the 8th/14th century Ibn Jazlah was translated into Turkish. In the 9th/15th century, Abu'l-'Abbās al-Ḥasanī (known as Sharīf al-Ṣaqillī) from Tunis wrote the *Kitāb al-aṭibbā'* (*The Book of Physicians*) which is concerned with drugs, followed by al-Qāsim al-Ghassānī, the Moroccan pharmacologist, and the author of the *Ḥadīqat al-azhār fī sharḥ māhiyyat al-'ushb wa'l-'aqqār* (*The Garden of Flowers on the Commentary upon the Essence of Plants and Drugs*). As already mentioned, the *Tadhkirah* of Dā'ūd al-Anṭākī contained a major section on drugs. In the 11th/17th century Madyan al-Qawṣīnī continued this tradition by composing the *Qānūn al-aṭibbā' wa nāmūs al-aḥibbā'* (*The Canon of Physicians and Laws of Friends*) while in the 12th/18th century 'Abd al-Razzāq al-Jazā'irī again from the Maghrib wrote the *Kitāb kashf al-rumūz* (*The Book of the Unveiling of Symbols*) basing himself mostly on Ibn Sīnā, Ibn al-Bayṭār and Dā'ūd al-Anṭākī. The practice of traditional pharmacology, moreover, has continued, especially in Egypt and North Africa, to this day, despite the spread of modern medicaments into this whole region since the last century.[83]

As for Persia and India, most of the figures already cited in conjunction with medicine were also concerned with pharmacology. Ghiyāth al-Dīn Shīrāzī's *Kitāb al-shāmil* includes major sections on drugs. The medical works of the Safavid period, which has been called 'The Golden Age of Pharmacology' by Elgood, also abound in studies of drugs. The *Ṭibb-i shāfi'ī* (*The Shāfi'ī Medicine*) of Muẓaffar al-Ḥusaynī[84] and the *Tuḥfat al-mu'minīn* written in Persia and the *al-Alfāẓ al-adwiyah* of 'Ayn al-Mulk composed in India are outstanding examples of pharmacological studies of this period contained in works which include medicine in general. It is of interest to mention also here the treatise written by Abu'l-Fatḥ Gīlānī, another Persian emigrant to India in the 10th/16th century, on the *qalyān*, or waterpipe, and the new drug which had just invaded the East, namely tobacco. This treatise is of interest in that it is the origin of the various forms of the waterpipe used today throughout the Islamic world. In Persia and especially India, pharmacology and its related fields have continued in use to this day more strongly than any other field of traditional medicine and many of the works here mentioned continue to serve both professional druggists and those experienced individuals who administer some of the simpler medicaments themselves for their family and friends.

The Compound Drugs

As far as compound drugs are concerned, they were usually treated in Islamic sources in the catalogue or listing of drugs which came to be known in Islamic languages as *aqrābādhīn* (from the Greek γραφίδιον meaning 'list' of drugs or a pharmacopoeia). In this field the influence of Galen was particularly strong. In the 3rd/9th century two *aqrābādhīns* appeared, one by Ṣābūr ibn Sahl of Jundishapur and the other by the philosopher al-Kindī.[85] Likewise, al-Rāzī pro-

82. This monumental work has been translated into both French and German. See L. Leclerc, *Traité des simples par Ibn el-Beithar, Notices et Extraits des Manuscrits de la Bibliothèque Nationale*, vols. XIII, 1; XXV, 1; XXVI, 1, Paris, 1877, 1881, 1883; and J. von Sontheimer, *Grosse Zusammenstellung über die Kräfte der bekannten einfachen Heil- und Nahrungsmittel*, vols. I and II, Stuttgart, 1840, 1842.

83. Also in faraway regions such as the Yemen, traditional pharmacology has continued in full force to the present day. There is a long tradition of studies on pharmacology in this region. In the 8th/14th century al-Malik al-Afḍal al-'Abbās ibn Yūsuf of the Rasūlī dynasty of the Yemen had written the *Kitāb al-lum'at al-kāfiyah fi'l-adwiyat al-shāfiyah* (*The Book of Sufficient Light on Curing Drugs*) based on the *Canon* of Ibn Sīnā. Both a written and a popular tradition on this subject have continued in the Yemen ever since but have been ignored until now and need to be fully studied.

84. This work is the primary source of Fr. Angelus's *Pharmacopoeia Persica*, written in the 11th/17th century, which is the first Western study of Persian pharmacology. The *Gazophylacium Persarum* of Angelus is also based on the *Ṭibb-i shāfi'ī.*

85. See M. Levey, *The Medical Formulary or Aqrābādhīn of al-Kindī.*

duced a greater and a lesser *Aqrābādhīn*, both translated by Gerard of Cremona into Latin. There is also a Latin work on this subject attributed to Johannes Mesuë, who is not Yuḥannā ibn Māsawayh but may be Māswayh al-Māridīnī who wrote on drugs at that time.

The *Canon* is as important for its *aqrābādhīn* as it is for its simples and its fifth book has served as reference for questions pertaining to compounds to this day.[86] But in compounds, as in simples, the works of Ibn Sīnā and al-Rāzī were not the end but rather served as models for later works, such as the 6th/12th century treatises of Ibn al-Tilmīdh, of Muḥammad ibn Bahrām al-Qalānisī – the most comprehensive work of its kind incorporating all the earlier sources – two important pharmacopoeias by Najīb al-Dīn al-Samarqandī,[87] and the *Kitāb minhaj al-dukkān* (*The Open Road to the Store*) which is nearly as comprehensive as the *Aqrābādhīn* of al-Qalānisī. Later works such as the *Ṭibb-i shāfi'ī* which is also called *Qarābādīn-i shāfi'ī* (*The Shāfi'ī Pharmacopoeia*), the *Tuḥfat al-mu'minīn* and the *Qarābādīn-i qādirī* (*The Qādirī Pharmacopoeia*) of Muḥammad Akbar Arzānī, the first two written in Persia and the second in India, are also important works on the subject and bring the study of the subject down to the period of the spread of Western medicine and pharmacology in the Islamic world.

Figure 85. A chicken being sacrificed to cure a snakebite.

Islamic Medicine Today

The brief survey of Islamic medicine presented here conveys to some degree the extent to which Islamic medicine is related to the traditional pattern of life of the Muslim peoples (and even religious minorities living among them). It also shows the long tradition of the study of medicine in the Islamic world and the remarkably wide basis upon which this medical tradition is established, a foundation which includes practically the whole medical knowledge of the civilizations preceding Islam, excluding those of the Far East. Finally, the continuous weakening of traditional medicine before the onslaught of the spread of modern Western medicine in the last two centuries is seen in most parts of the Islamic world. As a result, today, except for the subcontinent of India where traditional Islamic medicine and pharmacology continue on an intellectual level as well as on a popular one, in the heartland of the Islamic world where most of this medicine was cultivated and taught during the classical period – in such lands as Persia, Iraq, Syria and Egypt – only a few branches such as pharmacology and certain dietary habits continue, while the medical schools have become completely dominated by Western medicine and these countries converted into a market for the sale of Western-produced or, at least, Western-originated pharmaceuticals.

Strangely enough, just when the victory of

86. See J. von Sontheimer, *Zusammengesetzte Heilmittel der Araber. Nach dem fünften Buch des Canons von Ebn Sina aus dem Arabischen übersetzt*, Freiburg, 1845.

87. These are the *al-Qarābādhīn 'alā tartīb al-'ilal* (*The Medical Formulary according to the Order of Illnesses*) and the *Kitāb uṣūl tarkīb al-adwiyah* translated by M. Levey and N. al-Khaledy and already cited (note 39).

Plate 111. *Materia medica* used in contemporary Islamic medicine.

Western medicine seemed complete, rumours began in the Western world itself about the shortcomings of Western medicine and especially pharmacology. Despite their remarkable successes, practitioners of this medicine still cannot cure either a simple headache or a rheumatic pain better than did the masters of old. Certain reputable Western physicians began to search for other systems. Acupuncture spread rapidly in certain circles as did schools related to the Hippocratic-Galenic tradition. New interest is being shown in the use of herbs as medicaments. As a result, a greater degree of attention is being paid to Islamic medicine, combined with even more serious attacks upon the practice of Western medicine, leading to such recent 'iconoclastic' works as that of Ivan Illich.[88]

This situation in the West, the source of all the 'officially' accepted medicine in most Islamic countries, has now become combined with a new socio-economic problem. The process of modernization has caused many Muslim governments to seek to provide medical coverage for all their citizens, but both the rapid rise of population and the exorbitant cost of training physicians in the Western type of medical school, even if these graduates were not to wind up ultimately in Europe and America, make such a programme impossible. Moreover, medical care has become much worse in certain areas where the old *ḥakīms* have died out without anyone taking their place. There has, therefore, been a conscious effort in certain countries, such as Persia, to bring back traditional medicine in combination with programmes for the spread of rural medicine, although probably the inhabitants of cities are

88. We have especially in mind the thoroughly documented work of Illich, *Medical Nemesis*, London, 1974.

much more in need of it. Likewise, there is a notable rise in the use of traditional drugs wrapped and packaged in new forms.[89]

In conclusion, it can be said that Islamic medicine is fully alive in Pakistan and Bangladesh and among the Muslims of India, partly alive in the rest of the Islamic world in its popular and folk aspect and making a 'comeback' in certain areas where it has been on the defensive for a long time. Moreover, it is attracting even greater attention in the world at large as a vast treasury of medical wisdom and experience containing not only the fruit of the thought and experience of the Muslim physicians, but also all that Islam inherited from the ancient world. Islamic medicine is, despite everything, still a living tradition, still able to teach a great deal in fields as far apart as pharmacology and psychosomatic medicine to a humanity that has divorced the soul from the body and in its attempt to prolong man's earthly journey has almost destroyed the very equilibrium which has made this journey possible over the ages.

89. In Pakistan and India, such institutions as the Hamdard of Delhi and Karachi have been active in the field for decades, but in other places, such as Persia, making traditional drugs available in modern chemists' shops as well as the traditional '*aṭṭārīn* is a very recent phenomenon.

Chapter IX
Alchemy and Other Occult Sciences

The Occult Sciences in Islamic Civilization

Besides the 'open' and 'accessible' sciences discussed so far, the Islamic sciences include a category called the hidden (*khafiyyah*) or occult (*gharībah*) sciences, which have always remained 'hidden', both in the content of their teachings and in the manner of gaining accessibility to them, because of their very nature. The saying of René Guénon that there are no occult sciences but only 'occulted sciences' holds true as much for the Islamic world as for the West. These sciences in their unadulterated form – and not in their half-mutilated, present-day form in which their symbolism is forgotten – deal with hidden forces within the cosmos and the means of dealing with these forces. In a traditional world, these sciences were kept hidden in order to protect society from their being used, or rather misused, by the unqualified, much like esotericism itself, of which they are branches. The traditional occult sciences are, in fact, applications of cosmological sciences, and are understandable only in the light of a living esotericism having the metaphysical doctrines necessary to make lucid the symbolism they contain. Without the light of such an esotericism they become opaque and, in fact, dangerous channels for spreading chaos on the plane of external forms, both natural and human. The cultivation of the occult sciences in the modern world is a glaring example of such a case, where the singular lack of the light of wisdom has turned the 'occult sciences', whose principles have been totally forgotten, into major factors in the spread of disorder and chaos.[1]

In the Islamic world the situation has been completely different. While, on the exoteric level, the cultivation of the occult sciences, especially those dealing with prognostication, were forbidden or at least discouraged, on the esoteric level they became ancillaries to the purely esoteric doctrines of gnosis. Moreover, in the light of the esoteric dimension of the Quranic revelation, these sciences, some of purely Semitic origin and others inherited from the Hellenistic, Egyptian, Babylonian and Iranian worlds, became like shining stars in the firmament, providing so many keys for the contemplative understanding of the inner processes of the natural order.

1. On the role of the occult sciences divorced from their principles in the spread of chaos in the modern world, see R. Guénon, *The Reign of Quantity and the Signs of the Times*, trans. by Lord Northbourne, London, 1953, pp. 197ff.

The Nature of Alchemy

Without doubt, the most widespread and significant of these sciences in Islam was alchemy, which, as in the Latin West,[2] was considered at once a science and an art (*ṣināʻah*). Traditional alchemy is, in fact, a complete way of looking at things. It is at the same time a science of the cosmos and a science of the soul[3] and is related to art and metallurgy on the one hand and spiritual psychotherapy on the other. The alchemical point of view is based on the principle that 'everything is in everything', that everything penetrates everything[4] (*tadākhul*), and that therefore the substance of things can be transmuted so that their nature can be changed rather than only their accidents as is taught in Aristotelian natural philosophy.

To speak of alchemy is to speak of transmutation of the substance of things in the presence of a spiritual agent symbolized by the Philosophers' Stone. It means also, and above all, the inner transmutation of the subject, of man himself, who participates in the process of which only the external aspect is discernible. Alchemy is concerned with the material world, especially minerals and metals, but not considered solely in themselves. Rather, it sees in them the insignia of the cosmic intelligence and makes use of the alchemical processes concerning them as supports for the transformation of the soul. Alchemy is not a protochemistry, although the history of chemistry is inseparable from it. Nor is it a purely psychological science in the manner interpreted by C. G. Jung and his disciples. It is a science embracing at once the cosmos and the soul, based on the view of nature as a sacred domain whose processes of giving birth to precious metals and minerals[5] are accelerated by the alchemist through the power of the Spirit operating within his soul and making possible the final deliverance of the soul from all bondage and its transformation into gold, which alone among metals remains unaffected by the withering influences of natural forces. To seek in alchemy either a crude chemistry or a psychology in the modern sense of the word is to remain blind to the sacred view of nature and the doctrine of the unicity of the cosmos which form the foundation of all the traditional sciences, especially alchemy, and which stand at the antipode of the segmented and secularized world which forms the 'object or subject of study' of both modern chemistry and modern psychology.

Islamic alchemy, which reached its height at the beginning of its history with Jābir ibn Ḥayyān, contains a total 'philosophy of nature' related closely to the general philosophical outlook of classical Hermeticism, as well as a specific doctrine concerning the mineral kingdom and the transmutation of metals into gold. The basis of this natural philosophy is, as in Peripatetic physics, the doctrine of hylomorphism, the four natures or qualities and the four elements, although these are interpreted somewhat differently in the two schools.[6] The four natures combine in various permutations, as specified in Figure 86, to give rise to the two basic substances, or principles, of sulphur and mercury. These two principles are not, however, to be confused with the physical substances bearing the same name. Rather, the alchemical sulphur and mercury correspond to the masculine and feminine principles on the cosmic plane from whose wedding all creatures come into being. They correspond in many ways to the Yin-

2. As far as alchemy is concerned, Latin alchemy is both historically and conceptually a direct continuation of Islamic alchemy, as the name of the art itself from the Arabic *al-kīmiyā'* reveals. See Nasr, *Science and Civilization in Islam*, pp. 285ff.

3. The work of T. Burckhardt, which we consider the best contemporary account of alchemy, is in fact entitled *Alchemy – Science of the Cosmos, Science of the Soul*, trans. by W. Stoddart, London, 1967; Baltimore, 1971.

4. According to traditional Islamic metaphysics, the first determination of the Absolute (the level of *aḥadiyyah* according to the followers of the school of Ibn ʻArabī) is one in which all the Divine Names and Qualities are determined but as yet indistinct in such a way that every Quality is in every other Quality. It might be said that the alchemical point of view reflects this principial Reality on the level of cosmic existence.

5. The ideal of alchemy as a form of 'obstetrics' which delivers gold from the bosom of nature is an ancient one which Islamic alchemy inherited from its Alexandrian background. See M. Eliade, *The Forge and the Crucible*, trans. by S. Cossin, London, 1962, chap. 4.

6. On the theoretical structure underlying alchemy, see Burckhardt, *op. cit.*, Nasr, *op. cit.*, chap. ten; Eliade, *op. cit.*, R. Alleau, *Aspects de l'alchimie traditionnelle*, Paris, 1953; Fulcanelli, *Les demeures philosophales et le symbolisme hermétique dans ses rapports avec l'Art sacré et l'ésotérisme du Grand-Oeuvre*, Paris, 1930; G. Evola, *La tradizione esmetica*, Bari, 1948; M. Aniane, 'Notes sur l'alchimie, "Yoga" cosmologique de la chrétienté médiévale', in J. Masui (ed.), *Yoga, Science de l'homme intégral*, Paris, 1953, pp. 243–273; and E. Zolla, *Le meraviglie della natura – Introduzione all'alchemica*, Milan, 1975.

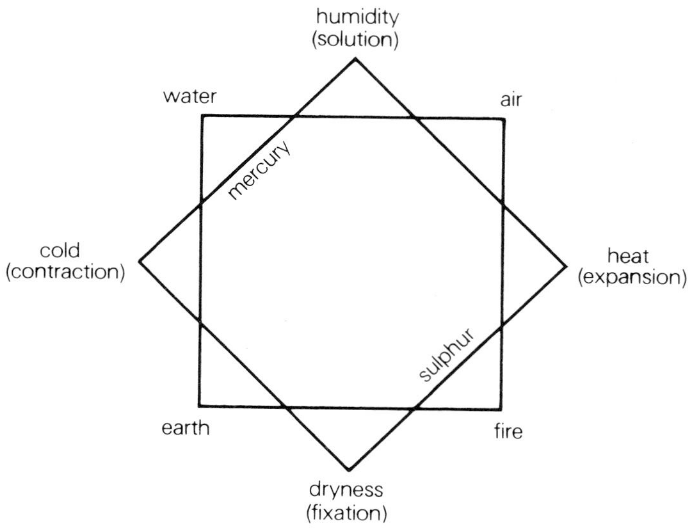

Figure 86. The four elements, natures and cosmic and alchemical principles.

Yang and Puruṣa-Prakṛti of Chinese and Hindu cosmologies considered on the lower planes of cosmic reality.

Hence, according to Jābirean alchemy, all metals come into being as a result of the wedding of sulphur and mercury in different proportions, and of course under particular celestial influences, which alone make this 'unnatural' and 'extra-terrestrial' substance which the metallic state signifies possible. That is why the metallurgist is always dealing with 'influences' which are not natural to the environment and which must be controlled through beneficent spiritual influences if they are not to cause disorder in the terrestrial *milieu*.[7] The use of the same symbols for metal and the planets in alchemy and astrology [♄ (Saturn and lead), ♃ (Jupiter and tin), ♂ (Mars and iron), ☉ (Sun and gold), ♀ (Venus and copper), ☿ (Mercury and quick-silver), ☽ (Moon and silver)] signifies the presence of celestial influences in the genesis of metals from the combination of sulphur and mercury. The metals are so many 'insignia' of the planets on the terrestrial plane.

According to Jābir, the key to the understanding of the structure of metals and, in fact, of all substances is the balance *(al-mīzān)*, which plays a crucial role in Islamic alchemy. The balance is not just a physical instrument to measure weights, and its presence in Jābirean alchemy is by no means the sign of the early appearance of quantitative analysis in the history of chemistry. Rather, the balance is the instrument which 'measures' the tendency of the World Soul towards a particular composition, the act of 'measurement' being meant here in its Pythagorean rather than modern sense.[8] The balance is, therefore, concerned with inner and outer qualities and with numeral symbolism, as well as with the symbolic letters of the Arabic alphabet.

According to Jābir, each metal possesses an outward (*ẓāhir*) and an inward (*bāṭin*) aspect, two qualities being manifested outwardly and two remaining inward. Gold, the most perfect of metals, is, for example, outwardly hot and humid but inwardly cold and dry while silver is its opposite. Jābir, moreover, divides each quality into four degrees and each degree into seven subdivisions, so that there are altogether twenty-eight parts, each of which corresponds to a letter of the Arabic alphabet. The four natures also exist in each metal according to the series 1:3:5:8, the sum being 17, which is the key to the understanding of the structure of the world. The series 1:3:5:8, as well as the numbers 17 and 28, are intimately bound to the magic square of nine houses

4	9	2
3	5	7
8	1	6

which if divided gnomonically will give the numbers 28 (4 + 9 + 2 + 7 + 6), 17 (3 + 5 + 1 + 8) and the series 1:3:5:8.[9] The numbers used by Jābir are closely related to the Pythagorean musical scale, to ancient Babylonian architecture, and also to the Chinese *Ming-Tang*, indicating early contacts with the Chinese tradition in this domain.

Jābir and other Islamic alchemists following him devised elaborate tables showing the correspondence of the letters of the alphabet with the degrees of the various qualities and the 'amount' of each quality existing in the metal in question. The name of the metal in Arabic is therefore connected through these tables to the very structure of the metal.[10] In Jābirean alchemy, the treatment of alchemical qualities is inseparable from the

7. See Guénon, *op. cit.*, chap. XXII; also Eliade, *op. cit.*, chap. 9.

8. On the meaning of the Jābirean balance, see H. Corbin 'Le livre du Glorieux de Jābir ibn Ḥayyān', *Eranos-Jahrbuch*, vol. XVIII, 1950.

9. On the Jābirean balance and the theory of composition of metals, see P. Kraus, *Jābir ibn Ḥayyān*, vol. II, 'Jābir et la science grecque', chap. V, pp. 187ff.; Nasr, *Science and Civilization in Islam*, pp. 258ff.; and Holmyard, *Alchemy*, London, 1957, pp. 66–80.

10. See Kraus, *op. cit.*, pp. 223ff.

science of numbers on the one hand and the science of letters (*al-jafr*) on the other. Every metal is constituted of the same qualities in differing internal and external proportions, and transmutation means the change of these proportions according to the tables devised and with the help of the cosmic balance which is itself the source for the tables.

It must be remembered, however, that alchemical transmutation is not simply a 'natural' process. It is the result of the direct intrusion of a higher principle upon the physical plane and a quickening of cosmic processes made possible only through the presence of forces from the worlds above in the same way that inwardly the transformation of the soul is possible only through the presence of the Spirit. This fundamental aspect of alchemy, which alone should clearly distinguish it from any form of proto-chemistry, is intimately bound to the elixir (from the Arabic *al-iksīr*) and also the Philosophers' Stone (*ḥajarat al-falāsifah*). The elixir is of different kinds, seven elixirs being enumerated by Jābir, some mineral, others vegetable and yet others animal, while the Philosophers' Stone is only mineral. But in both cases the necessity of their presence in the act of transmutation means the presence of a spiritual force not to be found by simply searching among natural substances. That is why the terms elixir and Philosophers' Stone imply something rare and precious, inaccessible save to the adepts. In Arabic and Persian, the term *kīmiyā'* itself, from which comes the word alchemy, means not only the art but also the substance whose presence makes transmutation possible, and even the fruit of transmutation, which is gold.

Alchemical transmutation is a process, a work consisting of various stages which are often summarized as blackening (*nigredo*), bleaching (*albedo*) and reddening (*rubedo*) of the 'stone' that is to be transmuted. It is achieved through nature itself but with the help of the art of alchemy and through the grace of God which is absolutely essential if the process is to be successful. The alchemists say that 'nature can overcome nature',[11] meaning that alchemy makes use of nature itself to bring about the transmutation of natural substances. But this overcoming of nature by nature is possible only with the help of the spiritual presence which transcends the natural order and yet is 'supernaturally natural'. The stages of the alchemical work imply death and resurrection, and dissolution and coagulation, in such a way that the base metal, disordered and chaotic, is transformed into gold, the solar metal and the symbol of perfection and harmony on the physical level. The work implies the dissolution of what is coagulated and the coagulation or crystallization of what is dissolved. The famous saying of the fifth and sixth Shī'ite Imāms in whose circle Jābir was trained, namely 'Our spirits are our bodies and our bodies our spirits' (*arwāḥunā ajsādunā wa ajsādunā arwāḥunā*) means, among other things, the alchemical transmutation which crystallizes and fixes the volatile spirit and dissolves the coagulated and dense body.

The famous alchemical *salva et coagula* not only concerns minerals and metals but is also directly connected with the spiritual alchemy through which the hardened heart of fallen man is dissolved and the amorphous aspects of his soul crystallized. The alchemical work *is* in fact an inward process through which the soul is transformed, but by making use of external metallurgical and alchemical processes as a support, thanks to the analogy between the microcosm and the macrocosm. While the base metal is melted in the athanor (from the Arabic *al-tannūr* or oven), the hardened crust of the soul of man which prevents him from reaching the fountain of life at the centre of his being is melted within the body, which is the microcosmic athanor, until the crust dissolves and ceases to be an impediment to the flow of the water of life. The death and resurrection of metals is an outward support for the death and resurrection of the soul, and the phoenix rising from its ashes is none other than the state of the soul of the initiate after it becomes freed from the prison of passions and limitation. The wedding of the sun and the moon or the king and the queen so often depicted in alchemical texts is, of course, the symbol of the wedding of the soul to the Spirit.[12]

Alchemy, like Tantrism, makes use of the cosmic forces themselves in order to transcend

11. See Burckhardt, *op. cit.*, chap. 9.

12. There are some vivid illustrations of this principle from mediaeval and Renaissance Western manuscripts in C. G. Jung, *Psychology and Alchemy*, trans. by R. F. C. Hull, New York, 1953, for example p. 316. The interpretation is, however, full of grave errors since the fundamental differences between Spirit and Soul are not emphasized by Jung.

the cosmos. It is a discipline whereby the male principle is devoured by the female principle to rise again in perfected form and to become wedded to the female principle in a union which itself is beyond all cosmic dualities. In this process, the mineral kingdom acts as a support for the alchemist, while the transformation within the being of the alchemist affects the external natural environment about him. The transformation of the soul of fallen man into the state of sanctity is a miracle which corresponds to the transmutation of base metal into gold. Both gold and the soul of the saint have become incorruptible within the world of generation and corruption where everything else withers away. They are both vice-gerents of the Spirit in this world, each on its own plane, and therefore correspond to each other in many ways. One is the fruit of inner alchemy and the other of outward alchemy. But ultimately there is a unity which embraces the inward and the outward and there is ultimately but one alchemy which makes possible both the inward and the outward transmutation.

Debates about Transmutation

The possibility of transforming base metal into gold was debated throughout Islamic history by Muslim scientists, philosophers and theologians, as it was in the West. Usually the theologians (*mutakallimūn*) opposed alchemy and the occult sciences in general, although some among them, such as the Muʿtazilite Qāḍī ʿAbd al-Jabbār and the Ashʿarite Fakhr al-Dīn al-Rāzī, wrote treatises on them. Most philosopher-scientists and physicians accepted the alchemical point of view, even if they did not believe in transmutation. Usually the Peripatetics opposed the possibility of transmutation while the Illuminationists accepted it.

Ibn Sīnā, for example, clearly opposed those who claimed to turn base metal into gold and wrote against them. Yet, the theory of the composition of metals which he presents in his *Shifāʾ* is based on the sulphur-mercury theory and is the same as that of the alchemists.[13] Ibn Sīnā was in fact taken to task by al-Ṭughrāʾī for his opposition to alchemy and the debate continued over the centuries. Usually in theological circles, those associated with Shīʿism, which early in its history integrated certain facets of Hermeticism into itself, were more sympathetic to alchemy than the Ashʿarite theologians, although there were notable exceptions. As for philosophy, schools which were of a more esoteric nature were naturally more interested in alchemy. In fact the highest and most profound interpretation of alchemy was to be given by the representatives of Islamic esotericism such as Ibn ʿArabī, who was himself entitled the 'red sulphur' (*al-kibrīt al-aḥmar*).

The Historical Development of Islamic Alchemy

While the origin of alchemy is hidden in the vast spans of prehistory, alchemy as a systematized discipline, with its written texts and established authorities, appears in Alexandria and China at almost the same time, namely just before the beginning of the Christian era. Islam was heir to the whole of the Alexandrian alchemical heritage and also, without doubt, had some contact with Chinese alchemy, from which it adopted many elements, including not only the numerological concerns already cited but also the meaning of the term alchemy itself, as both the art of transmutation and the substance which makes transmutation possible.[14]

The Muslim sources contain the names of nearly all the known Alexandrian alchemists as well as mythical figures associated with Hermeticism. The names of Agathodaimon, Isis, Kleopatra and Maria are often cited, as are those of Ostanes and Jāmāsb al-Ḥakīm, showing the strong Persian element which was already present in Alexandria.[15] Almost all the famous Greek philosophers from Pythagoras on were also cited as alchemical authorities as the well-known *Turba*

13. In traditional Islamic sources the wedding of the Holy Prophet and Khadījah is sometimes referred to as the conjunction of the sun and the moon.

14. S. Mahdihassan has gone so far as to claim that the word alchemy itself does not come from Egyptian and Greek sources (*chem* which is the Egyptian for black or the Greek verb *cheein* meaning to pour out) but from the Chinese *Chin-Ia*, which means the gold-producing juice of a plant. See Mahdihassan, 'Alchemy and its Chinese Origin as revealed by its Etymology, Doctrines, and Symbols', *Iqbal Review*, 1966, pp. 22ff. On Chinese alchemy itself see J. Needham, *Science and Civilization in China*, vol. V : 2, Cambridge, 1974.

15. The figure of Ostanes, the Persian, is of particular importance as the channel through which Persian influences penetrated into Alexandrian alchemical circles. See J. Lindsay, *The Origins of Alchemy in Graeco-Roman Egypt*, New York, 1970, chap. 7; also J. Bidez and F. Cumont, *Les mages hellénisés, Zoroastre, Ostanès et Hystaspe d'après la tradition grecque*, Paris, 1938.

Philosophorum (*Muṣḥaf al-jamā'ah* in its original Arabic of 'Uthmān ibn Suwayd and going back to a Greek model) shows.[16]

In addition to these figures the Muslims also knew and cited Alexandrian alchemists properly speaking such as Bolos Democritos, Zosimos, Apollonios of Tyana – whose *Sirr al-khalīqah* (*Secret of Creatures*) was so well known among Muslims –, Teukros and Stephanos of Alexandria.[17]

The most important source for Islamic alchemy, and in fact a major source of inspiration for certain of the other Islamic sciences and schools of thought, is, however, a number of treatises attributed to Hermes and known in the West as the *Corpus Hermeticum*.[18] What the mediaeval and even post-mediaeval West has known of Hermes comes essentially from Islamic sources rather than directly from Alexandrian ones, where, from the wedding of the Greek god Hermes and the Egyptian god Thoth, the figure of Hermes as the founder of alchemy and a whole 'philosophy of nature' came into being.

In Islamic sources the one Hermes of Alexandrian sources became three, hence the term Hermes Trismegistos (from the Arabic *al-muthallath bi'l-ḥikmah*), which has inspired so many philosophers and poets in the West. The three Hermes were considered by Muslims as prophets belonging to the golden chain of prophecy stretching from Adam to the Prophet of Islam. Hence Hermeticism was considered as a revealed doctrine and was easily integrated into the Islamic perspective because it was already 'Islamic' in the wider sense of the term as belonging to the chain of prophecy.[19] The first Hermes was identified with the ante-diluvian prophet Idrīs (or Akhnūkh). He lived in Egypt and built the pyramids. The second was entitled al-Bābilī, namely 'Babylonian'. He lived in Mesopotamia after the flood and was responsible for reviving the sciences. The third lived again in Egypt after the flood and taught men many of the sciences and crafts. The Muslims saw the three Hermes not only as founders of alchemy, but also of astronomy and astrology, architecture and many of the other arts, and finally of philosophy. The first Hermes is entitled by Muslim sources Abu'l-Ḥukamā' (the father of theosophers or philosophers).[20]

The Hermetic corpus in Arabic includes the celebrated *Tabula Smaragdina* (*The Emerald Table*), which appears also at the end of Apollonius of Tyana's *Sirr al-khalīqah*,[21] the *Kitāb al-Isṭamāṭīs* and the *Kitāb al-ḥabīb* (*The Book of the Friend*) all of which were very popular. There also developed a notable Islamic Hermetic literature which includes works of such diverse figures as Abū Ma'shar, Suhrawardī, Ibn 'Arabī and Afḍal al-Dīn al-Kāshānī. Hermetic writings formed a distinct corpus which played an important role in Islamic thought. Moreover, it was also influential in the West where its effect can be seen upon

16. On this important text of Latin alchemy see M. Plessner, 'The Turba Philosophorum, A Preliminary Report on Three Cambridge MSS', *Ambix*, vol. 7, 1959, pp. 159–163.

17. On the Alexandrian sources of Islamic alchemy see D. Chwolson, *Die Ssabier und der Ssabismus*, vol. I, pp. 781–792; E. O. von Lippmann, *Entstellung und Ausbreitung der Alchemie*, 2 vols., Berlin, 1919–1931; Ruska, *Tabula Smaragdina*, Heidelberg, 1926, pp. 6–68; Sezgin, *Geschichte der arabischen Schrifttums*, vol. IV, pp. 31–119; Ullmann, *Die Natur- und Geheimwissenschaften im Islam*, pp. 145–191.

18. For this corpus, which is not the same in Arabic as in Greek, see A. J. Festugière and A. D. Nock, *La révélation d'Hermès Trismégiste*, 4 vols., Paris, 1953 on; G. R. S. Mead, *Thrice-Greatest Hermes*, 3 vols., London, 1906 and 1949; and W. Scott, *Hermetica*, 4 vols., Oxford, 1924–1936.

19. See Nasr, *Islamic Studies*, chap. six, 'Hermes and Hermetic Writings in the Islamic World'. See also L. Massignon, 'Inventaire de la littérature hermétique', appendix IV to Festugière and Nock, *op. cit.*, vol. I; M. Plessner, 'Hermes' in the new *Encyclopaedia of Islam*; and A. E. Affifi, 'The Influence of Hermetic Literature on Moslem Thought', *Bulletin of the School of Oriental and African Studies*, vol. 13, 1949–1951, pp. 840–855.

20. More than any other figure Abū Ma'shar al-Balkhī is responsible as the source for the doctrine of the three Hermes, which was then reflected in different variations in numerous later works.

21. See Ruska, *op. cit.*, and Plessner, 'Neue Materialen zur Geschichte der Tabula Smaragdina', *Islam*, vol. 16, 1927, pp. 77–113.

writings as diverse as the *Parzival* epic[22] and the works of Giordano Bruno.[23]

Through direct contact and oral transmission as well as by means of translations of texts Muslims became heir to the tradition of Alexandrian alchemy and very early in their history founded a major new branch of the alchemical tradition which has come to be known as Islamic alchemy.[24] The earliest Muslim alchemist who had direct contact with Alexandrian, and perhaps Syriac, sources was the Umayyad Prince Khālid ibn Yazīd, whose name is often mentioned in later sources. Although his activities are clouded in some uncertainty, there is no doubt concerning his interest in alchemy. There are in fact treatises by him which still survive, as well as many which have been mentioned by later sources but which are no longer extant.[25]

Islamic alchemy reached its peak rapidly in the early 2nd/8th century in the circle of Imām Ja'far al-Ṣādiq, the sixth Shī'ite Imām, who was the teacher of Jābir ibn Ḥayyān.[26] As already mentioned, with Jābir, known in the West as Geber, Islamic alchemy reached a point never surpassed during the succeeding centuries. Jābir hailed from Kufa, spent much of his life in Tus, then came to Baghdad and died around the end of the 2nd/8th century in seclusion in either Kufa or possibly somewhere in Persia.[27] He wrote a very large number of works to which later followers of Ismā'īlism, who considered Jābir as their own, added many treatises following his teachings and in the spirit of his doctrines. Together, these works are called the Jābirean corpus and they constitute a major collection in the annals of Islamic science.[28] These include nearly every field of learning and especially alchemy where such works as the *Kitāb al-sab'īn* (*The Seventy Books*) and the *Kitāb al-mīzān* (*The Book of the Balance*) have served as the foundations of Islamic alchemy.[29] Altogether the Jābirean corpus, most of it still not studied thoroughly, is the most important single body of works on alchemy in Arabic and the main source not only of Islamic alchemy but even to a large extent of Latin alchemy.

The Barmakid family of viziers, who were patrons of Jābir, were themselves interested in alchemy and composed treatises on the subject. Also, in the early 3rd/9th century, 'Uthmān ibn Suwayd from Akhmīm (Panopolis) in Egypt composed the Arabic original of what was later to become one of the most famous of Latin alchemical texts, the *Turba Philosophorum*, which remained popular throughout the Middle Ages and the Renaissance.[30] It is of particular interest to note also that the Egyptian Sufi Dhu'l-Nūn al-Maṣrī, who was a contemporary of Ibn Suwayd, also wrote on alchemy, two of his treatises on the subject being mentioned by Ibn al-Nadīm. Nor was Dhu'l-Nūn the only Sufi master who wrote on

22. See H. and R. Kahane, *The Krater and the Grail; Hermetic Sources of the Parzival*, Urbana (Illinois), 1965; and Corbin, *En Islam iranien*, vol. II, Paris, 1971, chap. IV.

23. See F. A. Yates, *Giordano Bruno and the Hermetic Tradition*, London, 1964.

24. On the historical development of Islamic alchemy see Sezgin, *op. cit.*, pp. 120–299; Ullmann, *op. cit.*, pp. 192ff.; von Lippmann, *op. cit.*; Nasr, *Science and Civilization in Islam*, chap. ten; Holmyard, *Alchemy*, chap. 5; M. P. E. Berthelot, *La chimie au Moyen-Âge*, Paris, 1893; and A. Siggel, *Katalog der arabischen alchemisten Handschriften Deutschlands*, Berlin, 1949.

25. See the general study devoted to Khālid by Sa'īd Dīwajī, *al-Amīr Khālid ibn Yazīd*, Damascus, 1953.

26. Again, Ruska and others have cast doubt upon the alchemical teachings emanating from the circle of Imām Ja'far. But here, as in the case of Khālid ibn Yazīd and Jābir himself, later research by Sezgin and others has to a great extent substantiated, rather than repudiated, the traditional Islamic view.

27. A few years ago a tombstone was found in Western Persia with the name of Jābir on it, although traditional sources usually mention Tus or Kufa as his place of death. On the life of Jābir see Holmyard, *Alchemy*, pp. 66ff.; Holmyard, 'An Essay on Jābir ibn Ḥayyān', *Studien zur Geschichte der Chemie, Festgabe E. O. von Lippmann zum siebzigsten Geburtstage*, Berlin, 1927, pp. 28–37; Kraus, *Jābir ibn Ḥayyān*, vol. I; and Sezgin, *op. cit.*, pp. 132–231.

28. Sezgin, in the work already cited, has given detailed answers to many of the arguments of Kraus against the authenticity of the works contained in the Jābirean corpus. The new studies of the manuscript material by Sezgin have given a much greater historical reality to Jābir and his works than the ethereal picture of him depicted by Ruska and Kraus.

29. For a list of Jābir's writings, see Sezgin, *op. cit.*, pp. 231–269.

30. The Latin text of the *Turba* was published in Basle in 1572.

alchemy. Both al-Junayd and al-Ḥallāj, masters of the school of Baghdad, are also said to have written alchemical treatises, and works bearing their name have survived.

A new phase was begun in the history of Islamic alchemy by Muḥammad ibn Zakariyyā' al-Rāzī, whose influence was nearly as great in this domain as in medicine. A study of al-Rāzī's philosophical ideas reveals that he stood outside the mainstream of Islamic philosophy and negated among other things the distinction between the outward (*ẓāhir*) and inward (*bāṭin*) aspects of things and the process of spiritual hermeneutics (*ta'wīl*) which is the journey from the outward to the inward. Since alchemy is an eminently symbolic science of the cosmos, the negation of *ta'wīl*, and hence the symbolic interpretation of nature, meant also the transformation of the nature of alchemy itself. Al-Rāzī, more than any other Muslim alchemist, was responsible for the transformation of alchemy into chemistry, although he continued to use the language of alchemy.[31] His works such as the *Kitāb al-asrār* (*The Book of Secrets*) and the *Kitāb sirr al-asrār* (*The Book of the Secret of Secrets* – the *Liber Secretorum Bubacaris* in Latin) and the *al-Madkhal al-ta'līmī* (*Propaedeutic Introduction*) were studied as works on alchemy by later generations of Muslims because they continued to use the language of alchemy although in reality they are more texts of chemistry than alchemy. This is especially true of the *Kitāb al-asrār*, which by mistake has come to be known as *Sirr al-asrār*,[32] and which is the major opus of al-Rāzī on the subject. This work is definitely more concerned with chemistry than alchemy, despite the fact that the author follows Jābir on many points such as dividing metals into seven species including the 'chinese metal' (*khārṣīnī*). The later Muslim alchemists in general had not as yet had an experience of minerals and metals so emptied of their sacred content as to make possible the conception of chemistry in the modern sense. They, therefore, saw al-Rāzī as an alchemist, although some contemporary alchemists in Persia call a kind of imperfect transmutation of metal into gold the 'Rāzī transmutation'. Seen from the point of view of the later phases of the history of science, however, al-Rāzī must be considered as the founder of chemistry.

One of the most notable contributions of al-Rāzī to chemistry is his classification of substances. The well-known classification of substances into mineral, vegetable and animal is met with for the first time in his writings and he must be credited with this primary and all-important categorization.[33] Al-Rāzī also gave a careful description of many chemical processes such as distillation, calcination, filteration and the like, which are also seen in the writings of Jābir as well as in those of later alchemists, but which are particularly well described by al-Rāzī.[34] Being a physician, al-Rāzī was also interested in iatrochemistry and is traditionally credited with being the first person to separate, and make medical use of, alcohol, although this traditional view has not been proven by modern scholarship.

Ibn Waḥshiyyah was nearly contemporary with al-Rāzī, but wrote in a completely different vein. The famous author of occult works dealing especially with agriculture also wrote several treatises on alchemy, of which the *Kitāb al-uṣūl al-kabīr* (*The Grand Book of Principles*) may be cited as an example. He was followed in the 4th/10th century by Ibn Umayl, author of several alchemical works, the most famous of which is the *Kitāb al-mā' al-waraqī wa'l-arḍ al-najmiyyah* (*The Book of the Silvery Water and Starry Earth*). This work is among the most famous in the annals of Islamic alchemy and was also known in the West as *Tabula chemica*.

The great Peripatetic philosophers of the 4th/10th century, al-Fārābī and Ibn Sīnā, wrote on the elixir and other subjects related to alchemy but not on alchemy itself. But the philosopher and

31. See Nasr, 'From the alchemy of Jābir to the chemistry of Rāzī', in *Islamic Studies*, pp. 90–95. On Rāzī's chemical ideas, see also H. Sheybānī, *Kitāb al-asrār yā rāzhā-yi ṣān'at-i kīmiyā'*, Tehran, 1349 (A.H. solar).

32. See M. T. Danechepazhuh (ed.), *Kitāb al-asrār wa sirr al-asrār*, Tehran, 1964; U. I. Karimov (ed.), *Neizvestnoe socienie al-Razi 'Kniga Tainy Tain'*, Tashkent, 1957. Ruska, in his well-known study *Al-Razi's Buch Gehemnis der Geheimnisse*, Berlin, 1937, mistook the title of the *Kitāb al-asrār* for *Sirr al-asrār*.

33. See Holmyard, *Alchemy*, p. 89, for the details of this classification.

34. On various chemical processes, especially distillation, among Muslims, see R. J. Forbes, *A Short History of the Art of Distillation*, Leiden, 1970, pp. 28–54.

historian Ibn Muskūyah (usually known as Miskawayh) was actively interested in alchemy.[35] Alchemical treatises by him survive to this day and it is known that he spent much of his life in the quest of the Philosophers' Stone. Of the earlier Muslim philosophers, he was, with the exception of al-Rāzī, the person most devoted to the alchemical art.

The most noteworthy Islamic treatise on alchemical apparatus, the *'Ayn al-ṣan'ah wa 'awn al-ṣana'ā'* (*The Source of the Art and the Aid to the Students of Alchemy*) of Abu'l-Ḥakīm Muḥammad al-Kāthī, which was translated later into Persian from the original Arabic, belongs to the 5th/11th century.[36] Also to this period belongs Abū Maslamah al-Majrīṭī, to whom the well-known works, *Rutbat al-ḥakīm* (*The Sage's Step*) and the *Ghāyat al-ḥakīm* (*The Aim of the Wise*), famous in the West as the *Picatrix*,[37] are attributed. Abū Maslamah has been often mistaken even in Islamic works with the astronomer Abu'l-Qāsim Maslamah al-Majrīṭī who lived at about the same time in Spain. Meanwhile, in the East, the celebrated Sufi writer Abu'l-Qāsim al-Qushayrī left behind a treatise on alchemy, while al-Ghazzālī employed the term 'alchemy' in the title of his Persian work *Kīmiyā-yi sa'ādat* (*Alchemy of Happiness*). But, as far as is known, he did not write a work specifically on alchemy although many apocryphal ones on the subject are attributed to him.

During the 6th/12th century, alchemical works of major scope appeared again in both the eastern and western lands of Islam. In the East the vizier Mu'ayyid al-Dīn al-Ṭughrā'ī defended alchemy against sceptics and left behind several treatises on the subject including the *Kitāb mafātīḥ al-raḥmah wa maṣābīḥ al-ḥikmah* (*The Book of the Keys of Mercy and Lights of Wisdom*). In Andalusia Abu'l-Ḥasan al-Jayyānī, known as Afra' Ra's, who was a fine poet, composed several alchemical poems, the most famous being the *Shudhūr al-dhahab* (*Particles of Gold*). Also in the Maghrib, the celebrated authority on the occult sciences, Shams al-Dīn al-Būnī, devoted a large chapter of his *Shams al-ma'ārif* (*The Sun of the Divine Sciences*) to alchemy; likewise Muḥammad ibn al-Ḥājj al-Tilimsānī dedicated a section to alchemy in his primarily magical treatise, the *Shumūs al-anwār* (*Suns of Light*).

The most important alchemical work to follow this period is the *Kitāb al-'ilm al-muktasab fī zirā'at al-dhahab* of Abu'l-Qāsim al-'Irāqī,[38] which is essentially a summary of Islamic alchemy and based on Jābir, Ibn Umayl and others. Nevertheless, it is a well-written synopsis which continued to attract the attention of later alchemists, who wrote commentaries upon it. Among these commentators, the most important is 'Izz al-Dīn Aydamur al-Jīldakī, who lived in the 8th/14th century. His *Nihāyat al-ṭalab* (*The End of the Search*) is a commentary upon the *'Ilm al-muktasab*, while drawing also from earlier alchemical works. Al-Jīldakī is, in fact, particularly precious as a source for earlier Islamic alchemy.

In the 9th/15th century, Turkish writings on alchemy began to appear in addition to those of the Arabs and Persians. Among them, 'Alī Bek al-Izniqī, called the 'new author' (*al-mu'allif al-jadīd*), is the most important. He wrote many alchemical works, including the *Kitāb al-asrār fī hatk al-astār* (*The Book of Secrets Concerning the Rending of the Veils*), which includes discussions on cosmology. He also wrote on the balance (*al-mīzān*). Meanwhile, alchemical treatises continued to appear in the Maghrib with Abū 'Amr 'Abd al-Karīm al-Marrākushī writing on the Philosophers' Stone and other alchemical subjects. His treatise *Risālat al-ruḥāwiyyāt* (*Treatise on Edessan Inspirations*) is particularly interesting in that it describes the alchemical process in the form of a dream. In Persia, at the same time, Shahriyār Bahmanyār-i Pārsī was composing his *Tajārib-i shahriyārī* in Persian.[39]

35. See M. Arkoun, *Contribution à l'humanisme arabe au IVe/Xe siècle: Miskawayh (320/325–421)/(932/936–1030) philosophe et historien*, Paris, 1970.

36. This treatise has been translated with annotations into English by H. E. Stapleton and R. F. Azo, 'Alchemical Equipment in the Eleventh Century, A.D.', in *Memoirs of the Asiatic Society of Bengal*, vol. 1, 1905, pp. 47–71.

37. The Arabic text of this central work of both Islamic and Latin alchemy was edited by H. Ritter, Leipzig, 1933, and the text translated and analysed by Ritter and Plessner, *'Picatrix'. Das Ziel des Weisen von Pseudo-Mağrīṭī*, London, 1962.

38. See E. J. Holmyard, *The Book of Knowledge Acquired Concerning the Cultivation of Gold of Abu'l-Qāsim Muḥammad ibn Aḥmad al-'Irāqī*, Paris, 1923.

39. See M. T. Danechepazhuh, *Kitāb al-asrār*, which also contains the text of the *Tajārib-i shahriyārī*.

In the 10th/16th century, Bel-Mughus al-Maghribī wrote a short treatise on the history of alchemy from Adam to the Prophet of Islam showing its revealed nature. He then described how the art was transmitted from the Holy Prophet to ʿAlī and his family, then to Khālid ibn Yazīd and Imām Jaʿfar al-Ṣādiq. The author treats the transmission of alchemy as being like that of Sufism. In both there is a chain of transmission (*silsilah*) which alone makes their effective practice possible. Another fascinating figure of this period, Mīr Abu'l-Qāsim Findiriskī, but from the other end of the Islamic world, namely Persia, also wrote a treatise on alchemy. This remarkable sage taught the works of Ibn Sīnā in Isfahan and Sufism in India. He also commented extensively upon the *Yoga Vāsiṣṭha* and exchanged views with Hindu sages on various questions of gnosis.

From the 11th/17th and 12th/18th centuries, Western alchemical influences began to be seen in the Ottoman empire, as can be seen in such figures as Ibn Sallūm mentioned already. Still, traditional Islamic works also continued to appear, as seen in the works of Ḥasan Āqā Sardār who wrote commentaries on earlier alchemical works in Egypt. As for Persia, there alchemy as an inward science of the soul became a special subject of interest for the Shaykhīs, who have written numerous treatises on spiritual alchemy combined with Shīʿite gnosis during the past century. Likewise, some of the Sufi masters, especially of the Niʿmatallāhī Order, wrote on spiritual alchemy, one of the most famous among them being Muẓaffar ʿAlī Shāh Kirmānī.[40] To this day alchemy is practised in certain Sufi orders and by certain of the adepts although the use of its language is more prevalent among Sufis than the actual carrying out of its processes.

Alchemical Apparatus

Alchemists did, of course, deal with materials and, in fact, made use of all the technological know-how of the ancient Babylonians and Egyptians, especially in glass-making, dyes and metallurgy. But soon they developed their own distinct instruments which Muslims in turn inherited from the Alexandrians. The processes of calcination, sublimation, distillation, fusion and crystallization continued over the centuries as the main concern of the alchemists as far as the external aspect of alchemy was concerned, and so instruments to carry out these operations were developed and remained nearly unchanged over the ages. Many of the instruments described by al-Kāthī were also employed by Lavoisier and are, in fact, still found in chemical laboratories.

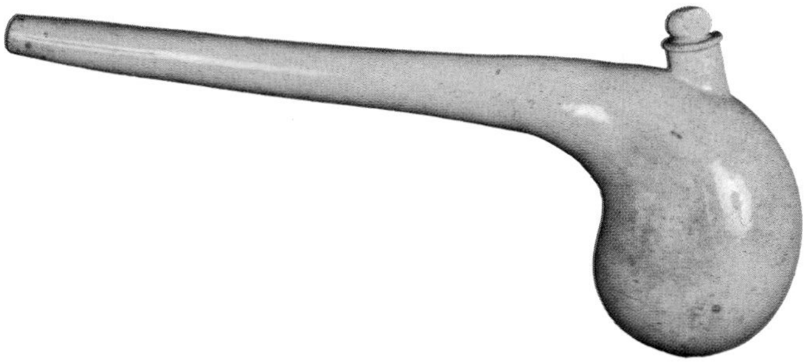

Plate 112. 18th-century alchemical retort by Josiah Wedgwood.

The most important alchemical instrument was the furnace, which is described in many alchemical manuscripts. The athanor, which is a special type of furnace, symbolizes the human body and reflects this correspondence even in its external form.[41] Another famous alchemical instrument is the still-head with a spout, known as the alembic (from the Arabic *al-inbīq*), whose form has remained unchanged over the ages and is still made in some places, such as Persia, in the same way that it has been made over the ages by both Islamic and Western alchemists. Another well-known instrument is the double-reflux, still used for redistillation and called the pelican because of its external resemblance to the bird of that name. Altogether alchemical apparatus marks an important chapter in the history of science as well as technology and is the basis of all later chemical apparatus.

40. See *Nūr al-anwār az baḥr al-asrār*, attributed to Muẓaffar ʿAlī Shāh Kirmānī, ed. by N. Subbūḥī, Tehran 1338 (A.H. solar). This work is a fine poem on alchemy and a masterpiece of its kind. Concerning the Philosophers' Stone the author says (p. 14):

چیست می دانی حجر مرآت ذات   مندرج اندر وی اسماء و صفات

Does thou know what is the Philosophers' Stone? The mirror of the Divine Essence,
In which are contained the Divine Names and Qualities.

41. On the significance of athanor, see Burckhardt, *Alchemy*, chap. 13.

Figure 87. Two stills and a condenser. Probably 18th century.

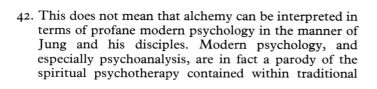

Plate 113. Contemporary alchemical apparatus from Persia.

Alchemy and Sufism

Already the names of several famous Sufi masters have been mentioned as authors of works on alchemy. The link between Sufism and alchemy is indeed a profound one. First of all, Sufism as a way of realization contains, like every authentic spiritual way, three elements: a doctrine, a method and an 'alchemy' which transforms the soul of man. On this level of meaning Sufism found in alchemy a ready-made language through which it was able to describe this aspect of its teachings. Moreover, Sufism contains within itself a spiritual psychotherapy intimately related to the aspect of alchemy as a science of the soul. The Sufi master in fact operates upon the base metal of the soul of the disciple and with the help of the spiritual methods of Sufism transforms this base metal into gold.[42]

There is yet another nexus between Sufism and alchemy. Many of the greatest of Sufi masters, such as Abu'l-Ḥasan al-Shādhilī and Shāh Ni'matallāh Walī, are said to have transmuted base metal into gold without any external aid but simply through a glance (*naẓar*), which, in the form of a miracle, 'translated' their inner state of sanctity unto the metal and affected through this

42. This does not mean that alchemy can be interpreted in terms of profane modern psychology in the manner of Jung and his disciples. Modern psychology, and especially psychoanalysis, are in fact a parody of the spiritual psychotherapy contained within traditional initiatic paths such as Sufism. See F. Schuon, 'The Psychological Imposture', *Studies in Comparative Religion*, Spring, 1966, pp. 98–102; and W. N. Perry, 'The Revolt against Moses', *ibid.*, pp. 103–119.

means the necessary change within the disciples for whom such an act was intended.[43] Altogether, it can be said that Sufism is a primaeval tree of which alchemy is a branch, or a garden of numerous flowers, in which alchemy is present as a perfume whose scent can be noted throughout the garden although belonging to only one species of the flowers present in the garden.

Alchemy and Islamic Art

As in the case of Sufism, in the arts, both plastic and audible, the relations with alchemy are so numerous as to need a separate treatise to do justice to them. Both traditional poetry and traditional music are intimately connected with the alchemical point of view through the effect they create upon the soul and the transformation they bring about within the soul. The traditional canons of both these arts deal with cosmological principles which are the same as those of alchemy and are concerned with processes which are akin to the Great Work. The end of both is the transformation of a base substance into a noble one. In certain great works of poetry and music the alchemical effect is quite evident, at least for the 'metal' which possesses the qualifications to be transmuted. Such works cannot be experienced without that break in the contractive aspect of the cosmic *milieu* and the expansion within the horizons beyond the material world which correspond very much to the stages of the alchemical work.

The same can be said of the plastic arts, of the harmony of forms in calligraphy and geometric design, whether they be connected with architecture or illumination of a manuscript. In all these cases there is a wedding between the alchemical or Hermetic and the Pythagorean points of view in the matrix of Islamic spirituality. Alchemy also plays a particular role in the harmony of colours and their symbolism. Without the knowledge of the alchemical effect of various colours those masterly symphonies of colour, such as Timurid mosques or Safavid carpets, would be inconceivable. Alchemy is the bridge between technology and the spiritual principles of Islamic art and is one of the keys to the understanding of the inner meaning of this art.

Alchemy and Medicine

Finally, as far as the rapport of alchemy with other disciplines is concerned, something must be said about the relation between alchemy and medicine. In Alexandria alchemy was concerned with the mineral kingdom and the cultivation of gold and in China mostly with plants and the attainment of longevity. Islamic alchemy contains both elements. It was not only the early masters, such as Jābir and al-Rāzī, who knew and practised medicine, but throughout Islamic history many of the alchemists were also practising physicians. Their knowledge of herbs served both a medical and an alchemical goal and they even made use of mineral drugs in their medical practice. The relation between alchemy and medicine in Islam has not been well studied, but there is no doubt that, in this field, Islamic alchemy occupies a place intermediate between the alchemy of Alexandria and that of China. Some Muslim alchemists showed little concern with pharmacology or other medical questions, whereas others saw in alchemy a means of regeneration which they also applied to human beings, combining the techniques of alchemy with those of medicine.

Islamic Alchemy Today

As already mentioned alchemy is by nature a hidden art. It is not therefore surprising that orientalists have not run across too many practising alchemists in their journeys through the Islamic world. It is known that in the 13th/19th

43. In one of the most famous verses of Persian poetry, that incomparable poet of the Persian language, Ḥāfiẓ, whose own verses possess a powerful alchemical effect, refers to the Sufi master in these terms:

آنان که خاک را به نظر کیمیا کنند
آیا شود که گوشهٔ چشمی به ما کنند

Those who turn dust into gold through a glance (*naẓar*),
Wouldst that they would cast upon us a corner of their eye.

A few years later, in a poem which most likely is an answer to Ḥāfiẓ, Shāh Ni'matallāh Walī, the founder of the Ni'matallāhī Sūfī order and one of the outstanding Sufi masters of Persia, wrote:

ما خاک راه را به نظر کیمیا کنیم

It is we who through our glance turn the dust of the path into gold.

The two verses show clearly the spiritual significance of alchemy and its rapport with the spiritual power of the Sufi master who, outside all 'natural processes', transmutes the lead of the fallen soul into gold, which symbolizes the state of the soul in remembrance of God and wed to the Spirit.

Plate 114. A contemporary alchemist at work.

century certain English Hermeticists travelled to Fez to renew their knowledge of the art, and a few practising alchemists were reported early this century in such areas as the Maghrib. But few realize that in those centres of the Islamic world where the traditional arts are still alive – in such cities as Yazd and Isfahan in Persia – alchemy still survives on a much larger scale than is outwardly suspected. Its dispensations, along with the more central grace issuing from Sufism itself, make the continuity of such arts as the weaving of traditional cloth possible.

A few real masters of the art survive along with many amateurish aspirants. The masters are well hidden and usually veil their activity by some kind of an outward occupation such as shopkeeping or the practice of medicine. Yet they are not wholly inaccessible for those who really seek them. To meet one of these masters is to be faced with the blinding evidence that alchemy is not simply a proto-chemistry, for in their presence one feels not as if one were in the presence of an ordinary chemistry teacher but as if one were bathing in the sun on a cool autumn day. They exhibit a spiritual presence, intelligence and inner discipline which proves that they are concerned above and beyond all charcoal-burning with the transformation of the base metal of the soul and the unveiling of the gold or the sun which shines at the centre of man's being, were he only to lift the veil that eclipses it before the outward eye.

The Other Occult Sciences

Islamic science was heir to a vast number of occult sciences, mostly of a divinatory nature, inherited from ancient Babylonia, Persia, Egypt, Alexandria and even Arabia itself.[44] These were usually classified by Muslim scholars as branches of the hidden or 'occult' (*khafiyyah*) sciences, along with alchemy and the like, in contrast to the open (*jaliyyah*) sciences, such as mathematics. Although dozens in number, the occult sciences were classified in the famous compendium of Ḥusayn 'Alī Wā'iẓ al-Kāshifī into the five sciences of *kīmiyā'* (alchemy), *līmiyā'* (magic), *hīmiyā'* (the subjugating of souls), *sīmiyā'* (producing visions) and *rīmiyā'* (jugglery and tricks). The first letters of the five words together form the words *kulluhu sirr*, which means, 'they are all secret'.[45]

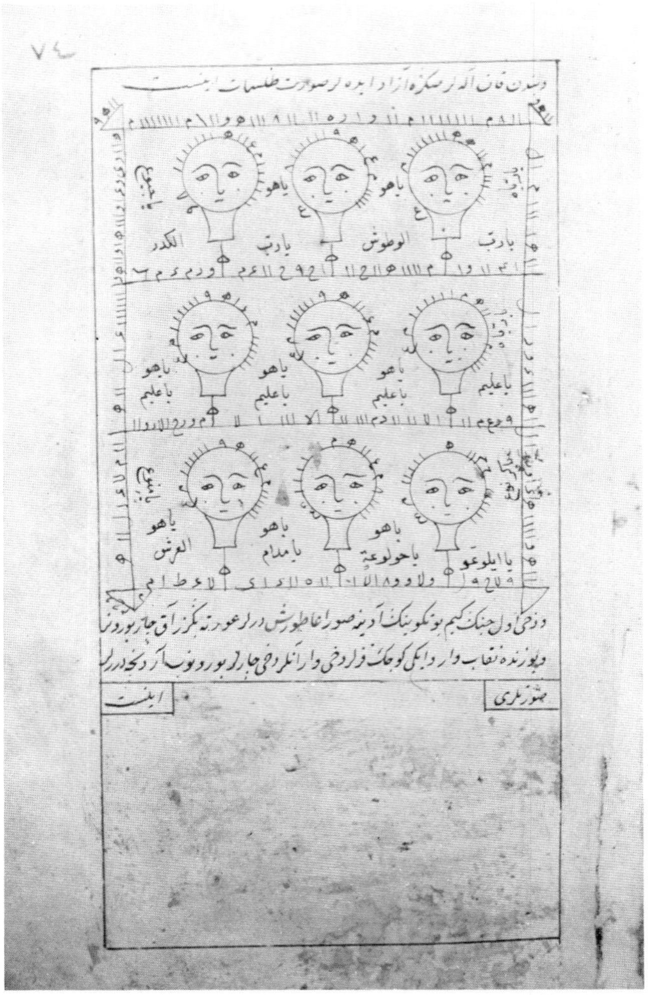

Figure 88. A page from a treatise on magic ('*ṭilism*' (talisman)).

Although this is a famous traditional classification which was followed later by Shaykh Bahā' al-Dīn al-'Āmilī, it is a simplified one. The texts on the occult sciences contain numerous other branches. Probably the most popular of the occult sciences was *jafr*, dealing with the numerical value of the letters of the Arabic alphabet and said to have been first cultivated by 'Alī ibn Abī Ṭālib. It

44. On the Arabic divinatory arts inherited by Muslims see T. Fahd, *La divination arabe; études religieuses, sociologiques et folkloriques sur le milieu natif de l'Islam*, Leiden, 1966.

45. On the occult sciences see Ullmann, *Die Natur- und Geheimwissenschaften im Islam*, pp. 359ff; S. H. Taqizadeh, 'The Open and Secret Sciences', in *Mélanges d'Orientalisme offerts à Henri Massé*, Tehran, 1963, pp. 383–387.

is used to this day for purposes ranging from interpreting the opening letters of the verses of the Holy Quran to casting evil spells. Almost as widespread is *raml*, or geomancy, which is said to have come down from the Prophet Daniel. Although it originally made use of pebbles of sand (hence the name, which in Arabic means sand), special instruments were later devised with various squares and dots from which future events are prognosticated. There is a special interest attached to the mathematics connected with geomancy, for it seems to be related to the structure of living things rather than to inert matter in the sense of modern physics.

Other occult sciences which have always been popular include physiognomy (*'ilm al-firāsah*) to which no less a figure than Fakhr al-Dīn al-Rāzī devoted a well-known treatise;[46] the interpretation of dreams, which has also been dealt with by philosophers and Sufis, one of the most famous treatises on the subject being by the 12th/18th century Sufi 'Abd al-Ghaniy al-Nābulusī; theurgy; all forms of magic, often making use of a combination of other occult sciences, especially *jafr*, as well as incantations; and even the interpretation of the twitching of various parts of the body (*ikhtilāj*). The latter practice, along with certain other popular practices, reveals late Turkish, Mongolian and Chinese influences within the Islamic world.

The occult sciences possess a vocabulary and language of their own and are impossible to interpret unless that language is mastered. They are all repositories of cosmological principles and have been interpreted over the ages in many ways and over a wide range as symbolic sciences by the sages as well as superstitions by those who have been unaware of their principles. In any case, their mastery, like that of alchemy, has been possible only on condition of realizing the principles

Plate 115. Instruments used for geomancy.

46. Y. Mourad, *La physiognomie arabe et le Kitāb al-firāsah de Fakhr al-Dīn al-Rāzī*, Paris, 1939.

of which they are so many contingent applications. Without the knowledge of these principles they have become reduced to the superstitions which most modern scholars take them to be. But in Islamic civilization, because of the presence of a living esotericism, they never became dangerous as channels for the spread of dark and demonic forces as they have become today in the Western world, where the knowledge necessary to understand them is, in general, lacking, and all scientistic attacks against them as superstition do not have the least power of stopping the ever-increasing interest shown in them. Only the sun can dispel darkness and turn a crystal made opaque in murky waters into a shining star. Anything else which claims to be the sun, without, however, possessing its inherent luminosity, cannot but add its own shadow to the spreading darkness.

Chapter X
Agriculture and Irrigation

It need hardly be mentioned that agriculture has formed the economic foundation of the sedentary regions of the Islamic world which have always been in conflict with, and at the same time in complementary relationship to, nomadic life. Agriculture has also provided the material backbone for the Islamic city which has been the site for the cultivation of the arts and sciences. Agriculture has not only been sanctioned by Islamic Law but encouraged as a direct religious activity. *Filāḥah* or *zirāʿah*, as agriculture is called in Arabic, was recommended by the *Sharīʿah* and practised by many eminent saints and religious scholars, going back to ʿAlī ibn Abī Ṭālib who was known for his intense interest and activity in planting trees. Likewise, many prophetic traditions have recommended agriculture to the extent that, according to one *ḥadīth*, it is a blessed act to plant a tree even if it be one day before the end of the world. The Muslims found in their own religious teachings the confirmation of earlier religions concerning the importance of agriculture for human life, earlier religions from Zoroastrianism where agricultural activity was an organic part of religious life to Hermeticism where the dictum that agriculture is the 'great alchemy' (*al-kīmiyāʾ al-ʿuẓmā*) is attributed to Hermes himself. The Muslims were heirs, in fact, not only to the older religious teachings concerning agriculture but also to the experience of millennia as found in all the earlier civilizations of Western Asia and the Mediterranean world, including Egypt, Babylonia, Persia, Byzantium, Rome and even the Yemen.

Irrigation

The climatic conditions of the Islamic world have made the problem of water of central concern for agriculture in a manner that is hardly conceivable for the European farmer for whom water has always been practically as plentiful as air. In the heartland of the classical Islamic world, from Sindh to Morocco, water has always been very scarce, except in certain limited regions such as Southern Arabia and the Sudan which are exposed to the monsoon and Mazandaran and Gilan in Northern Persia which have a semi-tropical climate.[1] In other places every conceivable means has been used to make maximum use of available water, and human ingenuity has applied itself to the question of irrigation in such a way as to make this science or art one of the most developed in the whole of Islamic civilization. It is enough to mention in this connection that the Arabic word for geometry is *handasah* which is derived almost certainly from the Pahlavi *handāzah*, a word denoting both computation and measurement of water canals, or simply irrigation.

In each part of the Islamic world the Muslims inherited the existing techniques of irrigation, some of which they preserved and others of which they modified and improved. Elsewhere, they expanded existing techniques or combined the experience in irrigation of different civilizations. In Egypt Muslims inherited several millennia of experience which they not only have kept intact until the present day but also improved upon as far as techniques of measuring the rise of the water of the Nile and similar problems are concerned. As early as the time of al-Ma'mūn, a nilometer was built along the Nile. It was rebuilt by al-Mutawakkil and restored over the ages. It continues to function to this day and is a reminder of the interest of Muslim engineers and scientists in Egypt over the centuries to deal with irrigation in the particular conditions of Egypt, which are not typical at all but present a special situation in the Islamic world.

In most other regions of the *dār al-islām* major river systems such as the Nile do not exist, and the problem has always been most of all to build reservoirs to preserve water rather than simply to measure the rise and fall of the level of a river. Dams were one way to create reservoirs in the path of smaller rivers. Most such dams were made of gravel and sand, yet with such strength that some of them have survived over the ages to this day. Others were built from stone and mortar often combined with the construction of a man-made basin. Some of the oldest of these reservoirs are to be seen in North Africa, such as the one near Qayrawan in Tunisia, which still survives. Likewise, the reservoir which provides water for Marrakesh represents a fine example of the construction of the traditional reservoir as it has existed everywhere in that region throughout Islamic history.

The use of reservoirs relies, of course, upon aqueducts which bring the water to the cities and villages for both agricultural and domestic use. Aqueducts were constructed throughout the Islamic world in connection with reservoirs, as well as with rivers and mountain springs. The oldest of these aqueducts is that of Mecca which was begun by Mu'āwiyah and which provided water for the holy city. In other regions the experience and techniques of Sassanid Persians, ancient Egyptians, Romans and Byzantines were employed and a vast network of aqueducts created in such regions as Andalusia and Persia which survive to a great extent to this day and which represent some of the most important feats of irrigation to be seen anywhere in the world.

Another problem with which Muslims, like their predecessors, were concerned with was, naturally, the question of raising existing water resources so as to make them accessible for either agricultural or domestic use. Here again they benefited from all the technological experience of their predecessors. In the former Byzantine province of Syria they mastered the use of the Noria wheel, which, in fact, continues to be used today in such cities as Hama. In the former territories of the Sassanids they learned the use of what has come to be known generally as the Persian wheel to draw water from wells. They perfected the use of this wheel and later took it to India where, under the Moguls, it became almost as popular as in Persia itself. Numerous other devices have also been used to elevate water, making use of human and animal sources of energy as well as the energy of running water itself and also the wind.

The technique of digging wells was also mastered rapidly, making use again of millennia of experience in such areas as Persia where, without wells, life in many regions would be impossible.

1. The central role of water and its vital connection with all life is emphasized in the Quranic verse, 'Have not those who disbelieve known that the heavens and the earth were of one piece, then We parted them, and We made every living thing of water?' (XXI; 30). Also in the Persian language the vital role of water in human life is reflected in two key terms. A desert devoid of human settlement is called *biyābān* (literally a place without (*bī*) water (*āb*), while a human settlement is called *ābādī* (literally a place where there is water). The suffix *ābād* which is found as a part of the name of cities from Allahabad and Hyderabad in India to thousands of villages, towns and cities in Afghanistan and Persia is related to the same word, and reflects the crucial role of water for all human settlements, and also its scarcity in Persia. Strangely enough, when Persian culture spread to India the same term continued to be used although water was plentiful in the sub-continent.

Plate 116. The Nilometer in Rawada Island at Fustat, near Cairo.

Plate 117. One of the oldest surviving man-made reservoirs in the Islamic world.

Figure 89. One of the oldest surviving man-made reservoirs in the Islamic world.

Plate 118. A reservoir near the city of Marrakesh.

Figure 90

يا غ افتاده جارى است جا رجسى در میان یاغ می باشد در بالای این پشته واقع شده طرف میان برب وجنوبی خوب
ه در وی است اطراف و تمام درحتهای باغ است درحتهای باغ نار هم هست و دراکر د حوض تمام سه برکه زار است جای صبغ
مین است در وقت زرد شدن نار جها بسیار خوب می ناید خیلی یاغ خوبی طرح شده و در طرف جنوب وه بیند

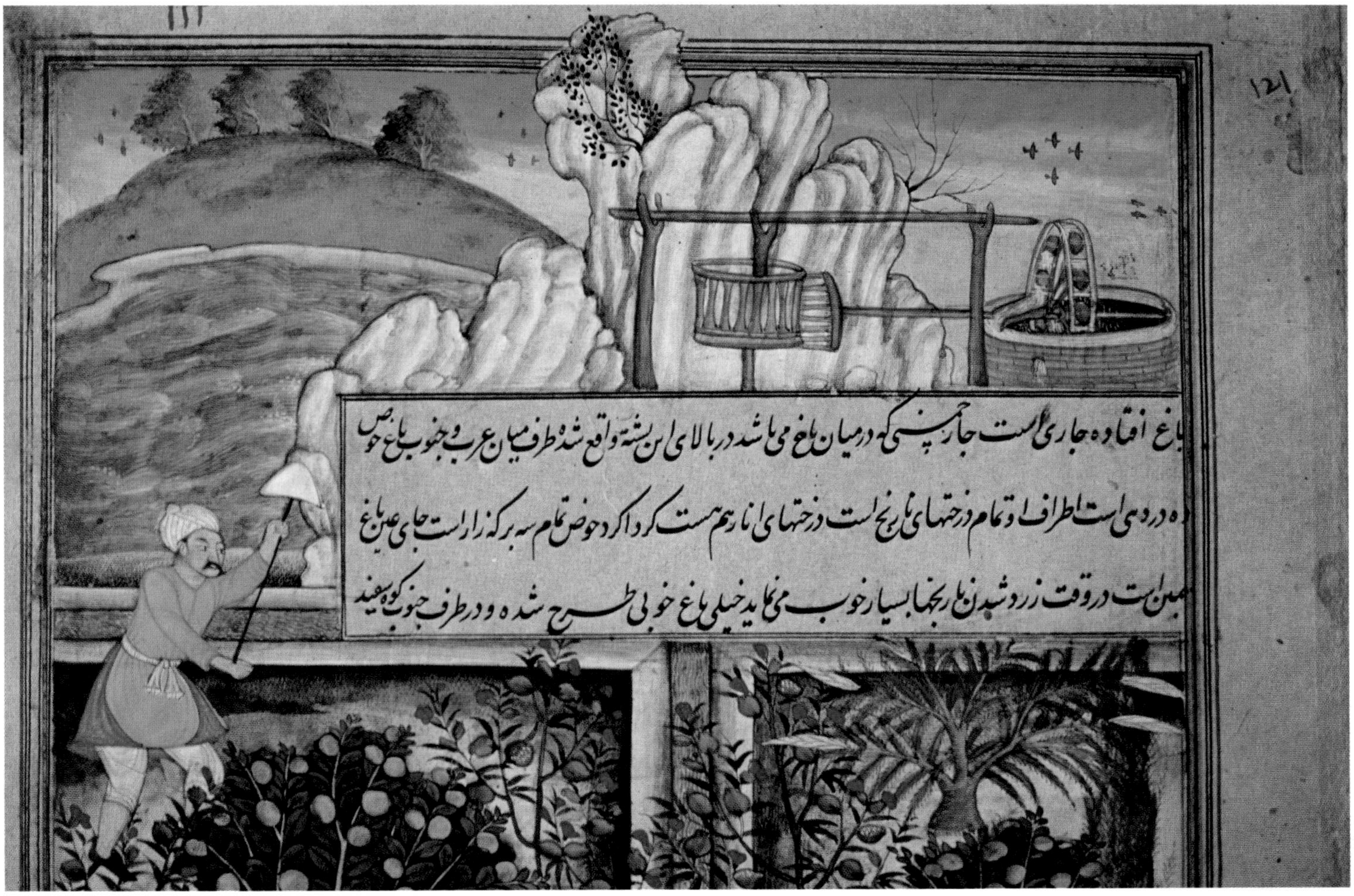

Plate 119. A device to lift water from a well in India.

Of particular interest in this context is the *qanāt* system, which is an ancient Persian invention found mostly from Syria to Afghanistan and occasionally in other regions, and surviving to this day in Persia itself and Afghanistan despite all the deep wells and electric pumps which have invaded these areas over the past decades. The *qanāt* system must be considered without exaggeration as one of the masterpieces of both architecture and engineering in traditional Islamic Persia.[2]

The word *qanāt* is most likely from the Accadian or Assyrian word *ḥanū*, meaning reed, a word which also entered into Greek and Latin and which is most likely the origin of the word canal. As for the underground canal system itself, which bears this name and which is also called *kahrīz* in Persian, it was a fully-developed system in pre-Islamic Persia. It was considered sacred and identified with the goddess Anahita. During the Islamic period it continued to preserve its religious aspect since water plays such a central role in Islamic rites. The *qanāt* system has been considered over the ages by Persians as having been the dowry of Fāṭimah, the daughter of the Holy Prophet. It has been revered as a God-given gift and its construction has been combined with religious ceremonies.

Moreover, during the Islamic period, all the known methods of mathematical calculation and engineering were put at the service of this art which brings water from high mountainous regions through underground canals to towns lying near deserts and deprived of local sources of water. To dig these canals, to determine their correct direction some fifty feet or more underground, to construct the canal with the correct inclination, to clean and repair a *qanāt* which sometimes continues for miles, and finally to determine where to begin the *qanāt* so that the original wells which provide the water will not dry easily is no simple task. These accomplishments are made possible only because of millennia of experience and of

Figure 90. A giant noria wheel from Hama, Syria.

2. On the *qanāt* see the article '*ḳanāt*' in both the old and the new *Encyclopaedia of Islam*. See also A. Smith, *Blind White Fish in Persia*, London, 1953, where the types of fish living in the *qanāts* are discussed.

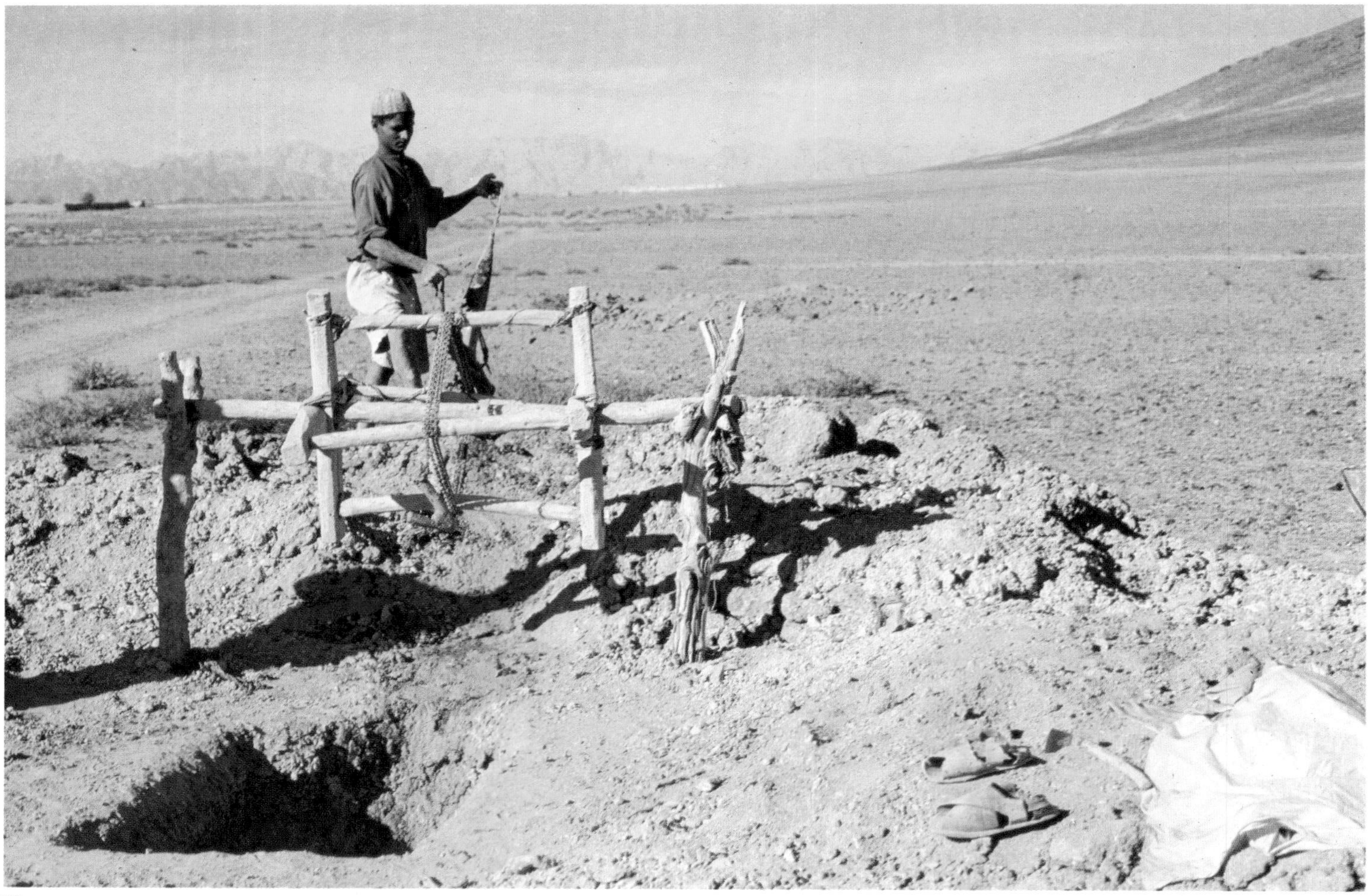

Plate 120

Plate 121

Plates 120, 121 and 122. The *qanāt* system – underground water channels used in dry areas.

science, as the unique work devoted to underground waters by the great mathematician al-Karajī to some extent reveals.[3]

Anyone travelling over Persia and Afghanistan cannot but be impressed by the immense human labour which has made possible the digging of hundreds or even thousands of wells at a distance of a few yards apart, all connected inwardly by the underground *qanāt* which is usually roofed over with brick and carefully constructed to make possible the continuous flow of water with the minimum amount of obstruction of various kinds, including silting and the caving in of the roof. Some *qanāts* extend over tens of miles, sometimes traversing forbidding deserts to bring the precious substance of life from high mountain springs and wells to the lowlands. Sometimes the *qanāts* appear overland as streams and disappear

3. See Karagi (Mohammad al), *La civilisation des eaux cachées*. Karajī describes in this opus not only the application of geometry and algebra to hydrology but also the instruments used by master well-diggers and *qanāt* builders (*muqannī*). Before him al-Khwārazmī also made reference to the relation between algebra

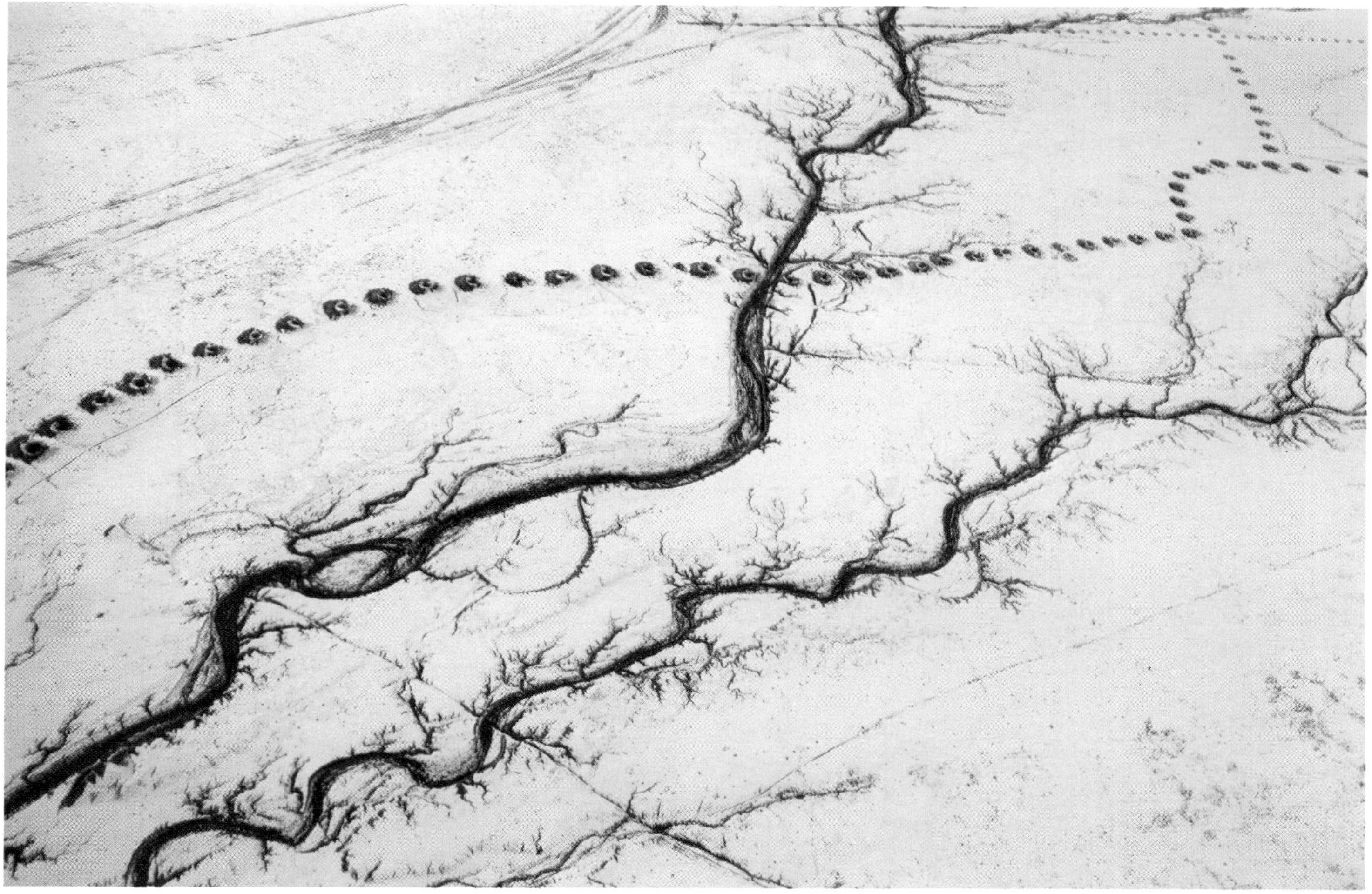

Plate 122

Plate 123. An open irrigation canal joined to a *qanāt* system.

again underground following the topography of the region in question. Altogether they represent a formidable achievement of man in drawing sustenance from nature in conformity with nature's own laws and with full consideration of the climatic peculiarities which have necessitated the *qanāt* system to begin with.[4]

Of course, not all Muslim villages and cities have relied principally on *qanāts*. Many have been blessed by rivers. In such cases the problem of irrigation became essentially reduced to devising an efficient and just method of dividing the water so as to irrigate the agricultural lands around the towns and also provide for the water within the towns themselves. The system of irrigation of the city of Baghdad, which does not survive today but which has been described in several mediaeval sources, is a splendid example of the way this

and hydrology although he did not devote a separate treatise to the subject.

4. For example, in the warm sun any open canal loses much of its water through evaporation while the underground *qanāt* reduces this loss to a minimum.

Plate 124. View of the River Zayandirud flowing through Isfahan.

Figure 91. View of the River Zayandirud flowing through Isfahan.

Plate 125. The internal water distribution system, for private dwellings, in the traditional city of Fez in Morocco.

problem was solved for a city adjacent to two major rivers. There are also a few treatises dealing directly with the distribution of water in other traditional Islamic cities and showing how each sought to solve this important problem.[5]

As far as an actual example of this type of irrigation is concerned, the city of Isfahan, which has a unique geographical situation, is of particular interest. Isfahan is an oasis in the middle of Persia surrounded on three sides by the desert; but from the Bakhtiyari mountains there flows through Isfahan the Zayandirud river which serves as the life-line of the city. The water of this river is divided, before entering the city, into many tributaries, some of which feed the surrounding agricultural fields and others of which flow through the city in the form of streams (*mādīs*), providing water for the city dwellers. The division of the water of this river in such a way as to satisfy justly the needs of both the agricultural fields and the city is still based on the tract written for this purpose by Shaykh Bahā' al-Dīn al-'Āmilī, the outstanding Safavid Sufi, theologian and mathematician. The original text of the tract, which survives in a private collection in Isfahan, shows the remarkable mathematical ingenuity of its author in solving such a complicated problem. The traditional system of irrigation survives also in certain other Muslim cities such as Fez where, in the old quarter, people still use the traditional canals which bring water into the city from nearby hills. Altogether, both in agricultural fields and within towns, the achievement of Muslims in the domain of irrigation is one of the most amazing features of the material aspect of Islamic civilization and in certain regions is not surpassed to this day.

5. See, for example, Qāsim ibn Yūsuf Abū Naṣrī Hirawī, *Risāla-yi ṭarīq-i qismat-i āb-i qulb*, ed. by Māyil Hirawī, Tehran, 1347 (A. H. solar), which deals with the division of water around and in Herat.

Agriculture

The religious sanction given to agriculture by the Holy Quran and the *Ḥadīth*, added to the variety of climates and geographical conditions which made up *dār al-islām* and the vast experience of millennia inherited by Muslims, incited them, from the beginning, to seek to improve and to intensify agricultural activity. Many plants were transferred from one region to another and stocks were improved through grafting and the like. Moreover, the religious character of this type of activity, which had existed since ancient times, continued to be reflected in early Arabic texts on agriculture. The spread of such products as coffee (from the Arabic *qahwah*), Seville oranges, cotton, sugar-cane, various kinds of melons, peaches and artichokes (from the Arabic *al-kharshūf*), to cite but a few examples, not only from one part of the Islamic world to another but also to Europe and ultimately to America attest to the worldwide influence of agricultural activity by Muslims. In such regions as Andalusia the Muslims transformed the whole pattern of agriculture and introduced a new set of plants which not only produced the Spanish garden, based ultimately on the Persian garden, but also changed completely the pattern of food production in the region.

Although in certain parts of the Islamic world there were large land holdings, there did not exist a system similar to the handing out of fiefs in mediaeval Europe, and therefore the use of the term feudalism cannot, strictly speaking, be applied to the Islamic world.[6] Nevertheless, because of other historical factors, large units of land owned by a single family or individual were to be found nearly everywhere until recent land reforms. But the agricultural activity, even on these large plots of land, was organized on a small, human scale, techniques usually revolving around the family unit. Thus, despite absentee-landlordism in some areas and repressions by certain landowners, agricultural life fortified family and other human ties.

A great deal of know-how in the form of simple but efficient technology was connected with traditional agriculture. For example, small water wheels using animal power and numerous types of mills, some using water and others wind, were developed. The origin of the windmill has, in fact, been traced to eastern Persia. Likewise, the various stages of harvesting and threshing of wheat and other products made use of simple machines often driven by animal power and making maximum use of a closely-integrated economy. Some of these techniques survive to this day despite the spread of mechanized agriculture.

A branch of agriculture which received special attention was the growing of fruit trees. Fruits themselves play, to this day, a greater role in the daily diet of Muslims than they do in that of most Westerners. They also fulfil an important medical role. Therefore, much effort was spent on improving the quality of various fruits by grafting them and developing new kinds of products in various ways. Also, because of the vividness of the Quranic image of paradise in which the symbolism of fruits plays an important role, the cultivation and use of fruits have always had a religious significance, and some, like pomegranates and mulberries, enjoy to this day a direct religious meaning.

Plate 126. A man being encouraged to cultivate the soil.

6. On land holdings in Persia see the classical work of A. K. Lambton, *Landlord and Peasant in Persia*, London, 1953.

Plate 127. A small water-wheel driven by a camel, in Afghan Turkistan.

Figure 92. A small water-wheel driven by a camel, in Afghan Turkistan.

Animal husbandry has been inseparable from agriculture. It is true that most of the daily products and wool have come from the nomads. But, to the extent that domestic animals are kept on farms, they function within the agricultural cycle of life. The same people have always cared for them who have cultivated the fields and have gathered the harvest. In contrast to modern agriculture where often separate organizations deal with husbandry and agriculture, in the Islamic world these two forms of activity have always been associated with a single mode of life. In fact the attempt to separate them over the past few decades in certain regions of the Islamic world has only led to unwelcomed economic and social results.

Plate 128. A simple cotton mill driven by a blindfolded cow, being urged on by the farmer.

Plate 129. The traditional method of threshing wheat, in Fars Province, Persia.

Islamic Treatises on Agriculture

As in other sciences, so in agriculture, in addition to inheriting the practical know-how and the oral traditions of their predecessors, the Muslims were also heir to the major written sources of Antiquity. They knew of the famous agricultural treatise of Bolos Demokritos through quotations.[7] The pseudo-Aristotelian treatise on agriculture, again known through the *Geoponica*, was also translated into Arabic. A very important source of Muslim writings on agriculture was the compendium of Vindanios Anatolios.[8] Also of importance is Kassianos Bassos, the Byzantine author, who was translated into Pahlavi as well as Arabic and through whom Muslims also came to know of Byzantine agricultural practices.

Probably the first author to have written a scientific treatise on agriculture in Arabic was Yuḥannā ibn Māsawayh, the well-known physician, who in his *Kitāb al-azminah* (*The Book of the Times*) dealt with the subject.[9] His student, Ḥunayn ibn Isḥāq, also wrote a treatise on agriculture. Moreover, in the Jābirean corpus there are several treatises devoted to various aspects of agriculture, usually combined with interest in alchemy and the other occult sciences.[10]

Early in the 4th/10th century there appeared a mysterious and, at the same time, very influential work by Aḥmad ibn Abī Bakr ibn Waḥshiyyah, entitled *al-Filāḥat al-nabaṭiyyah* (*Nabataean Agriculture*). This work is said to have been translated from 'Nabataean' by Ibn Waḥshiyyah in 291/904 and to have been compiled and edited by his student, Aḥmad ibn al-Zayyāt in 318/930. The work is syncretic in character and combines agricultural studies with magic, omens and similar considerations. It was read widely in the Islamic world and has also been the centre of a long controversy in the West since the 19th century, when many scholars, such as E. M. Quatremère, D. Chwolson, E. Renan, A. von Gutschmid and Th. Nöldeke debated its character and origin. More recently, the issue has been reviewed by M. M. Plessner and T. Fahd.[11] Views ranging all the way from ancient Babylonian origins to out-and-out forgery have been expressed. There is no doubt, however, that the work is a summary of a great deal of agricultural lore, including the religious dimension of agricultural activity, as it was known in the region of Mesopotamia and Syria in the pre-Islamic period and as it survived into the Islamic period. For this reason, and because of its wide dissemination, the *Nabataean Agriculture* remains a very important document for the study of Islamic agriculture, whatever may have been its origin or the sources of information of its author.[12]

7. The original text of this work is lost and even in the West it is known only through citations in the *Geoponica*, Pliny, etc.

8. See P. Sbath, 'L'ouvrage géoponique d'Anatolius de Berytos (IVe siècle), manuscrit arabe découvert', *Bulletin de l'Institut d'Egypte*, vol. 13, 1930–1931, pp. 47–54.

9. See G. Troupeau, 'Le livre des temps de Jean Ibn Māsawayh', *Arabica*, vol. 15, 1968, pp. 113–142.

10. On the history of agriculture among Muslims, see Ullmann, *Die Natur- und Geheimwissenschaften im Islam*, pp. 439ff.; also the article '*filāḥah*' by M. al-Shihabi *et al.* in the new *Encyclopaedia of Islam*.

11. On all the writings concerning this debate, see Ullmann, *op. cit.*, p. 441.

12. Because of Nöldeke's strong attack against the authenticity of this work and even doubt about its author, for some time interest in the other writings of Ibn Waḥshiyyah ceased. It has only been renewed recently by T. Fahd in many of his works. See especially his 'Retour à Ibn Waḥšiyya', *Arabica*, vol. 16, 1969, pp. 83–88. Early in the 19th century, a strange and fascinating work of the author was made known to the West by J. Hammer-Purgstall. See Ahmed ibn Abubekr bin Wahshih, *Ancient Alphabets and Hieroglyphic Characters Explained, with an Account on the Egyptian Priests, Their Classes, Initiation and Sacrifices.*

There also exists in Arabic the *Filāḥat al-rūmiyyah* (*Roman Agriculture*) which appeared shortly after the *Nabataean Agriculture* and which is attributed to Qusṭūs al-Rūmī. The two works have been complementary in the eyes of later Muslim readers although the *Roman Agriculture* has never gained the fame and popularity of the *Nabataean Agriculture*.

There are few fields in Islamic science in which a particular region of the Islamic world has held an almost complete monopoly such as one finds in the case of Andalusia in the field of agriculture. For several centuries, from the 4th/10th century onward, almost every important agricultural treatise written in the Islamic world came from Andalusia, which also from the point of view of the practice of agriculture shows achievements rarely seen elsewhere.[13] The first well-known treatise from this region was written in the 4th/10th century by Abu'l-Ḥasan al-Qurṭubī, who composed an agricultural calendar, the *Kitāb al-anwā'*. It was soon followed by *Kitāb al-filāḥah* (*The Book of Agriculture*) of the famous surgeon, Abu'l-Qāsim al-Zahrāwī. His student, 'Abd al-Raḥmān ibn Wāfid al-Lakhmī, known in Latin as Abencenif, also wrote a treatise by the same title which became famous in both the Islamic world and the West. It was translated into Catalan and served as a basis for the *Agricultura general* written in 1513 by Alonso de Herrera. Ibn Wāfid was also keeper of the royal botanical gardens in Toledo.

In the 5th/11th century, Abū 'Umar ibn Ḥajjāj al-Ishbīlī wrote several treatises on agronomy, of which the *Kitāb al-muqni'* (*The Convincing Treatise*) is the most famous.[14] His contemporary 'Abdallāh ibn Baṣṣāl from Toledo travelled extensively throughout North Africa and as far East as Mecca and Cairo. Then, upon returning to Spain, he composed a large volume entitled *Dīwān al-filāḥah* (*The Agricultural Dīwān*) and a smaller treatise the *Kitāb al-qaṣd wa'l-bayān* (*The Book of Concision and Clarity*).[15] Both these works are based on personal experience and observation and are devoted exclusively to agronomy without recourse to medical or magical discussions. The *Dīwān* consists of sixteen chapters devoted to every aspect of agriculture, including the use of various types of water, such as rainwater, river water, water drawn from cisterns, etc., for the irrigation of the soil. Ibn Baṣṣāl was also interested in the properties of the soil itself and discusses it in both his works. In 478/1085 Ibn Baṣṣāl put his vast agricultural knowledge into practice and constructed a botanical garden in Seville for the ruler al-Mu'tamid ibn 'Abbād.

Although the 5th/11th century marks, in a way, the peak of agricultural studies in Spain, important works continued to appear during the next two centuries. In the 6th/12th century the *Kitāb al-filāḥah* of Abu'l-Khayr al-Ishbīlī, which contains a general study of agriculture and special sections devoted to such common trees as vines and olive trees, became well known. This was followed during the 7th/13th century by what is perhaps the most famous agricultural treatise to issue from Andalusia, the *Kitāb al-filāḥah* of Abū Zakariyyā' ibn 'Awwām, which is also well known in the West because it was translated in the 19th century.[16] This work consists of thirty-five chapters in which some 585 plants, including 55 fruit-bearing trees, are studied. The work is based entirely on earlier sources such as Ibn Waḥshiyyah and Ibn Ḥajjāj for its agricultural knowledge. As for the section on animal husbandry which forms an important part of the book, it too is based on earlier zoological treatises such as those of Aristotle and al-Jāḥiẓ. Nevertheless, the work of Ibn 'Awwām is an important compilation and, along with the already cited treatises of Ibn al-Bayṭār on plants and their pharmacological properties, marks the sum of several centuries of study by the Muslim scientists of Spain in the field of plants and the agricultural, as well as medical, questions connected with the vegetable kingdom.

After Ibn 'Awwām, a few treatises on agriculture continued to appear in Andalusia such as the *Khulāṣat al-ikhtiṣār fī ma'rifat al-quwā wa'l-khawāṣṣ* (*The Synopsis of the Sum-*

13. For an incomparable study of the achievements of Islamic culture in Andalusia, including the domain of science, see T. Burckhardt, *Moorish Culture in Spain*, trans. by A. Jaffa, London, 1972.

14. See J. M. Millás Vallicrosa, 'Aportaciones para el estudio de la obra agronómica de Ibn Ḥaŷŷaŷ ye de Abū-l- Jayr', *Al-Andalus*, vol. 20, 1955, pp. 87–101.

15. See Ibn Baṣṣāl, *Libro de agricultura*, editado, traducido y anotado por J. M. Millás Vallicrosa y Mohamed Aziman, Tetuan, 1955; also J. M. Millás Vallicrosa, 'Los cinco últimos capitulos de la obra agronómica de Ibn Baṣṣāl', *Tamuda*, vol. 1, 1953, pp. 47–58.

16. This work was translated into Spanish by Banqueri in 1802, but became especially famous in the West thanks to the French translation of J. J. Clément-Mullet. See Clément-Mullet, *Le livre d'agriculture d'Ibn Awam*, 3 vols., Paris, 1864–1867. On Ibn 'Awwām, see also Meyer, *Geschichte der Botanik*, vol. III, pp. 260–266; and A. Miéli, *La science arabe*, Paris, 1938, p. 46.
Ibn 'Awwām was also widely known in the Islamic world and was translated into Turkish in the 10th/16th century.

mary concerning Knowledge of Powers and Properties) of Abū 'Abdallāh al-Awsī, known as Ibn al-Raqqām al-Mursī, whose work is essentially a summary of the *Nabataean Agriculture*. But the last chapter in the history of agriculture was connected with the eastern lands of Islam. In the 7th/13th and 8th/14th centuries two of the Rasūlī kings of the Yemen, 'Umar ibn Yūsuf and al-'Abbās ibn 'Alī, wrote treatises on agriculture, the second being responsible for the important opus, the *Kitāb bughyat al-fallāḥīn fi'l-ashjār al-muthmirah wa'l-rayāḥīn* (*The Book on the Object of the Desire of Agriculturalists concerning Fruit-Trees and Odoriferous Herbs*) which is a precious document reflecting agricultural knowledge in the Yemen, which had had a long tradition in this field. Also in the 8th/14th century Rashīd al-Dīn Faḍlallāh, the powerful Īl-Khānid vizier and the author of numerous works on history and medicine, devoted a section to agriculture in his *Kitāb al-akhbār wa'l-āthār* (*The Book of Notices and Vestiges*) which is an important source of knowledge for the practice of agriculture in western Persia at the time.[17] His contemporary, Jamāl al-Dīn al-Waṭwāṭ al-Kutubī, also devoted a large part of his *Kitāb mubāhij al-fikr* (*The Book to Delight the Mind*) to agriculture, including a discussion on soils.

From the 10th/16th century onward the writing of agricultural treatises became less common. In Persia, Qāsim ibn Yūsuf Abī Naṣr-i Anṣārī, known as Qāni'ī, composed a treatise in Persian entitled *Kitāb irshād al-zirā'ah* (*The Book of Guidance in Agriculture*) in the 10th/16th century. In the 11th/17th century two Turkish treatises appeared on the subject, the *Rawnaq-i būstān* (*The Splendour of the Garden*) of al-Ḥājj Ibrāhīm ibn Aḥmad and the *Ghars-nāmah* (*The Treatise on Planting*) of Kimānī. The Turks also wrote many works on the cultivation of flowers. The Arab provinces of the Ottoman empire also produced a few agricultural treatises at this time, one of the most notable being by the venerable Sufi 'Abd al-Ghaniy al-Nābulusī who, in the 12th/18th century, composed an all-embracing book on the subject entitled *Kitāb 'alam al-malāḥah fī 'ilm al-filāḥah* (*The Book of the Graceful Guidepost concerning the Science of Agriculture*).

As for India, there too, despite extensive activity by Muslims in agriculture and irrigation, much of whose results still survives, few works were written on the subject. Sections of the *Bābur-nāmah* (*The Book of Bābur*) by the founder of the Mogul empire, Bābur, are devoted to agricultural questions, especially problems of the soil. Also the eleventh chapter of the *Ganj-i bād āward* (*The Treasure Brought by the Wind*) of Amānallāh Ḥusayn Khān Zamān, written in the 11th/17th century, concerns agriculture. It is altogether strange that, despite the vast amount of activity carried out by Muslims in the sub-continent on irrigation, planting of trees, creation of gardens known as the Mogul gardens throughout the world and numerous works written by them on the medical properties of plants and fruits, so few works were devoted in that region to agriculture. The result of what they achieved in this field is there, however, to show that they possessed a great deal more knowledge in this field than they put into writing.

This relation between actual knowledge and its reflection in writing in fact is to be seen in the whole of the Islamic world as far as agriculture is concerned. There is a great deal more knowledge and know-how among those who practise agriculture even today than appears in the numerous works on the subject. The written documents are, of course, precious repositories of a millennial wisdom concerning man's relation with the earth, but they complement, even in this day of forgetfulness, the knowledge which lies in the hearts of men and which is transmitted orally and through the direct instruction of each new generation of villagers by the older members of the community or the family. In any case, both in its written and oral form, Islamic agriculture contains a precious treasury of know-how concerning the wise use of the soil, water, plants and animals which cannot simply be thrown away as some have tried to do, except at a price too forbidding for the human community to pay. After the unbelievably rapid destruction of the top soil, the turning of forests into deserts, the lowering of the water table through misuse and numerous other tragedies which modern man has succeeded in causing over the various continents during the past century or two, the teachings of traditional

17. See 'Abd al-Ghaffār Najm al-Dawlah, *'Ilm-i filāḥat-i dawra-yi mughul*, Tehran, 1324 (A.H. solar).

agriculture, of which the Islamic is one of the most important, become ever more significant. This is especially so since these teachings contain many elements that, if accepted and applied, can enable man to make wise use of the resources which make human life possible and which, if ignored, cannot but lead to the destruction of the equilibrium upon which human life on earth is itself based.

Part Five
Man in the Universe

Chapter XI
Man and the Natural Environment

Both Islamic science and its applications convey to those who are familiar with them a sense of harmony and equilibrium which is, in fact, directly reflected in the actual products of Islamic civilization, whether they be in the field of art in its narrow sense or in technology, agriculture, architecture and city planning. The continuous interaction between man and the natural environment which has always characterized life in various parts of the Islamic world, as elsewhere, does not give the observer a sense of aggressive destruction and a unilateral reaping of the resources of nature for the so-called needs of man. Rather, there is always the feeling that in this process of exchange, something is continuously returned to the natural cycle in such a way as to preserve the balance of life. The aspect of stability symbolized by the Ka'bah and so characteristic of all manifestations of the Islamic tradition and its civilization is also seen in the Islamic sciences of nature and their applications in various domains. When one meditates on classical Islamic civilization, one is struck by the fact that, despite its undeniable dynamism and energy, the element of stability completely dominated it. In studying the Islamic world one does not have a sense of an imminent collapse, of continuous crises in the natural environment, of disorder and dissolution and the like which now threaten all mankind. There is no doubt that here and there forests were destroyed or the top-soil was removed through malpractice, but this was on a small scale and appeared as an anomaly in contrast with the prevalent manner of living in harmony with nature. There was certainly nothing to compare with what the modern world has done to the natural environment in the span of only one century. There is, in fact, a feeling that, had it not been violently disturbed from the outside, the system inter-relating man and his environment in the Islamic world could have continued indefinitely, that the relations between nomadic and sedentary life, between agriculture and technology, between using the resources of nature and catering to nature's needs formed the life-providing rhythm within a living organism whose stability was guaranteed by the order, harmony and complementarity of these elements.

Today there is a great deal of talk about ecological equilibrium at the very moment when this God-given equilibrium is being destroyed by modern man in revolt against Heaven and against his own inner nature. The idea of ecological equilibrium is, however, far from being new. It forms one of the cornerstones of the traditional sciences of nature, including those of Islam. Modern science has grown during the past few centuries by forgetting the interrelation between things, by isolating a particular phenomenon, by analysing and finally generalizing the results of this analysis. In contrast, the traditional cosmological sciences, especially those of Islam, are based on the interrelation between things, on the unicity of nature, on synthesis and the vision of the whole within which alone the parts have meaning.[1] This is precisely what ecology aims to study, even if it limits its scope to the physical world. That is why it is so closely related to the philosophy of nature embedded in Islamic philosophy and science and is so alien to the prevalent 'philosophy of nature' in the West. The Islamic sciences may be said to be based on the profound intuition of the interdependence and interrelation of all things in the Universe, let alone the terrestrial environment, and their message for the modern world is, among other things, to remind man of the necessity of keeping in mind the central role of this harmony and equilibrium between opposites and the interrelation in every legitimate science of nature if this science is not to lead to the destruction of its own object of study.[2]

The equilibrium between man and nature in Islamic civilization is exhibited most directly in the human habitat whether it be a small village or a big city. Considering the problem of urbanism and all that urban centres signify in the present-day world as the foci of disorder and the origin of the forces which have caused the ecological crisis, the planning and construction of traditional Islamic cities and towns are of particular significance and worthy of special study. Today, much is being said about integrating architecture into the landscape and making it harmonious with nature. The villages and towns in the Islamic world, like those, in fact, of other traditional civilizations, had already achieved this end long ago. It is enough to travel in the southern regions of Morocco through Berber villages or along the green valleys of Mazandaran in northern Persia or, again, along the foothills of the majestic Alborz and Hindu Kush chains of mountains, stretching from eastern Anatolia through Persia to Afghanistan, to see how villages and towns have been thoroughly integrated into different types of landscape, creating living human units of settlement which are at once beautiful and efficient and which are in complete equilibrium rather than conflict with their natural environment. The science and know-how concerning landscaping and town-planning which have made these settlements possible have hardly ever been described in learned books. In fact as yet no manuscripts pertaining directly to these subjects have been discovered in any of the Islamic languages. The tradition has been passed on orally from one generation to another. There does exist, however, despite the lack of written records, a knowledge, a science, which makes such achievements possible. It is a science which draws from nearly all the disciplines described in this book, from cosmology and sacred geography to geometry, to irrigation and, on another level, even to astronomy and alchemy, not to mention the various forms of technology dealing with brick-making, tilework, metal-work, construction and so forth.

What is seen in the smaller towns is to be observed even in the great cities, the major urban units which have always been the centres of cultural activity for Islamic civilization.[3] Although cut off from nature to a certain extent through the very fact that it is made by man, the Islamic city has, nevertheless, always succeeded

1. On the central role of the doctrine of unity (*al-tawḥīd*) in the cosmological sciences to which we have already alluded in chapter I, see Nasr, *An Introduction to Islamic Cosmological Doctrines*, pp. 3ff. As for the question of equilibrium between man and his environment, as well as within Islamic society, see C. Coon, *Caravan, The Story of the Middle East*, New York, 1951, especially pp. 342ff.

2. Jalāl al-Dīn Rūmī has summarized the basic principle dominating the natural order in a single stanza:

صلح اضداد است اصل این جهان

The harmony between opposites is the principle of this world.

3. On the importance of the Islamic city and the study of its social structure, see I. Lapidus, *Muslim Cities in the Later Middle Ages*, Cambridge (U.S.A.), 1967; I. Lapidus, *Middle Eastern Cities*, Berkeley, 1969; A. H. Hourani and S. M. Stern (ed.), *The Islamic City*, Oxford, 1970. See also *Iranian Studies*, Summer-Autumn and Winter-Spring, 1974, devoted to the colloquium on Isfahan held at Harvard University in 1974, which includes numerous studies on one of the most important of Islamic cities, both architecturally and culturally. The studies range from irrigation to art style to religion and present one of the few cases of an all-embracing study of a Muslim city. For a unique study of another of the major Islamic cities seen from the point of view of the spiritual principles dominating every facet of traditional life, see T. Burckhardt, *Fes, Stadt des Islam*, Olten, 1960.

Plate 130. Human habitat completely integrated into its natural environment.

in preserving its equilibrium with the natural environment and the natural forces and elements, such as water, air and light, upon which human life depends. The architecture and city-planning of the Islamic city have never been in defiance of nature. The traditional Muslim architects, in contrast to many Muslim ones in the contemporary Islamic world, never tried to use large glass windows to allow the maximum amount of radiation through and then rely on the maximum amount of external energy to cool the rooms. The planning of their houses, mosques, streets, markets, bazaars, and all other basic elements of city life were such that they made maximum use of the factors provided by nature. Where there are hot deserts, narrow streets were built to protect the cool air of the night during the daylight hours. Where the temperature became very warm, such as around the central desert (Kavir) of Persia, use was made of wind towers to ventilate homes, of deep basements to serve as places of refuge for the summer and of deep underground cisterns to provide cool water. The use of wind towers in the central cities of Persia, such as Yazd, Kashan and Kerman, is particularly instructive and shows how the science of man has made maximum use of existing natural elements to create an architecture which is at once beautiful and efficient, one which reflects the principles of Islam and because of this trait – and not in spite of it – is in equilibrium with the environment. The same can be seen in the way light is used both metaphysically and architecturally in the traditional house and city where it is at once a reminder of the Divine Presence, a source of joy, the means for natural lighting of interior spaces and the source of heat. Altogether, the architecture of the Islamic city, like that of the small town, brings together nearly all the traditional sciences and technologies and, with the help of them, creates an atmosphere of peace and beauty in equilibrium with the environment and reflecting the innate

Plate 131

Plate 132

Figure 93. Details of a tower constructed to catch the wind and to ventilate the traditional house.

Figure 94. The traditional architecture of a water well in the dry regions of Persia.

Plate 131. A general view of the city of Kashan.

Plate 132. A general view of the city of Yazd.

harmony of the sciences, of which it is one of the major applications.[4]

Another facet of Islamic science connected directly with the problem of urbanism, as well as with the ecological crisis, is the use of energy. The Islamic world is becoming known to many people in the modern world as the area from which most of the main source of energy used today, namely petroleum, is imported. Also, strangely enough, only the recent rise of the price of this rare commodity, which the industrialized world was receiving for a nominal price until now, has turned the attention of many to alternative sources of energy such as the wind and the sun. But the Islamic world can, perhaps, help the industrialized world more in solving its energy problems by providing guidelines in the wise use of wind and solar energy than by providing it with the petroleum whose resources will in any case terminate soon. The Islamic world can also render the greatest service to itself by not forgetting its own traditional philosophy and methods of energy usage in favour of a way of living based on the squandering of both energy and natural resources.

The use of the sun to heat homes, of wind to turn mills or ventilate houses, of water to provide energy for small technologies and the like all reached a degree of efficiency and utility combined with beauty which is not often met with elsewhere. The philosophy behind the use of various forms of energy was based on two elements: to preserve as much energy as possible in any process and to use the most easily available form of energy requiring the minimum amount of disturbance of the environment. These ideas might appear as obvious and their application may be said by some to be making a virtue out of necessity. But even in cases where there were choices, the Muslim scientists, architects and engineers followed a way which would conform most closely to these principles. Modern technology makes use both of materials, namely various metals and synthetic substances, which are not natural to the terrestrial environment and of energy in such forms as fossil fuel, electricity and atomic energy which again are not a natural component of the environment on the

4. On the use of light, the elements and other natural factors in Islamic architecture and their significance from the point of view of the Islamic tradition, see N. Ardalan and L. Bakhtiyar, *The Sense of Unity, The Sufi Tradition in Persian Architecture*, Chicago, 1973.

Plates 133 and 134. Windmills in Khurasan.

surface of the earth, an environment upon which all forms of life depend, despite man's forgetfulness of this fact. No wonder that the rapid spread of this type of technology has led to an ecological crisis the like of which has never been seen in the history of the present human race.[5] The use of energy in Islamic civilization, and in fact in traditional civilizations in general, represents a completely different approach, one which can teach a great deal to those who have discovered that man cannot exhaust in a few hundred years the reserves which nature has taken, according to modern geology, millions of years to form[6] and yet hope to survive for long. Again, in this question, the main lesson of Islamic science is its emphasis upon the concept of equilibrium, on how to use energy on the surface of the earth without destroying the delicate ecological balance which governs that environment and which sustains life.

As far as the use of energy is concerned, a case of particular interest is that of transportation. The profit motive which dominates modern economies, not only capitalistic economies but also, indirectly, Communist ones, seeks to produce without end an ever greater quantity of material objects. To achieve this purpose, specialization is encouraged and specialization increases the amount of raw material and finished products which need to be transported. This, in turn, requires a greater use of energy and leads, moreover, to such problems as congested ports as well as city traffic which concerns mostly a particular type of transportation, namely that of manpower. Islamic civilization was always based on providing the maximum amount of happiness on earth possible in the light of man's ultimate felicity in the hereafter. Hence it did not seek after the maximum amount of production for its own sake. Rather, it aimed at local efficiency even when there was a choice to do otherwise.[7] It is true that spice and silk travelled from one end of the Islamic world to another and even beyond it to other lands such as Europe, but each city and town tried to have as complete and self-sufficient an economy as possible. This is to be seen to this day, especially in the traditional village where small industries such as carpet-weaving function side by side with agriculture. After the tragic flight of the population during the past century to big cities, causing the strangulation of many cities and the falling into ruin of many villages, several Muslim governments which had been discouraging this tightly integrated economy and were encouraging specialization on farms and in villages have now begun to return to the traditional Islamic idea. The modern industrialized world will also be forced sooner or later to reconsider its philosophy of transportation in the light of the energy crisis and think of a new form of economic and city planning in which there is the minimum rather than maximum amount of movement of people and objects,[8] and where a community can live at peace with its immediate natural environment with the minimum amount of external perturbation and the maximum amount of self-sufficiency.

Yet another feature of applied science and technology in the Islamic world is its intimate quality. Besides being inseparable from art (the word *ṣināʿah* in Arabic means both technology and art and is, moreover, related to the word *ṣunʿ* which means creation and which is directly connected with the Divine Name 'Creator' (*al-Ṣāniʿ*)), traditional technology is bound to forces and elements innate to the natural environment. It is also related to man in a way which is hardly comprehensible to those who identify technology with the modern machine driven by forces alien to the natural environment and possessed with

5. On the historical roots of the ecological crisis, see Nasr, *The Encounter of Man and Nature*, chap. II.

6. Modern geologists state that it has taken nature 400,000,000 years – whatever those 'years' mean – to form the existing fossil fuel deposits on earth and that at the present rate it will take man only four hundred years to exhaust these reserves!

7. We do not want to imply that this is unique to the Islamic world. It is found in all traditional civilizations and examples of it can still be seen in Hindu and Buddhist Asia in addition to the Islamic world.

8. The essay of I. Illich, *Energy and Equity*, London, 1974, has much to contribute to the discussion of this major problem.

9. See A. K. Coomaraswamy, *Christian and Oriental Philosophy of Art* (*Why Exhibit Works of Art?*), New York, 1956; W. Shewring, *Making and Thinking*, Buffalo, 1958; A. Gleizes, *Life and Death of the Christian West*, London, 1947; Eric Gill, *Autobiography*, New York, 1941; and numerous other writings of A. K. Coomaraswamy and E. Gill on the subject.

the capability of enslaving the spirit of man in contrast to traditional technology which was synonymous with the practice of art and also the crafts and which played a major role in freeing man's spirit.[9] What is of particular interest in the traditional technologies of Islamic civilization, along with their supporting social institutions, for today's world, which now speaks of the virtues of small technological units and 'tools for conviviality',[10] is their human dimension, their relation to identifiable village and community units and their ability to provide economic well-being without causing social disintegration. Many of the arguments found in the works of leading critics of modern science and technology such as L. Mumford, I. Illich and Th. Roszak[11] and suggestions made by them to improve the lot of modern man crushed by the weight of his own inventions are already found in practice and still as living institutions in certain parts of the Islamic world. As the Islamic states industrialize rapidly, they are for the most part falling into the same pitfalls as the industrialized states while vowing not to repeat their errors. Traditional technology in the Islamic world can, therefore, play a crucial role for the Islamic states themselves as well as for the West and should be considered much more seriously than it has been so far, now that the crisis caused by modern technology is beginning to reveal its most sinister aspects.

Finally, it is important to mention the strong awareness of life and its natural cycles which dominates so many aspects of Islamic thought and even traditional technological and economic theories and practices. Life is based on the interrelation between units and a continuous recycling of energy and materials through the chain of life in contrast to modern technology as supported by modern economic theories where the use of materials is usually seen as a one-way process through an assembly line ending finally in the junk heap. Again, as a result of the recent energy and resources crisis, the re-cycling of materials is being encouraged, at least in certain industries, but it is far from having become general practice. In contrast to the modern situation, in traditional technology, of which many examples can still be seen in the Islamic world, the maximum possible re-cycling of all materials has always been the rule rather than the exception. This has also been combined with a feeling of reverence towards all material bounties and a strong moral sense concerning waste and the squandering of the gifts of nature which are also the blessings of God. The use of every part of the sheep for purposes as far apart as feeding the family to providing fertilizer for the land to making strings for musical instruments is a case in point.

These and many other aspects of Islamic science and technology have guided, over the ages, the relation of the *homo islamicus* with his natural environment. Although he has made a profound effect upon this environment over the centuries, the member of *dār al-islām*, whether living in a city, a village or wandering as a nomad, has lived for the most part in peace and harmony with the world about him. He has taken the natural environment to be his lasting home and not a besieged country to be plundered and laid to waste. Paradoxically enough, he has felt at home on earth precisely because he has always been aware that he is but a traveller on a journey on the terrestrial plane and destined for another world.[12] He has lived in equilibrium with his environment because he has submitted himself to the universal laws which dominate all levels of existence and which are the metaphysical source of the laws governing the natural world. He has lived in peace and harmony with God and His Law and therefore with the natural environment which reflects on its own level the harmony and the equilibrium of the Universal Order.

10. See, for example, the thought-provoking works, *Small is Beautiful, A Study of Economics as if People Mattered* by E. F. Schumacher, New York, 1973, especially part II, and *Tools for Conviviality* by Ivan Illich, London, 1973.

11. This type of writing has increased greatly during the past two decades. See, for example, L. Mumford, *The Transformation of Man*, New York, 1956 and *The Myth of the Machine: I. Technics and Human Development*, New York, 1966; Th. Roszak, *Where the Wasteland Ends*, New York, 1973; and J. Ellul, *The Technological Society*, New York, 1964.

12. It might seem strange that everywhere throughout the world while man considered himself as an exile on earth he lived at peace with nature as if it were his permanent home and that when he began to consider himself as a purely earthly creature and the earth as his final abode he set out to destroy this home with unprecedented ferocity.

Chapter XII
Man in the Cosmic Order

An essential feature of the teachings of Islam, as reflected in its sciences as well as its philosophy and cosmology, is that equilibrium and harmony with the natural environment is not possible unless there is harmony with the total cosmic order and ultimately with the Metacosmic Reality. The Islamic sciences are so many applications of cosmological principles and therefore, while related on the one hand to the physical world and the natural environment, they are bound on the other hand intimately with the knowledge of a higher order. If they serve the various needs of man's terrestrial life and make possible his living in harmony with his natural environment, they are also means whereby man can journey across the levels of cosmic manifestation to attain ultimate freedom. Their 'utility' is, therefore, twofold: they concern human life here below and also the end of man as a creature destined for immortality. Moreover, their message revolves around the central theme of the utter dependence of the lower states of being upon those above and therefore the necessity to possess the higher knowledge and to live according to the norms of the world of the Spirit in order to be able to cultivate a legitimate knowledge of the world below and to live in harmony and equilibrium with it. If the Muslim sages of old were brought into the present-day world they would assert that the state of the modern world, ignorant of the higher forms of knowledge and rebellious against the Spirit, and yet possessing a vast knowledge of the physical world which has led along with other factors to complete disequilibrium *vis-à-vis* the natural environment, is a blinding proof of the truth contained in the message of the Islamic sciences.

The role of the Islamic cosmological sciences in situating man in the cosmic order is fulfilled through those aspects of these sciences which deal with the hierarchic structure of the Universe and of man and their inner correspondence and interrelation all pointing to a Reality which is at once transcendent and immanent, which lies beyond the macrocosmic order and at the heart of the microcosm. It is through the study and finally the experiencing of the stages of this hierarchy that man is led from the terrestrial abode from which these sciences begin to the spiritual empyrean where the source and origin of the traditional sciences is to be found.[1] All the studies concerning the minerals, plants and animals, numbers and figures, the elements and the heavens which have been outlined in the previous chapters are themselves contained within the hierarchic structure of knowledge. The visible world is seen as a symbol of the invisible levels of existence and the traditional man sees himself at the bottom of a hierarchy which leads through the three kingdoms to the angelic world and from there to the Divine Throne (*al-'arsh*) and the Divine Presence Itself. Although he is located at the centre of the Universe, which symbolizes his central role as God's vice-gerent on earth, he is also situated at the lowest level of existence, in a state which imposes upon him the sense of humility and servitude before the Divine Majesty (*jalāl*). The traditional cosmological schemes which are like mandalas to be meditated upon as well as to be studied, convey the two basic aspects of man's situation in the cosmic order: the centrality of his position and the lowliness of his state. Of these two aspects one corresponds to his function as God's vice-gerent (*khalīfatallāh*) and the other to his role as God's servant (*'abdallāh*). Man cannot be solely the one or the other without doing injustice to his own nature and the world about him.[2] But if he is aware of both aspects of his state and situation within the total cosmic order then he can both rule justly over the terrestrial environment and journey beyond the stars to the source of all existence.

The sciences of nature are like so many branches which lead to the trunk of the tree of cosmology itself whose roots are in turn sunk in the ground of the metaphysical principles which provide the tree with its life force. The sciences therefore not only provide for man's needs within a normal civilization but above and beyond that obvious function enable man to relate every particular aspect of physical reality from rivers and hills to various animal forms to the total scheme of cosmic reality in which man is able to situate himself in a meaningful sense. In contrast to modern man, traditional man, whether Muslim or otherwise, has certainly always known *where* he is and *where* he is going and the cosmological sciences have always aided him to chart his course in the perilous journey between his present position and final abode through the cosmic labyrinth.

If one were therefore to ask of what use are the Islamic cosmological sciences one could answer that besides providing the necessary background and knowledge for particular disciplines of practical import such as medicine and agriculture these sciences have a direct practical effect upon the inner life of man. They are directly related to man's real existential problem which is to traverse the perilous caves and valleys of the 'mountains' of the physical and psychic worlds to reach safely the sky of the world of the Spirit. Their eminently symbolic quality makes them a powerful aid to the exposition of metaphysical knowledge and gives them a validity beyond the significance of the physical sciences of a non-symbolic character which are affected by temporal change.

The masters of Islamic gnosis have provided many schemes in which the structure of the cosmos and the means for man to journey through it have been depicted often with great beauty. The *Manṭiq al-ṭayr* (*Conference of the Birds*) of 'Aṭṭār, the *Inshā' al-dawā'ir* (*Creation of the Spheres*) of Ibn 'Arabī, the *al-Insān al-kāmil* (*The Universal Man*) of 'Abd al-Karīm al-Jīlī and on a less gnostic and more philosophical level the visionary recitals of Ibn Sīnā[3] as well as numerous other works of a similar kind provide ample examples of cosmological schemes in which man is shown in his real situation in the chain of being at

1. The spiritual and the intellectual are ultimately the same especially in Islamic metaphysics where *'aql* in its highest sense is identified with both the Divine Intellect and the spiritual world. From the point of view of knowledge the principles of the traditional sciences are to be sought ultimately in the Divine Intellect while from the point of experience or existence they lead the traveller through the cosmic hierarchy to the spiritual world which is none other than the world of the Intellect (*ma'qūlāt*, intelligibles, and *mujarradāt*, spiritual beings, are nearly synonymous in Arabic).

2. See the series of articles by G. Eaton, 'The Only Heritage We Have', in *Studies in Comparative Religion*, 1974.

3. For a study of this aspect of the cosmological doctrines of Ibn Sīnā, see Nasr, *An Introduction to Islamic Cosmological Doctrines*, chap. 15, 'Nature and the Visionary Recitals'.

the lowest point of the arc of descent (*al-qaws al-nuzūlī*) and at the origin of the arc of ascent (*al-qaws al-ṣu'ūdī*).[4] These works also outline the means whereby man can traverse the states above him to reach the empyrean from which he has originally descended.

Traditional cosmology does not only concern the macrocosm but also the microcosm. It contains a complete knowledge of the soul as it does of the qualitative aspect of the Universe. Not only are there the earth, the seven heavens and the outermost heaven leading to the Metacosmic Reality, but there are also within man beside the physical body, the seven subtle organs or bodies (*laṭā'if*) which like the seven planets correspond to the various prophets of man's inner being[5] and the centre of the heart which, like the outermost heaven, is called the *'arsh al-raḥmān* (The Throne of the Compassionate) wherein resides the Divinity. The contemplation of the external cosmos is an aid to the penetration of the inner world thanks to the correspondence and analogy which bind them together. As metaphysics is the key to the understanding of cosmology, so is initiation the key which opens to man the door to the inner chambers of his own being.[6] By means of the initiatic path man enters ever more deeply within himself and at the same time through the higher levels of cosmic reality toward the Formless. His inner transformation includes the interiorization of the cosmic within his being and his freedom therefore embraces the deliverance of nature from the limitations imposed by cyclic conditions and its re-statement into its original state *in divinis* where nature is perennially a direct image of paradise.

The traditional cosmological sciences therefore concern man in an ultimate sense and on a level not to be compared with the modern sciences. The traditional cosmologies are related to man's inner perfection and to his ultimate end. They are inseparable from angelology and eschatology. They provide the background for that process of spiritual maturing which enables man to become God's vice-gerent in actuality rather than only potentially and thus to fulfil his role *vis-à-vis* nature as its protector and 'window' to the world of light.[7] The traditional cosmological sciences, therefore, not only provided a contemplative view of nature, but by enabling man to know where he is in the cosmic order and by aiding him to journey beyond the cosmos, helped in a direct manner to protect nature itself. The devastation of nature could not have come about until the traditional cosmological sciences were forgotten and the sacred view of nature upon which they are based became rejected as remnants of 'primitive animism'.

The destruction of nature in modern times is due also to another factor which is directly connected with the very nature of modern science in contrast to the traditional sciences. The Islamic sciences which have been outlined in this book, like other traditional sciences, never sought to satisfy the thirst for the Infinite in the realm of the finite. They were based directly on metaphysics and made no claim to usurp its place. They presented a 'finite science' of the finite and the relative domain of reality and left the quest for the Infinite and the Absolute to metaphysics and gnosis which alone can satisfy this thirst in a real manner. In contrast, modern science has sought to quench this profound thirst for the Infinite on its own level of finiteness forgetting the limits which have always been set upon the sciences from on high. And this has led to an explosion

4. Some Islamic metaphysicians like Jalāl al-Dīn al-Dawānī have interpreted these two arcs as the arc of presence (*al-qaws al-ḥuḍūrī*) and the 'arc of consciousness' (*al-qaws al-shu'ūrī*). This appellation contains a profound significance as indicating the two poles of existence and knowledge through both of which man is related to his origin.

5. The Sufi 'Alā' al-Dawlah Simnānī in fact speaks explicitly of the Adam, Abraham, Moses, Christ, etc., of man's being (*Ādam wujūdika* and so on). See H. Corbin, *En Islam iranien*, vol. III, chap. IV. The seven subtle bodies, usually combined with the symbolism of the seven colours, form an important part of the teachings of many schools of Sufism especially those descended from Najm al-Dīn Kubrā. See *ibid.*, p. 290; also Corbin, *L'homme de lumière dans le soufisme iranien*, Paris, 1971, where comparisons are also made with similar ideas among Western Hermeticists and esotericists in general including Goethe.

6. We do not mean to imply by any means that a knowledge of the cosmological sciences is a requirement for spiritual attainment. There have been many saints over the centuries who have had no knowledge of them. But a complete tradition cannot do without them for they play the role mentioned above for certain intellectual and spiritual types for whom the aid of this aspect of traditional teachings is indispensable.

7. See Abu Bakr Siraj Ed-Din, *The Book of Certainty*, New York, 1970.

of the most dangerous kind which now threatens the very harmony of the natural order.[8] The lack of quest for infinity on the level of finitude which is to be observed in the history of the Islamic sciences is profoundly connected with the structure of Islamic cosmological and meta-

Plate 135. Man and the macrocosm.

8. 'Science is natural to man but it is important above all else to choose between the different levels, in the light of the axiom: "My kingdom is not of this world"; all useful observation of the herebelow expands science, but the wisdom of the next world limits it, which amounts to saying that every science of the Relative which does not have a limit which is determined by the Absolute, and thus by the spiritual hierarchy of values, ends in super-saturation and explosion.' F. Schuon, *Logic and Transcendence*, p. 135.

physical doctrines. It also contains a lesson about what the boundaries of any legitimate science can be, a lesson which modern science should heed before its misled search for the Absolute and the Infinite in the relative and the finite order results in the complete destruction of the bound and finite world that is the sole subject of study of this science.

By placing each existent where it belongs in the hierarchy of universal existence Islamic metaphysics and cosmology were able to create an extensive science of the physical and of the psychic worlds which far from destroying nature only accented the equilibrium that exists in the cosmic order and emphasized the harmony between man and his environment. While the Islamic sciences taught man a great deal about the world about him and enabled man to rule over this world, they also set limits to his power to destroy the earth and pointed in a thousand ways to the fact that man's end is to journey to a world beyond and not to be satisfied through pride or ignorance with imprisonment within the cosmic crypt which man's forgetfulness has made to appear as his natural state. They provided a science of things which enabled man to contemplate the forms of nature rather than to destroy them before the altar of his passionate nature. These sciences enabled those who mastered them and their metaphysical principles to remember and never to forget that there is no reality except the Ultimate Reality (*Lā ilāha ill'Allāh*), that all cosmic manifestation from the sand pebbles of the desert to the angels are 'sent' by that Reality (*Muḥammadun rasūl Allāh*) and that before that Reality they are literally nothing. For this reason the Islamic sciences, beyond all their historic and scientific importance for the Islamic world as well as other civilizations, have been for the Islamic tradition itself an affirmation of Divine Unity (*al-tawḥīd*) and on the highest level aids to the realization of this Unity. For this reason above all others they still contain a message of the greatest actuality for mankind which is so deeply in need of re-discovering this Unity and of living and knowing according to the Light It has always cast and will always cast upon human existence.

wa'llāhu aʿlam

Notes to Illustrations

All photographs not otherwise credited are by Roland Michaud.

Chapter I

Figure 1a. Quran II; 255.

Figure 1b. Quran XXIV; 35.

Figure 1c. Quran XXXIX; 9.

Figure 1d. Quran XLI; 53.

Figures 2a, 2b and 2c. These sayings are a small number of the large amount of *Ḥadīth* recorded in the canonical collections of Sunnis and Shīʿites alike concerning the primacy of knowledge in the Islamic perspective.

Figure 3. Prepared by S. H. Nasr.

Chapter II

Figure 4a. See al-Fārābī, *Catálogo de las ciencias, edición y traducción castellana por Angel Gonzales Palencia*, 2nd ed., Madrid: Publicaciones de la Facultad de Filosofia y Letras, Universidad de Madrid, 1953, *passim.*

Figures 4b and 4c. From *Nafā'is al-funūn fī ʿarā'is al-ʿuyūn* by Shams al-Dīn Muḥammad al-Āmulī, ed. by Ḥajj Mīrzā Abu'l-Ḥasan Shaʿrānī, Tehran, 1377 (A. H. solar).

Figure 5. Al-Azhar University is one of the oldest Islamic institutions of learning, founded by the Fāṭimids in the 4th/10th century and still the major centre of religious learning in the Sunni world.

Figures 6, 7 and 8. From the 11th/17th century Persian MS No. 14709, in the Islamic Museum, Cairo.

Figure 9. From A. Ashtarī, 'Pazhūhishī dar kashf-i raṣadkhāna-yi Marāghah', *Faḍā'*, Tīr, 1354 (A. H. solar), pp. 24 and 31.

Plate 1. A typical scene in which a few of the younger students beginning their study of the religious sciences gather in a small group in a madrasah around the master to recite correctly and to interpret the meaning of the Holy Book and other important traditional texts. Since this course is being held in winter, the students are sitting round a table covered by a thick blanket inside which is a hearth filled with burning charcoal and called a *kursī* in Persia, and a *ṣandalī* in Afghanistan. This traditional heating system is still very prevalent in Persia and Afghanistan and, strangely enough, in certain parts of Spain.

Plate 2. Picture of the courtyard of the most ancient and influential university and adjoining mosque of North Africa founded eleven centuries ago.

Plate 3. One of the most beautiful monuments of Timurid architecture, built by a Timurid princess from her personal wealth and endowed heavily to support religious students. The school continues to this day as a major centre of learning in Persia.

Plate 4. One of the many notable schools in Samarqand built by the descendants of the Timurids. It survives today only as an historical monument. Early 11th/17th century.

Plate 5. Ghaẓanfarāqā Madrasah in Istanbul from the 11th/17th century MS No. H.889 in the Topkapı Library, Istanbul.

Plate 6. One of the many important centres of learning built in Ottoman Turkey in which the teaching of medicine and the treatment of patients took place along with the instruction of students in the usual subjects taught in Muslim universities. The hospital even had a special section devoted to psychologically unbalanced patients.

Plate 7. Perhaps the largest centre for the practice of traditional Islamic medicine in India today. Photograph by Robert Harding.

Plate 8. From the 9th/15th century Persian MS No. F.1418, in the University Library, Istanbul.

Plate 9. A miniature depicting a Mawlawī Sufi centre with the dervishes occupied with the recitation of Sufi poetry and the performance of the Sufi dance. From the 10th/16th century MS No. H.1365, in the Topkapı Library, Istanbul.

Chapter III

Figure 10. From *al-Futūḥāt al-makkiyyah* based on the study of T. Burckhardt, *Clé spirituelle de l'astrologie musulmane d'après Mohyiddin ibn Arabi*, Paris, 1950 and 1974.

Figure 11. From Sayyed Ḥaydar Āmulī, *Le Texte des textes (Naṣṣ al-nuṣūṣ)*, ed. by H. Corbin and O. Yahya, Tehran and Paris 1975, diag. 23, p. 461.

Figure 12. From S. H. Nasr, *An Introduction to Islamic Cosmological Doctrines*, Cambridge (U.S.A.), 1964, p. 71.

Figure 13. From *Shams al-ma'ārif al-kubrā* by Shams al-Dīn al-Būnī, Cairo, n.d., p. 291.

Figure 14. From *Kitāb al-tafhīm* by al-Bīrūnī, 12th/18th century MS No. 6565, in the Majles Library, Tehran.

Figure 15. From a manuscript in the Institute of Oriental Studies, Tashkent, Uzbek Soviet Republic.

Figure 16. From a MS in the Egyptian National Library, Cairo.

Figure 17. From a MS in the Egyptian National Library, Cairo.

Figure 18. From the 10th/16th century Turkish MS No. 6605, in the University Library, Istanbul.

Plate 10. From the 9th/15th century Egyptian MS No. 4689, in the University Library, Istanbul.

Plate 11. From the *Gūy u Chawgan (The Ball and the Stick)* of 'Ārifī, 10th/16th century MS No. 1941, in the Museum of Islamic and Turkish Art, Istanbul.

Plate 12. From the *'Ajā'ib al-makhlūqāt (Wonders of Creation)* of Muḥammad al-Ṭūsī, 10th/16th century Persian MS, in the Egyptian National Library, Cairo.

Plate 13. From the 10th/16th century Persian MS No. 1404, in the University Library, Istanbul.

Plates 14 and 15a. From the 6th/12th century MS No. 1702, in Leiden University Library, reproduced from the *Monumenta Cartographica*, by Yūsuf Kamāl, fascicule 2, vol. III, Leiden, 1932.

Plates 15b and 16. From the Persian translation of *al-Masālik wa'l-mamālik* by al-Istakhrī, 8th–9th/14th–15th century MS No. 1331, in the Central Library, Tehran University.

Plates 17 and 18. From Aya Sophia MS No. 2577, in the Süleymaniye Library, Istanbul.

Plate 19. From the *Dīwān-i lughat al-turk*, 9th/15th century MS, in the Millet Library, Istanbul.

Plate 20a. From the National Museum, Damascus, Syria.

Plate 20b. From the Turkish and Islamic Art Museum, Istanbul.

Plate 20c. From the Ni'matallāhī Khānaqāh, Tehran.

Plate 21. From the Topkapı Library, Istanbul.

Chapter IV

Figure 19. From the 9th/15th century Persian MS No. 2127, in the Topkapı Library, Istanbul. The MS contains both the Arabic text of the *Materia Medica* of Dioscorides and its 9th/15th century translation.

Plate 22. From British Library MS Or. 2784, f96r.

Plates 23 and 24. From the 12th/18th century MS No. 6471, in the Majles Library, Tehran.

Plate 25. From the 7th/13th century MS No. 1266 of the botanical and pharmaceutical encyclopaedia of Ibn al-Bayṭār, in the Ahmadiyyah Library, Aleppo, Syria.

Plate 26. From the Arabic MS and its Persian translation No. 2127, in the Topkapı Library, Istanbul.

Plates 27, 28, 29 and 30. From the 9th/15th century Persian MS No. 2127, in the Topkapı Library, Istanbul. See note to Figure 19 above.

Plates 31, 32 and 33. From the 9th/15th century MS No. R.1022, in the Topkapı Library, Istanbul.

Plate 34. From a 10th/16th century MS, in the New Delhi Museum.

Plates 35 and 36. Early 11th/17th century Mogul MS from the School of Jahāngīr, in the Freer Art Gallery, Washington DC.

Plate 37. From the album of Mehmet II, MS No. H.2153 (109a), in the Topkapı Library, Istanbul.

Plate 38. From the 12th/18th century MS No. 6471, in the Majles Library, Tehran.

Plates 39, 40 and 41. From the 9th/15th century Egyptian MS No. 4689, in the University Library, Istanbul.

Chapter V

Figure 20. Figure from *Shams al-ma'ārif al-kubrā* by Shams al-Dīn al-Būnī, p. 227.

Figure 21. From MS No. 98, in the Egyptian National Library, Cairo.

Figure 22. R.A.K. Irani, 'Arabic Numeral Forms', *Centaurus*, vol. IV, 1955, pp. 1–12.

Figure 23. From the 10th/16th century MS of the *Book of Wonders*, in the Egyptian National Library, Cairo.

Figure 24. In the Islamic Museum, Cairo.

Figure 25. From *Khayyāmī-nāmah* by J. Homā'ī, vol. I, Tehran, 1346 (A.H. solar).

Figure 26. From the 9th/15th century Persian MS No. 1359, in the Millet Library, Istanbul.

Figure 27. From *Ḥakīm 'Umar-i Khayyam bi 'unwān-i 'ālim-i jabr* by Gh. Moṣāḥab, Tehran, 1339 (A.H. solar), pp. 153–154.

Figure 28. From the *Kashf al-ghunūm wa'l qurāb fī sharḥ ālāt al-ṭarab*, 8th/14th century MS No. 3465, in the Topkapı Library, Istanbul.

Figures 29, 30 and 31. From an 8th/14th century MS No. 4720, in the Majles Library, Tehran.

Figure 32. From the Arabic MS No. 1206, in the Ahmadiyyah Library, Aleppo, Syria.

Figure 33. Islamic geometric patterns in comparison with the picture of a beryllium molecule as deduced by X-ray defraction analyses. Prepared by Keith Critchlow.

Plate 42. From Esad Efendi MS No. 3638, in the Süleymaniye Library, Istanbul.

Plate 43. From the 9th/15th century Persian MS No. 1359, in the Millet Library, Istanbul.

Plate 44. From the Gök Medresse, Sivas, Turkey.

Plate 45. From the Friday Mosque, Kerman, Iran.

Chapter VI

Figure 34a. From al-Bīrūnī, *The Co-ordinates of Cities*, trans. by S. Ali, Beirut, 1966, pp. 248–253.

Figure 34b. From *Tuḥfat al-ajillah fī ma'rifat al-qiblah* by Ḥaydar Qulī ibn Pīr Muḥammad Khān Sardār Kābulī, trans. by S. H. Nasr, Tehran, 1319 (A.H. solar), pp. 19–20.

Figure 35. From *al-Āthār al-bāqiya 'an al-qurūn al-khaliyah* by al-Bīrūnī, 8th/14th century MS Or. 161 f6v, in Edinburgh University Library.

Figure 36. From the resumé of the *Almagest* of Ptolemy, 4th/10th century, MS No. 8093, in the National Library, Tunis.

Figures 37 and 38. From the *Ṣuwar al-kawākib*, 9th/15th century Arabic MS No. 197, in the Majles Library, Tehran.

Figure 39. From the *Ṣuwar al-kawākib*, 11th/17th century MS No. 196, in the Majles Library, Tehran.

Figure 40. From *Kitāb al-tafhīm* by al-Bīrūnī, MS No. 6565, in the Majles Library, Tehran.

Figure 41. From the 8th/14th century MS of a collection (*Majmū'ah*) of Naṣīr al-Dīn al-Ṭūsī on mathematics and astronomy, MS No. 1346, Central Library, Tehran University.

Figure 42. From *Kitāb al-tafhīm* by al-Bīrūnī, MS No. 6565, in the Majles Library, Tehran.

Figures 43, 44, 45 and 46. From *Risālah mu'ayyanah* and *Ḥall-i mushkalāt-i mu'ayyanah* contained in the *Majmū'ah* on mathematics and astronomy, MS No. 1346, Central Library, Tehran University.

Figure 47. From an 8th/15th century MS No. 4720, in the Majles Library, Tehran.

Figure 48. From E. S. Kennedy, 'Late Medieval Planetary Theory', *Isis*, vol. 57, 1966, pp. 367, 369, 374; and Victor Roberts, 'The Solar and Lunar Theory of Ibn ash-Shāṭir', *ibid.*, p. 429.

Figures 49 and 50. From the Ulugh Beg Museum, Samarqand, Uzbek Soviet Republic.

Figure 52. From the Qarawiyyīn Mosque, Fez, Morocco.

Figures 54, 55 and 56. From *Kitāb al-tafhīm* by al-Bīrūnī, 12th/18th century MS No. 6565, in the Majles Library, Tehran.

Figures 57 and 58. J. A. Repsold, *Zur Geschichte der astronomischen Messwerkzeuge,* Leipzig, 1908–14; A Miéli, *Panorama General de Historia de la Cienca II, El Mundo Islamico, y el occidente medieval cristiano,* Buenos Aires, 1946.

Figures 59 and 60. Persian geared astrolabe made in Isfahan in 618/1221 by Muḥammad b. Abī Bakr ibn Muḥammad al-Rāshidī al-Ibarī, in the Museum of the History of Science, Oxford.

Figure 61. Made by Raḍī al-Dīn Muḥammad ibn Sayyid 'Alī al-Ḥussaynī, probably 12th/13th century, in the Museum of the History of Science, Oxford.

Figure 62. From a collection of miscellanea, 9th/15th century MS No. B.411, in the Topkapı Library, Istanbul.

Figure 63. From a Persian MS in the Ni'matallāhī Khānaqāh Library, Tehran.

Figure 64. From the *Majmū'ah* of al-Ṭūsī, MS No. 1346, in the University Central Library, Tehran.

Plate 46. A 12/18th century instrument in the Aleppo Museum, Syria.

Plate 47. From the Turkish translation of *'Iqd al-jumān fī ta'rīkh ahl al-zamān* of Maḥmūd ibn Aḥmad al-'Ayn, MS No. TY5953, in the University Library, Istanbul.

Plate 48. From the *Ṣuwar al-kawākib,* 9th/15th century Arabic MS, in the Malek Library, Tehran.

Plates 49, 50, 51, 52, 53, 54, 55, 56, 57, 58, 59 and 60. The signs are from a collection of MSS as follows: Aries, Gemini, Libra, Pisces from *Ṣuwar al-kawākib,* of al-Ṣūfī, 11th/17th century MS No. 197, in the Majles Library, Tehran.
Virgo and Capricorn from *Ṣuwar al-kawākib* of al-Ṣūfī, 11th/17th century MS No. 196, in the Majles Library, Tehran.
Cancer from *Ṣuwar al-samāwiyyah,* Reza Library, Rampur, India. Photograph by Robert Harding.
Taurus, Leo, Scorpio, Sagittarius and Aquarius from *Ṣuwar al-kawākib* of al-Ṣūfī, 9th/15th century MS, in the Malek Library, Tehran.

Plate 61. One of several figures of this kind which appeared in Islamic astronomical and astrological treatises after the 7th/13th century. From the *Wonders of Creation* of Muḥammad al-Ṭūsī, 10th/16th Persian MS, in the Egyptian National Library, Cairo.

Plate 62. From *Kitāb al-tafhīm* by al-Bīrūnī, MS No. 6565, in the Majles Library, Tehran.

Plate 63. From the 9th/15th century Persian MS of the *Wonders of Creation* in the Egyptian National Library, Cairo.

Plate 64. From the original MS of the *Zīj* in the Salar Jang Museum, Hyderabad, Deccan, India. Photograph by Robert Harding.

Plate 65. From the *Shāhanshāhī-nāmah,* 10th/16th century, MS No. FY1404, in the University Library, Istanbul.

Plates 66, 67, 68 and 69. Photographs by Robert Harding.

Plate 70. From the Qarawiyyīn Mosque, Fez, Morocco.

Plate 71. Opposite the Bū 'Ināniyyah Madrasah, Fez, Morocco.

Plate 72. Special sundial said to have been built by Bahā' al-Dīn al-'Āmilī in the Shah Mosque in Isfahan.

Plate 73. Seljuk astrolabe of the 6th/12th century in the Islamic and Turkish Art Museum, Istanbul.

Plate 74. Andalusian astrolabe from Seville of the 7th/13th century in the Islamic and Turkish Art Museum, Istanbul.

Plates 75 and 76. The front and back of an Egyptian astrolabe of the 7th/13th century in the Islamic and Turkish Art Museum, Istanbul.

Plate 77. Moroccan astrolabe in the Qarawiyyīn Mosque school.

Plate 78. 12th/18th century Persian astrolabe in the Archaeological Museum, Tehran.

Plate 79. Isfahan is one of the few cities in the Islamic world where the tradition of astrolabe-making is still kept alive. Both real astrolabes and models of them are made by the traditional craftsmen.

Plate 80. A Persian celestial globe (not spherical astrolabe), made by Ja'fair ibn Umar ibn Dawlatshāh al-Kirmānī, 764/1362–3, in the Museum of the History of Science, Oxford.

Plate 81. In the Islamic and Turkish Art Museum, Istanbul.

Plate 82. In the Museum of Mevlana in Konya, Turkey.

Plate 83. From the *Nuṣrat-nāmah,* 10th/16th century MS No. M.1365, in the Topkapı Library, Istanbul.

Plate 84. From the *Shāhanshāhī-nāmah,* 10th/16th century MS No. FY1404, in the University Library, Istanbul.

Plate 85. From the *Mashāriq al-anwār al-sulṭāniyyah* by Muḥammad Ḥasan al-Ḥusaynī, 13th/19th century MS No. 7197 (temporary catalogue), in the Majles Library, Tehran.

Plates 86 and 87. From the 9th/15th century MS No. R1976, in the Topkapı Library, Istanbul.

Plate 88. From the *Wonders of Creation* by Muḥammad al-Ṭūsī, in the Egyptian National Library, Cairo.

Chapter VII

Figure 65. From 'Ibn al-Haytham's work on Optics, A Commentary', by Mustafa Nazif Bey, in *Ibn al-Haitham*, ed. by Ḥakīm Muḥammad Sa'īd, Karachi, 1970, pp. 286–287.

Figure 66. From H. J. J. Winter and W. 'Arafāt, 'Discourse on the Concave Spherical Mirror', *Journal of the Royal Asiatic Society of Bengal*, vol. XVI, no. 1, 1950, pp. 2–3, and S. H. Nasr, *Science and Civilisation in Islam*, pp. 131–132.

Figures 67, 68 and 69. From the *Kitāb mīzān al-ḥikmah* of al-Khāzinī, ed. by Mudarris Raḍawī, Tehran, 1346 (A.H.solar). From E. Wiedemann, 'al-Mīzān', in the *Encyclopaedia of Islam*, 1st ed., Leiden, 1913–42.

Figure 70. From British Library MS Add.23, 391 (ff. 22v–23r.).

Figures 71 and 72. From a Maghribī MS No. 98, in the Egyptian National Library, Cairo.

Figure 73. From a treatise by Fatḥallāh Shīrāzī, in M. A. Alvi and A. Rahman, *Fatḥallāh Shīrāzī*, New Delhi, India, 1968, Fig 2.

Plates 89, 90 and 91. From the *Kitāb fī ma'rifat al-ḥiyal al-ḥandasiyyah* of al-Jazarī, 7th/13th century MS Ahmet III 3472, in the Topkapı Library, Istanbul.

Plates 92 and 93. From the *Kitāb fī ma'rifat al-ḥiyal al-ḥandasiyyah* of al-Jazarī in the Süleymaniye Library, Istanbul.

Plate 94. From the *Wonders of Creation*, 9th/15th century Persian MS in the Egyptian National Library, Cairo.

Chapter VIII

Figure 74. Bath-house adjacent to the Mihrimāh Mosque.

Figure 75a. From S. H. Nasr, *An Introduction to Islamic Cosmological Doctrines*, p. 253.

Figure 75b. Based on M. Ullmann, 'Jābirean writings', *Die Medizin im Islam*, p. 99.

Figure 76. Copyright Science Museum, London.

Figure 77. From a collection of miscellanea, 9th/15th century MS No. B.411, in the Topkapı Library, Istanbul.

Figure 78. From a Persian medical MS in the Ahmadiyyah Library, Aleppo, Syria.

Figure 79. From *Tashrīḥ-i manṣūri*, 13th/19th century MS No. 450, in the University Central Library, Tehran.

Figure 80. From a treatise on ophthalmology in the Egyptian National Library, Cairo.

Figure 81. From the *Kitāb al-taṣrīf* (Book of Concession) of al-Zahrāwī in the Khudābakhsh Library, Patna, India. Photograph by Robert Harding.

Figure 82. From the Museum of the History of Medicine, Tughluqābād, Delhi, India. Photography by Robert Harding.

Figure 83. From *al-Āthār al-bāqiya 'an al-qurūn al-khaliyah* by al-Bīrūnī, 8th/14th century MS Or. 161 f6v, in Edinburgh University Library.

Figure 84. From the *Jarrāḥiyyat al-khāniyyah*, the Turkish surgical treatise by Sharaf al-Dīn ibn 'Alī, 9th/15th century MS No. T.79, in the Millet Library, Istanbul.

Figure 85. In Islam animals are never 'slaughtered'; they are only allowed to be killed ritually (*dhibḥ*). In the case above there is no question of a particular magical act being involved; it concerns only using a hen, whose neck has just been cut ritually, to treat someone bitten by a dangerous snake. From the 9th/15th century MS No. Ahmet III 2127, in the Topkapı Library, Istanbul.

Plate 95. The hospital at Divriği, Turkey.

Plate 96. Labābīdī bath-house from the Mamluk period in Aleppo, Syria.

Plate 97. Timurid miniature of the School of Behzad from Jāmī's *Haft-awrang*, in the Kabul Library, Afghanistan.

Plate 98. The Ganj 'Alī Khān bath-house built during the 13th/19th century in Kerman, Persia.

Plate 99. From a collection of miscellanea, 9th/15th century MS No. B.411, in the Topkapı Library, Istanbul.

Plate 100. From *Tashrīḥ-i manṣūrī*, 13th/19th century MS No. 450, in the University Central Library, Tehran.

Plate 101. From the 11th/17th century Persian MS No. 14709, in the Islamic Museum, Cairo.

Plates 102 and 103. From the *Tashrīḥ-i manṣūrī* by Manṣūr ibn Muḥammad Aḥmad, 11th/17th century Persian MS No. 5266, in the Majles Library, Tehran.

Plate 104. From a treatise on ophthalmology in the Egyptian National Library, Cairo.

Plates 105, 106 and 107. From the *Jarrāḥiyyat al-khāniyyah*, the Turkish surgical treatise by Sharaf al-Dīn ibn 'Alī, 9th/15th century MS No. T.79, in the Millet Library, Istanbul.

Plate 108. From British Library MS Or. 2784, f101v.

Plate 109. Prepared by S. H. Nasr.

Plate 110. From the 7th/13th century Arabic MS No. Ahmet III 2127 from Mosul, Iraq, on Dioscorides, *Materia Medica*, in the Topkapı Library, Istanbul.

Plate 111. From the Museum of the History of Medicine, Tughluqābād, Delhi, India. Photograph by Robert Harding.

Chapter IX

Figure 86. Prepared by S. H. Nasr.

Figure 87. From the Museum of the History of Science, Oxford.

Figure 88. From the Turkish *Da'wat nāmay-i firdawsī*, 10th/16th century MS No. 208, in the University Library, Istanbul.

Plate 112. From the Museum of the History of Science, Oxford.

Plate 113. From a private collection in Isfahan.

Plate 114. In certain regions of the Islamic world there are still practising alchemists. Here one can see a Persian alchemist at work in his *atelier*.

Plate 115. From the Ni'matallāhī Khānaqāh Library, Tehran.

Chapter X

Figure 89. The reservoir near Qayrawan in Tunis, in the 3rd/9th century during the Aghlabid Dynasty.

Figure 90. The Muslims adopted the noria wheel, originally invented by the Romans, and it survives to this day, especially in the cities of Syria, such as Hama.

Figure 91. The river is spanned by several bridges which are used to this day, both for transportation and for regulating the flow of the water of the Zayandirud.

Figure 92. From Afghan Turkistan.

Plate 116. This monument, built by al-Ma'mūn and then restored in the time of the caliph al-Mutawakkil the Abbasid, shelters the graduated scale by which the rise and fall of the water of the Nile is measured.

Plate 117. The reservoir near Qayrawan in Tunis, built in the 3rd/9th century during the Aghlabid Dynasty.

Plate 118. The Minara reservoir, one of the largest existing reservoirs in Morocco.

Chapter XI

Figure 93. One of the many towers of this kind in Kerman, Persia.

Figure 94. The architecture of this edifice, situated between Na'in and Yazd, shows that with the help of the wind, which ventilates the inside space through the four towers and the closed dome, a minimum amount of precipitation results, and the water is kept remarkably cool.

Plate 119. From the *Bābur-nāmah*, a 10th/16th century MS in the National Museum, Delhi, India.

Plate 120. Work being carried out in Afghanistan. Traditional methods continue to be used to this day in Persia and Afghanistan to construct and clear *qanāts*.

Plates 121 and 122. Two *qanāts* which carry water from the mountain-sides to the low plateaux in the region lying between Isfahan and Kashan. The *qanāt*, or *kariz*, system from Iran is also called *foggra* in the Sahara.

Plate 123. Open *qanāt* in Afghan Sistan.

Plate 124. The river is spanned by several bridges which are used to this day, both for transportation and for regulating the flow of the water of the Zayandirud.

Plate 125. In Fez, Morocco.

Plate 126. From *al-Āthār al-bāqiyah* of al-Bīrūnī, 12th/18th century MS No. 2132, in the Majles Library, Tehran.

Plates 127 and 128. From Afghan Turkistan.

Plate 129. A wagon with wooden or iron beaters is generally used, but in some areas a threshing-board drawn over the grain by animals is preferred.

Plate 130. This little Afghan village, between Kabul and Jalalabad, is one of the many examples of this kind.

Plates 131 and 132. The cities of Kashan and Yazd, two of the oldest in Persia, are situated in one of the dryest and hottest regions of the country. Therefore, in their city planning they have to make the maximum use of the little water and the great deal of air and wind that are available to them in order to make human life possible. In this view the central role of towers (*bādgīr*) constructed to catch the wind is to be seen.

Plates 133 and 134. The windmills are said to be of Persian origin. They still serve, as in these examples from Khargird in Persian Khorasan, and near Herat in Afghan Khorasan, to convert easily accessible and natural means of energy for simple technological devices.

Chapter XII

Plate 135. From MS No. 1973 in the Turkish and Islamic Art Museum, Istanbul.

Glossary

Note

1. All words are of Arabic origin except where indicated otherwise.
2. The definite article *al-* is ignored for the purpose of alphabetical listing.

ābādī (Persian), a place where there is water; a human settlement

adwār, cycles, especially of universal existence and cosmic events associated with cosmic history

aḥadiyyah, singularity, a term of the school of Ibn ʿArabī denoting the first determination of the Absolute

aḥjār, see *ḥajar*

amlāḥ, salts, one of the classes of minerals according to Ibn Sīnā

aqrābādhīn, lists of drugs; pharmacopoeia, usually concerned with compound drugs

arithmaṭīqī, a term for the science of numbers derived from the Greek

al-arqām al-hindiyyah, Indian numbers

al-ʿarsh, throne; the Divine Throne

ʿarsh al-raḥmān, the Throne of the Compassionate, the centre of the heart and the outermost heaven wherein 'resides' the Divinity

ātishak-i farangī (Persian), 'Frankish fire', syphilis

al-ʿaṭṭār, druggist

awāʾil, the early (sciences), as classified by al-Āmulī and others

awākhir, the late (sciences), as classified by al-Āmulī and others

awqāf, religious endowments, pl. of *waqf*, relating to institutions such as schools, libraries and other educational establishments

al-awzān waʾl-maqādīr, weights and measures

al-aʿyān al-thābitah, the immutable essences

āyāt, signs or portents (of God); aspects of nature to be contemplated rather than simply analyzed

baḥr al-fārs, the Persian Sea, i.e. the Indian Ocean

bandar (Persian), port

barakah, grace, issuing directly from the Quranic revelation

barzakh, a measure of distance, derived from the Pahlavi *farsang*

bāṭin, inward (aspect)

bīmāristān (Persian then Arabic), place of the sick; hospital

biyābān (Persian), a place without water; a desert

Dār al-funūn, the abode of sciences, name of a new university established in Tehran during the Qajar period where modern medicine was taught

dār al-islām, the world of Islam

dhāʾibāt, solubles, one of the classes of minerals according to Ibn Sīnā

dhāt al-ḥilaq, zodiacal armillaries

dhāt al-rubʿayn, azimuthal quadrant

dhawq, tasting (of the Truth), which with *kashf* leads to gnosis *dhikr*, invocation (of the Name of God). By means of speech man imitates the act of creation; thus invocation plays a central role in the 'reversal' of the cosmogonic act and the return of man to his origin

al-dīn al-ḥanīf, the primordial tradition, to which Islam in a fundamental sense returns

falak, planetary orbit

farsang (Pahlavi), a measure of distance (about four miles)

filāḥah, agriculture

fiṭrah, nature; the profoundest and primordial nature of man

gharīb, occult (used of sciences)

ghasaq, darkness; the absence of light, and 'matter' in the view of the Illuminationists as opposed to the 'substance' of the world which is considered to be light

al-ḥaḍarāt al-ilāhiyyat al-khams, the Five Divine Presences, the spiritual psychic and physical worlds as depicted by Ibn 'Arabī

ḥadīth, saying; the Prophet's sayings which are a commentary and extension of the teachings of the Quran. In Shī'ism, *ḥadīth* includes both the sayings of the Prophet and the Imāms

ḥajar (pl. *aḥjār*), stone, also the Philosophers' Stone; one of the classes of minerals according to Ibn Sīnā

ḥajarat al-falāsifah, the Philosophers' Stone

ḥakīm, wise-man or sage; the traditional physician and philosopher as well as master of most of the other traditional sciences

ḥammām, bath

handasah, geometry, probably derived from Pahlavi *handāzah*, denoting both computation and measurement of water canals or simply irrigation

handāzah, see *handasah*

al-ḥarakat al-jawhariyyah, transubstantial motion, the idea developed by Mullā Ṣadrā which made motion a property of the substance of physical objects and not only of their accidents

ḥifẓ al-ṣiḥḥah, prophylaxis; hygiene and public health

al-ḥikmat al-muta'āliyah, transcendent theosophy, the school dominant in Persia today whose foundation was set by Mullā Ṣadrā

hīmiyā', the subjugating of souls, one of the occult sciences

ḥisāb al-ghubārī, 'dust board' computation, so called because dust was spread on a board and numbers traced on it

ḥisāb al-jummal, a method of computation based on the sexigesimal system using the letters of the alphabet to symbolize numbers

ḥisāb al-munajjimīn, the arithmetic of astronomers, a term used to describe the sexigesimal system

ḥisāb al-yad, finger computation

ikhtilāj, twitching; the interpretation of the twitching of various parts of the body and a branch of the occult sciences

ikhtiyārāt, selections; in astrology the selecting of propitious moments for undertaking an important event

al-iksīr, elixir

'ilm, knowledge, considered sacred in Islam as all knowledge ultimately concerns some aspect of God or His theophanies

'ilm al-'adad, science of numbers, later often used interchangeably with *'ilm al-ḥisāb* (q.v.)

'ilm al-anwā', science of the appearance of the first light of the moon as it enters each mansion by means of which meteorological phenomena and terrestrial events were predicted

'ilm al-falak, science of the planetary orbits; astronomy

'ilm al-filāḥah, agriculture

'ilm al-firāsah, physiognomy, one of the branches of the occult sciences

'ilm al-hay'ah, astronomy

'ilm al-ḥisāb, science of reckoning; see also *'ilm al-'adad*

'ilm al-ḥiyal, science of stratagems or ruses; that branch of science which deals with mechanical devices, gadgets, automata etc., usually related in the Muslim mind with the occult sciences and magic

al-'ilm al-ḥuḍūrī, presential knowledge, sapiential wisdom or gnosis

al-'ilm al-ḥuṣūlī, acquired knowledge, comprising the two classes of formal knowledge (*al-'ulūm al-naqliyyah* and *al-'ulūm al-'aqliyyah*, q.v.)

'ilm khawāṣṣ al-ashyā', science of the properties of things; being closely interwoven with mineralogy, it is not limited merely to what is measurable but is based on a vast vision wherein manifest and occult aspects and properties of things are all real and react with each other and with man in the Universe

'ilm al-miqāt, science of fixed moments, for determining the times of prayer

'ilm al-nabāt, science of plants, botany

'ilm al-nujūm, science of the stars; astronomy

al-inbīq, alembic

al-insān al-kāmil, Universal Man, in whom the fullness of the human state is realized and through whom multiplicity returns to Unity

ishrāq, illumination, name of a school founded by Suhrawardī which developed its own distinct doctrines where the very substance of the world is light and matter darkness or the absence of light

i'timād, support; a theory of projectile motion by which the motion of one object by nature engenders the motion of another after it

al-jabr, algebra, meaning originally restoration and amplification of something incomplete

jadhr, root (algebra)

al-jafr, the sacred and esoteric science connected with the numerical symbolism of the letters of the Arabic alphabet

jaliy, open (used of sciences); contrasted with the hidden or occult sciences

jism, material; the *corpus* of the cosmologist of Antiquity, being a level of existence standing below the worlds of the Spirit and the psyche

juz' lā yatajazza', a particle which is indivisible; atom

kabārit, sulphurs, one of the classes of minerals according to Ibn Sīnā

kaḥḥāl, ophthalmologist

kahrīz (Persian), underground canal system

Kalām, theology

kashf, vision, which with *dhawq* leads to gnosis

khafiy, hidden (used of sciences)

khānaqāh (Persian), Sufi centre for initiatic and spiritual practices where esoteric and sometimes exoteric sciences are taught. *Zāwiyah* in Arabic

khāriq al-'ādah, that which breaks the habit, i.e. of the mind in its perception of external reality; miracles

al-kharshūf, artichoke

khārṣīnī, Chinese metal; one of the seven species of metals according to al-Rāzī and others

Khawārij, a group opposed to 'Alī and Mu'āwiyah, who for centuries opposed both Sunnis and Shī'ites

khilāfah, vice-gerency, i.e. of man as God's representative on earth and the representative of all earthly creatures before God

khulafā' rāshidūn, rightly guided caliphs, being the four who followed Muḥammad immediately – Abū Bakr, 'Umar, 'Uthmān and 'Alī

al-kibrīt al-aḥmar, red sulphur; an alchemical term and an epithet of Ibn 'Arabī

al-kīmiyā', alchemy

al-kīmiyā' al-'uẓmā, the great alchemy, also name for agriculture (attributed to Hermes)

kishwar (Persian), region, of which there are seven and into which the world is divided according to the ancient Persians

al-kulliyāt, general principles (of medicine)

külliye, a Turkish term for an educational and scientific complex

kun, 'be', the creative act of God according to the Quran

laṭā'if, subtile organs or bodies, of which there are seven in man beyond the physical body

laylat al-mi'rāj, night of ascent, when the Prophet made his nocturnal ascent to the Divine Proximity from Jerusalem

laylat al-qadr, the night of power, during which the Quran was revealed

līmiyā', magic, one of the occult sciences

mādīs (Persian), streams subdivided from the Zayandirud river and flowing through the city of Isfahan, which provide water for the inhabitants

madrasah, place for lessons; an institution associated with the mosque and which developed into a university for religious sciences but also for many of the intellectual sciences

māl, square (algebra)

manāzil al-qamar, the stations of the moon which are twenty-eight in number

mandala (Sanskrit), representation of the cosmic scheme used as a contemplative aid for the adept

masā'il, questions, being in astrology enquiries into the life and activities of someone absent

massa, to rub or touch with the hand and possibly the origin of *massage*

mawālīd, kingdoms, of which there are three in the natural world

mawsim, monsoon

mayl, inclination, a concept developed by Ibn Sīnā to explain projectile motion

Ming-Tang, the magic square according to which the Chinese empire was divided and which is also found in early Islamic alchemy

mi'rāj, see *laylat al-mi'rāj*

al-mīzān, balance

al-mu'allif al-jadīd, the new author, name given to the Turkish alchemist 'Alī Bek al-Iznīqī

al-mu'allim al-thānī, the Second Teacher, referring to al-Fārābī, who gave order to and classified the sciences

mufradāt, simples, drugs in their natural and simple state or pharmacognosy

muḥāwarī, daily discourse, comprising sciences such as history, genealogy etc.

muḥtasib, he who reckons, being a person responsible for the correct use of weights and measures in commercial transactions in the traditional Muslim city

munajjimūn, astronomers or astrologers and often both

muqābalah, balancing, i.e. of the two sides of an equation

murakkabāt, compounds, drugs as usually understood today in contrast to simples

mutakallimūn, theologians

muthallath bi'l-ḥikmah, thrice (great) in wisdom, Hermes Trismegistos

nafas, breath; related to *nafs* (soul)

nafas al-raḥmān, the Breath of the Compassionate; in Sufi terminology, the very 'stuff' or substance of the Universe which 'produces' created beings like human breath which then produces words and sounds

nafs, soul, the *anima* of the cosmologists of Antiquity, being a level of existence between the Spirit and physical bodies; souls are also the inner forces which govern the life patterns of the kingdoms of the natural world

al-nafs al-nāṭiqah, the rational soul, being the rational faculty which distinguishes man from the animals in a fundamental and not just an accidental manner

nākhudā (Persian), captain of a ship

al-nasī', intercalation, postponement of a sacred month

naw', the appearance of the first light of the moon as it enters each mansion; pl. *anwā'*, see *'ilm al-anwā'*

naẓar, glance

al-nujūm, stars

qahwah, coffee

qanāt, underground water system especially of Persia

al-qaws al-ḥuḍūrī, arc of presence; an appellation of some metaphysicians which along with *al-qaws al-shuʿūrī* (q.v.) corresponds to *al-qaws al-nuzūlī* (q.v.) and *al-qaws al-ṣuʿūdī* (q.v.)

al-qaws al-nuzūlī, arc of descent, extending from the Origin, through the various links in the chain of being, to man

al-qaws al-shuʿūrī, arc of consciousness, see *al-qaws al-ḥuḍūrī*

al-qaws al-ṣuʿūdī, arc of ascent, stretching from man, through the higher states of being, to God

qiblah, the direction of Mecca

al-qudamā' al-khamsah, the five eternals; principles of an independent cosmology developed by al-Rāzī which included time and space

al-Qur'ān al-tadwīnī, the recorded Quran; the written Quran

al-Qur'ān al-takwīnī, the Quran of creation; the created world

quwwat al-ḥarakah, momentum

raml, sand; geomancy, originally making use of pebbles of sand although special instruments were later devised

rīḥ, wind or air; in the Galenic doctrine, through the air breathed by the organism the life-force enters the body

rīmiyā', jugglery and tricks, one of the occult sciences

rūḥ, spirit; the Divine Centre of the Cosmos; that level of existence between the Origin and the Universe corresponding to the *spiritus* of the ancients. In medicine the spirit descends upon the mixture of humours and is the subtle body between the physical body and the force of life from the world above

al-ṣafīḥah, a type of astrolabe in which the two stereographic projections of the circles of the equator and ecliptic were presented on the same surface

salām, peace

samāʿ, 'what is heard' being that part of natural philosophy in which the principles are discussed

al-samā', the sky

samāwāt, the heavens

al-Ṣāniʿ, see *ṣināʿah*

shahādah, attestation, the fundamental testimony of Islam

Sharīʿah (Sacred) Law, promulgated by Islam and governing human life whereby man can live in conformity with ultimate Reality

sharʿiyyāt, the sciences of law

shay', thing, used for the unknown in algebra and which became the modern *x* through Spanish

siddhāntas (Sanskrit), astronomical compendia, referred to by Muslims as *sindhinds*

ṣifr, zero, whence cipher

silsilah, chain; especially in Sufism and alchemy the transmission from authority to authority

sīmiyā', producing visions; one of the occult sciences

ṣināʿah, art and technology; the root is related to *ṣunʿ*, creation, and *al-Ṣāniʿ*, the Creator, thus binding traditional technology to forces and elements innate to the world of creation

sindhinds, see *siddhāntas*

siyāq, a popular method of calculation still fairly prevalent in the bazaars of Persia

ṣunʿ, see *ṣināʿah*

ṭabīʿiyyāt, natural philosophy, which included the life and earth sciences as well as physics

tadākhul, everything penetrating everything, being the principle of alchemy

al-tannūr, oven; athanor where base metal is melted

al-tawḥīd, unity; the interrelatedness of all that is brought into being, the doctrine of Unity

ṭibb al-a'immah, medicine of the Imāms; the class of works in Shīʿism associated particularly with the fifth, sixth and eighth Imāms and complementary to prophetic medicine

al-ṭibb al-nabawī, prophetic medicine; that particular branch of medicine concerning the traditions of the Prophet on medicine; also called *ṭibb al-nabī*

ṭibb al-nabī, see *al-ṭibb al-nabawī*

ṭūfān, storm, whence typhoon

al-ʿulūm al-ʿaqliyyah, the intellectual sciences; knowledge acquired through the God-given intelligence of man on both the level of intellect and reason

al-ʿulūm al-gharībah, the occult sciences

al-ʿulūm al-khafiyyah, the hidden sciences, i.e. the occult

al-ʿulūm al-naqliyyah, the transmitted sciences; knowledge acquired through the path of revealed truth which after its revelation is transmitted from one generation to the next

wajd, bliss, see *wujūd*

waqf, see pl. *awqāf*

wujdān, consciousness, see *wujūd*

wujūd, Being, which is at once also consciousness (*wujdān*) and bliss (*wajd*), qualities present in the cosmos because the cosmos is a manifestation of the Principle

ẓāhir, outward (aspect)

zāwiyah, Arabic equivalent of Persian *khānaqāh* (q.v.)

zīj (from Sanskrit via Pahlavi), originally meant 'straight lines', was used in conjunction with astronomical tables because of lines drawn up in such works to tabulate the results of observations, hence astronomical tables

zirāʿah, agriculture

Select Bibliography in European Languages

Abu Bakr Siraj ed-Din, *The Book of Certainty*, London, 1952.

Ardalan, N., and Bakhtiar, L., *The Sense of Unity. The Sufi Tradition in Persian Architecture,* Chicago, 1973.

Arnaldez, R., and Massignon, L., 'La science arabe' in R. Taton (ed.), *La Science antique et médiévale (des origines à 1450)*, vol. 1 of the editor's series *Histoire générale des sciences*, Paris, 1957; English translation by A. Pomerons as *Ancient and Medieval Science*, New York, 1963, and London, 1965.

Averroes, *Tahāfut al-tahāfut*, transl. by S. van den Bergh (E. J. W. Gibb Memorial Series 19), London, 1954.

Avicenna Commemoration Volume, Calcutta, 1956.

Barthold, V. V., *La Découverte de l'Asie*, transl. by B. Nikitine, Paris, 1947.

Al-Battānī, *al-Zīj al-ṣābi*, ed. and Latin transl. by C. Nallino, 3 vols., Milan, 1899–1907.

Berthelot, M., *La chimie au Moyen-Âge*, 3 vols., Paris, 1893.

Al-Bīrūnī, *The Book of Instruction in the Elements of the Art of Astrology*, transl. by R. R. Wright, London, 1934.

Al-Bīrūnī Commemoration Volume, Calcutta, 1951.

Browne, E. G., *Arabian Medicine*, Cambridge, 1921.

Browne, E. G., *A Literary History of Persia*, 4 vols., London, 1902–24.

Burckhardt, T., *Alchemy*, transl. by W. Stoddart, Olten, 1960.

Burckhardt, T., *Fes, Stadt des Islam*, Olten, 1960.

Burckhardt, T., *Moorish Culture in Spain*, transl. by A. Jaffa, London, 1972.

Campbell, D. E. H., *Arabian Medicine and Its Influence on the Middle Ages*, 2 vols., London, 1926.

Carra de Vaux, B., *Les penseurs de l'Islam*, 5 vols., Paris, 1921–26.

Clagett, M., *Archimedes in the Middle Ages*, Madison, 1964.

Clagett, M., *The Science of Mechanics in the Middle Ages*, Madison, 1959.

Clément-Mullet, J., *Essai sur la minéralogie arabe*, Paris, 1869.

Corbin, H., Nasr, S. H., and Yahya, O., *Histoire de la philosophie islamique*, vol. 1, Paris, 1964.

Datta, B., and Singh, N. A., *A History of Hindu Mathematics,* parts I and II, Bombay, 1962.

Dreyer, J. L. E., *A History of Astronomy from Thales to Kepler,* 2nd ed., New York, 1953.

Dictionary of Scientific Biography, New York, 1969.

Duhem, P., *Le système du monde : histoire des doctrines cosmologiques de Platon à Copernic*, 10 vols., Paris, 1913–59; especially vols. II and IV.

Dunlop, D. M., *Arabic Science in the West*, Karachi, 1958.

Elgood, C., *A Medical History of Persia and the Eastern Caliphate*, Cambridge, 1951.

Eliade, M., *The Forge and the Crucible*, transl. by S. Corrin, New York, 1962.

Encyclopaedia of Islam, 1st edition, London and Leiden, 1908–38; new edition, Leiden and London, 1960 on.

Evola, G., *La Tradizione ermetica*, Bari, 1948.

Gruner, O. C., *A Treatise on the Canon of Medicine of Avicenna, Incorporating a Translation of the First Book*, London, 1930.

Hamarneh, S., *Bibliography on Medicine and Pharmacy in Medieval Islam*, Stuttgart, 1964.

Hartner, W., *Oriens-Occidens: Ausgewählte Schriften zur Wissenschaft- und Kulturgeschichte. Festschrift zum 60. Geburtstag*, Hildesheim, 1968.

Haskins, C. H., *Studies in the History of Medieval Science*, New York, 1960.

Hirschberg, J., *Die arabischen Augenärtze nach den Quellen bearbeitet*, Leipzig, 1904–5.

Hirschberg, J., *Die arabischen Lehrbücher der Augenheilkunde*, Berlin, 1905.

Holmyard, E. J., *The Arabic Works of Jābir ibn Ḥayyān*, vol. I, Paris, 1928.

Ibn Yūnus, *Al-zīj al-kabīr al-ḥākimī (Le Livre de la grande table Hakémite)*, ed. and transl. by J. J. A. Caussin de Perçeval, in *Notices et extraits des manuscrits de la Bibliothèque Nationale*, vol. VI (1), Paris, 1804, pp. 16–240.

Al-'Irāqī, *Kitāb al-'ilm al-muktasab fī zirā'at adh-dhahab*, ed. and transl. by E. J. Holmyard, Paris, 1923.

Karpinski, L. C., *Robert of Chester's Latin Translation of the Algebra of al-Khwarizmi*, New York, 1915.

Kasir, D. S., *The Algebra of Omar Khayyam*, New York, 1931.

Kennedy, E. S., *A Survey of Islamic Astronomical Tables*, Philadelphia, 1956.

Kennedy, E. S. and Pingree, D., *The Astrological History of Māshā'allāh*, Cambridge, 1971.

Krachkovski, J. J., *Istoria Arabskoi Geograficheskoi Literatury*, Moscow–Leningrad, 1957.

Kraus, P., *Jābir ibn Ḥayyān. Contribution à l'histoire des idées scientifiques dans l'Islam*, 2 vols., Cairo, 1942–3.

Kraus, P., 'Raziana', *Orientalia*, N.S. 4 (1935), pp. 300–34, N.S. 5 (1936), pp. 35–36, 358–78.

Kushyār ibn Labbān, *Principles of Hindu Reckoning*, transl. with introd. and notes by M. Levey and M. Petruck, Madison, 1965.

Leclerc, L., *Histoire de la médecine arabe*, 2 vols., Paris, 1876, photo-reprint New York, 1960.

Levey, M., *The Algebra of Abū Kāmil*, Madison, 1966.

Levey, M., *The Formulary or Aqrābādhīn of al-Kindī*, Madison, Milwaukee and London, 1966.

Levey, M., and al-Khaledy, N., *The Medical Formulary of al-Samarqandī and the Relation of Early Arabic Simples to Those Found in the Indigenous Medicine of the Near East and India*, Philadelphia, 1967.

Luckey, P., *Die Rechenkunst bei Ǧamšīd b. Mas'ūd al-Kāšī*, Wiesbaden, 1951.

Al-Mas'ūdī, *El Mas'udi's Historical Encyclopaedia Entitled 'Meadows of Gold and Mines of Gems'*, London, 1841.

Mattock, J. N., (ed.), *Tract Comprising Excerpts from Aristotle's Book of Animals (Arabic Technical and Scientific Texts 2)*, Cambridge, 1966.

Mattock, J. N., and Lyons, M. C., (eds.), *Hippocrates: On Endemic Diseases, (Arabic Technical and Scientific Texts 5)*, Cambridge, 1969.

Mattock, J. N., and Lyons, M. C., (eds.), *Hippocrates: On the Nature of Man, (Arabic Technical and Scientific Texts 4)*, Cambridge, 1968.

Meyer, E. H. F., *Geschichte der Botanik*, vol. III, Konigsberg, 1856.

Meyerhof, M., *Las Operaciones de Catarata de 'Ammār ibn 'Alī al-Mauṣilī, Oculista de el Cairo*, in five languages including English, Barcelona, 1937.

Meyerhof, M., and Sobhy, G. P., (eds. and transl.), *The Abridged Version of 'The Book of Simple Drugs' of Aḥmad ibn Muḥammad al-Ghāfiqī by Gregorious Abu'l-Faraj (Barhebraeus)*, 4 vols., Cairo, 1932–40.

Miéli, A., *La science arabe et son rôle dans l'évolution scientifique mondiale*, Leiden, 1938, 2nd ed. Leiden, 1966.

Millás Vallicrosa, J. M., *Assaig d'història de les idees físiques i matemàtiques a la Catalunya medieval*, Barcelona, 1931.

Millás Vallicrosa, J. M., *Estudios sobre Azarchiel*, Madrid–Granada, 1943–50.

Millás Vallicrosa, J. M., *Nuevos estudios sobre historia de la ciencia española*, Barcelona, 1960.

Mingana, A. (ed. and transl.), *Book of Treasures, by Job of Edessa*, London, 1935.

Nallino, C. A., *Raccolta di scritti editi e inediti*, 6 vols., Rome, 1939–48; vol. 5: *Astrologia, Astronomia, Geografia*.

Nasr, S. H., *An Annotated Bibliography of Islamic Science*, vol. I, Tehran, 1975.

Nasr, S. H., *Al-Bīrūnī, an Annotated Bibliography*, Tehran, 1973.

Nasr, S. H., *The Encounter of Man and Nature, the Spiritual Crisis of Modern Man*, London, 1968.

Nasr, S. H., *An Introduction to Islamic Cosmological Doctrines*, Cambridge (U.S.A.), 1964; London, 1976.

Nasr, S. H., *Science and Civilization in Islam*, Cambridge (U.S.A.), 1968; New York, 1970.

Needham, J., *Science and Civilisation in China*, Cambridge, 1951 on.

Neugebauer, O., *The Astronomical Tables of al-Khwārizmī*, Copenhagen, 1962.

Neugebauer, O., *The Exact Sciences in Antiquity*, Providence, 1967.

O'Leary, De L., *How Greek Science Passed to the Arabs*, London, 1964.

Peters, F. E., *Allah's Commonwealth*, New York, 1973.

Peters, F. E., *Aristotle and the Arabs, the Aristotelian Tradition in Islam*, New York and London, 1968.

Pines, S., *Beiträge zur islamischen Atomenlehre*, Berlin, 1936.

Pingree, D., *The Thousands of Abū Ma'shar*, London, 1968.

Plessner, M., 'Storia delle scienze nell'Islam' in *La civiltà dell'Oriente*, vol. III, pp. 449–92, Rome, 1958.

Al-Qazwīnī, *The Zoological Section of the Nuzhatu-l-Qulub of Hamdullah al-Mustaufi al-Qazwini*, transl. by J. Stephenson (Oriental Translation Fund, New Series, vol. XXX), London, 1926.

Reinaud, J., *Géographie d'Aboulféda*, 2 vols., Paris, 1848–83; especially vol. I, *Introduction générale à la géographie des orientaux.*

Rhazes, *The Spiritual Physick of Rhazes*, transl. by A. J. Arberry, London, 1950.

Rosenthal, F., *Das Fortleben der Antike im Islam*, Zurich and Stuttgart, 1965.

Ruska, J., *Tabula smaragdina*, Heidelberg, 1926.

Ruska, J., and Kraus, P., *Dritter Jahresbericht mit einer wissenschaftlichen Beilage der Zusammenbruch der Dschābir-Legende*, Berlin, 1930.

Sarton, G., *Introduction to the History of Science*, 3 vols., Baltimore, 1927–48.

Sayılı, A. M., *The Observatory in Islam*, Ankara, 1960.

Schroeder, E., *Muhammad's People*, Portland, Me., 1955.

Schuon, F., *Dimensions of Islam*, transl. by P. Townsend, New York, 1969.

Schuon, F., *Logic and Transcendence*, transl. by P. Townsend, New York, 1975.

Schuon, F., *Understanding Islam*, transl. by D. Matheson, London, 1963.

Sezgin, F., *Geschichte des arabischen Schrifttums*, Leiden, 1970 on; especially vols. III, IV, and V.

Sharif, M. M. (ed.), *A History of Muslim Philosophy*, 2 vols., Wiesbaden, 1963–66.

Smith, D. E., and Karpinski, L. C., *The Hindu-Arabic Numerals*, Boston and London, 1911.

Stapleton, H. E., Azo, R. F., and Hidāyat Ḥusain, M., 'Chemistry in Iraq and Persia in the Tenth Century A.D.', *Memoirs of the Royal Asiatic Society of Bengal*, vol. XII (6), 1927.

Stapleton, H. E., and Hidāyat Ḥusain, M., 'Three Arabic Treatises on Alchemy by Muḥammad ibn Umail al-Tamīmī', *Memoirs of the Royal Asiatic Society of Bengal*, vol. XII (I), 1933.

Steinschneider, M., *Die arabischen Übersetzungen aus dem Grieschischen*, Graz, 1960.

Steinschneider, M., *Die europäischen Übersetzungen aus dem Arabischen bis Mitte des 17. Jahrhunderts*, Graz, 1956.

Suter, H., *Die Mathematiker und Astronomen der Araber und ihrer Werke*, Leipzig, 1900, new ed. 1902, reprint Ann Arbor, 1963.

Ullmann, M., *Die Medizin im Islam*, Leiden, 1970.

Ullmann, M., *Die Natur- und Geheimwissenschaften im Islam*, Leiden, 1972.

Vernet, J., *Der Islam in Europa*, Bussum, 1973.

Von Grunebaum, G. E., *Islam – Essays in the Nature and Growth of a Cultural Tradition*, London, 1955.

Waite, A. E., *The Secret Tradition of Alchemy, Its Development and Records*, New York, 1926.

Walzer, R., *Greek into Arabic*, Oxford, 1962.

Wiedemann, E., *Aufsätze zur arabischen Wissenschaftsgeschichte*, 2 vols., Hildesheim, 1970.

Woepcke, F., *L'Algèbre d'Omar Alkhayyami*, Paris, 1851.

Wolfson, H. A., *Crescas' Critique of Aristotle: Problems of Aristotle's Physics in Jewish and Arabic Philosophy*, Cambridge (U.S.A.), 1929.

Yuschkewitsch, A. P., *Geschichte der Mathematik im Mittelalter*, Leipzig, 1964 (original Russian in Moscow, 1961).

Yuschkewitsch, A. P., *Die Mathematik der Länder des Ostens im Mittelalter*, Berlin, 1963.

Index

Index

Index

Index

nautical geography, 43; geography, 42, 45; Islamic idea of the goal of science, 133; Ptolemy attacked during R., 106; *Turba Philosophorum*, 199; wedding of soul to spirit in alchemy, 196 (f12)
Renan, E., 221
Renaud, H. P. J., 173 (f29), 188 (f80)
Reports on China (Akhbār al-Ṣīn) of Sulaymān the Merchant, 40
Reports on India (Akhbār al-Hind) of Sulaymān the Merchant, 40
Resumé of Astronomy of Thābit Ibn Qurrah, 133
Revision of the Optics, The (Tanqīḥ al-manāẓir) of Kamāl al-Dīn al-Fārsī, 142
Rhazes, see Muḥammad ibn Zakariyyā' al-Rāzī
"Rhetorics", branch of logic, 15
Richter, P., 185 (f73)
rīmiyā' (jugglery and tricks), 206
Risālah dar tiryāq (Treatise on Theriaca) of Kamāl al-Dīn Ḥusaynī, 183
Risālah fī anwā' al-ḥijārah wa'l-jawāhir (Treatise on Various Types of Stones and Jewels) of al-Kindī, 53
Risālah fī anwā' al-jawāhir al-thamīnah wa ghayrihā (Treatise on Various Types of Precious Stones and other Types of Stones) of al-Kindī, 53
Risālah fī anwā' al-suyūf al-ḥadīd (Treatise on Various Kinds of Steel Swords) of al-Kindī, 53 (f14)
al-Risālat al-muḥīṭiyyah (The All-Embracing Treatise on the Circumference) of Ghiyāth al-Dīn Jamshīd al-Kāshānī, 81
Risālat al-ruḥāwiyyāt (Treatise on Edessan Inspirations) of Abū 'Amr 'Abd al-Karīm al-Marrākushī, 201
Ritter, H., 201 (f37)
Robert of Chester, 85
Roger II, 42
Roger, The Book of (Kitāb al-rujārī) of Abū 'Abdallāh al-Idrīsī, 42
Rome, 209
Roman, aqueducts, 210; baths, 157 (f8); botany, 54
Roman Agriculture (Filāḥat al-rūmiyyah) of Qusṭūs al-Rūmī, 221 (f12)
Rosen, F., 85 (f27)
Rosenfeld, B. A., 81 (f17), 82 (f22), 85 (f26)
Rosenthal, F., 14 (f8)
Roszak, Th., 234
Royal Astronomical Tables (Zīj-i shāh or *Zīj-i shahriyār)*, 11, 97
Royal Book, The or *The Perfection of the Art (Kitāb al-malikī* or *Kāmil al-ṣinā'ah* Lat: *Liber Regius)* of 'Alī ibn al-'Abbās al-Majūsī, 172, 177
rūḥ (spirit), 28, 160, 161
al-Rūḥ (the Spirit), 28 (f6)
Rules of Treatment (Dastūr al-'ilāj) of Sulṭān 'Alī Gunādī, 183
Rūmī, see Jalāl al-Dīn Rūmī
Ruska, J., 53 (f12), 198 (f17), 199 (f26), 200 (f32)
Rutbat al-ḥakīm (The Sage's Step) of Abū Maslamah al-Majrīṭī, 201

Sabaeans, 98; Sabaeanism, 11; *Sabaean Tables*, 99
Sabaean Tables, The (Zīj al-ṣābī) of Abū 'Abdallāh al-Battānī (Albategnius), 99
Sabra, A. I., 79 (f12), 84 (f23), 95 (f2), 140 (f20)
Sābūr ibn Sahl, 189
Sabziwārī, 135
Sachau, E., 80 (f14)
Sa'dān, A., 78 (f6), 79 (f9)
Sadīd al-Dīn al-Awfī, *Jawāmi' al-ḥikāyāt (Collected Stories)*, 68
Ṣadr al-Dīn Shīrāzī (also called Mullā Ṣadrā), *Asfār al-arba'ah (The Four Journeys)*, 138; classification of the sciences, 14; knowledge and existence, 13 (f3); *Mafātīḥ al-ghayb (Keys to the Unseen)*, 163; "natural philosophy", 139; physics, 135; plants in the resurrection, 59; Safavid theosopher, 138
Sadīd al-Dīn al-Kāzirūnī, 181 (f61)
al-ṣafīḥah, al-Zarqālī, 123
Safvat, D., 86 (f31)
Safavid, *Asfār al-arba'ah (The Four Journeys)*, 138; astronomical instruments, 114; automata, 145; carpets, 204; medical revival, 183; Mīr Dāmād, 15; Mullā Ṣadrā, 138; out of three great Islamic empires, 4–5; outstanding medical works of the period, 189; mathematics, 19; Safavid Persia, 15; science of numbers, 81; Shāh Sulṭān Ḥusayn, 120; study of animals, 69; Sufi: Shaykh Bahā' al-Dīn al-'Āmilī, 217
Sage's Step, The (Rutbat al-ḥakīm) of Abū Maslamah al-Majrīṭī, 201
saḥarik al-hindī, see Caraka
Sa'īd Dīwajī, 199 (f25)
Saladin, see Ṣalāḥ, al-Dīn al-Ayyūbī
Ṣalāḥ al-Dīn al-Ayyūbī (Saladin), 155, 181
Salé, 155
Salem, Adib E., 4 (f5)
Saliba, Dj., 75 (f1)
Ṣāliḥ ibn Sallūm, *Ghāyat al-itqān fī tadbīr badan al-insān (The End of Perfection Concerning the Regimen of the Body of Man)*, 184
Samanids, 178
Samarqand, 17; *madrasah* at S., 17; observatory, 105, 112, 114; Ulugh Beg, 112
al-Samarqandī, see Abū Ḥāmid Muḥammad al-Samarqandī, and Najīb al-Dīn al-Samarqandī
San'a, 17
Sanā'ī, 134; *Ḥadīqat al-ḥaqīqah (The Garden of Truth)*, 68; *Mi'rāj-nāmah*, 31 (f9)
al-Ṣāni' ("Creator"), 233
Sanjarī Tables, The (Zīj-i sanjarī) of 'Abd al-Raḥmān al-Khāzinī, 105
Sanskrit, *Kalīlah wa Dimnah*, 11, 50 (f3), 62; 'Alī ibn Rabban al-Ṭabarī, 176; background of Islamic pharmacology, 187; Indian numerals, 78; medical sources, 155 (f4); origin of *zīj*, 98 (f11); pharmacological names, 188; translations into Persian, e.g. *Ṭibb-i sikandarī (The Medicine of Sikandar)*, 183; transmission of culture, 12
di Santillana, G., 126 (f32)
Sardār Kābulī, 93
Sarjīs of Resh'aynā, 173
Sarton, G., 48, 48 (f19), 145 (f27)
Sassanids, Anūshīrawān, 174; aqueducts, 210; astrology, 127; astronomy, 97, 98; development of Jundishapur, 11; extensive knowledge of drugs, 185; geography, 38; *"qanāts"*, 52; works translated, 96
Sāte' al-Hosrī, M., 52 (f9)
Satisfying Book on Indian Arithmetic, The (Kitāb al-muqni' fi'l-ḥisāb al-hindī) of Abu'l-Ḥasan al-Nasawī, 79
Sayılı, A., 20 (f15), 112 (f22), 142 (f21)
Sayyid 'Alī Ra'īs, *al-Muḥīṭ (The Circumference)*, 45; entitled Kātib-i Rūm, 45; second Ra'īs, 45
Sayyid Ḥaydar al-Āmulī, Shī'ism, 31
Sayyid Zayn al-Dīn Ismā'īl al-Ḥusaynī al-Jurjānī *Aghrāḍ al-ṭibb (The Aims of Medicine)*, 182; *Dhakhīra-yi khwārazmshāhī (Treasury dedicated to the King of Khwārazm*, 182; *Yādigār-i ṭibb (Medical Memoranda)*, 182
Sbath, P., 221 (f8)
Schacht, J., 77 (f4), 179 (f58), 180 (f59)
scholastic, 139, 178
Schramm, M., 140 (f20)
Schumacher, E. F., 234 (f10)
Schuon, F., 3 (f2), 14 (f5), 28 (f3), 203 (f42), 238 (f8)
sciences, *gharībah* (occult), 193; *khafiyyah* (hidden), 193; *Kitāb iḥṣā' al-'ulūm (The Enumeration of the Sciences)* of Abū Naṣr al-Fārābī, 14; sciences of law *shar'iyyāt)*, 16; science of weights, 15; *al-'ulūm al-'aqliyyah* ("the intellectual sciences"), 5 (f11), 14, 92, 105, 182; *al-'ulūm al-naqliyyah* ("the transmitted sciences"), 5 (f11), 14
scientia sacra, 3
Scot, Michael, *Abbreviatio Avicennae de animalibus*, 63 (f30)
Scrutinization of what the Eyes Perceive, The (Kitāb al-istibṣār fī mā tudriku-hu'l-abṣār) of Shihāb al-Dīn al-Qarāfī, 142 (f21)
Secretum Secretorum (Latin trans. of *Kitāb sirr al-asrār*) by Roger Bacon, 53, 200
Section of the Ratio, The, of Apollonios Pergaeus, 77
Sédillot, L. A., 99
Seemann, H. J., 123 (f29)
Segal, 81 (f17)
Selection of the Age, The (Nukhbat al-dahr) of Shams al-Dīn al-Dimashqī, 42
Selim II, 184
Seljuks, 4, 96, 155
Semitic, 12, 138, 193
Seneca, 142
Servetus, 180
Servier, J., 9 (f13)
Seventy Books, The, Kitāb al-sab'īn in the Jābirean corpus, 199
Severus Sebokht of Nisibis, astrolabe, 120
Seville, 112, 218, 222
sexigesimal system, 78
Seyāḥat-nāmah (Travel Accounts) of Ewliyā Čelebi, 45
Sezgin, F., 54 (f19), 56 (f20), 62 (f23), 77 (f4), 172 (f26), 173 (f30), 175 (f34), 198 (f17), 199 (f24)
Shāfi'ī Medicine, The (Ṭibb-i shāfi'ī) of Muẓaffar al-Ḥusaynī, 189
Shāfi'ī Pharmacopoeia, The (Qarābādīn-i shāfi'ī) of Muẓaffar al-Ḥusaynī, 189
Shah, M. H., 179 (f57)
Shahādah, 31
Shāh Ismā'īl, 183
Shāh-nāmah (Epic of Kings), of Firdawsī, 68
Shāh Ni'matallāh Walī, 203, 204 (f43)
Shāh Sulṭān Ḥusayn, 120
Shahriyār Bahmanyār-i Pārsī, *Tajārib-i shahriyārī*, 201
al-Shāmil fi'l-ṣinā'at al-ṭibbiyyah (The Comprehensive Work on the Art of Medicine) of 'Alā' al-Dīn ibn al-Nafīs, 180
Shams al-Dīn al-Akfānī, 54; *Kitāb ghunyat al-labīb 'ind ghaybat al-ṭabīb (The Refuge of the Intelligent during the Absence of the Physician)*, 181
Shams al-Dīn al-Būnī, formulae/numbers, 79; Hermetic ideas, 31; *Shams al-ma'ārif (The Sun of the Divine Sciences)*, 201
Shams al-Dīn al-Dimashqī, natural history compendium, 49–50; *Nukhbat al-dahr (The Selection of the Age)*, 42; study of animals, 63
Shams al-Dīn Muḥammad al-Āmulī, 15, 16; *Nafā'is al-funūn fī 'arā' is al-'uyūn*, 16; *Nafā'is al-funūn (Precious Elements of the Sciences)*, 15
Shams al-Dīn al-Nuwayrī, 59, 63
Shams al-ma 'ārif (The Sun of the Divine Sciences) of Shams al-Dīn al-Būnī, 201
Shānāq, see *Cānakya*
Sharaf al-Dawlah, 99

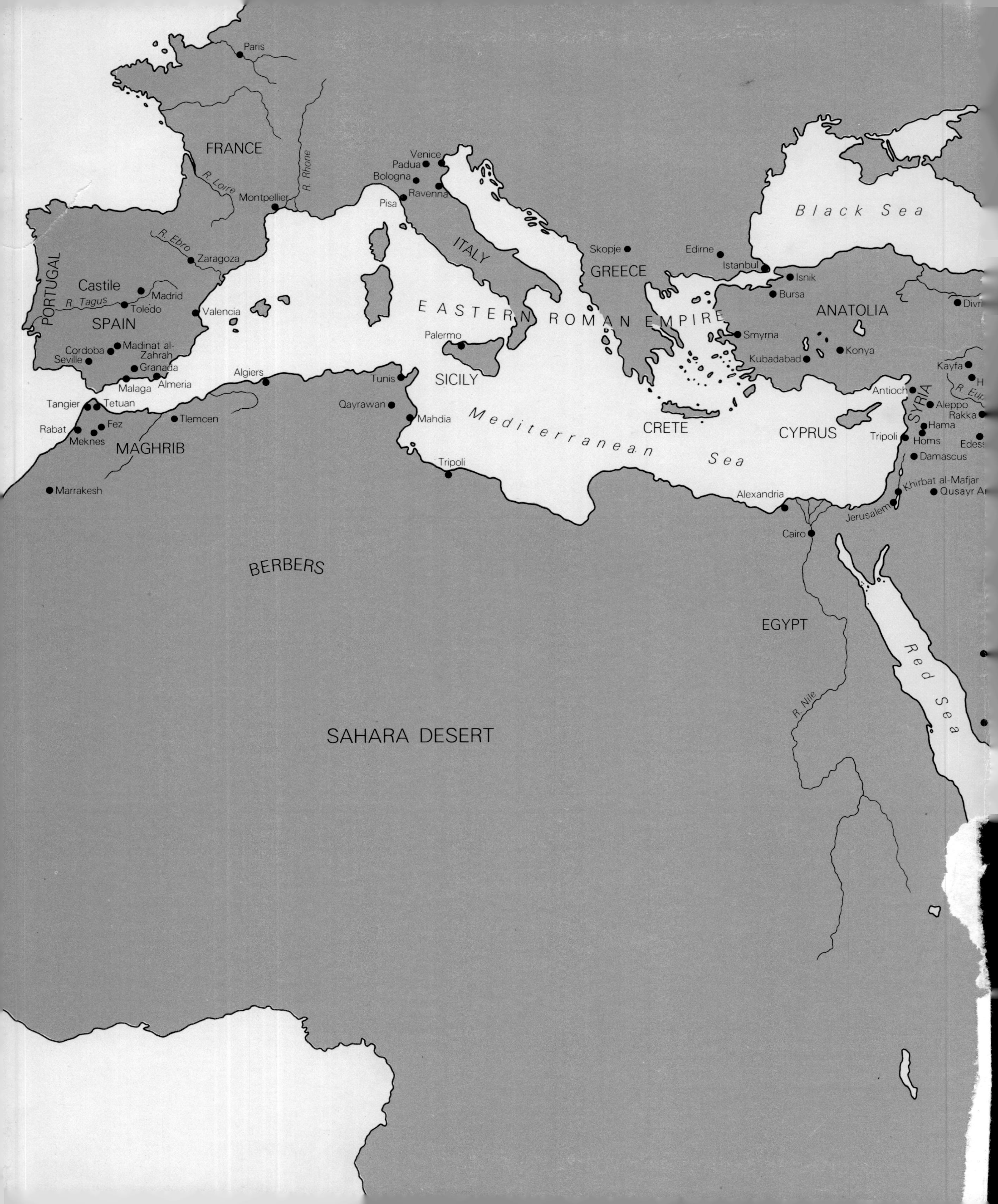
Paris
FRANCE
R. Loire
R. Rhone
Montpellier
Venice
Padua
Bologna
Ravenna
Pisa
ITALY
R. Ebro
Zaragoza
PORTUGAL
Castile
Madrid
R. Tagus
Toledo
SPAIN
Valencia
Cordoba
Madinat al-Zahrah
Seville
Granada
Malaga
Almeria
Algiers
Tangier
Tetuan
Rabat
Fez
Meknes
Tlemcen
MAGHRIB
Marrakesh
Tunis
Qayrawan
Mahdia
Tripoli
Palermo
SICILY
EASTERN ROMAN EMPIRE
Mediterranean Sea
Skopje
GREECE
Edirne
Istanbul
Isnik
Bursa
Black Sea
ANATOLIA
Smyrna
Konya
Kubadabad
CRETE
CYPRUS
Kayfa
Antioch
SYRIA
Aleppo
Rakka
Hama
Homs
Tripoli
Damascus
Khirbat al-Mafjar
Jerusalem
Alexandria
Cairo
BERBERS
EGYPT
R. Nile
Red Sea
SAHARA DESERT